Disability, Human Rights,
and Information Technology

PENNSYLVANIA STUDIES IN HUMAN RIGHTS

Bert B. Lockwood, Jr., *Series Editor*

A complete list of books in the series is available from the publisher.

DISABILITY, HUMAN RIGHTS, AND INFORMATION TECHNOLOGY

Edited by

Jonathan Lazar

and

Michael Ashley Stein

UNIVERSITY OF PENNSYLVANIA PRESS

PHILADELPHIA

Copyright © 2017 University of Pennsylvania Press

All rights reserved. Except for brief quotations used
for purposes of review or scholarly citation, none of this
book may be reproduced in any form by any means without written
permission from the publisher.

Published by
University of Pennsylvania Press
Philadelphia, Pennsylvania 19104-4112
www.upenn.edu/pennpress

Printed in the United States of America
on acid-free paper

10 9 8 7 6 5 4 3 2 1

A Cataloging-in-Publication record is available from
the Library of Congress.

ISBN 978-0-8122-4923-1

CONTENTS

Foreword ... ix
   H. E. Ambassador Luis Gallegos

Introduction ... 1
   Jonathan Lazar and Michael Ashley Stein

PART I. PARTICIPATION AND INCLUSION

1. Standards Bodies, Access to Information Technology, and Human Rights ... 11
   Judy Brewer

2. Accessible ICTs and the Opening of Political Space for Persons with Disabilities ... 24
   Janet E. Lord

3. Web Accessibility for People with Cognitive Disabilities: A Legal Right? ... 41
   Peter Blanck

4. The Intersection of Human Rights, Social Justice, the Internet, and Accessibility in Libraries: Access, Education, and Inclusion ... 58
   Paul T. Jaeger, Brian Wentz, and John Carlo Bertot

PART II. GOVERNMENT AND GOVERNANCE

5. Public Financing of Information Technology and Human Rights for People with Disabilities ... 73
   Deborah Kaplan

6. Using Provincial Laws to Drive a National Agenda:
   Connecting Human Rights and Disability Rights Laws   94
   Ravi Malhotra and Megan A. Rusciano

7. Access to Justice   111
   Fredric I. Lederer

8. Open Government and Digital Accessibility   125
   Timothy Elder

PART III. SPECIFIC APPLICATIONS AND TECHNOLOGIES

9. E-Books and Human Rights   143
   Jim Fruchterman

10. Accessibility and Online Learning   158
    Mary J. Ziegler and David Sloan

11. Who Owns Captioning?   182
    Raja Kushalnagar

12. Information Privacy and Security as a Human Right
    for People with Disabilities   199
    Jonathan Lazar, Brian Wentz, and Marco Winckler

13. How Does Inaccessible Gaming Lead to Social Exclusion?   212
    Joyram Chakraborty

PART IV. INTERNATIONAL DEVELOPMENT

14. The Pivot Model of Policy Entrepreneurship: An Application
    of European Ideas in the Global South   227
    G. Anthony Giannoumis, Mirriam Nthenge, and Jorge Manhique

15. The Accessibility Infrastructure and the Global South   244
    Joyojeet Pal

16. ICT Access, Disability Human Rights, and Social
    Inclusion in India   263
    Sanjay S. Jain

Notes   279

Contributors   327

Index   339

FOREWORD

H. E. Ambassador Luis Gallegos

Information and communication technology (ICT) is changing our world. Ubiquitous mobile telephony, television, computers, tablets, software, websites, the Internet of Things, electronic kiosks, and digital interfaces of home or office appliances have transformed the way human beings communicate, learn, work, and play around the world—not only in the developed North but also among countries in the developing South.

And while the availability of sophisticated information technology used to be restricted to governments and the corporate world, billions of individual users benefit from it today. I personally was educated with paper and pencils, but today, with my family spread around the globe, instant electronic free communications are a daily reality. These would have been unthinkable only a few years ago. On a given day I interact from Quito, Ecuador, with Europe, the Americas, and Asia.

This collection of essays that Jonathan Lazar and Michael Ashley Stein have coedited, *Disability, Human Rights, and Information Technology*, comes at a very important and timely moment in the quest for inclusive societies. It underlines the imperative to ensure equal access to ICTs among the one billion persons living with disabilities around the world. The challenge is obvious: can anyone participate equally in society today without being able to communicate with a mobile phone, watch important news on TV, have access to emergency communications, or use a computer, e-reader, ATM, or website? Are there any activities, from work to education or justice, that can be conducted without interfacing with ICTs?

As is abundantly demonstrated in this book, ICTs can present insurmountable barriers for persons with disabilities or, to the contrary, can offer unprecedented solutions to accommodate persons with sensorial, cognitive, or physical limitations. The good news is that there are solutions today allowing persons with most types of disabilities to use ICTs ranging from mobile telephony to TV, kiosks, software, or websites, and assistive technologies leveraging the power of ICTs have made giant steps forward because of unprecedented and increasingly inexpensive solutions such as voice recognition, screen reading, and text-to-speech, as well as multiple alternative modes of electronic communications. However, as discussed in the following chapters, the actual awareness of, availability of, and required support for those technologies to fully benefit persons with disabilities are still severely lagging in most regions for essential types of activities, and subtle legal, societal, or economic barriers remain.

The urgency of this challenge is pressing indeed. Beyond essential accommodations that remove accessibility barriers, the use of technology also ends more fundamental forms of discrimination by leveling the field for those excluded because of their "differences," enabling new forms of communication and interaction that reveal their creativity and strengths in all aspects of human endeavors. Technologies are therefore an essential success factor for the full inclusion of persons with disabilities and the full realization of their rights.

December 13, 2016, marked the tenth anniversary of the approval by the United Nations General Assembly (A/RES/61/106) of the Convention on the Rights of Persons with Disabilities (CRPD) and its Optional Protocol. This is a good time for all stakeholders to engage in taking stock of where we are, what has been achieved, and what needs to be done to promote and protect the rights of persons with disabilities.

The CRPD has the merit of offering a universal framework that makes social changes possible while elevating disability rights to a prominent role in the process of inclusion of and nondiscrimination against one billion persons with disabilities. I have always believed that a person may be born with a disability or may acquire it by sickness, accident, war, or for whatever other reason, but certainly as we age, we will have a disability. I mention this because the universality of disability in the human condition is not considered one of the main reasons that brought us to the halls of the UN in New York to advance the cause of rights of persons with disabilities. But I believe that it should be. It is not, therefore, a problem of a minority; it is a problem of all of us.

Article 9 of the CRPD stipulates that "to enable persons with disabilities to live independently and participate fully in all aspects of life, States Parties shall take appropriate measures to ensure to persons with disabilities access, on an equal basis with others, to the physical environment, to transportation, to information and communications, including information and communications technologies and systems." It goes on to outline that states parties shall also take appropriate measures to promote other forms of assistance and support to persons with disabilities to ensure access to information; to promote access to new information and communication technologies and systems, including the Internet; and to promote the design, development, production, and distribution of accessible information and communications technologies and systems at an early stage, so that these technologies and systems become available at minimum cost.

As we measure, in cooperation with disabled persons' organizations around the world, progress made by states parties in promoting ICT accessibility in accordance with Article 9, contrasting results appear: progress occurs in laws, regulations, policies, or programs, but the actual availability of accessible ICTs for persons with disabilities remains limited, in large part because of weak capacities among states parties to implement their commitments. A majority of countries, for instance, do not have any substantial implementation of accessible TV, accessible mobile telephony, or accessible websites.[1] Less than a third of states parties take accessibility into account in their public procurement of ICTs, while the other two-thirds do not, unwittingly creating new barriers for millions of citizens and public workers with disabilities, in large part because of lack of awareness.[2]

With such data points in mind, a very important contribution of this book, thanks to the depth and variety of its sectorial analysis of ICT accessibility, will be to help close this gap in awareness among states parties and other stakeholders. By exploring multiple facets of issues and solutions in ICT accessibility, it will also further facilitate imagining new steps toward equal access by persons with disabilities to information and knowledge.

The impact of information technology on our lives is hard to predict in both a positive and a negative sense. But as an optimist, I believe in the use of technology to bridge the social gaps in our societies. I am also certain that the access of persons with disabilities to these technologies will open up new horizons in their lives, from education to employment, from inclusive development to a more rights-based legal system.

Our world is changing and should change at an equal pace for persons with disabilities in all fields of human endeavor. The chapters in this book will contribute to the better understanding of the importance of those critical linkages among human rights, disability, and information technology.

Introduction

Jonathan Lazar and Michael Ashley Stein

People with disabilities have a civil and human right to access the same digital content at the same time and at the same cost as people without disabilities. In a majority of cases, technology solutions already exist to make that situation a reality. Furthermore, when digital content is incorporated into the initial design and manufacture of information and communication technology (ICT), it can be made accessible to persons with disabilities at little or no added cost. To illustrate, when web content is designed from the start to be accessible, the expected costs are only 1 to 2 percent of the costs of the overall web design project.

An example of easily attained inclusion via provision of a standardized technological feature in a popularly used device is the incorporation of text-to-speech modality in iPhones, iPads, and other iOS devices. Text-to-speech functionality, known colloquially as a screen reader, comes standard on Apple devices at no additional cost to purchasers. Making digital devices, e-books, and web content accessible allows equal access for people with disabilities and also increases the customer base for companies who then sell their products, services, and technologies to an increased number of consumers. Some retailers, notably Wal-Mart, have long recognized the business case for maintaining fully accessible websites.

Yet despite the ready availability and minimal cost of technology to enable people with disabilities to equally access ICT—as well as the increasing use of that technology by consumers without disabilities—prevailing practice around the globe results in the exclusion of those individuals. This is true both for the public sphere, where open access to government is one measure of transparency and legitimacy, and for the private sector, which has a vested economic self-interest in engaging the largest possible number of consumers. The arbitrary and irrational nature of these circumstances is frustrating and perplexing.

Notably, despite clear legal obligations under Section 508 of the Rehabilitation Act to make technology purchased, developed, or acquired by the U.S. federal government accessible to users with disabilities (including public-facing systems like websites and internal technology for federal employees), many federal websites remain inaccessible. This is equally true of American state and local government websites operating under similar legal obligations—Section 504 of the Rehabilitation Act and Title II of the Americans with Disabilities Act (ADA)—even those mandated with providing emergency evacuation and assistance information. Moreover, there is very little transparency in federal, state, and local governments in terms of documenting the accessibility of technologies or how the accessibility process is managed. In consequence, some prominent disability rights advocacy groups have taken action to remedy glaring problems. For instance, the National Federation of the Blind (NFB) filed a lawsuit in February 2016 against the U.S. Department of Health and Human Services because electronic communications were inaccessible between the agency and blind users. The NFB likewise participated in a lawsuit against the New York State Board of Elections in June 2016, precipitated by the state's inaccessible online voter registration.

Strikingly, some companies go beyond neglecting their legal and social obligations to include consumers with disabilities and actively resist making their hardware, software, and websites accessible. Amazon provides a case study in recalcitrance. Since the Kindle e-book device was first introduced in 2007, there have been multiple problems related to accessibility through various iterations of the device despite repeated efforts by disability rights advocates to educate Amazon about these barriers. Subsequently, and in response to Amazon's continued and conscious exclusion of users with disabilities, the disability rights community persuaded federal government officials to cancel millions of dollars of contracts for Kindle devices as being in violation of federal law prohibiting disability discrimination. In March 2016, Amazon signed an agreement with the NFB to make its products more accessible.

Peapod is another example of a company that actively refused to address the needs of consumers with disabilities in spite of clear economic benefits. Much like people without disabilities, there are people with disabilities who prefer ordering their groceries online and having them delivered to their homes and offices. Nevertheless, despite several requests from consumers with disabilities that Peapod make its website and mobile app accessible, the company refused to do so. In November 2014, after an investigation, the U.S. Department of Justice entered into a settlement agreement with Peapod that required the online store to provide equal access to customers with disabilities by making its website and mobile app accessible.

Why do government agencies and departments violate their legal and fiduciary duties by resisting making otherwise publicly available information accessible and available to members of the public with disabilities? Why do otherwise rational income-maximizing companies break laws and work against their own self-interest by refusing to make their websites accessible to consumers with disabilities? Such actions are flummoxing.

* * *

New technologies create interesting questions at the intersection of human-computer interaction, disability rights, civil rights, human rights, international development, and public policy. Indeed, more frontiers of human-computer interaction are unsettled than resolved, and this is especially true when they involve persons with diverse disabilities. Some quandaries arise where technologies have advanced ahead of existing laws and policies, as is the case in considering the intellectual property implications of captioning. Other complexities arise where legal norms have been established but not yet implemented, or where legal rights are defined, but clear technical implementations are not yet established, for instance, interface accessibility for people with cognitive impairments. Additional questions arise in allocating limited resources, especially within the context of developing countries. Cutting across all these fields are issues relating to the promulgation and enforcement of standards; and always undergirding these issues are the crucial matters of cultural recognition, acceptance, and inclusion of persons with disabilities in societies.

This book addresses the globally pertinent issue of equal access to and inclusion in ICT by persons with disabilities. Within the United States, as touched on earlier, the right to equal access is expressed in terms of antidiscrimination prohibitions under both the Rehabilitation Act and the ADA. More globally, this right is implicit in several human rights instruments, features prominently in Articles 9 and 21 of the Convention on the Rights of Persons with Disabilities (CRPD), which went into operation in May 2008, and is the subject of the Marrakesh Treaty to Facilitate Access to Published Works for Persons Who Are Blind, Visually Impaired, or Otherwise Print Disabled, which has now opened for State ratification. The right to access ICT, moreover, invokes cross-cutting civil and human rights issues, among them freedom of expression, freedom of information, political participation, civic engagement, inclusive education, the right to access the highest level of scientific and technological information, and participation in social and cultural opportunities. Accordingly, the authors of each chapter have been encouraged to consider relevant domestic laws (including the respective national-level human and civil rights of persons with disabilities), international human rights, disability studies, and technological, sociological, and cultural perspectives. The authors have likewise been encouraged to provide appropriate international examples to illustrate these concepts in a global setting.

* * *

In February 2015, we convened an exploratory seminar at the Radcliffe Institute for Advanced Study at Harvard University on the topic "Frontiers in United States Law: Equal Access to Information Technology for People with Disabilities." The seminar examined legal questions at the intersection of human-computer interaction and disability rights law in the United States and focused primarily on topics that have not been clearly decided by legal statutes or case law. The participants chosen were a cross section of scholars in computer science and law, civil and human rights advocates, practitioners, and government policy makers. Five themes were examined at the seminar: captioning and legal ownership, accessible instructional materials in higher education, technology access for people with cognitive impairments, e-book access for people with print disabilities, and access to courtroom documents and technology. Some of the participants and their work are included in chapters of this book.

The exploratory seminar focused on legal and technical issues arising within the United States. The scope of this volume is broader, however, than the exemplary discussion we enjoyed over those two days at Radcliffe. The focus of this collection goes beyond ICT accessibility in the United States to include Europe and parts of the developing world. This book is likewise broader in considering the role of international law, and especially human rights, in enabling access to ICT on behalf of the globe's one billion persons with disabilities. Although many of the chapters cut across multiple themes, we present the chapters in four sections: "Participation and Inclusion"; "Government and Governance"; "Specific Applications and Technologies"; and "International Development."

We are excited to have a group of distinguished, knowledgeable, and passionate authors address many fundamental topics at the intersection of disability rights, civil rights, human rights, intellectual property, international development, human-computer interaction, accessibility, public policy, and sociology. At the same time, and because of limitations of space, it is not possible to cover every potential topic of interest as much as is deserved and desired. For example, inclusive health care and transportation are two fields that come to mind as crucial to the intersection of disability rights and the use of technology, especially as they relate to independence. In addition to the topics covered in the book, there are a number of important and interesting but underresearched and consequently unresolved topics that we hope researchers will address in the future. For now, we sketch out four areas in dramatic need of further exploration: accessible educational testing; telecommunications laws as human rights enablers; consumer rights laws as human rights enablers; and North-South/South-North development transfers.

Accessible Educational Testing

In the past, education tests were primarily written and occasionally oral. Now, a large and ever-increasing percentage of educational testing is offered via computer. In theory, computer use should create a level playing field, allowing people with various disabilities to equally take part in these standardized assessments. However, many educational tests are technically inaccessible to people using assistive technology and may also contain questions that are biased against people with disabilities. Furthermore, there are still some institutions that believe that individuals who take tests using assistive technology ought to have their use of assistive technology marked on their record by a statement that they took the exam under "nonstandard conditions," thereby flagging their disability and denigrating the test results. The increased reliance on standardized testing throughout K–12 education, as well as the importance of testing for admission to college and graduate school, makes this topic especially urgent for increased study.

Telecommunications Laws as Human Rights Enablers

When people reflect on ICT accessibility, they correctly think of the relevant laws as being those of disability rights, human rights, or civil rights. Yet there is potential for telecommunication law, the statutes and policies regulating communication devices and transmissions, to be used also for improving equal access to technology and content for people with disabilities. For instance, disability rights laws can cover the purchasers of technology, such as government agencies and recipients of government funding. However, telecommunication laws that regulate the manufacturing of devices can outlaw the manufacturing or distribution of inaccessible devices. Doing so shifts the onus of assuring accessibility from the purchaser to the manufacturer. In the past, telecommunication laws have been responsible for requiring relay service, as well as captioning, for people who are deaf or hard of hearing. Recent telecommunication laws, such as the U.S. Communications and Video Accessibility Act, specifically require accessibility of smartphones, among other devices. Likewise, the U.S. Federal Communications Commission has stated that Internet service providers are required to provide equal access for people with disabilities. It is expected that the ongoing development of policies related to net neutrality, for instance, will have an impact on equality of access for people with disabilities. This area is rapidly evolving, with enormous implications for people with disabilities.

Consumer Rights Laws as Human Rights Enablers

Consumer rights laws have the potential to be used as tools for increasing human and civil rights. Government compliance monitoring, related to consumer rights, often examines topics such as consumer fraud and consumer privacy. The U.S. Federal Trade Commission, for instance, "protects consumers by stopping unfair, deceptive or fraudulent practices in the marketplace."[1] When users with disabilities pay higher prices for services or receive a lower quality of goods relative to consumers without disabilities, there may be a violation of existing consumer protection laws. When consumers are not given information about whether a device or software application is accessible, a situation arises where the consumer with a disability must first make a purchase and then afterward determine whether the technology is accessible. This practice can be viewed as deceptive and parallels truth-in-labeling laws where consumers have the right to know what they are being sold. Other areas of consumer protection may include identity theft and consumer scams that target people with disabilities. The potential of consumer rights laws to protect the human and civil rights of people with disabilities has not been adequately researched.

North-South/South-North Development Transfers

An underexamined law and development issue that is central to the notion of creating and disseminating accessible ICT for persons with disabilities is the transfer of actual technology between states, nonstate private actors, or some combination of these entities, as well as the sharing of recommendations and best practices for using those technologies.[2] These matters were addressed for the first time by a human rights treaty in the CRPD, which contains an article on international cooperation requiring such collaboration between states. Yet little practical information and guidance have been developed on how to implement this mandate in the context of limited resources, whether state or privately funded. For instance, it seems quixotic and inappropriate to premise dissemination of information regarding basic services, such as availability of vaccinations or location of clean water and sanitation, on the possibility that people in Botswana will have iPads with Internet access (even if some do). However, a radio transmission or a mobile phone app might provide this same information in a more immediately practical manner, although access to those technologies themselves requires certain disability-specific accommodations. In this respect, it is important not to strike a colonial attitude but to acknowledge that although many technological transfers will flow from the North to the South, many innovations and creative solutions will be generated and disseminated from the South to the North. Thus, although many localities in the United States have established emergency evacuation notices in case of natural disaster, those notices are frequently inaccessible to users with disabilities. Conversely, the government of Ecuador deployed a network of fieldworkers using GPS technology to identify and be able to subsequently assist persons with disabilities across that country, including those living in hard-to-reach terrain, in the event of natural disaster. This is only one example of the underexplored phenomena of developing states, precisely because they lack resources, developing creative and more cost-effective use of ICT to enable persons with disabilities.

* * *

We are grateful to the Radcliffe Institute for Advanced Study at Harvard University for supporting the exploratory seminar that served as a foundation for this book. We thank our university homes, Towson University Department of Computer and Information Sciences for Jonathan and Harvard

Law School and the University of Pretoria Faculty of Law Centre for Human Rights for Michael, for supporting us in this work. We acknowledge with gratitude the immense efforts of our chapter authors and express appreciation to the editors at the University of Pennsylvania Press. We likewise acknowledge the generosity of artist Robert Tinney for granting permission to use his classic artwork on technology and disability for the cover of this book. Jonathan also would like to thank Howard and Ann Georgi for their support in providing non-ICT accommodations on his multiple trips to Harvard to work on this book. On a final note, we praise, thank, and encourage our colleagues in the various communities in which we work who inspire us to continue pushing for a more inclusive world of technology.

PART I

Participation and Inclusion

CHAPTER 1

Standards Bodies, Access to Information Technology, and Human Rights

Judy Brewer

Introduction

The Web has been a focal point of accessibility-standardization efforts since 1997 through work within the World Wide Web Consortium (W3C)[1] Web Accessibility Initiative (WAI),[2] and increasingly also through work throughout the Web community. The scope of work done through WAI has ranged from promoting awareness of the need for accessibility of the Web, to development of guidelines and technical specifications, coordination with research communities, and coordination with other standards organizations to ensure international harmonization of accessibility standards. During this time, accessibility of information on the Web has improved greatly. However, many accessibility barriers remain; and although many Web innovations improve accessibility, new barriers are still often inadvertently introduced as technologies advance.

This chapter explores the landscape of Web accessibility from the perspective of development of accessible information and communication technology (ICT) standards. It examines the importance of addressing accessibility support in mainstream technologies from the design stage onward; the need to engage different stakeholder groups, including end users, at the design table; and the challenges of addressing accessibility for people with disabilities within the intensely competitive and constantly evolving technology sector.

The Relevance of Standardization to Ensuring Accessibility of ICT

For many people who have worked on human rights, including disability rights, standards organizations may not be the first vehicle one thinks of when considering options for influencing the design of key technologies. Standards bodies are sometimes considered relevant primarily for capturing established practices in their fields rather than as a venue through which to help shape social aspects of technology design.

Yet because ICT occupies such a central role in society and the pace of technology change is constantly accelerating, it has become critically important to ensure that accessibility requirements are addressed at the design stage of ICT product and service development. After they have been released to the market, accessibility products and services may be difficult to retrofit—and by then, people with disabilities have already been left behind by the latest innovations. Standards bodies provide an opportunity to address accessibility principles early in the pipeline of emerging technologies.

Most ICT requires some degree of standardization in order to ensure interoperability with other parts of the technology infrastructure. Some standards organizations provide an effective setting in which to solicit perspectives and help articulate requirements from across a global community.

W3C WAI has been instrumental in developing guidelines and specifications that address a wide variety of user needs for accessibility and has been able to achieve broad international consensus on these. It also provides a coordinated process of accessibility review of mainstream Web standards in areas as diverse as graphics, media, mobile web, payments, security, digital publishing and e-readers, geolocation, automotive navigation, TV, and more. It has also enabled identification of potential accessibility barriers at early stages in the design process, when problems can still be relatively easily addressed. For accessibility requirements that require dedicated specifications or application programming interfaces (APIs), W3C provides a forum in which accessibility experts and advocates can work hand in hand with developers of mainstream technologies to ensure architecturally compatible design approaches for accessibility requirements. This aspect of WAI work is pursued through the Accessible Platform Architectures (APA) Working Group (previously the Protocols and Formats Working Group).[3]

Accessibility of ICT as a Human Right

Today, some of the most critical tools of society—for education, employment, commerce, health care, civic participation, entertainment, and more—are those used in the information society. The Web is one of the most important tools for communication and interaction, facilitating access to and integration into society. In the relatively short span of twenty-five years, the Web has evolved from an interesting and nice-to-have luxury to an essential means of interacting with the world. Even in areas that are off the electric grid or devoid of landline telecommunications, or both, access to the Internet and the Web through mobile devices has been increasing rapidly. There is a growing commitment to providing low-cost or no-cost global Internet services that will help reach the great majority of the world's population.[4] Although the availability of digital technology has increased access to information for many people with disabilities, the accessibility of that newly available information is still inconsistent, so for people with disabilities it is sometimes possible to get to Web content but not possible to perceive, understand, or interact with that content. If access to the Internet and the Web becomes nearly ubiquitous, yet unaddressed accessibility barriers in ICT remain, this could paradoxically exacerbate social and economic inequities that are already present for people with disabilities just at the time when the digital environment is finally providing the tools and opportunity to undo those inequities.

This need for the tools of the information society to be accessible to people with disabilities is articulated in the Convention on the Rights of Persons with Disabilities (CRPD), adopted by the United Nations in 2006. The CRPD restates, with specific reference to the needs of people with disabilities, basic rights that people without disabilities in many countries have been able to take for granted for years but that people with disabilities have often been denied.

Articles 9 and 21 of the CRPD, among a number of other provisions, address the right of accessibility to information and to the tools of the information society for people with disabilities. To paraphrase the portions relating to ICT from these two articles, the CRPD directs that state parties to the convention shall take appropriate measures to ensure persons with disabilities access, on an equal basis with others, to information and communications, including information and communications technologies and systems, and electronic services and emergency services (from Article 9(1)(b)).[5]

Additionally, the CRPD directs that states shall take all appropriate measures to ensure that persons with disabilities can exercise the right to freedom of expression and opinion, including the freedom to seek, receive, and impart information and ideas on an equal basis with others and through all forms of communication of their choice, including information in accessible formats and technologies, and communications (from Article 21(a, c, e)).[6]

In these two articles, it is significant to note that both the tools of the information society and the rights and freedoms afforded by these tools to people with disabilities were important to the framers of this convention, and that these are just as important as the many other rights enumerated in this treaty, including access to education and to the built environment. For people with disabilities around the world, the CRPD has been an important milestone in societal recognition of equal status.

Prior to the development of the CRPD, some countries already had treaties, legislation, or policies that promoted or required accessibility of the Web, or, more generally, of accessibility of information and communication systems. In some countries, these have taken a civil rights approach; in other cases, they have focused on procurement approaches that require accessibility of ICTs purchased or acquired for government usage. The first of these was Section 508,[7] originally added to the U.S. Rehabilitation Act in 1986 and amended several times since then. In 2014, the European Norm 301 549, which also took a procurement approach, was adopted in Europe.[8] An increasing number of countries have already developed or are developing similar policies.

Examples of Accessibility Barriers and Requirements for Web Content

The scope of Web accessibility encompasses a broad range of functional requirements across different disabilities and the needs of older users. For someone who is hard of hearing or deaf watching a web-based TV broadcast that is interrupted by an announcement of emergency evacuation information, access to real-time streaming captions or sign language can be lifesaving. For a student with a visual disability taking an exam based on interpretation of complex visual data, description of visually presented information embedded in an infographic may be essential to fair assessment of her or his knowledge. For someone with an intellectual disability who is trying to interpret health-care information from a website, consistency of navigation menus and understandability of language used on a Web page may be important. For someone with limited fine motor control who is trying to fill out and submit an online financial form before it expires and she or he has to restart the process, an option to extend the time to fill out a form may be critical. For someone with a photosensitive seizure disorder, being able to avoid strobing lights in web content may be important. For an older user who may have changes in vision, hearing, dexterity, or short-term memory, or a combination of these changes, accessibility support on the Web may be useful regardless of whether that individual considers herself or himself to have a "disability."[9]

The Web can be made accessible for persons in all of these situations, but to do so requires several things working together in concert. It requires web-accessibility guidelines that set out accessibility requirements; features in web specifications that support provision of accessibility information, such as captions and descriptions of images; browsers or mobile applications that can render the embedded accessibility information; content authors who provide the necessary accessibility information; an awareness of the benefits of using a common set of guidelines internationally; policies to ensure that accessibility guidelines are used; and evaluation tools and processes to assess whether a website conforms to accessibility.

Information on many websites is dynamic and interactive. For instance, Web users may need to expand nested menus or drag and drop objects on a Web page. For people who are using computers with assistive technologies such as screen readers or voice recognition, compatibility between browsers or mobile applications and assistive technologies may be essential to accessing information on a Web page or in Web applications, or completing tasks such as filling out and submitting forms. Use of accessibility-supporting specifications such as Accessible Rich Internet Applications (ARIA) 1.0[10] in the design of these websites can enable accessibility of dynamic and interactive content on websites.

Accessibility also needs to intersect well with other aspects of technology usage, such as privacy, security, internationalization, and the operation of these technologies across different devices and platforms. For instance, people who are blind may need their screen readers to voice pronunciations from phonetic dictionaries for multiple languages, and they may need to ensure that security provisions do not disrupt interoperability between browsers and assistive technologies. Assistive technologies may require more direct access to the core functions of an application, which may be interpreted as attempts to hack into the system itself, triggering a shutdown of the system. These kinds of considerations can be identified and addressed by accessibility application programming interface mapping (accessibility APIs, AAMs) developed through joint work between accessibility groups and other working groups within W3C.

Elements of a Standards-Development Process That Can Support Inclusive Design

The process used in developing standards can have a significant impact on outcomes with regard to needs of end users, including people with disabilities. In August 2012, W3C was an inaugural signatory to the principles of Open Stand, along with the Internet Society, the Internet Engineering Task Force (IETF), the Internet Architecture Board (IAB), and the Institute of Electrical and Electronics Engineers (IEEE).[11] Open Stand's modern paradigm for standards[12] recognizes characteristics of standardization processes that have contributed to the success of the Internet and the Web. These include the following:

1. Cooperation
2. Adherence to principles (due process; broad consensus; transparency; balance; openness)
3. Collective empowerment
4. Availability
5. Voluntary adoption

W3C's standards-development process has encompassed elements of these principles since its founding in 1994 and has continued evolving with regard to openness, transparency, and availability, for instance, through its pioneering royalty-free patent policy.[13] The W3C process[14] has been instrumental in ensuring an effective environment for developing accessibility standards.

Several mechanisms have helped ensure that the perspectives of multiple stakeholders in accessibility standards are represented throughout the development process. These include broad public review with openness and transparency to ensure accountability, and inclusion of invited experts as well as representatives of member organizations. Additionally, reliance on a consensus-oriented decision process has ensured that standards are decided primarily on the merit of arguments rather than the standing of particular organizations or national-body representatives regardless of their expertise in a given technical domain.

An important aspect of this standards-development process is W3C's multistage development process for technical reports.[15] It starts with a series of iterative working drafts, eventually followed by an implementation-testing period ("Candidate Recommendation") during which the working group identifies and then tests implementations of each feature in the draft specification to ensure conforming and interoperable implementations. The Candidate Recommendation period in some cases requires an extensive test suite with potentially up to tens of thousands of tests to encompass the full scope of features in a large specification, as was the case with HTML5.[16] This has allowed adjustment of accessibility barriers after the design has stabilized but before the standard has been finalized. During the subsequent Proposed Recommendation stage, the W3C membership reviews the near-final draft standard for acceptability within the standards field. The final stage, a W3C Recommendation, is recognized internationally as a Web standard. Some W3C standards are also endorsed by the International Standards Organization (ISO), as was W3C's Web Content Accessibility Guidelines 2.0 in 2012.[17]

Timing of accessibility reviews is an important factor. It is generally considered that early identification of potential accessibility solutions is most cost-effective. Until 2015, W3C maintained a Last Call Working Draft (LCWD) stage that immediately preceded the implementation-testing stage of Candidate Recommendation and was important for ensuring reviews of cross-cutting features such as accessibility support, internationalization, privacy, security, and more. This stage provided an opportunity to review potential accessibility impacts in a stable draft because not all accessibility problems are fully evident in the earliest versions of a specification. The elimination of the LCWD stage increased the challenge of accessibility reviews in that a specification now starts undergoing implementation testing at the same time as the specification's features are becoming stable. Although these changes bring the standards-development process more into alignment with more agile development approaches that have become central to the increasingly fast-moving and competitive development of technology, they mean reviewing the accessibility support of a moving target.

Why Multistakeholder Involvement Is Critical

Development of accessibility guidelines for Web technologies, and accessibility reviews of technical standards under development, require the participation of all relevant stakeholder groups. These include representatives from industry, the disability community, research, education, and government. There is a growing pool of accessibility experts who work within industry or in nongovernmental organizations (NGOs) and who may or may not be end users of the technologies. Direct end-user representation can provide important information on prioritization as well as design of features. The membership of W3C has become increasingly diverse over the years, for instance, expanding to reflect the needs and interests of a growing number of accessibility-focused businesses and some disability organizations. The "Invited Expert" provision in the W3C process allows further flexibility where necessary to ensure representation of stakeholder viewpoints not included among the membership. As with accessibility of the built environment, people with disabilities have an expectation of inclusion—"nothing about us without us"—and direct user participation can be critically important in ensuring that user needs are clearly understood.

For instance, when developers are considering approaches for enhancing accessibility of the user interface for browsers or other user agents, they often suggest approaches that automatically detect technologies an end user has installed, thereby potentially exposing a combination of settings and assistive technologies that may in turn reveal an individual's disability. If this information is exposed in a nonsecure way, for instance, while a person with a disability is in a public location using a mobile device, it could put the individual at physical risk, even though the user never gave permission for that information to be stored or exposed. User involvement in technology design can be valuable for a better understanding of user requirements and concerns.

In order to ensure that accessibility solutions have global relevance, it is also important to ensure representation from different national and language groups to address the needs of different scripts and character-based languages, including Chinese, Japanese, and Korean, and the need for bidirectionality, for instance, for Arabic and Hebrew. In some cases, web-accessibility experts have worked extensively with W3C WAI working groups to ensure that language-specific needs are fully addressed and to support harmonization among guidelines, such as with the Web Accessibility Infrastructure

Committee, which is part of the Japanese Industry Standards Association in Japan.[18] Authorized translations of Web Content Accessibility Guidelines (WCAG) 2.0 are available in a number of languages.[19] The W3C Policy for Authorized Translations[20] describes how to develop additional authorized translations of WCAG 2.0, as well as other WAI and W3C documents. Increased emphasis on cross-time-zone collaboration facilitates participation in an asynchronous environment. Interested contributors and implementers from around the globe provide additional avenues to ensure that these issues are addressed.

Key Areas of Focus for Accessibility Guidelines

There are several areas of importance for development of accessibility guidelines. One is accessibility of Web content and applications; another is accessibility of authoring tools used to produce Web content; a third is accessibility of browsers, mobile devices, and e-readers. To some extent these are artificially distinct areas, since many applications blur the boundaries between content, the authoring process for creating and producing content, and user agents that render content. For instance, authoring tools such as wikis and blogs contain content, render content, and also provide a means to directly author content. Potential updates to guidelines in the future are likely to address these three areas in combination.

The W3C accessibility standard that has most frequently been adopted or referenced around the world is WCAG 2.0.[21] These guidelines address accessibility of web content and applications—essentially the information on web pages and in applications that are used on computers and mobile devices. WCAG 2.0 includes four principles: that content should be

- perceivable—that information and user interface components must be presentable to users in ways that they can perceive;
- operable—that user interface components and navigation must be operable;
- understandable—that information and the operation of the user interface must be understandable; and
- robust—that content must be robust enough that it can be interpreted reliably by a wide variety of user agents, including assistive technologies.[22]

Each WCAG 2.0 principle is associated with one or more guidelines, which provide the basic goals that authors should work toward in order to make content more accessible to users with different disabilities. Associated with the guidelines are multiple testable success criteria designed to be used where requirements and conformance testing are necessary. The success criteria are supported in turn by informative techniques, including techniques that are sufficient for meeting the guidelines, and optional advisory techniques. This layering of principles, guidelines, normative success criteria, and informative techniques[23] allows technology-neutral general principles that can remain stable over time, while the informative-techniques layer can evolve with emerging technical standards. All three W3C WAI guidelines use a similar layered structure in which the success criteria are the normative portion against which conformance testing may be performed.

The set of principles in WCAG 2.0 has also proved relevant beyond the traditional web, for instance, for mobile applications, digital publishing, and many of the newer technologies that have been converging with the Web. Nearly all the provisions of WCAG 2.0 apply to the mobile environment; and the majority of mobile-application accessibility requirements that are not addressed by WCAG 2.0 are addressed by User Agent Accessibility Guidelines (UAAG) 2.0. Gap requirements for mobile accessibility are under consideration for normative extensions to WCAG 2.0. Normative extensions are also under consideration to increase existing coverage for cognitive and learning disabilities and for low-vision accessibility requirements.[24] "Guidance on Applying WCAG 2.0 to Non-Web Information and Communications Technologies (WCAG2ICT),"[25] a W3C WAI Working Group note, maps the relevance of WCAG 2.0 across additional areas, such as accessibility of documents.

Authoring Tool Accessibility Guidelines (ATAG) 2.0, finalized as a W3C recommendation (web standard) in 2015, addresses two critical aspects of accessibility of the Web for people with disabilities. One aspect is accessibility of the user interface for authoring tools because these need to be accessible to people with disabilities. For instance, a web developer with low vision may need to adjust the size of the font in the editing window independently from the default font size intended for the eventual content of a website. Another aspect of ATAG 2.0 is support for production of accessible web content. In this function, ATAG 2.0 is complementary to WCAG 2.0. In both of these cases, the primary audience for ATAG 2.0 is developers of authoring tools, since the goal is to greatly facilitate how accessible web content can be authored. The range of authoring tools that ATAG 2.0 addresses is quite broad, including not only WYSIWYG ("what you see is what you get") HTML editors but also every kind of authoring tool from blogs and wikis to image editors, media editors, and content management systems (CMSs).

UAAG 2.0[26] addresses accessibility of browsers, browser extensions, readers, aspects of mobile applications not covered by WCAG 2.0, and interoperability with assistive technologies. It further addresses what user agents need to do to facilitate perception of content, operability of content, understandability of content, and programmatic access to content. Accessibility of browsers and user agents remains a concern to people with disabilities—especially the need for more consistent support for key features across different browsers, since the expectations that an individual with a disability may encounter for using a particular browser may vary from the workplace to school and to other settings. UAAG 2.0 was finalized as a Working Group note in 2015.

Although the complexity of test-suite development and full testing of UAAG 2.0 was a barrier in completing candidate recommendation work, multiple implementations were identified for all but a few of the accessibility provisions in these guidelines. Major changes in browsers and the browser-development process mean that different approaches may be needed to address browser accessibility in the future, but they may also mean new opportunities for automating more aspects of accessibility as the capabilities of browsers and other user agents become more advanced.

A fourth area of guidelines currently under development is provisionally called the Web Technology Accessibility Guidelines (WTAG).[27] This area addresses guidance for accessibility support directly in Web specifications themselves and is intended to help address the scalability problem of needing to ensure accessibility support in an ever-increasing and diversifying set of web technologies under development at W3C. The majority of technical standards and specifications on which the Web is based have been developed at W3C. Since technical specifications tend to proliferate rapidly to address every aspect of web usage, a large number of draft specifications must be tracked over the course of a given year, and accessibility experts must identify, analyze, and address all accessibility barriers before those specifications are finalized.

Initial development of WTAG includes a set of reference requirements for accessibility features and considerations for the design of different kinds of web technologies, as well as a checklist to facilitate self-review by working groups seeking to identify accessibility considerations early in their development processes. It particularly focuses on accessibility of any user interface specifications and the need for accessibility application programming interface mappings (AAMs). Use cases are expected to play a significant role as part of the WTAG resources. These can be helpful for developers in that they highlight design requirements that may be unfamiliar to some engineers without being prescriptive about how those requirements must be met. For instance, design requirements are part of the Media User Accessibility Requirements (MAUR),[28] which has been instrumental in addressing user requirements for accessible audio and video on the Web. In societies where there is still segregation between the lives of people with and without disabilities—which, despite recent improvements in human rights for people with disabilities, remains the case around much of the world at present—there is often a lack of familiarity with the specific needs of people with disabilities. User scenarios and use cases are not only a valuable starting point for articulating accessibility requirements but can also be good instruction for helping engineers who wish to understand the diversity of ways in which people with disabilities may interact with technology.

The Importance of Conformance-Evaluation Approaches

Assessing the conformance of a website or web application to accessibility standards is an important aspect of ensuring accessibility. It is relevant not only on the scale of individual websites and applications but also across entire market sectors when one is endeavoring to assess system-wide progress, or lack thereof, on accessibility.

It is possible to get a quick indication of potential accessibility problems on websites by following the tips in "Easy Checks,"[29] a WAI resource page that explains how to use existing browser settings for an initial inspection of a website. However, this approach will identify only a sampling of potential problems on a website, and is no substitute for conformance testing. Alternatively, one can use one of the many automated or semiautomated testing tools listed in the Web Accessibility Evaluation Tools List.[30] However, automated tests alone cannot provide a thorough assessment of conformance to WCAG 2.0, since some accessibility provisions require assessment by a human expert. A comprehensive conformance evaluation currently requires a knowledgeable human expert, often using one or more evaluation tools.

Coordination with the Research Community

Accessibility barriers often emerge at the edge of mainstream design. A research approach can help in better understanding needs and potential approaches to addressing barriers in unknown territory. Because of the need to keep up with and ideally keep ahead of the rapid pace of technical innovation, there has often been insufficient opportunity to research questions that might help move the field forward.

The research needed may include exploring less well known and less studied use cases or developing more specialized features than the average consumer might need. In some areas, such as accommodation of visual disabilities, there is a long history of well-articulated user requirements and well-proven strategies for addressing them—for instance, the detailed work on representation of information in complex images that has been done by the Diagram Project.[31] For other disabilities, user requirements are less well known, and there is a need for more focused research. Within W3C/WAI work, one response to this need has been establishment of the Cognitive and Learning Disabilities Accessibility Task Force,[32] which has taken on an effort to collect research on accessibility approaches for the broad spectrum of cognitive disabilities, including intellectual disabilities, memory impairments, and the autism spectrum. This task force has been instrumental in collecting and assessing relevant research that in some cases was not well known in the web-accessibility field.

Conclusion

There is a great need for work by people familiar with accessible technologies and accessible design principles across all these areas, and the need will only increase as the role of ICTs expands in the future. Many different types of expertise are needed at the table—whether it is help promoting understanding of the need for accessibility, working with the engineers and innovators who are designing new approaches to accessibility, or studying how and why accessible design of ICTs can be successfully implemented on a global scale. A starting point for work in this area is the Web Accessibility Initiative home page,[33] which links to guidelines, specifications, and other resources, including educational resources on Web accessibility.

CHAPTER 2

Accessible ICTs and the Opening of Political Space for Persons with Disabilities

Janet E. Lord

Introduction

Societal exclusion of persons with disabilities from political life persists as a serious contemporary human rights challenge. Although information and communication technology (ICT)[1] has the potential to pry open political space for persons who are isolated from political decision making in all sorts of ways,[2] absent attention to ICT accessibility, additional barriers can be created and further entrench the exclusion of marginalized groups from political engagement in their communities. For election practitioners, whether and how to use modern ICTs is a major focus of attention, particularly in regard to voter registration and identification, e-voting, processing of results, and the use of open-source technology in election administration. In some contexts, ICTs enhance efficiencies in the electoral cycle, but ICTs can also introduce difficult challenges, including the adoption of inappropriate and inaccessible technologies and lack of qualified staff to work with ICTs.

For persons with disabilities, ICT accessibility emerges as a concern in a wide variety of contexts in democratic societies; and those areas affecting social and economic development have deep implications for citizen participation and the exercise of political rights.[3] A primary concern is ensuring that voting procedures, facilities, and materials are accessible.[4] Related are e-government processes and services, including those that register voters, engage the public in consultation and decision making, and provide civic and voter education. Both civil society education and advocacy and political party campaigning and platform dissemination are additional dimensions of ICT accessibility in political spaces. Too often, ICT barriers limit individual decision making and communal participation for individuals with disabilities.[5] These arise not as a consequence of technological obstacles and shortcomings but because of socially driven decisions or failures to embrace accessibility.[6] In that sense, inaccessible ICTs reflect social choice and not inevitable technological constraint. To the extent that ICTs constrain and limit participation, whether of individuals with disabilities or other marginalized groups, concentrations of power by those with access are facilitated, and the potential for governmental abuse is greater.[7]

This chapter explores the role of ICTs in advancing (or retrenching) political space for persons with disabilities. It begins by reviewing ICT accessibility barriers that limit access to and usage of political processes. In so doing, it examines the particular salience of a disability human rights perspective on the issue of ICTs and their potential to facilitate or constrain the participation of persons with disabilities in political and public life.[8] Second, it sets forth the Convention on the Rights of Persons with Disabilities (CRPD) framework in the context of ICT and political participation. Thereafter, it examines the role of ICTs in electoral processes by examining points of ICT intervention along the entirety of the electoral cycle. It also highlights some rich and innovative practices advocates have advanced to secure implementation of the CRPD in this context and to make active and engaged citizenship real for persons with disabilities. It concludes by identifying key areas of policy making and programmatic activities to implement CRPD requirements for ICTs in political life.

ICT Exclusion

General international human rights documents provide no specific protection against discrimination on the basis of disability, nor do such instruments contain positive measures intended to bring about substantive equality for persons with disabilities.[9] Early human rights instruments, such as the 1948 Universal Declaration of Human Rights, do, however, emphasize political equality generally and the right to seek, receive, and impart information, as well as the right to benefit from scientific progress. To that extent, they provide an important point of departure for the consideration of ICT accessibility for persons with disabilities and indeed for all persons.

There are a multitude of barriers that persons with various types of disabilities may experience in accessing ICTs.[10] Many of these affect the exercise of rights to participate in political and public life. ICT access is hindered by direct barriers presented in using ICT (for example, the inaccessible electronic voting machine or government service information or service provision via web page) and also by indirect barriers posed by legal, attitudinal, and physical dimensions that facilitate or inhibit ICT access.

Too often, fundamental aspects of political engagement are supported by inaccessible ICTs. Television is a central conveyor of political campaign messaging and voter information but is too often inaccessible to persons who are deaf when it is delivered without closed captioning (scrolling text across a television set). Notably, closed captioning provides access to information not only to people who are deaf or hard of hearing but also to those who cannot access the language used or those in the process of learning to read.

Election commissions routinely provide automated information on voting and candidates provide information on their platforms by telephone, posing barriers for those who cannot hear or those who require plain language or need support in understanding the information provided. In addition, mobile phones now routinely provide voter information, but they are not always accessible, for instance, to persons with vision impairments absent features such as text-to-speech. Emergency evacuation plans are relevant for electoral contexts, but too often security considerations inhibit access, while emergency procedures fail to be accessible.

Although the introduction of e-voting (the use of electronic means in elections to cast or count votes) can advance accessibility and seriously improve human voter-assistance systems by allowing independent ballot casting and safeguarding secrecy of the vote, they must be designed with accessibility features in place. Too often, they fail to effectively communicate the voting process to voters accessing via audio media or are physically designed in a way that does not meet the current consensus on accessible design as crafted by the technology industry, the disability community, and leading national government institutions. One disabled persons' organization (DPO) representative, speaking in relation to blind voters who had used a California e-voting machine, reported that "very few of our members were able to vote privately, independently, despite Santa Clara County's supposed accessible touch screens."[11] Survey results of fifty blind voters detailed barriers experienced in using the audio technology intended to guide them through the ballot and then cast a vote in secret. These included poor sound quality, delayed response time, braille that was positioned so awkwardly that it could be read upside down, and meaningless audio directives, such as one requiring blind voters to press a yellow button, which, for one blind voter, was decidedly unhelpful because yellow had no meaning for him.[12]

The introduction of technology poses other barriers as well, for instance, where voting machines have instructions posted too high to be read by persons of short stature or persons using wheelchairs, requiring that voters ask for assistance and inhibiting independent voting and secrecy. In voting districts using paper ballots, automated scanners for the ballots may also be used and require the voter to manually feed ballots into the scanner. Too often scanners are high or awkwardly positioned, requiring assistance and thereby compromising both independence and secrecy of the vote. Website navigation, whether for an election commission, a political party, a government site, or a political action group, may be constrained for some users in a variety of ways: constant flickering poses concentration barriers for individuals, complex layout of information is difficult to understand, and readers using screen-reader technology may be unable to access documents that contain image files a screen reader cannot understand.

All these examples illustrate the kinds of barriers that can seriously undermine participation in political and public life for persons with disabilities where ICT accessibility is not addressed. It should also be recognized that some members of the disability community are particularly marginalized by confronting severe discrimination in exercising their right to participate in the political process. Women with disabilities, for instance, are all too often not afforded the chance to attend school or to work, and their opportunity to engage in political decision making is thereby undermined. Even if ICTs are made accessible, social barriers will often serve to undermine disabled women's access because they may have restricted mobility within their community, lack the skills to use technology, or face other barriers. Persons with mental disabilities are also frequently denied the right to vote, sometimes on the basis of arbitrary exclusion at the polling place.

Stigma and false assumptions about what individuals can or cannot do may be even more pronounced where ICTs are being utilized.

ICTs in the CRPD Framework

The CRPD responds to ICT marginalization in several ways. Its reflection of the social model, in combination with its recognition of both individual and collective disability human rights, offers a framework within which ICTs may be used to facilitate political participation consistent with principles of nondiscrimination, accessibility, and universal design.[13] ICT accessibility falls within the ambit of nondiscrimination in several respects. First, the duty to provide reasonable accommodation may be achieved through ICT access measures, such as activating an accessibility feature of an e-voting machine to accommodate a user. Second, positive measures provided to ensure equality, such as ICT access measures in developing an election commission website, are expected in order to facilitate equality. Third, the failure to provide reasonable accommodation where required in an individual case and where it would not represent an undue or disproportionate burden (e.g., placing ballot machinery on a high table out of the reach of a wheelchair user) constitutes discrimination.

Several of the CRPD's specific substantive rights either explicitly or implicitly make reference to accessible ICTs,[14] including provisions on political participation, access to information and freedom of expression, and access to education. Equally, accessibility of ICTs applies in respect to CRPD implementation measures.[15] Shoring up protections for persons with disabilities in ICT, the Marrakesh Treaty to Facilitate Access to Published Works for Persons Who Are Blind, Visually Impaired or Otherwise Print Disabled, adopted in 2013, responds to the barriers experienced by persons with print disabilities. These protections have salience for protecting the right of persons with disabilities to participate in political and public life.

ICT Accessibility Practices to Advance Political Participation

ICTs play a critical role in advancing citizen participation in the electoral cycle and other realms of democratic engagement. ICT products, contents, and services are already universally used to facilitate political participation and will continue to do so. Most ICT applications in the political-engagement realm (whether in e-voting, accessing e-government, or engaging in online political action) can be made readily accessible to most users. In order to do so, however, ICTs must make provision for alternative modes of interaction, provide outputs in multiple formats, support customization of configurations and settings, and be made compatible with assistive technology. Some rough guidelines provide texture to ICT accessibility in operationalizing accessibility and are clearly essential as election events become increasingly reliant on ICT for many aspects of implementation.

The point of departure for implementation of ICT-accessibility measures is ICT usability, roughly defined as "the extent to which a product or service can be used by a person with a disability as effectively as it can be used by a person without that disability."[16] Users of ICTs must be able to (1) perceive, (2) understand, and (3) operate ICT products, content, and services.[17] These three elements of usability[18] are important in making assessments of ICT accessibility in exercising political rights, for instance, the way voting equipment is designed, its use, and where it is located or placed for the user.

ICT products, content, and services may be regarded as accessible if they can be used by all individuals equally, irrespective of disability. Like reasonable accommodations generally, ensuring full access can be (and frequently is) straightforward. It may include measures such as providing textual descriptions for images on election commission and other government websites (to aid blind persons using screen readers or persons experiencing comprehension barriers) or pictorial guides to portray step-by-step election procedures, or text/video-messaging services for deaf persons or for persons who cannot read the language.

A range of ICTs exists to carry out communication in ways that facilitate participation in political and public life. These include television and radio, fixed and mobile telephony, text messaging and short message service (SMS), and Internet-based resources and services such as e-mail communication, websites, video, instant messaging over the Internet, interactive training tools, Voice over Internet Protocol services, web conferencing, social media that allow for instant communications, instant photo/video capture and sharing, and satellite communications. Perhaps the most beneficial aspect of ICT use to facilitate citizen participation and voice is the ability to create and deliver content in multiple formats through multiple media.

Conceptualizing the election process cyclically underscores that elections form part of an ongoing political process as opposed to isolated events. At the most general level, the electoral cycle is divided into three main periods: the preelectoral period, the electoral period, and the postelectoral period. The electoral cycle has no fixed starting or ending points, nor do the three periods and the segments within the cycle. In theory, it may be said that one cycle ends when another begins. However, some postelectoral-period activities may still be ongoing when activities related to the subsequent electoral cycle commence. Similarly, some segments, such as civic education and support to political parties, cut across the whole cycle and are therefore to be considered ongoing activities throughout all three periods. Electoral components (and stakeholders) are interdependent, and therefore, the breakdown of one aspect (for example, the collapse of a particular system of voter registration) can negatively affect another, including the credibility of the election itself, and thus the legitimacy of the elected government and the democratization process of a partner country and its overall development objectives. The discussion that follows identifies points of intervention not only in terms of casting ballots, but at various points throughout the electoral cycle.

Legal Frameworks

Ensuring legal-framework compatibility with ICT accessibility principles hinges on a variety of factors, including whether and how election law and ICT regulation intersect and whether the legal framework is sufficiently developed and flexible enough to address ICT accessibility in the electoral context, among others. There are many areas in which independent election commissions, local and national governments, and technology providers need to intervene and work to implement ICT accessibility through policy and government processes, as well as through other channels. A key component of successful engagement is participation of persons with disabilities and DPOs, for instance, through a disability task force or similar structure, as in the (Australian) Victorian Electoral Commission's (VEC) Election Access Advisory Group, which meets regularly to review implementation of the commission's Disability Action Plan.[19]

Of particular import are laws that prohibit discrimination in cyberspace, together with implementing regulations or implementation guidelines. Election-specific codes and regulations ought to expressly incorporate standards by reference or adopt them specifically. Specific government regulations may affect the adoption of technology for use by election bodies, whether by limiting procurement of goods by type (accessible ballots or e-voting machines) or place of manufacture or requiring that technology purchases be vetted or approved by appropriate authorities external to the election-management body. An election-accessibility task force or DPO panel can reduce the likelihood of the procurement of inaccessible ICTs.

The applicable regulatory environment may accordingly foster or constrain the implementation of accessible ICTs by electoral administration bodies and other stakeholders. Any standards and restrictions on technology acquisition should be identified early on to avoid conflicts, select appropriate technology, and implement changes smoothly. In other instances, implementation of ICTs in the electoral context will require legislative and regulatory reform, as in the introduction of digital voter-registration systems and use of electronic voting (e-voting) systems.

Equally important is ensuring that, where needed, legislative changes are implemented before budgetary allocations to develop and implement new systems and new technologies. In some instances, legislation may foster funding for ICT access. In the United States, the first law to specifically address voting technology was the Help America Vote Act of 2002 (HAVA), established, among other things, to fund the replacement of punch-card voting systems.[20] In other countries, election commissions are pressing for law reform to support more flexible forms of electronically assisted voting for specific target groups at all elections.[21] Since legislation can have a significant impact on the type of technology that can be used for an electoral process, it is advisable to request legislators to use language that allows some flexibility in the choice of technology by election administrators. Moreover, it is essential that such reform processes adhere to disability legislation and accessibility standards.

Finally, ICT accessibility must be considered in the context of election-related disputes. The legal framework must identify and empower existing bodies, such as courts and election commissions, or new institutions, such as electoral courts, to properly and quickly handle violations of political rights of persons with disabilities. Electoral complaints mechanisms must accommodate claims relating to inaccessibility of voter materials in the ICT realm that prevent users with disabilities from exercising their political rights.[22] ICT accessibility in relation to electoral-complaint rules and procedures relates to ensuring that the format and formal requirements for election complaints are clear and specified in the election law or in implementing regulations that are developed by election-management bodies, and that information is readily accessible. Although an official form provided for the filing of election complaints may facilitate access, it may also hinder access if it is difficult to find on a website, is not readable by screen-reading technology, or is confusing or written in complex language.

Preelection Technical Assessments

Preelection technical assessments are tools used by election bodies, international development agencies, and other election stakeholders to assess the electoral environment, together with political, economic, social, and security issues that may affect political campaigns and election procedures, and to make recommendations.[23] Too often, however, assessments of the accessibility of an electoral system to persons with disabilities are not included within general assessment frameworks but exist as a one-off or ad hoc effort, if at all.[24] It is the rare preelection technical assessment that includes ICT accessibility in its framework at all, much less a comprehensive review of ICT and disability law and policy more generally. Some election bodies are including ICT accessibility in their standard accessibility audit tool for polling centers, a practice that needs to be expanded, along with the practice of including ICT access in preelection technical assessments.

Civic and Voter Education

Websites, Facebook, and other social media are increasingly used for voter education and information.[25] Efforts to reach young voters focus on horizontal interaction (music, video clips, and so on) rather than top-down voter-education efforts in order to reach youth most effectively via the Internet. Many of these efforts are designed to be as interactive as possible in order to best capture the attention of young people. In some country contexts, for instance, rural areas in developing countries, the Internet is often not an ideal medium in the context of developing democracies because of a lack of accessibility. Instead, other more traditional methods of voter education, as well as SMS technology, are advocated.

In Kenya, the deaf community promoted sign language interpretation for television stations, including its use in elections. The Kenya National Association of the Deaf staged a demonstration outside the Nation Centre in February 2013, demanding that all television stations make their programming fully accessible by providing either sign language interpretation or closed captioning or subtitling. Use of SMS media has the potential to significantly enhance access to information for deaf persons who are able to use such technology. The Rwanda National Association of Deaf Women initiated an SMS media program to make government programs, including election information, known to deaf people. In Congo, deaf advocates responded to a ban on SMS texting by the government initiated after public unrest, claiming that it was being used to "incite ethnic hatred, insurrection and xenophobia" around presidential and parliamentary elections. The advocates argued that the measure affected many Congolese deaf persons because this was a primary mode of communication for many, and that the measure essentially condemned deaf Congolese people to indefinite isolation.[26]

The VEC's Disability Action Plan includes a range of interventions aimed at promoting the accessibility of civic and voter education, many with ICT implications. Among them are (1) the development of an e-mail network through which to promote and distribute electoral information and education to Victorians with a disability; (2) promoting a wheelchair-accessibility rating system on the VEC's website and providing a voting-center finder, along with press advertisements that list all voting centers in the state; and (3) a communication campaign during electoral periods specifically to promote accessible venues and accessibility initiatives.[27]

Voter Registration

In many countries, election bodies are turning to online voter registration on the grounds that online efficiencies result in a decrease in administrative burdens, enhanced data accuracy of voter rolls, and significant cost savings.[28] Election officials are now routinely using the Internet to register voters, display voter lists or individual voter-registration records, and communicate polling-station assignments to voters.[29] Information entered in real time at registration centers into direct data capture devices can be transmitted to a centralized voter registry, often via the Internet. Displays of voter lists via the Internet, along with individual voter-registration records, allows, among other things, citizens to check the voter lists and verify their accuracy. It stands to reason that such systems could also capture information regarding reasonable accommodations needed, generating information about accessibility, allowing for assignment to an accessible polling site, and capturing much-needed data about reforms to enhance accessibility.

For eligible voters, an online voter-registration system may represent an easy and quick way to register.[30] At the same time, absent attention to web accessibility, online voter registration may serve to disadvantage individuals with disabilities, persons with low literacy, and persons who have little or no online access.[31] A study of European Union countries found that of twenty-eight EU member states, only ten election websites complied with website accessibility standards, and six had none at all.[32] As voter registration becomes increasingly administered online, it is important to ensure that it will ease the process of registration for all voters and not create additional barriers.

Ballot Casting and Accessible Voting Equipment

Ballot casting around the world increasingly falls within the domain of e-voting machines, a category of ICT under the umbrella of "electronic kiosks."[33] The accessibility elements of key concern include (1) physical accessibility, which may prevent a user from having any access at all to the machine because of its placement; and (2) user interface accessibility, or enabling all actions required to use the voting machine, including pressing buttons, responding to audio instructions, using keypads or touchscreens, and the like.[34]

Persons who have a permanent or temporary condition that restricts their mobility may confront barriers along the pathway to a voting machine, including, for example, steps, posts, or signage, making it difficult or even impossible to access the machines. These obstacles can likewise pose problems for people with restricted vision. Accordingly, the pathway to some or indeed all e-voting machines must be free from obstacles such as steps, bins, or signage that would obstruct the progress of users who are either walking or using a mobility aid such as a wheelchair or motorized scooter. This includes the path into any room or area containing the e-voting machine. The user should be able to operate the kiosk from a clear, flat area large enough to maneuver mobility aids such as a wheelchair or buggy. There should be provision for adequate lighting.

The operable parts of an electronic voting machine, like other electronic kiosks, may consist of a number of discrete components, each raising discrete accessibility issues, such as (1) labels and instructions; (2) smart cards; (3) displays; (4) keypads; and (5) touchscreens.[35] These operations should be possible with minimal grip, pushing and pulling strength, or twisting of the wrist. Users should be able to access all of these from whatever position and orientation they find themselves in naturally when using the voting machine, and ideally, this should be a single position that does not require the person to reorient himself or herself during the operation.[36]

In the United States, federal law and state requirements mandate that voting systems be equipped for voters with disabilities, affording the same opportunity to vote privately and independently and requiring that every precinct must have at least one accessible voting machine available. In Massachusetts, for example, voting machines use electronic marking devices with audio-cue capacity for visually impaired voters. They will also magnify the ballot or display the ballot in high contrast for voters with low vision and produce an oral report to the voter to disclose the choices selected before the voter prints the ballot.[37] In Western Australia, computer software called Vote Assist allows electors with visual impairments to listen to an audio recording, and by following the instructions and using a numeric keypad, they can cast their vote, obtain a printed ballot paper, and place the ballot paper in the ballot box, thereby preserving both independence and secrecy. A U.S. Government Accountability Office (GAO) 2005 report highlighted the range of options for voters who are blind, including braille keyboards and audio interfaces, voice-recognition capability to allow voters to make selections orally, and the accommodation of voters with neurological disabilities by offering head-movement switches and "sip-and-puff" plug-ins for voting machines. This last technology employs a mouth-held straw with which the voter issues switch commands—hard puff, hard sip, soft puff, and soft sip—to provide signals or instructions to the voting machine. This and other ICT, such as e-voting technology, that facilitate voting for persons with disabilities may also address the needs of voters living in remote areas or overseas voting. The U.S. government has addressed the widespread need to accommodate voters posted abroad (military, civilian personnel) through the introduction of fully accessible online voting.[38]

E-voting machines are clearly not the sum total of ICT at work in voting centers. In many instances, additional devices may be used to assist in the voting process. Election-management bodies may also include a standard stock of voting aids, including fat pencils, magnifying sheets, closed-circuit television (CCTV) units for enlarging views of voting material, talking boards where possible, and seating, in order to further facilitate access. To be sure, as with any disability accommodation or accessibility measure, ICT accessibility will be driven by the local context and will also hinge inevitably on individual needs and preferences, posing challenges for election bodies that can be adequately addressed only with ongoing and consistent user input.

Notwithstanding moves toward e-voting, many electoral bodies are nervous about the validity and security of elections and are promoting a turn back to paper-based ballots instead of the direct recording electronic voting devices. This is of some consequence for accessibility, especially for people with print disabilities, because it reinstalls barriers that were already removed (since many times states are not purchasing the paper-ballot devices that allow access to the blind). A recent case from the U.S. state of Maryland illustrates well this tension between security and accessibility. The state had failed to certify an accessible version of its online ballot-marking tool, citing concerns about possible voter fraud. This prompted a lawsuit in which it was argued that absent certification, persons with visual disabilities would be denied meaningful access to the absentee-ballot voting process in the upcoming election. A U.S. district court ruled that the state was required to make the system accessible.[39]

Procurement of Election Technology

Vital to ensuring access to political processes, whether voting or other public decision-making processes, is ensuring that technology associated with such participation complies with ICT-accessibility obligations by implementing appropriate public procurement rules that include ICT-accessibility considerations. Although public procurement is not specifically referenced in the CRPD, it is nonetheless covered in Article 4 (for example, general obligations concerning conformity with the CRPD by public authorities and institutions), together with ensuring the implementation of all rights in the treaty in all policies and programs of government (Article 4(3)). Procurement in the context of ICTs and political participation processes thus falls squarely within this ambit. Recent research, however, suggests that public procurement is underused to prompt ICT-accessibility implementation.[40]

The procurement of election-related ICTs is a central component of planning for accessibility by all users. DPOs are often able to find innovative and frugal solutions to address specific challenges, such as providing portable screen readers or other assistive software that can be carried around and used on multiple computers by persons with disabilities who are forced to use cybercafes or service centers.[41]

In Canada, the issue of ICTs and ensuring that accessibility is given due attention in the procurement of products (including, for example, voting machines) was the focus of a detailed assessment. A task force recommended that governments at all levels use the force of procurement to promote and encourage the adoption of universal design standards for accessibility, and that only materials complying with such standards should be purchased. The Accessible Procurement Toolkit, published by the government's Assistive Devices Industry Office, supports the process as a web-based application that delivers accessibility requirements and standards to apply to a purchase of mainstream products and services. The overall objective is to ensure that products meet "universal design" principles and help the procuring organization meet its mandated obligation to purchase more accessible goods and services.[42] Other countries are similarly responding: for example, Ireland, where an ICT procurement tool kit provides guidance on procuring goods and services.[43]

For many developing countries, especially those emerging from conflict or transitioning to democracy, the procurement of election materials (voting machines, ballots, and other materials) is financed by international donors who may not take accessibility into account. Some donors have sought to respond to this issue. The U.S. Agency for International Development, for example, has adopted two directives relating to procurement; although it is not specific to ICTs, one of those directives does remind responders to solicitations that their programs should not present barriers to persons with disabilities.[44] More rigorous monitoring could amplify such efforts and highlight the issue of ICT accessibility, among other measures to ensure that development programs are benefiting persons with disabilities.

Training of Election Officials and Other Election Stakeholders

Many training packages use ICTs in the delivery of training to election officials and other election stakeholders. Indeed, a multicountry survey of election-official training approaches reveals that typical training formats very often include PowerPoint slides and transparency masters, videos and DVDs, interactive CDs, and website training.[45]

Beyond ensuring that such training formats are accessible to election workers and other stakeholders with disabilities, the content of the training must likewise adequately cover accessibility issues. Some electoral commissions have disability action plans that require a specific section of a training module to cover universal access awareness and sensitivity training for election staff and that senior officials receive training on the setup of a voting center to ensure adequate space in the layout, as well as ensuring that lower-height voting compartments are used, which can be critical for accessing election technology. Voter-information staff might further receive training on running a communication campaign during electoral periods specifically to promote accessible venues and accessibility initiatives. These might highlight, for example, customized settings on voting machines, such as setting the font size larger or activating assistive technology such as screen readers, screen magnification, or voice-recognition software for input, among others.[46] A task force focused on ICT accessibility in Canada, for example, recommended that departments and agencies of government at all levels train their personnel to be aware of the specific needs of print-disabled Canadians, such as the availability of multiple format materials, and in the use of the related assistive technology.[47]

Political Campaigning and Running for Office

Voters with disabilities need information on political party manifestos, candidates, and campaign events to make an informed decision. As candidates for office, likewise, persons with disabilities need to have a level playing field in order to be competitive. Partnerships between DPOs and political parties represent an important avenue for dialogue and relationship building.

Self-advocates with intellectual disabilities in Ireland developed an innovative program that sought to expand the accessibility of political party platforms and campaign information. The project website, My Opinion, My Vote, developed information in easy-to-read formats and standards for political parties and others to follow in ensuring information accessibility in the political participation context.[48] In Louisiana, the federally mandated protection and advocacy system created a comprehensive guide on accessibility in the context of political campaigns, directed primarily at candidates and political parties, to help ensure the accessibility of their campaign messaging to persons with disabilities.[49]

Televised debates are a routine feature of political campaigns but all too often are inaccessible to deaf viewers. The election-management body in Guatemala provided professional sign language interpreters for debates so that deaf and hard-of-hearing constituents could access the debates on television. Similarly, in Serbia in 2012, owing to DPO pressure, televised debates between presidential candidates featured a sign language interpreter.[50] Deaf advocates are continuing to achieve these advocacy successes in countries around the world.[51]

Before the July 2012 elections, Mexican DPOs developed a disability rights platform with priority issues to share with presidential candidates. The coalition published and disseminated these proposals on its website and promoted them on social media platforms.[52] Down Syndrome Ireland launched a campaign to engage its members in the European Union parliamentary electoral process, presenting and posting online easy-to-read documents.[53]

Although the CRPD upholds the right of persons with disabilities to run for public office on the basis of equality, the playing field is often not level. Canadian disability rights advocate Steven Estey encountered firsthand the financial costs associated with running a political campaign: "The real issue for me in that campaign was that disability related costs were not covered, so I had to raise the money for the campaign and access costs—so it is a disincentive for a local organization to field a disabled candidate since they are on the hook for additional costs."[54]

Conclusion

The disability rights advocacy that helped forge international consensus resulting in the adoption of the CRPD continues through implementation processes around the world. Although progress is beginning to be made, more needs to be done to ensure that ICTs are made accessible in an ever-broadening array of applications designed to advance political inclusion. A report issued for the High Level Meeting on Disability and Development, held at the United Nations in September 2014, stresses the importance of ICTs for the inclusion of persons with disabilities, including in political life.[55] Thus ICT accessibility is beginning to emerge on the international disability and development agenda, and democracy-promotion activities supported by bilateral and multilateral donors must adhere to prevailing standards in this context.

As the foregoing illustrates, work undertaken to expand accessibility to political processes through ICTs presents opportunities for persons with disabilities, but it is by no means assured. Some developments are hopeful manifestations of agency and engaged citizenship that can be developed in order to further advance ICT inclusion. Nonetheless, rapid ratification of the CRPD, which has created space for domestic law and policy change, poses a challenge where rapid reform does not keep pace with advances in ICT.

Although ICT applications and ICT services can pose insurmountable barriers if they are not designed in an accessible way, new ICT solutions can facilitate unprecedented access to political life for persons with disabilities. Examples in this regard include text-to-speech applications allowing persons to access the digital version of otherwise inaccessible print documents, GPS and GIS technology, image recognition, near field communications, and Internet connectivity. These and other ICTs represent new enabling technologies that support multiple entry points for political engagement by persons with disabilities, as well as other marginalized groups.[56]

CHAPTER 3

Web Accessibility for People with Cognitive Disabilities: A Legal Right?

Peter Blanck

Introduction

This chapter explores how a legal right to web accessibility is necessary for people with cognitive and other disabilities to fully participate in the information age. I consider definitions, legal challenges, and rights that are discussed more fully in *eQuality: The Struggle for Web Accessibility by Persons with Cognitive Disabilities*.[1] I also reflect on new disability law and policy developments in the United States and internationally since *eQuality* was published. Full and equal access to the Internet's World Wide Web ("web") is an enabler of basic human and civil rights.[2] The web supports the freedoms of speech, association, and civic engagement.[3] But although it is fundamental to exercising one's rights of citizenship,[4] access to the technological tools of the Internet alone is not sufficient to guarantee web equality. Overly complex interfaces, lack of information alternatives (for example, symbols along with text, captions instead of audio), and the inability to transform content presentation all prevent effective use of the tool that is the Internet's web. Technology access alone is not web-content equality.

I have described web *eQuality* as the opportunity for full and equal enjoyment of web content across all its technologies and interfaces: "Full and equal enjoyment of the web is to have the meaningful and reasonably comparable opportunity to enjoy—access and use—web content, and to not be excluded from that prospect on the basis of cognitive and other disabilities, either by individuals, organizations, or through the design of web technology."⁵ Web technology has the unique potential to reduce attitudinal, behavioral, and structural barriers encountered by individuals with a range of cognitive, physical, and sensory capabilities. I take a civil and human rights approach to disability and frame web equality within the norms and legal obligations of the Americans with Disabilities Act (ADA) and the UN Convention on the Rights of Persons with Disabilities (CRPD). The power of the web is in its potential to mitigate barriers to knowledge that drive and inform human cognition, speech, and ideas. The web increases the opportunity for individuals and collectives to share knowledge, but structural barriers such as poverty and a lack of access to technology continue to stand in the way of full access to the information society.

Presently, to approach web equality, people with a range of disabilities require modifications and accommodations in service design when it is reasonable and feasible to provide them. These accommodations alone do not and cannot guarantee that in all circumstances people with disabilities will have the same outcomes from their activities on the web. In this sense, web equality does not necessarily equate to content impartiality because there may be judgment at some point before the end user to determine what information will be offered and how. Although it is expected that content transformations and substitution of equivalent information will be directed by the end user, there is still a filtering process that may raise concerns about how web content is selected. Will certain alternate content be favored over another, and if so, why?

I use the term "web *eQuality*" to emphasize two essential ideals. The first is the conception of equality and justice under law. Thus in the ADA there may be found a justiciable right to web equality for persons with cognitive and other disabilities. The second is the conception of "*e*lectronic quality," which signifies that the meaningful and objective opportunity for the comparable use of web content by people with disabilities is possible, with particular reference in this chapter to people with cognitive disabilities. The right to enjoy digital knowledge is encompassed by freedom from discrimination as a consequence of disability and is established by the ADA and recognized in the CRPD.

Rights of People with Cognitive Disabilities

In the United States, the ADA has been in effect for more than twenty-five years, and there has been a concordant growth in disability rights worldwide.

For example, China passed a national-level disability rights law concurrent with the ADA, and several countries, including the United Kingdom and Australia, adopted domestic disability protections modeled on the ADA. Nevertheless, web equality for people with cognitive disabilities has received limited attention, and when it has been examined, it has faced resistance and pushback. Under the ADA, the right to web equality, like other rights assuring nondiscriminatory access to society, is considered on an individualized basis in circumstances involving human-computer interaction. People with cognitive and other disabilities who choose to engage with the web must have the prospect for reasonably equivalent and comparable use of its electronic content (not simply separate access to it), as do others without disabilities in the same situation.[6]

Nondiscrimination in the full and equal enjoyment of web content offered by commercial entities is addressed by the ADA's Title III, which covers services offered by "public accommodations," including those of online service providers. Freedom from discrimination because of disability in the use of the online activities of public accommodations (and of state and local governments under the ADA's Title II) and the corresponding obligation to make modifications within reason to ensure that services offered are equally enjoyable are among the central means by which people with disabilities meaningfully participate in the digital information society.

The ADA's preamble establishes its mandate as ensuring equal opportunity, inclusion, independent living, and opportunity for economic self-sufficiency.[7] The web is a major driver of these principles, particularly for people with cognitive disabilities.[8] For this reason, the lack of equal opportunity to participate on the web, whereby separate access to web content becomes the default means for interaction, is inherently not equal for people with cognitive and other disabilities who aim to enjoy such services.

The World Wide Web Consortium (W3C) defines equivalent web content as that which is an "acceptable substitute," adaptation, and alternative that "fulfills essentially the same function or purpose as the original content upon presentation."[9] Alternative content removes reliance on any one mode and cognitive mechanism for comprehension; for instance, text can be heard instead of seen, audio can be read instead of heard, images can be described instead of seen, and so on. This seemingly complex suspension of modal reliance often is achieved simply in web content, as well as in other digital content. An illustration of a common adaptation is transformations in presentation, such as text enlargements and higher contrasts.

Practically speaking, the enjoyment of web content must be considered in context. This is why laws like the ADA approach such fact-based determinations on a case-by-case basis and not in terms of prescriptive compliance with web-content technical standards and functional performance criteria. This also is the reason that American courts tend to view web equality in accord with notions of the equivalent opportunity to participate regardless of disability. The concept of web equality embodies the comparable choice to participate online, with or without appropriate supports and adjustments, and without discrimination on the basis of disability.

Given historical and present attitudinal discrimination, web equality is a means to ensure that disability is respected as an element of human diversity. The ADA accords people with disabilities individual and collective rights to web equality regardless of obvious or hidden individual characteristics that may subject them to invidious and paternalistic forms of prejudice and discrimination. Article 9 of the CRPD likewise conceives of web accessibility as the opportunity to have equivalent access to and use of web content, and for individuals not to be excluded unreasonably from that prospect because of disability.

Global Context

The human rights of disabled people set out in the CRPD are recognized by more than 165 nations that have ratified the treaty. The CRPD reflects a commitment by member states to value active citizenship by people with disabilities. Article 1 of the CRPD states as its purpose "to promote, protect and ensure the full and equal enjoyment of all human rights and fundamental freedoms by all persons with disabilities, and to promote respect for their inherent dignity." People with disabilities are people with physical, sensory, mental, or cognitive impairments who face societal barriers that "hinder their full and effective participation in society on an equal basis with others" without such conditions.

The CRPD (Article 9, Accessibility) establishes obligations for states parties to ensure comparable access to communications technology. Although the United States has yet to ratify the CRPD, the ADA directs that in a free society, people with disabilities have the equal right to use online materials to learn, work, play, communicate, shop, and participate fully in their communities. Furthermore, other countries are evolving their own approaches and legislative responses to web accessibility. Israel, for example, requires that private and public entities providing services available to the public on the Internet make those websites accessible by October 2016. Kenya, as noted in Chapter 14 by Giannoumis and colleagues, also requires web accessibility.

Web Ubiquity

Almost half (42 percent) of the world's seven billion people use the web.[10] Web usage is accelerating for people who previously have faced barriers to it, including people with cognitive disabilities and those who are aging (or who acquire cognitive disabilities with age), people living in poverty, and others who face economic and political restrictions on web access. More people use mobile and tablet devices to access the web than desktop PCs.[11] In 2014, there were more than one billion smartphones and tablets bought worldwide, and this number was set to double.[12]

Web Content

Web content is online digital information derived from human and machine operations and transferred to users by various means. Nonetheless, the definition of web content is far from clear for purposes of legal analysis.[13] Social networking websites often distinguish among web content, online data, and metadata ("data that explain or describe other data"). They are all forms of knowledge-based digital information that allow for online participation and the sharing of electronic text, images, and other modes of communication, as expressed in computer code, data, and semantic information in machine-readable formats. The W3C's Web Content Accessibility Guidelines (WCAG, presently in version 2.0) conceives of web content as the "information and sensory experience to be communicated to the user by means of a user agent (e.g., a browser), including code and markup that define the content's structure, presentation, and interactions."[14]

User-Based Content

The web's architecture enables online service providers to organize and maintain digital information about users in computer code. One common form of such metadata collection is cookies, which are tracking devices that create summaries of user data.[15] Other metadata derive from the use of the web and its applications, such as information about electronic book (e-book) usage and purchases made online.

Location-based web content and services may be offered using metadata, such as information retrieved from a device's global positioning system (GPS) and Internet service provider (ISP). This information may be used by the web service to provide a user with information such as advertisements tailored to user preferences and choices in situ. "Click data" from the user's interaction with an advertisement are assessed to determine an ad's effectiveness and resultant closure of e-sales.

Websites create other data from user information; for instance, using GPS and sensors that collect location information and provide real-time information and content feedback to the user. Many e-commerce organizations sell this content to third-party enterprises for marketing and other purposes. This web content is dynamic, in part because it is user generated and collected via multiple sensors and offered in multiple formats from text, photos, movies, and audio. User-based content exemplifies the extraordinary capacity of online service providers to provide personalized and customized experiences to individual visitors and to respond to the needs and preferences of the individual.

Semantic Content

The web's inventor, Tim Berners-Lee, and his colleagues conceived of the web as a responsive (experiential) and machine-assisted "Semantic Web." The Semantic Web refers to a common structure for understanding and processing web content with the assistance of computer algorithms (rules for computer processing).[16] The conception of the Semantic Web draws on advances in natural language processing (NLP: computers drawing meaning from human language) and the ability of machines to recognize human speech and convert it to electronic text.

The Semantic Web is a conceptual, machine-based framework that enhances access to and use of web content by diverse users. It does this by aiding in the understanding, organization, and interpretation of digital information. Intelligent web design conceived presently has not replicated and may never replicate the intricate state of human knowledge processing and interaction; however, it has the promise to make web content accessible and usable (in its broadest form, universally usable) by people with cognitive and other disabilities. The Semantic Web, along with other innovations, will support web enjoyment that is individualized and contextualized in consideration of a user's preferences, skills, motivation, and use of assistive technology (AT) and myriad applications across desktop and mobile platforms, operating systems, and devices.

The capacity for semantic and user-based content to form both universal and individualized web content for people with cognitive disabilities is supported and increasingly delivered through cloud computing.[17] The cloud allows web users ubiquitous access as they move through contexts and setting, and interact with web-enabled and interconnected devices. Through access to software stored in the cloud, users are not tied to one access configuration, location, device, and form of AT. Cloud computing enables a user to use AT and invoke preferences on any enabled device. No longer are persons bound to a device that has AT or preferences installed; instead, they may enjoy the freedom of web-content equality in an information-technology ecosystem that undergoes continuous change (for example, updating of content) and leverages the exponential power of computer data mining, search capacity, and semantic content generation and interpretation.

Cognitive Disabilities and the Web

Besides discrimination and technological barriers, there are structural reasons that people with cognitive disabilities face exclusion from the web. Poverty and lack of inclusive education, inadequate job training, and negative expectations limit the opportunity to access computer technology and services provided online. There are associated barriers facing those across the spectrum of disability in transportation, health care, recreational activities, and housing. The examination of cognitive disability and web *eQuality* involves consideration of arguably the largest metagroup of people with disabilities. Admittedly, within cognitive disabilities there are individual disparities in access to and use of online services. There is evidence that for some populations of people with cognitive disability, such as people with Down syndrome, transformations of content or interface may not be needed, but the key success factor is the presence of structured technology training, which often is not present.[18] Nonetheless, there is a general lack of commitment to web equality for persons with cognitive disabilities despite the fact that technological advances for persons with cognitive disabilities complement and extend access strategies for people with visual, hearing, dexterity, and other conditions.[19] Many presupposed barriers to web equality not only are surmountable but also are capable of resolution for individuals with diverse intellectual and developmental impairments.

As mentioned, digital code enables software to convert web content to speech for screen-reading functions and audio information to text for captioning. People with cognitive disabilities benefit from these conversions. As is the case for blind people who use screen readers and deaf people who use captioning to access web content, people with cognitive disabilities profit from conversions that format text to audio and the reverse, as well as from the opportunity to use content presented in multiple communication modalities and to alter the viewing format of the information presented. This is the case where text alternatives for audio information are presented as captions and include important nondialogue audio information, such as sound effects.[20] Even perceived barriers for people with cognitive disabilities, such as passwords, can be overcome.[21]

Sometimes, however, people with cognitive disabilities face additional challenges in the use of web content as expressed purely in text alternatives. A user's reading level affects comprehension and understandability, as well as the processing of text. People with cognitive impairments who may have hearing impairments often have lower levels of linguistic capabilities, especially if a gestural language such as American Sign Language (ASL) is their first language. Some people may require ASL or other sign languages not based on English grammar to aid in web-content usability and comprehensibility. Consequently, within the domain of content transformation, there is a need to consider an array of characteristics.

Although the WCAG does not currently include deep guidance related to cognitive impairment, the Cognitive and Learning Disabilities Accessibility Task Force of the Web Accessibility Initiative presently is examining how future versions of the WCAG may include enhanced information for users with cognitive and intellectual disabilities.[22] If the task force's recommendations are adopted, they should have a positive impact around the world. For instance, recent drafts have suggested modifications to WCAG 2.0 such as ones to (1) enable as many users as possible to understand sites and use them; (2) prevent users from making mistakes and facilitate their correction; (3) help users focus and restore context if attention is lost; and (4) minimize the cognitive skills required to use sites' content. In addition, earlier guidelines released in 2013 by WebAIM for assessing and making websites accessible to individuals with cognitive disabilities provide basic guidance (www.webaim.org) on the issues; however, they have resulted in little change within the industry.

What Are Cognitive Disabilities?

Braddock and colleagues describe a cognitive disability as "a substantial limitation in one's capacity to think, including conceptualizing, planning, and sequencing thoughts and actions, remembering, interpreting subtle social cues, and understanding numbers and symbols."[23] The term "cognitive disability" covers conditions that may be based on the interaction of biology and environment over the life course—autism, intellectual and developmental disabilities, traumatic brain injury, brain injury acquired from aging, physiological and environmental conditions, post-traumatic stress disorder, dyslexia and learning disorders, and print-related disabilities.[24] These conditions coexist with sensory and physical impairments and with mental health conditions (for example, depression and bipolar disorder) and have a diversity of causes, severity, and presentation. Cognitive disability is affected separately and in combination by individual characteristics, environmental demands, and social supports.

Although in some instances cognitive disability may be associated with lower levels of intelligence as defined by standard tests and measures of daily functioning, this is not necessarily the case. Many individuals with cognitive disabilities have average or high levels of daily life functioning and intellectual skills. These individuals, whether with dyslexia or autism, experience limitations in social and communication abilities due to a range of factors. Moreover, contrary to popular belief, the majority of individuals with cognitive disabilities have conditions that are relatively mild or moderate.[25] This having been said, the experience of severe cognitive disability over the life course is not a presumption against the same opportunity for individual preference and choice in daily life, often with human and technological supports in certain circumstances. For people with cognitive disabilities, autonomous choice takes on new meaning when decision making is bolstered by web-based supports across the life cycle to maximize independence.[26]

Cognitive Load

The process and rate involved with the delivery of electronic text determine the cognitive load that the information presents to an individual and that person's capacity to meaningfully acquire the information. Cognitive load is affected by how online tasks (websites) are designed and presented, as well as by individual characteristics.

The proliferation of online devices, services, and multitasking has made cognitive load a crucial performance issue of the information age.[27] In interacting with a web service, there is an expected distribution of cognitive load generated across the population of users. Unfortunately, web services typically are designed to be accessible and usable by a limited range of distribution of web users and often by an idealized "normal user" without consideration of cognitive disability and the effects of other factors: environment, task, and individual and collective interaction.

Disability antidiscrimination laws set parameters to define when the "range of usage" is unfairly limited because of disability and hence is discriminatory. To date, these have been used in ADA actions by the blind and deaf communities and to a lesser extent by persons with cognitive disabilities. The requirement for reasonable modifications is meant to mitigate unfair restrictions as long as they do not alter the essence of the task or present an undue burden to the content producer. This conception applies across disability types and functional severity, although cognitive disabilities by definition directly implicate issues of cognitive load.

Although screen-reader software and augmentative technologies may transform electronic content to aural presentation and vice versa, the structure of the website, its navigability, and the complexity of its organization may independently affect comprehensibility and cognitive load.[28] Cognitive load or capacity is tested when one is considering multimedia and dynamic (constantly updated) web content and interactions across platforms and interfaces. Cognitive disabilities may result in memory-processing limitations that affect attention capabilities, which reduce the ability to perform sequenced web-based tasks.[29] Without the opportunity for alternatives, augmentations, and feedbacks, web use is effectively limited.[30]

In principle, accessible and usable web design offers the opportunity to reduce unnecessary cognitive load, especially those substantive and presentational formats that are cumbersome or nonessential to the meaning of web content.[31] Of course, "unnecessary" cognitive load is a relative term and often depends on the perspectives of the content owner and producer and the individual user.

Universal Design

When the opportunity for web-content accessibility and usability is possible in the broadest sense, it trends toward "universal design" (UD), which enables participation by diverse users to the maximum degree possible. For instance, reductions in task complexity and conveyance of information in alternative channels of communication reduce cognitive demands and thereby increase accessibility and usability because capacity is effectively deployed and not expended on extraneous tasks and decision-making processes. Individual cognitive capacity may be increased with the use of customization strategies that allow for tasks to be broken down into accessible components that are presented in multiple modalities.

In theory, UD exists when there is an equivalent opportunity for diverse individuals to use web content easily, comprehensibly, and within reasonable bounds. In practice, UD represents an aspiration to achieve equal and individualized participation regardless of disability and other human characteristics.

Universal Design and Web *eQuality*

Without web *eQuality*, people with cognitive and other disabilities often find themselves on the wrong side of the digital divide.[32] This means a lack of access to comparable web content across multiple devices, platforms, and browsers (for example, lack of cross-platform compatibility). The lack of functional and equivalent access to web content affects individuals across the spectrum of disability, as well as other "nonstandard" web users. However, people with cognitive disabilities are among those most profoundly affected by web-content inequality. This is because, as a general proposition, web *eQuality* for people with cognitive disabilities necessitates consideration of the meaning of web content.

For instance, a web user with memory-processing limitations likely will benefit from the opportunity to choose clearer and more concise language, which requires developers to consider the meaning of text-based web content they employ.[33] It is essential, therefore, to examine the purpose of web content and the design of the online service itself. Analysis requires examination of the "equivalent enjoyment of web content" from the perspective of content owners and designers and content users and their environments.

Given the web's inclusive UD possibilities, it is fitting to aim for a principled basis in law for web equality for people with cognitive disabilities. This is not to divert attention from web equality for those with other disabilities; rather, it is to focus attention on particularly stigmatized individuals. Moreover, the potential UD benefits of web-content equality for those with cognitive disabilities transcend cognitive conditions and apply to other coexisting conditions, such as sensory and mobility-related impairments.

For people with cognitive disabilities, there may be at least two recognized metafunctional dimensions of web-content equality: (1) ease of use of web content, for instance, in navigational and multimedia access and operability, and (2) comprehensibility of web content, for instance, in its understandability and substantive usability. These dimensions are not zero-sum choices or independent of each other. Rather, they reflect a continuum of user experience to be considered in context, with or without the use of AT and other supports.[34] They are multidimensional concepts that are influenced by and affect individual preferences and differences and interaction with semantic content on the web. Individuals with similar backgrounds and characteristics may prefer different ways to interact with web content in various situations and conditions.[35]

Preference in web use, however, does not necessarily equate to simplification (and is relative to context), and greater comprehensibility (or simplicity) is not necessarily synonymous with intellectual challenge and cognitive demands. For instance, although people with autism may experience differences in sensory and speech processing and sensitivities to the human voice, these characteristics in social communications are not necessarily tied to individual intelligence and capabilities.[36] Nevertheless, for many people with cognitive disabilities, ease of use and simplicity are directly tied to the nature of web-content accessibility and usability.[37]

Toward Web *eQuality*

Optimistically, before too long, binary views of web accessibility and usability will be relics of the past. Instead of one-size-fits-all web content for standard users, there will be opportunities for autopersonalization one-size-fits-one content, reflecting a globalized alignment of the web as an enabler of human rights as envisioned by the CRPD.[38] Even with such technological optimism, there are complexities to the mass customization of web content, such as the need for developers to maintain design simplicity and ease of use with the proliferation of niche technologies, which is where open-source ecosystems that promote universal access and use will come into play.

Hardware and software architectures will coexist with smart environments—homes, schools, libraries, workplaces, and health-care centers. Embedded ambient intelligence will converge in cloud infrastructures, and web content will be semantically responsive and intuitive and less design and code dependent.[39] Content will be available in on-demand services on and in the person (through wearables and nanorobotics made by personalized 3-D printers) in homes (through automation and appliances), schools (with online teaching materials), and workplaces (with job training and advancement programs).[40] The web will provide options for collaborative crowd-sourced feedback and services for individuals, groups, and communities from the management of health care and financial transactions to emergency preparedness for natural and human-made disasters. Digital cooperatives not only will enhance the sharing and development of knowledge but also will be central to the management and growth of a free and open information society.[41]

Functional *eQuality*

As online activities increasingly are personalized, the WCAG 2.0 and other standards likely will trend toward functional use criteria for universal applicability.[42] Corresponding concepts of accessibility and usability will fade and will be replaced by a paradigm shift toward innovation in web content regardless of disability. The inventor of the web, Tim Berners-Lee, understood this centrality of choice and cohesiveness to web-content equality when he said that its "flexibility and openness" make it possible "to transform content for purposes other than that for which it was originally intended."[43] This transformational capability leads toward meaningful and autonomous engagement in the web ecosystem.

Coming technologies will progressively support inclusive web content that will undergird a cloud-driven Semantic Web, a "social-semantic" web that will provide the opportunity for contextually aware multichannel communications, using facial expressions and tone of voice, eye blinks and movements, gestures, and sign languages.[44] The W3C and other groups are developing complementary tools to support the inclusive web, such as the Web Ontology Language (OWL V.2) for web applications to process content.[45] Ontologies are vocabularies of content—terms, words, microformats, and metadata—organized by rules and relationships to other terms. When these capabilities are combined with collective and machine-based knowledge from cataloging and search capabilities, they offer personalized opportunities for people to interact with web content, even with constant informational updating. Legal and policy regimes domestically and transnationally will need to keep pace with these advances to support harmonization and innovation in web-content ownership, licensing, and open-source agreements.

Raising the Floor for People with Cognitive and Other Disabilities

Cloud-based educational, job-training, financial, and leisure programs and services increasingly act as daily life supports for people with an array of cognitive disabilities. The cloud has the potential to augment communication, memory, and concentration skills in real time by aiding in customization and operability across digital devices, browsers, and systems.[46] The Raising the Floor (RtF) Consortium and its partners engaged with the Global Public Inclusive Infrastructure (GPII) initiative are developing a real-time cloud-based ecosystem for customized user profiles to enhance online access for people with cognitive and other disabilities.[47] The goal is to provide autopersonalized options for users to simplify operations and interfaces, and to make web operations adaptable and compatible across devices for individuals with disabilities who use AT.

Rtf[48] is developing a MasterList (database) of strategies to support universal solutions for web-content equality. These entries are applicable to individuals with cognitive disabilities, such as cloud-based solutions for customized dictionaries in multiple languages, usage profiles to share with others, and customized cues for prompting use and function. Other solutions allow for customizing keyboard and voice controls for text and input entry, along with use of specialized "hotkeys" (shortcuts to simplify actions). Error-prevention, correction, and recovery solutions are provided. Privacy functions allow for automatic and preset assessments of website credibility and authenticity for trusted websites. Security functions are presented to support ease of use and comprehensibility for a range of users in e-commerce, social media, and gaming functions. The use of GPS navigation provides for way finding and use of mobile devices in real time, as well as aiding in information processing and comprehensibility of content.

The RtF and similar projects are making online technologies more universally available to people with cognitive and other disabilities. These technologies also benefit people with lower reading skills and digital literacy, as well as individuals with lingual and age-related barriers. These efforts build on the principles in the ADA and the CRPD to promote web *eQuality* as an enabler of active citizenship. They also support the evolving Semantic Web and the Internet of Things (IoT, such as web-activated household appliances), whereby online services are shifting from user-driven interfaces to the IoT's hybrid of interfaces between users and intelligent machines. For example, rather than programming a website to interact with a particular AT, a developer will program household appliances to interact with cloud-based autopersonalization services. The objective is to allow users with diverse backgrounds and skills, and under varying conditions, to access the IoT through platforms and input devices the user chooses, anyplace and anytime.[49]

Conclusion

Vast numbers of individuals with disabilities and divergent interests increasingly are using the web. The trend is toward use of mobile devices with cloud infrastructures over the life course.[50] In the past, many of these individuals were among those least able to participate online and to exert pressure for web content *eQuality*. This is the reason that members of a new generation of disability advocates are vigorously defending their right to the web.[51] Recent legal cases illustrate the ongoing struggle for web equality across platforms, apps, and services offered, such as Massive Open Online Courses (MOOCs), IoT devices, and crowd-sourced apps.[52]

For instance, in 2015, U.S. disability advocates—individuals who are deaf or have hearing impairments, along with the National Association of the Deaf (NAD)—sued Harvard University and the Massachusetts Institute of Technology (MIT) under the ADA.[53] They alleged that these universities' online web-based content (for example, in MOOCs) was not captioned and was often unintelligible, making the information inaccessible and incomprehensible.[54]

While the Harvard and MIT cases were awaiting determination, later in 2015, the U.S. Department of Justice (DOJ) reached a settlement with edX Inc., a not-for-profit provider of MOOCs created by Harvard and MIT in 2012. This enterprise is an online platform for a consortium of sixty partnering universities providing hundreds of courses to over three million individuals worldwide.[55] The DOJ had alleged violations of the ADA's Title III because edX's website and platform for providing MOOCs were not fully accessible to individuals who are blind or have low vision, who are deaf or hard of hearing, or who have physical disabilities affecting manual dexterity (for example, videos without captions, and information not usable and lacking compatibility with screen-reader software applications). The allegations did not include a claim that edX's online platform and apps and related activities and services were not fully accessible to individuals with cognitive and learning impairments. Nonetheless, the settlement remedies adopted will benefit individuals across the spectrum of physical, sensory, and cognitive disabilities. For example, edX will modify its website platform and mobile applications to conform to the WCAG 2.0 AA, and it will provide guidance, best-practice examples, and authoring tools to entities that create and post edX courses to ensure that the course content offered is accessible.

The edX agreement does not necessarily resolve all the accessibility issues alleged in the Harvard and MIT litigation mentioned earlier. Universities and other online providers still must provide their information and course materials to edX and content-management service providers in formats that are capable of accessible digital transmission. However, the edX agreement puts universities and online information providers on notice that they must offer information in accessible formats when they are using the tools and means made available by edX and other like entities.

In 1935, the public library of Webster City, Iowa, introduced the idea of home delivery of books to people with physical disabilities.[6] Before the rise of the Internet, libraries were broadly committed to promoting equal access and education for patrons with disabilities by providing materials in alternative formats and creating built environments that were accessible.

In 1961, the American Library Association (ALA) crafted the first of a series of standards to ensure the equal service of patrons with disabilities, and the comprehensive Library Services for People with Disabilities Policy is now fifteen years old. Following the lead of the ALA, the majority of public, academic, and school library mission statements articulate a commitment to equal access and services for all patrons, explicitly including people with disabilities.[7] Most of these libraries have also long been committed to the acquisition of new assistive technologies as they become available— braille materials, large-print materials, talking books, reading machines, video enlargement, screen readers, e-books, and screen magnifiers, among many others.[8] The Library of Congress, for example, now serves the information needs of 700,000 people with disabilities in the United States through a wide variety of formats.[9] Since the rise of the Internet as a central part of both library services and patrons' information behavior, libraries have worked to promote access and education for people with disabilities through new resources on their own websites, through online resources and databases, and through new technologies and devices.[10] This long-term commitment to equity for people with disabilities has also been part of a maturation of the overall stance and activities of libraries collectively in the United States, which have become more obviously institutions committed to promoting social justice and human rights in their communities through access, education, and social services.[11] To illuminate the unique and vital contributions of libraries to promoting equality, rights, and justice for people with disabilities, this chapter will discuss the roles of information in rights and justice, the roles of libraries in rights and justice, and the specific ways libraries promote equality, rights, and justice of people with disabilities in the age of the Internet.

Information, Human Rights, and Social Justice

The concept of human rights is the belief that all individuals deserve certain equal rights as members of society, while the implementation of human rights is tied to specific legal and policy mechanisms that promote equality. Effective implementation of human rights depends on systems of social justice, which are the social and societal structures that foster equality based on the laws and policies. For the purposes of this discussion, human rights are "a legally enforceable set of expectations as to how others, most obviously the state, should behave toward the rights bearers."[12] Social justice can be understood as a set of both formal rules (legal, political, and economic) and informal rules (moral sanctions and conventions),[13] as well as the institutions that help implement these rules.[14]

Information issues relate to human rights and social justice in many ways: the relationship of information to rights and justice; social, cultural, economic, legal, and political forces shaping information and rights; the impacts of rights on information professions, practices, standards, and cultural institutions; and information access and use by disadvantaged populations.[15] As information and related technologies have become increasingly essential to education, employment, social interaction, and civic participation, greater emphasis has been placed on the idea that information can be seen as a necessary human right and a core part of social justice. Arguments have been made that information access, information literacy, intellectual freedom, freedom of expression, and other information behaviors fall under the category of rights and justice in the age of the Internet.[16] At the tail end of the last millennium, Kofi Annan, the seventh secretary general of the United Nations, stated, "People lack many things: jobs, shelter, food, health care, and drinkable water. Today, being cut off from basic telecommunications services is a hardship almost as acute as these other deprivations, and may indeed reduce the chances of finding remedies to them."[17] Fifteen years later, this observation still holds true.

Information and the Internet can now be seen as being central to human rights—the ability to obtain, communicate, and disseminate information is necessary for many human rights to be possible.[18] A leading scholar of human rights identified one of the most significant challenges to human rights as "equal access to information and communication."[19] The intersection of rights, justice, and information includes issues of expression, access, privacy, intellectual property, participation, assembly, race, gender, and sexual orientation, among others.[20] Among the principles of the UN Universal Declaration of Human Rights (UDHR), issues of privacy, nondiscrimination, due process, education, access to public services, mobility, work, development, peace, and women's rights are all affected by the relationships of rights, justice, and information. Information has been described as "the linchpin right" that holds the others together, particularly in the online context.[21]

In short, "human rights remain unattainable in the absence of free and equitable access to reliable information.... When individuals and communities are denied information, it becomes much easier to exploit and suppress them."[22] Since the 1990s, many nations have adopted right-to-information laws in recognition of the importance of information to so much of daily life.[23] To see how information is a significant and pressing issue in this area, a look at the UDHR is instructive. Information technologies were still fairly new when the United Nations issued the UDHR in 1948. Since its passage, however, the idea of human rights has been evolving and adapting to social, cultural, and technological change. Although the computer, the Internet, and mobile devices were developed long after the UDHR was originally drafted, many of the principles articulated there relate directly to information, communication, and technology; many more rely on information, communication, and technology to support the principles. Most items directly stated as rights are now either entirely dependent on or enabled by information access and digital literacy, including such major activities as education, employment, and civic participation.[24] For example, freedom of speech, press, assembly, and expression are far more practicable when they involve a literate populace with access to information technologies. The human rights to education and development are possible without access to and use of information technologies, but they are much more effective with these technologies.

Article 19 of the UDHR most explicitly deals with issues of information, enshrining rights to "freedom of opinion and expression" and to "seek, receive and impart information and ideas through any media," as well as the freedom from "interference" in seeking and exchanging information and ideas. On the basis of this article and many other parts of the UDHR, the ability to access and use the Internet for purposes of education and expression has been identified as a human right in many quarters. Not long after use of the World Wide Web became commonplace, scholars of law, information, technology, and education began making arguments that universal Internet access is a necessary part of human rights.[25]

The UN has also emphasized disability rights through its Convention on the Rights of Persons with Disabilities (CRPD). The impact of the language in the CRPD has a direct correlation to the services and information that are provided by libraries throughout the world.[26] Also on the international level, the Marrakesh Treaty to Facilitate Access to Published Works for Persons Who Are Blind, Visually Impaired, or Otherwise Print Disabled was signed in 2013 to focus on the challenges that copyrights can impose on the process of creating and maintaining accessible published works.[27] The treaty provides for copyright exceptions and has been signed by more than fifty countries. It needs to be ratified by at least twenty members to fully enter into force.

Information and the Internet can now be seen as being central to human rights, such as the ability to obtain, communicate, and disseminate information.[28] As Internet-enabled technologies have become more mobile and omnipresent—and vital to education, employment, civic engagement, communication, and entertainment—these arguments have matured into assertions that the abilities both to successfully access and to successfully use the Internet are human rights.[29] These rights are significant for both technologically advanced nations and those that are still developing the infrastructure for widespread Internet access. In technologically advanced nations, the issue is making the existing Internet infrastructure more inclusive, including making it equally accessible to users with disabilities. In nations still developing their Internet infrastructure and working to make Internet access widely available, the issue is building an infrastructure that is inclusive from the outset, including being equally accessible to users with disabilities.

Libraries, Human Rights, and Social Justice

The ALA, the International Federation of Library Associations and Institutions (IFLA), the United Nations Educational, Scientific, and Cultural Organization (UNESCO), and other information professional and governmental organizations have adopted Article 19 of the UDHR and the principles of information access as a human right into their bylaws and policies. The Internet Society, an organization that bills itself as "the world's trusted independent source of leadership for Internet policy, technology standards, and future development," declared the ability to use the Internet to be a human right in 2011. Also in 2011, a UN report explicitly discussed Internet access as central to supporting Article 19 and enabling many other aspects of the UDHR.[30] The IFLA-led Lyons Declaration on Access to Information and Development called on the UN to make information literacy and digital inclusion central to its human rights and development agendas, building on the assertions in the 2006 Alexandria Proclamation that the UN and individual nations should make information literacy a central part of their goals.[31] This is an essential effort for the cause of international human rights because an estimated 60 percent of individuals worldwide still lack this critical aspect of human rights.[32]

In the past fifteen years, arguments have been made for the central role of educational and cultural heritage institutions—especially public libraries, school libraries, and academic libraries—in ensuring human rights related to the Internet in an age so dependent on information and technology.[33] Overall, many ALA policies and bodies have been created with a human rights and social justice focus, such as those that address services to disadvantaged groups, persons with disabilities, and the poor, as well as the many associations for different service needs and populations within the ALA.[34] It is recognized that there is a direct relationship between the lack of employment opportunities for people with disabilities and the increase in poverty that can result from unequal societal opportunities.[35]

It has been argued that libraries themselves should be seen as a human right;[36] however, the situation is far more complex. Simultaneously acting as institutions that facilitate both human rights and social justice places libraries in a unique and tremendously important position that librarians themselves have difficulty articulating. Thus far, unfortunately, libraries have seldom framed their activities in the terminology of human rights or social justice, even though they are the organizations most focused on the good of the whole community and all the individual members of the community. Often, when library activities are framed in terms of human rights and social justice, the focus is limited to topics such as the ways in which libraries can help other organizations or groups in their human rights and social justice activities.[37]

However, the human rights and social justice functions of libraries absolutely define what libraries have evolved into in the age of the Internet. Embracing these existing roles and the accompanying terminology will enable libraries to better explain what they do and how they contribute to society, formulate ways to better help their patrons and their communities, and advocate for the support that they so desperately need.

A great number of the contributions of libraries to human rights and social justice involve using technology to make impacts in their communities. The key contributions of libraries to human rights and social justice include ensuring information access, literacy, and digital inclusion. These are necessary for equity and social inclusion and are also foundations of all human rights, either being rights in themselves or underlying rights. Human rights depend on systems of social justice for effective implementation; to be relevant, systems of social justice need to be built on a framework of recognized human rights. Libraries support both rights and justice and in many contexts directly ensure rights and justice. Libraries are community anchors that promote social justice and human rights through a wide range of activities, including education and literacy, social inclusion, social services, community outreach, partnerships with other community groups, and provision of access to printed materials, electronic materials, and the online environment. Although the contributions may vary by type of library, all libraries—public, school, academic, and others—make myriad, clear contributions to human rights and social justice. Few (if any) other institutions are capable of serving as many rights and justice roles as libraries. As a community good, libraries can meet as many individual and community needs as the financial, political, and other support to provide sufficient staffing, space, and infrastructure will allow. Even though they are already filling these human rights and social justice roles—ensuring access, inclusion, and equity for individuals and entire communities—the members of the library profession do not speak of libraries as institutions of rights and justice or frame library activities as promoting rights and justice.

If the members of the library profession were to embrace the reality of the roles that they are already playing, it would provide many new potential opportunities to connect their activities to members of the public; to positively influence the perceptions of policy makers, politicians, and funders; and to articulate the reasons that libraries remain vital and necessary institutions in the time of smartphones and social media. Libraries and library professionals are not the only ones whose well-being depends on the library profession better expressing and advocating its human rights and social justice activities. These activities at each individual library benefit many different service populations and community groups, often groups that are otherwise unserved, including the homeless, the unemployed, immigrants, non-English speakers, the socioeconomically disadvantaged, older adults, and persons with disabilities.

Many individuals, many populations, and many organizations in a community—that is, a large segment of each community—depend on the human rights and social justice roles that libraries fulfill. Without libraries, most of these rights and justice needs would go unmet. Libraries are filling these roles for the benefit of their communities, and so they also need to articulate and advocate these roles for the benefit of their communities. Continued success as institutions of rights and justice depends on embracing and articulating these roles.

Libraries, People with Disabilities, and Human Rights

The assertion that Internet access is a human right by many different information professional groups, nonprofits, and international agencies presents a clear opportunity to frame online accessibility for people with disabilities as an issue of human rights and social justice. As long as the Internet has existed, people with disabilities have been excluded more extensively than any other population because of a combination of barriers resulting from socioeconomic challenges, social biases, and inaccessible design choices.[38] Although the legal system in the United States has recently begun to pay greater attention to the accessibility of the online environment and Internet-enabled devices, the search for online equality—"Internet justice"—remains elusive for people with disabilities.[39]

One of the institutions that has been most essential in supporting the ability of people with disabilities to have access online is the library. Libraries have a long history of developing unique programs and collections to promote information access of and social inclusion for people with disabilities.[40] Although state libraries devoted to serving patrons with disabilities in the state may be the most obvious examples of libraries that provide information, programs, and services to promote rights and justice for people with disabilities, virtually all libraries—public, academic, and school—provide information, programs, and services to promote inclusion of people with disabilities in their communities.

Public library programs and services provide a telling example of the current support of equal access for all in meeting important online information, communication, and interaction needs. The 2014 Libraries and Digital Inclusion survey emphatically demonstrates the roles of libraries and the technology access and education that they provide in supporting human rights and social justice in their communities.[41] Its findings highlight that all public libraries (100 percent) provide free public Internet access, and all public libraries (100 percent) provide free access to online educational databases. Almost all public libraries (96.5 percent) provide homework assistance, digital reference services are available in 91.5 percent of public libraries, and most libraries (89.5 percent) provide access to e-books. In addition, a majority of libraries (55.1 percent) offer online language-learning course and tools, a majority of libraries (53.3 percent) offer workspaces for mobile workers, and the average public library outlet has twenty Internet-enabled workstations.

All these elements of the hardware, software, and educational infrastructure at public libraries support their roles as institutions of human rights and social justice. The provision of all these services and resources for free makes it possible for many members of their communities to be included and have equal opportunities in regard to information, communication, education, employment, social support, health, and myriad other rights under the UDHR. In some communities, the needs for the services listed here are quite pronounced.

The results of the survey also demonstrate that these contributions to human rights and social justice extend far beyond the infrastructure and space of public libraries. The educational roles of public librarians actively expand their roles in human rights and social justice.[42] For example, education and learning programs—including basic literacy, digital literacy, summer reading, continuing education, foreign-language instruction, and maker spaces—are offered in 99.5 percent of public libraries, and technology training is provided in 98 percent of public libraries. Employment-resource training, assistance, and programs are available in 95 percent of public libraries, and community, civic engagement, and e-government training, assistance, and programs are available in 75 percent of public libraries. Also, health and wellness programs are offered by 57.9 percent of public libraries, and assistance in finding and assessing health insurance plans is available in 37.3 percent of public libraries. Although these programs and services benefit many community members in many different groups, the provision of free public Internet access, the necessary assistive technologies to support that access, and digital literacy instruction are uniquely important to people with disabilities.

People with disabilities face tremendous barriers to use of the Internet, including lack of affordable hardware, inaccessible Internet service providers (ISPs), and incompatibility of software with assistive technologies.[43] For these reasons, the percentages of people with disabilities in the United States who use the Internet are staggeringly low in comparison with the rest of the population—less than half in regard to owning a computer at home, having household access, home use, and use outside the home.[44] This is a population that has the lowest levels of Internet usage in the United States because of the inability to afford access at home, the inability to afford the necessary computing and assistive devices at home, lack of access to digital literacy and inclusion, or a lack of accessibility of the content of the Internet.[45]

People with disabilities often have unique access needs, particularly finding devices and software that provide equity of access for people with disabilities. In regard to physical access, libraries not only provide hardware and broadband access but also frequently provide assistive technology, including screen readers, large-print book collections, audio books, and more. Many libraries have designated computers for patrons with disabilities or even accessible computer labs. These services enable patrons with disabilities to use materials otherwise inaccessible to them. Universal design for learning is increasingly a central goal of libraries as well, leading to the development of accessible spaces and materials for patrons.[46]

Additionally, given the staggeringly high levels of unemployment among people with disabilities and the greater frequency of interaction with government programs, library emphasis on help with online job applications and interaction with e-government is of particular importance to people with disabilities. The access and education in libraries address many of these major needs of literacy and inclusion, including education, civic participation, and employment.

To serve patrons with disabilities, many libraries have focused on making technology access equitable. Among public libraries, 72.3 percent offer public access computers compliant with the standards of the Americans with Disabilities Act (ADA), and 48.9 percent of public libraries purchase only licensed resources that are accessible to people with disabilities.[47] This commitment to accessible technologies is spread across all types of libraries, but large urban public libraries and small rural libraries have the highest levels of accessible technologies available.[48] The large urban libraries have the largest budgets and technology staffing to help support accessibility, while the small rural libraries have the smallest number of technologies to make accessible.

Beyond offering the various programs and services described above, many libraries and library organizations have also developed specific programs and services to promote online equity for people with disabilities in their communities. Several studies have demonstrated that library websites are far more likely to be accessible than websites for schools, government agencies, universities, corporations, and nonprofit organizations.[49] Most libraries provide assistive technologies for patrons with disabilities, with some even having adaptive technology labs and special computer rooms,[50] and many libraries offer computer literacy and digital inclusion courses specifically for people with disabilities.[51] An example of these types of classes is the One-on-One Basic Computer Training for Visually Impaired (and Sighted) Individuals offered by the George W. Covington Memorial Library in Mississippi.[52]

Digital library partnerships, such as the HathiTrust, are exploring new areas for collaboration on accessible digital resource provisions.[53] The Association for Research Libraries (ARL) created the Web Accessibility Toolkit to assist research libraries with digital accessibility and promote greater digital inclusion.[54] Some libraries also host "Accessibility Hackathons" that "bring together young adults with disabilities, and companies that develop accessibility solutions, to provide mentorship and create new adaptive technology solutions,"[55] and several libraries have even recently opened accessible maker spaces for patrons with disabilities.[56]

Certain specific libraries have devoted a great deal of time and innovation to promoting access for patrons with disabilities. The robust adaptive services program at the Washington, D.C., Public Library is one example. Its patrons can access adaptive technologies, receive training in these technologies, participate in groups and meet-ups, and use an "Internet Classroom," designed to help patrons learn adaptive technologies on their own.[57] The Baltimore County Public Library (BCPL) is another example of a library that has attempted to proactively improve access for patrons who are blind or have low vision. It has recently noted the need to more publicly highlight the services that it offers these patrons, and it engaged a researcher at Towson University to assess its level of accessibility and to provide advice on technological advances that could further expand its services for patrons with disabilities. The College of Staten Island Public Library and the Pennsylvania State University Libraries are just two other examples of libraries and library systems that have been addressing the need to provide more inclusive and accessible library information and services. Some state-level libraries, such as Maryland's Library for the Blind and Physically Handicapped, have taken statewide leadership on promoting accessibility for patrons with disabilities.[58] Although these kinds of services cannot address all the numerous accessibility problems encountered by persons with disabilities, for many persons with disabilities, these educational programs and technology access are the key to an online world that the general population takes for granted.

Challenges and Opportunities

In regard to major challenges and future opportunities for improvement, libraries must be aware of their legal responsibilities in regard to accessibility and patrons with disabilities. The lawsuits and settlements by several libraries in recent years, including the inaccessible "Nook" lawsuit against the Free Library of Philadelphia[59] and the Justice Department settlement with the Sacramento Public Library Authority over inaccessible e-readers,[60] serve as examples of this priority.

Although libraries in the United States have placed a great deal of emphasis on serving patrons with disabilities, they need to work more to expand such notions to libraries in other parts of the world. The United States has been the leader that many other nations have tried to follow in many aspects of librarianship,[61] but the same has not been true in regard to services to people with disabilities. This point is made clear by *A History of Modern Librarianship*.[62] The book features long sections on the history of libraries in Europe, Africa, Australasia, and the United States and Canada, but only the section on the United States has anything to discuss about services to people with disabilities. There certainly are efforts in other nations, but they are not nearly as commonplace or as central to librarianship as they are in the United States.

Libraries also must continue to adapt and improve their services to people with disabilities, particularly in the electronic environment. As was noted earlier, libraries generally have far more accessible online presences than primary and secondary schools, colleges and universities, government agencies, corporations, and nonprofits.[63] However, the levels of accessibility for library websites and online services still leave a great deal of room for improvement. Being the most successful among a weak field is not enough to promote true equality. Libraries must continue to work toward developing and updating the online materials they create to be inclusive of people with disabilities and compatible with the assistive technologies that they rely on.

These efforts should also include increased research about accessibility as a focus at specific institutions and across all types of libraries at the national level. Both practitioners and scholars should be contributing to and collaborating on such research. More research will provide a better picture of the access successes and areas of needed improvement for all types of libraries, as well as the means to better articulate their larger roles in human rights and social justice to funders, politicians, service communities, and individual patrons. Such research can further help provide improved ways to share innovations and best practices among libraries.

Finally, ongoing accessibility challenges continue to emerge in regard to digital databases and online subscription services that libraries offer their patrons. The challenge is sometimes related to the third-party vendor that provides the access to the databases and subscription services. Libraries must be proactive in demanding and advocating for the accessibility of those information systems if they are to be equally available to all the patrons of the library.

Conclusion

Libraries and library associations have been central to the cause of human rights in social justice, particularly in the digital era. In ensuring free access to the Internet, educational resources, health and wellness programs, employment training, and even physical workspaces for mobile workers, they provide the foundation for human rights in many parts of the developed world. The broad range of community activities that are supported by the infrastructure of libraries also helps promote many human rights and social justice causes. Many libraries have also been proactive in their approach to inclusion by providing devices and software for people with disabilities. Given the significant population worldwide that still lacks access to the positive benefits of the Internet, it is hoped that libraries can be an essential component of the dissemination of this growing human right. Because of the critical impact that libraries can have on the areas of daily life that form the foundation for the cause of many areas of human rights and social justice, this critical intersection of libraries and human rights should serve as a reminder of the societal value of libraries, a call for increasing global support for libraries, and an inspiration to many libraries as they seek to enrich and extend their impact on the people whom they serve.

PART II

Government and Governance

CHAPTER 5

Public Financing of Information Technology and Human Rights for People with Disabilities

Deborah Kaplan

Introduction

The Convention on the Rights of Persons with Disabilities (CRPD) specifically defines accessibility to include ICT. As countries begin to implement the convention, they will need to address their technology operations. Section 508 of the Rehabilitation Act in the United States and the EC Mandate 376 form the foundation for a global movement, built on the work and successes of the early adopters. International cooperation and collaboration, forming a global community of practice on ICT accessibility, will be the most effective way to move forward.

The Relationship Between Government and ICT Accessibility

As information technology has developed and become ubiquitous, with ICT present in virtually all aspects of life, accessibility for people with disabilities has become a stronger and stronger imperative. Basic human rights are thwarted when an individual with a disability attempts to accomplish a mundane task but cannot do so because of inaccessible design. The experience of the past several decades teaches us that accessibility cannot be assumed as a natural outcome from the private market. Private companies have not completely ignored accessibility,[1] but barriers to all kinds of ICT are common, and lack of accessibility has historically been the norm. Because of this market failure, government is turned to as a necessary influencer for change.

In the background to the Regulatory Assessment for the 2000 Section 508 standards, the U.S. Access Board describes this market failure and why government initiatives such as Section 508 are necessary to remedy the failure:

> Manufacturers of electronic and information technology have an economic incentive to sell accessible products to buyers with disabilities. However, there are costs for sellers and buyers to identify and to negotiate with one another. If these transaction costs are too high, manufacturers will not know the accessible products buyers with disabilities would like to purchase. Mutually beneficial trades among buyers and sellers will not occur, resulting in a market failure.
>
> The Federal government can correct this potential market failure. The Federal government can invest resources to identify the needs of individuals with disabilities for accessible products and communicate those needs to manufacturers. Manufacturers then can produce accessible products. In section 508, Congress required the Access Board to identify the needs of individuals with disabilities and required Federal agencies to procure accessible products that meet those needs.[2]

Government has two roles to play. The legislative arm of government establishes policies that can directly or indirectly affect the accessibility of technology. It can enact requirements or mandates for technology accessibility, and it can also create incentives to reward companies that follow accessibility standards. In addition, the administrative arm of government can establish programs to make it easier to implement accessibility standards. The Americans with Disabilities Act, which covers many different aspects of how private and public entities operate, requires that private commercial websites be accessible. The Accessibility for Ontarians with Disabilities Act requires that government and private companies follow WCAG 2.0 for websites and web content, communications with the public, and public emergency information. These laws impose accessibility as a mandate.

Laws that require the administrative arm of government to assure accessibility when purchasing, developing, or using ICT intend to create an incentive for the private sector. Most technology companies regard the government as a very attractive and lucrative market. When the government includes accessibility as a technical requirement in its purchasing practices, accessibility becomes a business advantage to those companies that can demonstrate that their products meet the accessibility standards.

There is a very important ethical and moral aspect of the role of government with respect to technology accessibility. Governments should conduct business in a way that is above reproach. If the government imposes a mandate on the private sector, it should be a model in the implementation of that mandate in its own operations. In addition, the government often has a major role in offering information, technical assistance, and direct support to people with disabilities. All these functions are carried out through ICT, whether the government uses a website, a mobile app, or presence on social media.

Often people with disabilities depend on getting information and services from the government, and timeliness and accuracy can be vitally important. Accessibility barriers can have very serious consequences. People with disabilities are employed by governments as well. In many countries, the government employs a higher percentage of people with disabilities than most private employers. For most jobs, ICT plays a central part in how the work gets done. This has implications for much more than the government's public website. In order for employees with disabilities to be able to perform well, the government's intranet site, software systems, e-mail, applications, documents, and hardware technology all need to be accessible. The requirement for accessibility of all the ICT a government purchases, develops, or uses involves more than the government's procurement processes. Fulfilling this requirement means establishing an enterprise-wide accessibility program with many facets. In order to fully and effectively carry out the intent of laws mandating government ICT accessibility, it is necessary to put into effect a broad, far-reaching program with connections to most of the operations of the enterprise.

Section 508 in the United States

Section 508 was added to Title V of the Rehabilitation Act in 1986. Title V of the Rehabilitation Act includes laws that were some of the first civil rights protections for people with disabilities in the United States. Section 501 requires federal agencies to engage in affirmative action and nondiscrimination in hiring and employment of people with disabilities. Section 502 created the U.S. Access Board to handle enforcement of the federal Architectural Barriers Act and to develop standards for accessibility. Section 503 requires affirmative action and prohibits discrimination by federal government contractors. Section 504 prohibits discrimination by recipients of federal grants and financial assistance.

The original language of Section 508 required the General Services Administration (GSA) to develop and adopt guidelines to ensure that federal employees with disabilities can use electronic office equipment with or without special peripherals.[3] At that time, computers were used primarily for office functions, and assistive technology was less widely used. Section 508 did not require development of standards to define accessibility, and there were no provisions to enforce it. Federal agencies did not have realistic guidance on how to implement it, and it was not a priority. Disability advocates began to push for changes that would make the law more effective.

In 1998, the Rehabilitation Act was amended, and a stronger version of Section 508 was added. It specifically applies when agencies are developing, procuring, maintaining, or using electronic and information technology. It is important that the scope of Section 508 is broader than procurement or acquisition of ICT because federal agencies often develop software, apps, or systems in-house or through a contract with a developer. Agencies also develop their websites. When technology is maintained or upgraded, accessibility must be considered. In this way, older systems and technologies can be made accessible, and accessibility that exists in an earlier version of ICT can be preserved.

The new law required the development of technical standards defining accessibility by the U.S. Access Board, which empaneled a group of academic technology experts, industry representatives, and people from disability organizations to prepare a draft.[4] Congress specifically required the Access Board to review and revise the standards over time so that they would not become outdated.[5]

The revised law requires the Department of Justice to conduct biennial reviews of the state of federal implementation of Section 508's requirements and to publish the results in a report to Congress.[6] The Department of Justice has conducted these reviews and published reports in 2001, 2003, and 2012.

The GSA and the Access Board were given the authority to provide technical assistance to federal agencies and the public about Section 508 and how to implement it. The GSA has established a website[7] that includes a wide variety of documents and other information and resources. The Access Board also has established a website about the Section 508 standards. The U.S. CIO (Chief Information Officer) Council established an Accessibility Community of Practice (earlier referred to as a committee) that fosters collaboration and consistency of practices across the federal government. It published a Section 508 "Best Practice Library"[8] and conducts a regular webinar series.

In 2013, the Office of Management and Budget (OMB) of the White House issued the Strategic Plan for Improving Management of Section 508.[9] It requires each federal agency to conduct an initial baseline assessment of key indicators of Section 508 performance, based on a template developed by the U.S. CIO Council Accessibility Community of Practice. Agencies file reports every six months on the same measures so that progress can be documented. Agency CIOs have been asked to explain poor performance in annual information technology (IT) reviews by the OMB.

The law allows individuals to file administrative complaints with the federal agency that is the subject of the complaint. It specifies that agencies should use their Section 504 complaint process. Section 508 also specifically states that individuals can file civil lawsuits in court for violations of the law.[10]

Key Elements of Public Procurement and Accessibility

Policy

A written policy is essential to the establishment of an effective accessibility program. The policy gives authority to the accessibility program's leaders and communicates to all the other programs and employees that accessibility is a priority for the government. The written policy is the basis for resolving any resistance or questions from other departments; it is the official communication that pushes change forward. It provides continuity of accessibility efforts so that there is a policy framework in place when there are changes in leadership. The elements listed below provide the basis for a complete program. Each country or agency's policy will also need to be consistent in format and approach with the general manner in which policies are locally stated.

An accessibility policy should address the following:

1. Purpose/goals: There should be a clear statement of the desired eventual outcome, such as "All members of the public, regardless of disability status, should have equal access to the information, services, and benefits provided by XX Government when they are provided by IT." All the relevant goals should be included.
2. Authority: This is usually a list of all the laws, ordinances, proclamations, and so on that provide the government with the legal basis for establishing this policy.
3. Policy: This is the essence of the policy, a statement of the broad expectations for accessibility of technology. For example, "All websites, both Internet and intranet, will comply with the WCAG 2.0 Level AA standards," and "All software, applications, and systems that are developed will be accessible, and accessibility will be considered throughout the development process, including at the earliest stage." The statement of policy makes explicit all the areas of operation that are affected. The rest of the policy describes different aspects of a program that are designed to accomplish the policy statements.
4. Roles and responsibilities: Many different offices are involved in accessibility, for example, the web-development and maintenance organization, the procurement and acquisitions office, the IT-management organization, IT support, software and systems development, and human resources or employment. A strong policy names each entity that must be involved and sets forth the specific responsibilities of each. These include responsibilities for governance and collaboration.
5. Governance: With so many different entities playing their own essential roles, it is important to explicitly describe the way in which decisions will be made, policies will be interpreted, conflicts will be resolved, guidance will be established, and best practices will be identified. Leadership of the governance body or bodies should be identified.
6. Accountability: It is critical to establish ways to measure how well the government or agency is complying with the policy. The first step in measuring progress is establishing a baseline from which measurable accomplishments can be recorded. Analysis of the baseline will

lead to a plan for improvement, with specific steps to be taken by the various offices given responsibilities in the policy. Then regular reports should be required that will show whether the plans have been implemented and whether improvements in accessibility have occurred.

Top-Level Support

In order to have a truly effective accessibility effort, top-level support that is real rather than simply lip service is essential. Many different parts of the enterprise need to cooperate and coordinate the work on accessibility; all need to receive the message that accessibility is a priority. Otherwise, competing priorities will receive their attention and resources.

In addition, there will be instances where achieving an important accessibility outcome will necessitate taking a stand over protests from others within the organization. In 2008, the California State University (CSU) system caught the attention of the higher education world in the United States by standing firm on a decision not to allow its campuses to adopt iTunes University because of widespread accessibility problems. The CSU chief information officer personally stood behind this decision despite pressure from several campuses and from Apple, and he visited the Apple offices in Cupertino, California, to deliver the message.[11] He also offered assistance to Apple to remedy the deficiencies, which Apple did resolve, to the benefit of users with disabilities beyond the CSU system. Without the strong support of the California State CIO, the accessibility achievements would not have occurred.

Accessibility Officer

One of the key participants in the roles and responsibilities section of the policy is the accessibility officer. The accessibility officer manages the accessibility effort and makes sure that key functions have needed resources and that the plan is implemented. The accessibility officer supports and leads the governance functions, bringing the necessary parties to the table to make decisions and to issue guidance. The accessibility officer leads the metrics and reporting effort, making sure that information is collected and analyzed.

The report data and analysis are the basis for allocating resources, setting training goals and strategies, and making many other decisions. The accessibility officer is the key advocate for accessibility within the organization, always evaluating the culture to determine how to advance accessibility in a way that is compatible with the values and the established ways in which things get done. The accessibility officer is aware of the strategic direction and challenges of the organization and is looking for potential advantages to be aware of, as well as possible barriers that can be anticipated.

Procurement and Acquisitions

Government purchasing is a highly structured activity. Unlike private companies, the government is not concerned only with getting the best deal or finding the best technical solution for a need. Because public money is being spent, the government must be able to demonstrate that its purchasing processes and decisions are not affected by corruption or personal influence. There are preferences for small businesses and businesses owned by women, veterans, and minorities. The processes for purchasing ICT are established in many different regulations, with specific steps to be followed in a very specific order.

Government offices specialize in the various procurement processes, and there are procurement specialists for different processes and programs. They are experts in government purchasing rules and processes, but they are not experts in accessibility. Accessibility is one criterion that must be applied to a purchase, much like other technical specifications. There must be specific accessibility requirements for conformance with the applicable accessibility standards. The procurement specialists need assistance to determine which standards to apply, and when different bids are considered, they need assistance to evaluate the actual accessibility of the bids. Then they need contractual language to make sure that accessibility will be assured after the product is accepted, for future upgrades or for procedures to follow if accessibility problems are discovered when the product is used.

Accessibility is also an important consideration in acquisition of services, such as software development or preparation of online training. In selecting a vendor, the government entity needs to evaluate the accessibility capability of each applicant. The request for bids should also make it clear that the desired product must be accessible, and it should specify which standards will apply. In order to be sure that the resulting product will be accessible, it is good practice to schedule accessibility reviews periodically during the product-development process so that any accessibility problems can be identified and remedied during the development process, not at the end. Products should not be accepted until accessibility is assured.

Software-Development Process

Whether software and apps are developed in-house by government staff or by an outside contractor or vendor, accessibility requirements should be identified during the design process, and accessibility needs to be checked multiple times during development. In the older Waterfall software-design process, accessibility should be treated the same way in which we expect it to be included in the design of a physical building. The accessibility requirements should be fully implemented in the final product. A major shortcoming of Waterfall from an accessibility perspective is that testing for accessibility can occur only at the end of the process, after the product has been fully built. Remedying any problems that are found can then be costly and time consuming.

The Agile development process and other more streamlined processes that are based on continuous checkpoints and improvement are well suited for inclusion of accessibility. Because there are numerous predefined points in the development process for assessing progress, an accessibility expert can be included as one of the stakeholders to be involved. At each stage, the accessibility challenges or goals can be identified and the degree of compliance can be measured. From this assessment, a plan can be developed that will be implemented, and then the product will be reassessed at the next checkpoint.

Web Accessibility

Web accessibility is the cornerstone of any public accessibility program. A government's website is often its most publicly visible presence. Members of the public depend on it for information and for communicating directly with government agencies. Because of this, it is usually the first target of the government's accessibility program. There is general global consensus that WCAG 2.0 standards should apply.

The government's intranet site is just as important as the public-facing website. Many governments employ more people with disabilities than the private sector, and barriers to the intranet can make it difficult for employees to perform well in the job, have access to training, engage in common employment activities, and participate in many other important aspects of the job.

Anything hosted on a website should be accessible. This can include items like templates, databases, videos, podcasts, and apps or software. Many of these items can be difficult to remedy for accessibility, so it is important to have processes in place to screen for accessibility before something is added to the website.

Accessible Content or Documents

Websites are used by governments to publish documents. Publication of physical documents still occurs, but electronic publication and dissemination are very common. Early accessibility laws, such as the Americans with Disabilities Act, were written when printed documents were the norm. Accessibility of print materials requires making alternative formats available, such as braille, large print, audio recordings, or an electronic accessible version.[12]

Electronic documents need to follow the same general accessibility requirements as websites and software. Achieving accessibility within a particular electronic format, such as Word, Excel, PowerPoint, or PDF, requires an understanding of how to apply a particular accessibility requirement within the workings of that format. For example, the technique for adding an alt tag for a graphic image is different within various formats. Because of this, guidance is available[13] for how to make documents accessible for popular formats, and the techniques for checking and remedying documents for accessibility are also available.

One of the most significant challenges for document accessibility is that document authors can be found throughout the government, and they have widely variable technical skills and experience. Incorporating accessibility into the original document-authoring process is the most effective and least costly way to achieve document accessibility. However, reaching all document authors and ensuring that they have the needed skills is a very big undertaking. Many document authors are not very well versed in using the authoring software, such as Word or Excel, and they lack the overall skill set to take advantage of the tools built into the software that can make accessibility fairly easy. They need training in how to maximize their authoring software and in how to include accessibility in the authoring process.

Many U.S. agencies started out in an ad hoc manner without a full plan for reaching the goal of accessibility of documents. They brought on outside firms with accessibility skills to remedy inaccessible documents. This approach makes sense as a way to manage a large backlog of documents that require remediation, but it is not a cost-effective way to make sure that new documents will be accessible. Leaving accessibility to the last step of authoring and publishing documents is a very costly approach. A more strategic approach should include establishment of document-authoring training goals, with accessibility included as a key element of the training; establishment of a document-accessibility monitoring program; and remediation as a last resort.

Training

Accessibility needs to be recognized as a valued job requirement and skill for many different employees within the government: policy makers and administrators, procurement and acquisitions staff, contract administrators, technology managers, software developers, human resources staff, document authors, and others. It is not fair or even possible to hold people accountable for their role in assuring accessibility if training is not made available to assist them to develop and mature the necessary skills.

Some accessibility training courses are well suited to be only about accessibility. For these, the subject matter is complex, and there are a variety of incentives for the appropriate staff to sign up. Technical skills for accessibility are an example. For other subjects, it may make more sense to include accessibility as a section or module in a course that has a broader scope. For example, if the government or agency offers training courses for all employees about how to use authoring/publishing software such as Word or PDF, accessibility should be included as a key aspect of the training. Document authors should be encouraged to develop basic document-authoring skills, and accessibility should be regarded as a basic skill rather than as something separate or special. Similarly, if procurement staff are expected to attend training about key functions of their jobs, accessibility should be included.

In-person training is often preferred for transferring accessibility skills, but it is impractical in a large enterprise such as a government entity. Approaches such as a train-the-trainer program or online modular videos are better at delivering consistent content to a wide and dispersed audience. One of the challenges for the accessibility field is delineating a progression of skills needed for different levels of expertise that an accessibility professional can follow in order to move from an entry level to more advanced positions.

Evaluation/Testing/Validation

The goal of accessibility for end users with disabilities cannot be assured without evaluation of the accessibility of the ICT involved.[14] Evaluation can be used for independent validation of the accessibility claims of vendors, software developers, document authors, and others who attest to the degree that their product conforms to the relevant accessibility standards. There are two different broad types of accessibility evaluations: (1) technical evaluations of websites, software applications, and other specific products and (2) evaluations of the accessibility of the companies or programs that develop products. There are also different levels of attestations that can be used or required.

Testing specific products for accessibility can be done informally by having an end user with a disability try to use the website or product in question. The problem with informal testing is that the results are not useful for communicating where the barriers can be found or for developing a remediation approach. The results of informal testing cannot be shared with others very well, since the results are difficult to replicate or compare with other tests.

More formal testing should include several basic elements: (1) determination of what core requirements will be tested, (2) a repeatable testing methodology, (3) determination of what tools will be used, (4) a report of the results using a standard framework and using all these elements, and (5) recommendations for remediation. The purpose of the testing should affect the nature of the report and recommendations. If the tests are conducted for the acquisition of ICT from a vendor, the report needs to provide enough information to justify the recommendation whether to purchase the ICT. If the purpose of the test is to provide information and feedback to ICT developers, the report results need to be in a more technical format, with more details that can be used by developers and engineers and with specific recommendations for how to remedy accessibility problems.

Once an accessibility testing unit is established within an enterprise, it often experiences a high level of demand, especially if accessibility must be verified before the website, application, or system is allowed to become operational. Federal agencies in the United States that have experienced this problem are moving toward a solution involving training and certifying their technical staff to conduct the testing using a standard testing methodology, referred to as the Trusted Tester approach.[15] This expands the number of certified testers and disperses them throughout the agency; in this way, the software-development group, for example, has its own accessibility testing capacity within its staff members.

In the United States, within the procurement process, vendors have been required to include a self-certification document in an ICT contract bid, referred to as a VPAT (Voluntary Product Accessibility Template), to attest to the extent to which their product conforms to the Section 508 standards.[16] Self-certification is not a very reliable method because it is not possible to distinguish valid claims from inaccurate or misleading ones. Under the accessibility procurement program developed by the EU, member countries are encouraged to consider applying a range of levels of conformity attestations.[17] The EN ICT Accessibility Procurement Toolkit points to relevant International Standards Organization (ISO) standards. The standard "EN ISO/IEC 17000:2004" defines five types of attestations:

1. A first-party declaration is a statement issued by a supplier or manufacturer that fulfilment of specific requirements has been demonstrated.
2. A Supplier's Declaration of Conformity (SDoC) is a first-party declaration with details compliant with the standard EN ISO/IEC 17050. A Supplier's Declaration of Conformity can be substantiated by supporting documentation for which the supplier is responsible. Anyone should be able to repeat the verification and arrive at the same result using this information.
3. A second-party attestation is an attestation of conformity issued by a second party, usually the buyer or user of the product. Mostly, this term applies to a company controlling its subcontractors or a large buyer or government agency carrying out the assessment itself.

4. EN ISO/IEC 17000:2004 defines third-party conformity assessment activity "as performed by a person or body that is independent of the person or organization that provides the object and of user interests in that object."
5. A conformity-assessment body of any type (first, second, or third) can apply for accreditation. Accreditation is the procedure by which an authoritative body gives formal recognition that a body or person is competent to carry out a specific conformity assessment.

The tool kit also provides several different factors that may affect which level of attestation to require. The value of the types of attestations other than self-certification is that they are inherently more credible. With higher levels of credibility, the need for the government entity to perform its own testing is lower.

Another method of accessibility assessment involves measuring the strength of the vendor's internal accessibility program. The National Association of State Chief Information Officers (NASCIO) has issued a two-part policy brief[18] about an approach called Policy-Driven Adoption for Accessibility. Developed by state accessibility leaders from Massachusetts, Minnesota, and Texas, this method examines a vendor's capacity to

1. develop, implement, and maintain an ICT accessibility policy;
2. establish and maintain an organizational structure that enables and facilitates progress in ICT accessibility;
3. integrate ICT accessibility criteria into key phases of development, procurement, acquisitions, and other relevant business processes;
4. provide a process for addressing inaccessible ICT;
5. ensure the availability of relevant ICT accessibility skills and other resources within (or to) the organization; and
6. make information regarding ICT accessibility policy, plans, and progress available to customers.

For procurement organizations, the responses can be used to assess the vendor's ability to produce accessible offerings and to gauge confidence in the quality of a vendor's VPAT or other accessibility documentation. If repeated measures of the same vendor are conducted over time, progress and improvement can be determined. For vendors, a self-assessment using the same measures can guide the implementation of organization-wide accessibility programs and initiatives and help achieve long-term accessibility in product lines and offerings.

Accountability/Reporting

Ultimately, public programs are accountable to the citizens of the country, whose taxes are used to carry out government functions. In particular, the public should be able to find out how effective accessibility programs are. What percentage of government websites are found to be accessible? How many contracts for ICT include language requiring accessibility? What percentage of software systems undergo accessibility testing during the development process? How much of an agency's budget is dedicated to the accessibility effort?

To be able to produce answers to these questions, government accessibility programs should conduct the same type of self-assessment that is referred to in the previously described NASCIO Policy-Driven Adoption for Accessibility method. The arm of the government responsible for carrying out government-wide policies should communicate what information is to be collected and how often. A regular periodic schedule for filing reports is the best method. An analysis of the results should be made public, and that analysis should be used to make strategic improvements.

The requirement of filing a regular report helps the people who manage the operations of accessibility focus on key goals. The visibility of the results creates internal and external pressure on the enterprise to demonstrate progress. Operationally, accessibility is more a process than a goal; it needs continuous attention and dedication of resources.

Complaints and Help-Desk Function

What can an end user with a disability do when ICT cannot be accessed or used? The first avenue for employees is to contact the IT support office; this general source of support should be useful for employees with disabilities. The IT support office, or help desk, can help define the problem and begin to determine its basis and solution. There are many possibilities, including poorly functioning assistive technology, incorrect settings, accessibility flaws, or problems not based on accessibility at all. If the IT support staff cannot find a solution, they can refer the user to an appropriate technical expert with knowledge about accessibility and the particular systems and apps in use. The IT staff should receive basic training in accessibility and assistive technology in order to be able to serve in a first-level problem-solving function.

Governments need to provide members of the public with a point of contact to report problems with the accessibility of public-facing ICT. Reported problems need to be referred to the appropriate staff members with expertise in both the ICT involved and accessibility. When such a problem is resolved, it is important to communicate back to the individual who reported it. Data about the types of problems reported and their resolution should be collected. Analysis of these data can reveal underlying technical problems that require a systemic solution. The data can also identify areas of the enterprise that need strengthening in accessibility. There are numerous ways in which the data can be used to understand how well the accessibility program is functioning.

A more formal complaint process should be available for individuals when the accessibility problem has not been fixed. Governments are operated by bureaucracies, which are infamous for getting bogged down in lengthy processes and for dropping the ball. A more formal complaint process should be administered by an arm of the government that does not have a conflict of interest or a perceived reputation to protect. The complaint process should be transparent; the complainant should be informed about the status of a complaint, and there should be a timeline for resolution.

Section 508 Standards Published in 2000

The Section 508 standards were issued in 2000, shortly after WCAG 1.0. The scope of the Section 508 standards is broader than WCAG. The technical standards were divided into six separate categories of ICT:

1. Software applications and operating systems
2. Web-based intranet and Internet information and applications
3. Telecommunications products
4. Video and multimedia products
5. Self-contained, closed products
6. Desktop and portable computers

The standards provide that each federal agency shall ensure that ICT complies with applicable sections of the standards unless doing so would impose an undue burden on the agency. Undue burden is defined very broadly: "Undue burden means significant difficulty or expense. In determining whether an action would result in an undue burden, an agency shall consider all agency resources available to the program or component for which the product is being developed, procured, maintained, or used." In instances where undue burden is found to exist, agencies are required to provide the information and functionality through an alternative means of access.[19]

Section 508 establishes an exemption for national security systems.[20] The standards provide a detailed definition of this exemption and also set forth an exemption for "back office" equipment used only by service personnel for maintenance, repair, or similar purposes.[21] They provide that Section 508 does not require a fundamental alteration of a product or its components; for example, a small portable device would not be required to include a large screen display.

Within each category, there are technical specifications and performance-based requirements relevant to the particular type of technology. These categories have become difficult to apply over time because technology has changed with the emergence of new platforms and functionalities that overlap, such as embedded video.

The Subpart with Functional Performance Criteria[22] applies to overall product accessibility. The provisions cover operation, including input and control functions, operation of mechanical components, and access to visual and audible information.

The standards also require that access to information, product documentation, and end-user support be accessible.[23] These include user guides, instructions, and customer or technical support communications.

New Regulations on Section 508

In early 2015, the U.S. Access Board issued proposed revisions to the Section 508 standards for public comment, and a final rule was issued in January 2017.[24] The final rule directly incorporates WCAG 2.0 as a requirement, with a greater focus on functional performance criteria than in the previous rule. Unlike the prior Section 508 regulations, which focused on separating out the different types of products and technologies, the new regulation focuses more on functions and user goals. Among other features, the new regulation clarifies the coverage (e.g., document accessibility is clearly included in this regulation), limits the use of alternate text-only pages, and harmonizes more with international standards and usage of terminology. Federal agencies will have until January 2018 to comply with the new requirements, but there is a safe harbor provision for legacy systems and content which have not been modified or updated and comply with the existing 508 standards. It is unclear if the new White House administration will in any way modify the new Section 508 regulation.

Global Perspective

The United States has the most mature and complete government accessibility program in the world in Section 508, which has been in effect since 1986. Other countries have begun to implement laws that require that government agencies make their websites accessible,[25] and some have also begun to put in place laws requiring accessibility in procurement and development of technology.[26] The laws vary in what is required to be accessible and the extent to which there are means to hold the governments accountable for measuring compliance.

The Convention on the Rights of Persons with Disabilities (CRPD)[27] was adopted by the United Nations in 2006 and has been ratified by over 150 countries. Many programs and laws have been initiated across the globe as a result, although much more will need to be done in order to attain its broad goals. The CRPD defines accessibility specifically to include access to information and communication technology. Article 9, the section that defines accessibility, requires governments to ensure that persons with disabilities have equal access to "information and communications, including information and communications technologies and systems, and to other facilities and services open or provided to the public." In addition, governments are also required to take appropriate measures to "develop, promulgate and monitor the implementation of minimum standards and guidelines for the accessibility of facilities and services open or provided to the public ... promote access for persons with disabilities to new information and communications technologies and systems, including the Internet ... and promote the design, development, production and distribution of accessible information and communications technologies and systems at an early stage, so that these technologies and systems become accessible at minimum cost."

Many countries have incorporated accessibility into their web-development policies and practices, including testing for accessibility with tools and manual methods. In 2006, the list of countries included Australia, Austria, Belgium, Brazil, Canada, Denmark, Finland, France, Germany, Hong Kong, Ireland, Italy, Japan, Korea, Luxembourg, the Netherlands, New Zealand, Norway, Portugal, Singapore, Spain, Sweden, Thailand, and the United Kingdom. The European Union has also adopted a web accessibility policy.[28] Most countries have not seriously begun to incorporate accessibility into their business processes related to ICT. Fortunately, WCAG 2.0 provides a common framework for approaching web accessibility, allowing for shared practices and techniques. Accessibility is a common challenge; each country does not need to adopt its own approach. A global community of practice is possible, in which accessibility experts and practitioners share tips, solutions, and new innovative ideas. Technology is constantly evolving at a rapid pace, and the accessibility community has the best chance of keeping up through international collaboration.

As countries across the globe move forward in implementing the CRPD, their focus is moving beyond web accessibility into government procurement and broad accessibility practices. This chapter has detailed the elements that need to be addressed. Ontario, Canada, has moved beyond web accessibility in its policy requirements. It will need to include program metrics in the implementation of the broad policy goals, with regular reporting on these metrics, in order to move beyond aspiration and ad hoc accomplishments.

Japan has developed ICT-accessibility standards in response to legislation affecting procurement by all government entities at all levels of government. The Japan Industrial Standards Committee (JISC) developed a seven-part standard that harmonizes with WCAG 2.0. Programmatically, however, the procurement process simply requires that one sentence about accessibility be included in a request for bids. Self-reporting by vendors is accepted, and there are no comprehensive accessibility guidelines for government agencies.[29]

The European Union has spent several years planning for implementation of broad accessibility requirements. In 2014, the European Standardization Organizations (CEN, European Committee for Standardization; CENELEC, European Committee for Electrotechnical Standardization; and ETSI,

European Telecommunications Standards Institute) published the first European standard on accessibility requirements for ICT products and services, EN 301 549. It is intended in particular for use by public authorities and other public-sector bodies during procurement to ensure that websites, software, and digital devices are more accessible.[30] EU member countries are required to adopt these standards by 2016 (during 2016, countries were in different stages of adopting the standards.) In 2005, the EU Commission issued Mandate 376, which requires all EU countries to harmonize their procurement practices with respect to public procurement of ICT. Accessibility practices will be included in this broad European harmonization of procurement practices. To support the accessibility requirement, the EU has published a tool kit[31] that offers guidance and tools that can be used by government agencies through the different stages of procurement.

The European approach is based on sharing resources and collaboration. The work undertaken by the Irish, described in the following paragraph, which predated the EU initiative, influenced the process and resources now available across Europe. Similarly, the Canadian procurement process incorporates some of the Irish resources. Accessibility of ICT is complex and requires unique qualifications; countries will be more successful if they build on the work and accomplishments of others.

In Ireland, Section 27 of the Disability Act of 2005 requires the head of a public entity to ensure that services provided and goods supplied to the public are accessible to people with disabilities. Exceptions are available when doing so is not practicable, would be too expensive, or would cause an unreasonable delay.[32] This law covers many different types of purchases, including ICT. The Irish National Disability Authority has an online IT Procurement Toolkit[33] with extensive information and resources covering preparation of a request for bids, assessment of bids, integrating accessibility into software development, accessibility evaluations, and maintaining accessibility. Specific language for inclusion in documents is also provided.

The Global Initiative for Inclusive ICTs (G3ict) is an advocacy initiative established by the United Nations Global Alliance for ICT and Development to promote the implementation of the CRPD elements related to accessibility of ICT. Its white paper about public procurement, "CRPD Implementation: Promoting Global Digital Inclusion Through ICT Procurement Policies & Accessibility Standards,"[34] contains a very strong recommendation for the adoption of a global accessibility standard for procurement purposes. Noting that the Section 508 and the EN 301 549 standards are very close but not completely harmonized, G3ict calls for a universal standard that builds on both in order to enable countries of the Global South to move forward rapidly.

The countries of the EU and other countries across the globe have looked to Section 508 in the United States as an inspiration for their own goals and aspirations. It is to be hoped that they can avoid some of the early pitfalls of Section 508: lack of program metrics and regular reporting, fragmented testing methods and operations, failure to incorporate accessibility into technology development, and overreliance on self-certification from vendors, to name a few. It will be important for countries to recognize that accessibility requires an enterprise-wide approach and that it is an essential skill area for many involved in technology development and operations.

Conclusion

The Convention on the Rights of Persons with Disabilities cannot be truly implemented without major advances in every country in the accessibility of technology used by governments. Technology is almost as essential as water or air; human rights cannot be realized without access to technology. Even though each country is unique, with its own laws, history, and procedures, there are many common challenges and solutions in regard to ICT accessibility. Countries should not just attempt to copy the work of others; they should strive to make improvements. This can be done successfully only by discerning what aspects of an existing accessibility program need improvement. Collaboration between accessibility experts and managers can yield the most benefit for all. Successes and lessons learned should be shared on a global basis.

CHAPTER 6

Using Provincial Laws to Drive a National Agenda: Connecting Human Rights and Disability Rights Laws

Ravi Malhotra and Megan A. Rusciano

Introduction

Federal states present significant challenges to effective implementation of international human rights and provision of consistent domestic protection to vulnerable groups, such as people with disabilities. This chapter explores one such federal state, Canada, which has federal and provincial human rights laws that cover all jurisdictions, but disability rights laws in only a very small number of provincial jurisdictions. We argue that although the landmark Accessibility for Ontarians with Disabilities Act, 2005 (AODA), holds out much promise for the future, we should also pay attention to successful litigation, such as *Jodhan v. Canada*,[1] in which a blind woman successfully sued the federal government for its failure to make websites accessible to people with print disabilities. In making a successful equality rights claim under Section 15 of the Canadian Charter of Rights and Freedoms, *Jodhan* establishes the basis for future claims at both the federal and the provincial level.

We first explore the implications of the Accessibility for Ontarians with Disabilities Act, 2005, for the ICT sector. Information and communication technology will become increasingly important as society shifts to conducting more and more of daily life online. From electronic banking and shopping to teaching a class through the Internet and even health care, ICT is now ubiquitous. Full inclusion of people with print disabilities and hearing impairments in society requires robust provisions that systematically address and rectify barriers in ICT technology that impede the full inclusion of people with disabilities. We then examine the use of litigation as a strategy for driving a national agenda for equality in the ICT sector. Given the limited examples of provincial disability rights legislation across Canada, progressive judicial decisions have gained utility as resources for Canadian advocates to advance and propel the disability rights agenda. In particular, Donna Jodhan's successful challenge to the federal government's inaccessible websites for visually impaired users represents just one example of how a progressive judicial decision can incite a useful and transformative dialogue about the barriers that reinforce discrimination against persons with disabilities. We argue that the *Jodhan* decision proffers an example advocates can advance to promote the rights of persons with disabilities, even in jurisdictions without disability rights legislation, by employing progressive litigation strategies that aim to address the discriminatory nature of the "disability divide" and promote social inclusion more broadly.[2] We close with some brief concluding remarks.

Regulation by Statute: The Accessibility for Ontarians with Disabilities Act

Since 1982, the Human Rights Code in Ontario, Canada's largest province by population, has prohibited discrimination on the basis of disability.[3] This allows applicants to bring forward any complaint to the Human Rights Tribunal of Ontario, especially since Ontario adopted a direct-access model that eliminated the role of the Ontario Human Rights Commission as a gatekeeper to screen complaints.[4] Because Canada is a federal state, the first question that must be determined is whether a particular matter falls within federal or provincial jurisdiction. If it is a federal matter, then jurisdiction falls to the Canadian Human Rights Commission. Because Canadian federalism is relatively decentralized, many powers that are granted to the federal government in other jurisdictions, such as the United States, fall under provincial jurisdiction in Canada.[5] That having been said, many issues of concern for ICT, such as telecommunications, are typically classified as federal powers.[6] Although disability discrimination claims in the ICT sector remain largely undeveloped in Ontario, disability discrimination has become the most common ground alleged in cases before the Human Rights Tribunal.[7] Given the state of information technology in 1982, it is hardly surprising that human rights cases that raised these issues were litigated in the 1980s. A 2003 history of advocacy organizing by blind organizations in Canada makes essentially no mention of ICT issues beyond the relatively low-technology issue of obtaining an exemption on a levy imposed on behalf of copyright holders and producers on blank cassettes.[8] Yet today, ICT encompasses numerous technologies that are part of everyday life and allow people with disabilities to work, go to school, and play in the community. Electronic banking is now indispensable to the economy, and many other services are increasingly using technology. Without full ICT inclusion, people with disabilities will fall further and further behind and be unable to effectively participate in daily life and compete in the marketplace.

Disability rights advocates nevertheless campaigned for a provincial statute specifically relating to disability in light of the success and influence of the Americans with Disabilities Act (ADA) and the painfully slow progress that had been achieved by people with disabilities through twenty years of applications via the human rights complaint process in the 1980s and 1990s. The international impact of the ADA, generating disability statutes of broader or narrower scope in many jurisdictions around the world in a relatively short time, may plausibly be regarded as an example of what legal scholar Harold Koh has insightfully called "transnational legal process." Transnational legal process refers to how public and private actors interact in various public and private forums domestically and internationally to create, adapt, enforce, and internalize norms of transnational law.[9] The case can be made, in line with the thinking of scholars associated with expressive theories of law, that the ADA showcased the importance of equality and inclusion for people with disabilities and therefore has gradually helped make the prohibition of disability discrimination an international legal norm by encouraging other states to follow through with comparable domestic legislation.[10]

The Ontarians with Disabilities Act

The first initiative was a false start with a seriously flawed piece of legislation known as the Ontarians with Disabilities Act (ODA).[11] Enacted in 2001, the

ODA may be traced in part to general dissatisfaction with the many barriers people with disabilities experienced in all areas of Canadian life, including ICT, employment, and transportation. Advocates such as the lawyer David Lepofsky campaigned tirelessly for effective disability rights legislation that would systematically remove barriers and facilitate equality rights for people with disabilities.[12] A more specific if somewhat symbolic influence, emblematic of the theory articulated by Koh, was a talk given by renowned American disability rights advocate Justin Dart in 1992 in Ottawa, the Canadian capital, and later published in the influential magazine of the Toronto-based disability legal clinic ARCH. Dart, chair of the President's Committee on Employment of People with Disabilities, argued in his speech that disability rights had to be enforceable rights that promoted equality without compromise.[13] A third dimension that warranted careful attention was the realization that the nature of federalism in Canada required the passage of an effective disability rights law at the provincial level. Unlike the United States, many key powers, such as the regulation of most employees, hotels, services, and health care, are accorded to the provinces in Canada. This meant that advocacy and organizational activity needed to be undertaken at the provincial level.[14]

In 1994, four years after the historic passage of the ADA in the United States, the ODA Committee was formed to lobby for a strong and effective piece of disability rights legislation in Ontario. Its immediate goal was to support a private member's bill advocating an Ontarians with Disabilities Act by a Deaf member of the Ontario legislature, Gary Malkowksi.[15] Evocative of expressive theories of law, the advocacy of the statute created the movement that raised awareness of disability issues but did not see the bill enacted.[16]

After the election of a Conservative government in Ontario in 1995, the ODA Committee faced a chilly reception in lobbying for disability legislation. In 1998, facing the prospect of another upcoming election, the government proposed a very short piece of legislation, Bill 83, which would have simply required government ministries to indicate what barriers they intended to remove in the following year. There was no enforcement mechanism or obligation to consult with people with disabilities. The bill was vigorously opposed by disability rights activists, and the government ultimately abandoned it a few weeks later.[17]

Finally, after years of lobbying, the reelected Conservative government enacted the ODA in 2001. Unfortunately, the ODA was a deeply flawed piece of legislation that had little to contribute to ICT issues, apart from a vague commitment to ensure accessible government websites.[18] First, unlike the ADA, the ODA applied only to the government and the broader public sector, such as hospitals, school boards, and universities and colleges.[19] At a time when governments everywhere are downsizing and job creation is primarily in the hands of the private sector,[20] this was an immense roadblock to improving the quality of life of people with disabilities. Indeed, it is clear that no significant progress can be made in ICT without a legislative framework that encompasses the private sector. Second, the ODA did not require accessibility or mandate barrier removal.[21] The ODA was consequently a pale copy of the ADA with little chance of making a difference in the lives of people with disabilities.

The AODA

After the election of the Liberals in 2003, Ontario eventually enacted the Accessibility for Ontarians with Disabilities Act[22] in 2005, becoming the first Canadian province with such legislation.[23] Although the AODA is far more robust than the ODA, it has always been explicitly premised on the gradual adoption of standards to make Ontario an accessible society by 2025. Consequently, as of this writing, it is at a relatively early stage of development. The AODA contains regulations that are relevant to those seeking an inclusive ICT sector. Building an inclusive ICT sector is central to equality for people with disabilities because it will allow people with disabilities to fully participate in electronic commerce, banking, and learning. As governments of all political stripes place more emphasis on small business and entrepreneurship to grow the economy, access to ICT will become that much more critical for people with disabilities to attain equality. The law sets up accessibility standards for both the public and the private sector in customer service, information and communications, employment, transportation, and the design of public spaces (the built environment). The first standard is articulated in the Customer Service Standard and relates to the use of service animals, training for staff of providers of goods and services, and notification of temporary disruptions.[24] The final four standards were consolidated into one regulation, known as the Integrated Accessibility Standards Regulation (IASR).[25] One feature that sets it apart from the ADA and its emphasis on litigation as a means to achieve conflict resolution is the extent to which the AODA relies on compulsory training on accessibility for many public-sector employees and volunteers, including hospital workers, school-board employees, and academics.[26] Given the fact that the Canadian public sector is relatively large, this means that the day-to-day knowledge of accessibility acquired by a public-sector worker may, over time, be significant in acting as a catalyst for further improvements to attain accessibility and substantive equality.

However, the legislation was unfortunately designed with a very long and complex phase-in period. Some requirements on obligated authorities do not come into effect for many years.[27] Not surprisingly, private-sector stakeholders, including ones in the ICT sector, have delayed the attainment of accessibility by lobbying in favor of standards with lengthy timelines, while disability rights advocates have sought clarity to ensure a timely implementation of accessibility.[28] The issue of agency capture of regulators has generated a large literature that cannot be addressed here.[29] However, it is problematic that corporate stakeholders have been able to successfully argue for a framework in which many more years will elapse before enforcement on obligated authorities begins, especially when one considers the fact that the disability community has sought the adoption of regulatory standards for some twenty years. There are also real questions about the efficacy of the enforcement mechanism. The AODA envisions daily fines of up to $100,000 for noncompliance, but it is far from clear in what situations such fines would actually be imposed.[30] Because it is too early for any discussion of case law, the focus here is statutory.

Understanding the Regulations

For the purposes of this chapter, the key regulations are the subsections of the IASR dealing with information and communications, which are contained in Part II of the regulation. This standard is articulated through eleven sections (which are organized under the headings Sections 9–19). For contextual purposes, Table 6.1 presents the overall structure of the IASR.

Before proceeding with the analysis, it should be made clear that provisions of the Convention on the Rights of Persons with Disabilities (CRPD) may be applied in interpreting the regulations. Canada ratified the CRPD in 2010 but has not adopted specific implementing legislation. Although there is still some ambiguity in Canadian courts about the requirements for a

Table 6.1. The Integrated Accessibility Standards Regulation

Part I	General provisions (applicable to all sectors)	Sections 1–8
Part II	Information and communication standards	Sections 9–19
Part III	Employment	Sections 20–32
Part IV	Transportation	Sections 33–80
Part IV.1	Design of public spaces and standards	Sections 80.1–80.44
Part V	Compliance	Sections 81–86.1

ratified international treaty to take effect, we argue that ratification by Parliament is sufficient for courts to interpret legislation and subordinate regulations in accordance with the CRPD.[31]

Section 9 of the IASR sets out various definitions for key terms, such as "communications" and "information."[32] Where information or communications are unconvertible, an exception may be granted provided that the person requesting the data is given an explanation why accessibility is impossible and is given a summary of the data.[33] In our view, the terms are generally defined broadly, allowing for more widely encompassing regulation of obligated organizations. Moreover, this definitions provision should be understood and interpreted robustly through the prism of Articles 9, 21, and 30 of the CRPD. Article 9 is a broad provision on accessibility requiring states parties to take appropriate measures to ensure access for persons with disabilities on an equal basis.[34] Article 9(1)(b) stipulates that states parties shall undertake measures to identify and eliminate obstacles and barriers to accessibility for people with disabilities in the context of information and communications, including electronic services.[35] Article 21 concerns freedom of expression and opinion and access to information. It requires states parties to take all appropriate measures to ensure the provision of information in accessible formats and technologies in a timely manner and with no extra cost. It also encourages private entities to provide services, including on the Internet, in an accessible format for people with disabilities. It also promotes use of sign languages.[36] Finally, Article 30 requires states parties to take all appropriate measures to ensure that people with disabilities enjoy access to cultural materials in accessible formats, access to television, films, theater, and other cultural activities, and access to places for cultural performance or service.[37] Collectively, these articles suggest that the pivotal Section 9 provision of the IASR should be interpreted broadly, at least to the extent that its ambit includes government, by the courts and administrative tribunals in order to comply with Canada's international commitments.

Section 10 of the IASR stipulates that Sections 9, 11, 12, and 13 apply to all obligated organizations.[38] Section 11 requires that organizations that have processes for receiving and responding to feedback ensure that they are provided in an accessible format upon request. Section 11 also makes clear that obligated authorities must also comply with the requirements of the Customer Service Standard, allowing for the various standards to work in tandem to provide accessibility.[39] Given that many Canadian universities continue to have inaccessible mechanisms for students to evaluate faculty teaching, an interesting question is whether Section 11 would cover faculty evaluations.

Section 12 lies at the heart of the ICT accessibility requirements set out in the IASR. Section 12 requires every obligated organization to provide or arrange for the provision of accessible formats upon request. This must be done at no additional cost in consultation with the requesting party to ensure the suitability of the format.[40] The public must be notified about the availability of accessible formats and communication supports.[41] Although disability rights organizations such as Citizens with Disabilities–Ontario have criticized the vagueness of the timelines,[42] Section 12, at least on its face, encourages speedy compliance through the use of the phrase "in a timely manner."[43] The section also sets out a schedule for compliance depending on the size and character of the organization.[44] Again, this provision should be interpreted broadly in light of Canada's international treaty commitments pursuant to Articles 21 and 30 of the CRPD to ensure that people with disabilities promptly receive the services they require.

Section 13 requires organizations that produce emergency plans, procedures, or public information to make them available in accessible formats with appropriate communication support.[45] This is critical for the inclusion of people with disabilities in the event of floods, earthquakes, or terrorist attacks. Again, the vagueness of the timeline for obligated organizations has been criticized.[46] Section 14 sets out a key provision mandating accessible websites and web content. As we will see in more detail later in this chapter, access to websites that are inclusive is essential in order for people with disabilities to thrive in education, employment, and recreation. Section 14 requires obligated organizations to ensure that their websites and web content conform to the WCAG 2.0 at Level AA within a stipulated time frame. The schedule varies depending on the size and nature of the organization.

Exemptions from the standards are accorded for specific success criteria such as live captions and prerecorded audio descriptions for various lengths of time. All web content published after January 1, 2012, is subject to the provision.[47] Although this section has the potential to lead to dramatic change, the stipulated timeline for large organizations is very long. Unfortunately, designated public-sector organizations and large organizations are granted until 2021 to modify existing websites to conform to the WCAG 2.0 Level AA standard.[48]

Section 15 relates to ICT requirements in the educational sector. Educational inclusion lies at the foundation of equality for people with disabilities. Without proper educational tools that are fully inclusive, students with learning disabilities or sensory impairments may find themselves facing tremendous barriers in obtaining an education at both the public school and the postsecondary level. Section 15 requires obligated educational or training institutions, upon notification, to provide educational or training resources in an accessible format in consultation with the requesting party. It also requires that student records and program descriptions be made available in an accessible format.[49] Section 16 requires training of educators at school boards, universities, and colleges with respect to accessible program or course delivery.[50] This innovative provision, which goes well beyond typical human rights statutes, may have a long-term potential to transform attitudes about students with disabilities. Section 17 requires producers of educational or training materials to make textbooks and print-based supplementary learning resources available in alternative formats.[51] However, once again, for the category of learning resources, the timeline is long. Producers have until 2020 to comply with the requirement.[52] Section 18 requires academic libraries to make their collections, with some exceptions for categories such as archival materials, available in alternative format.[53] In the case of digital or multimedia resources, however, the deadline for compliance is 2020.[54] Finally, Section 19 requires public library boards to provide accessible materials or arrange for their provision where they exist.[55] As a whole, the provisions offer some genuine possibilities for change in the future. The commitment to training, in particular, has great potential to change attitudes on the ground and is not something that is required under, for example, the ADA. However, the generally lax timelines throughout are frustrating.

It is also worth noting that there are ICT elements embedded in other parts of the IASR. For instance, Section 26, in Part III of the IASR dealing with employment, requires employers, upon request, to provide materials in an accessible format to allow an employee do her or his job. An employer must also make information that is generally available to employees available in an accessible format.[56]

Advocates continue to identify barriers that pose difficulties for people with disabilities and violate the AODA. For instance, in 2012, disability rights advocates questioned the accessibility of a new website produced by the Durham Region Transit. The website produced many barriers for visually impaired and print-disabled users when it was assessed in accordance with the WCAG 2.0 Level AA standard. As one article correctly pointed out, this is the internationally recognized standard for web design.[57] Unfortunately, the excessively lenient timelines set out in the AODA did not require compliance with this standard until 2016.[58] As a result, new websites, in this case with important information concerning public transportation, may have been created without allowing equal access to this information by people with disabilities.

The Alliance for Equality of Blind Canadians produced a powerful critique of the AODA in 2011. At that time, the alliance warned that the timelines were too lengthy. It also cautioned that the government's approach of phasing in a requirement of compliance with WCAG 2.0 Level AA only gradually was misguided. It argued that this means that obligated organizations will have to train staff twice with respect to Level A and then Level AA. The alliance went so far as to suggest that the requirements were so weak that they provided less accessibility than is already required under the Ontario Human Rights Code, the Charter of Rights and Freedoms, and the CRPD.[59]

In April 2015, the Canadian government announced that it would accede to the World Intellectual Property Organization's Marrakesh Treaty to Facilitate Access to Published Works for Persons Who Are Blind, Visually Impaired, or Otherwise Print Disabled. The Marrakesh Treaty was adopted in 2013 and requires states parties to create exceptions to copyright law in order to facilitate access to published works for people with visual impairments and print disabilities.[60] It was expected to dramatically increase the availability of books in alternative formats for people who require them. Hundreds of thousands of books in fifty-five languages will be made available to people with print disabilities.[61] This could enhance the quality of life of Canadians with print disabilities from all walks of life. Although Canada had already taken some steps toward copyright reform, further modifications to copyright law are necessary to bring Canada into full compliance with the treaty.[62] In June 2015, the government introduced the Support for Canadians with

Print Disabilities Act in Parliament. The proposed bill would have established a clearer exception to copyright infringement for the reproduction of materials for those with perceptual disabilities. Unfortunately, the bill died when Parliament was recessed for the summer break and the subsequent ongoing federal election campaign.[63]

Legislative standards, however, can do only so much. Sometimes the publicity and legal remedies resulting from one high-profile litigation case can advance the law more dramatically than a mountain of regulations that are poorly understood or ignored by key policy makers. Direct lobbying sometimes can result in significant change. For instance, blind advocates Chris and Marie Laporte Stark were successful in persuading the Royal Bank to make automated teller machines (ATMs, known as ABMs in Canada) accessible to people with print disabilities. This design was then copied in the United States. They were also successful in persuading financial services and telecommunications companies to issue statements in multiple formats.[64] These small measures can have a tremendous effect on the quality of life of people with print disabilities. In the modern world, access to an ATM may well mean the difference between living independently and securing a job and a life of dependency.

Canada's leading cross-disability advocacy organization, the Council of Canadians with Disabilities, founded the Access to Technology Committee in 2007 (it was dissolved in 2014, and its functions were transferred to the Social Policy Committee). It made submissions to various governmental agencies, such as the Canadian Radio-Television and Telecommunications Commission (CRTC), on a variety of topics relating to accessibility, including the need to ensure accessible television program content and equipment, barriers in set-top boxes that do not meet universal design standards, and the need for increased access to captioned television programs with higher-quality captioning.[65] Interestingly, the Access to Technology Committee specifically referred to the right contained in the CRPD to cultural life.[66] As mentioned earlier, Article 30 of the CRPD mandates, inter alia, that people with disabilities enjoy access to cultural materials in accessible formats and access to television programs, film, theater, and other cultural activities in accessible formats.[67]

Additionally, between 2003 and 2007, the Council of Canadians with Disabilities was an active partner in the Disability and Information Technology Research Alliance, led by Deborah Steinstra and funded by the Social Sciences and Humanities Research Council (SSHRC). This work led to a special issue of the *Information Society International Journal* on barrier removal.[68] We now turn to an analysis of one key litigation battle concerning access to ICT, *Jodhan v. Canada*.

Jodhan v. Canada

Donna Jodhan is an accessibility advocate for people with visual impairments. She is a systems engineer with a degree in business administration and a diploma in management from McGill University.[69] She resides in Ontario and owns her own consulting business, which provides recommendations to clients about their products' accessibility to users with special needs, specifically persons with visual impairments.[70] Jodhan is also legally blind.

In 2004, Jodhan attempted to access a government website to fill out a job application. However, she was unable to do so on her own and ultimately required sighted assistance to complete the application.[71] She was also unable to create an online profile for her job application because pop-up windows emerged when she used the website, which prevented her screen reader from being able to navigate the page.[72] More broadly, she found that in her various attempts to navigate other government websites, the online material was not accessible to screen-reader technology, nor was it compliant with W3C standards for accessibility.[73]

Eventually, she retained David Baker of Bakerlaw to initiate a charter challenge against the federal government, alleging that it systematically failed to "implement the accessibility standards for the visually impaired" for its online services in contravention of her equality rights under Section 15 of the charter.[74] Throughout his career as a disability rights advocate, David Baker has worked to advance litigation that exposes the barriers to social inclusion that persons with disabilities face and has remained a critical ally of the disability rights movement by engaging with a myriad of topics within the field.[75] Bakerlaw took on Jodhan's case pro bono and relied on the now-defunct Court Challenges Program to secure funding for Jodhan's case.[76]

Before the start of litigation, the government was working to comply with international standards on web accessibility, including WCAG 2.0.[77] Starting in 1999, the government introduced a project to allow all Canadians "to acquire information and services, on their terms, and according to their needs" online and developed a communication policy to ensure that these communications were accessible.[78] It implemented this policy through what was called the Common Look and Feel (CLF) Standard, monitored by the Treasury Board. These standards continue to ensure accessibility for persons with visual impairments and are built on international guidelines, including the Web Content Accessibility Guidelines. Jodhan argued that the government also failed to comply with its own standards in violation of her Section 15 rights.

The case went before the Federal Court and was later appealed to the Federal Court of Appeal. The Federal Court found that the government did not properly maintain accessible websites, was not meeting its own accessibility standards, and should update the CLF Standard to refer to WCAG guidelines.[79] The court held that the government failed to safeguard Jodhan's Section 15 rights when it argued that Jodhan could fill out her job application over the phone with the help of sighted assistance and when it failed to monitor its websites.[80] When the government provided services through various channels, all of these channels had to be accessible.[81] The court noted that Section 15 of the charter protects equal access to and the benefit of the law, and, in this case, "the benefit of the law is access to government information services," which includes "the benefit of online access."[82] Indeed, the court found that equal access required access to the Internet, and that persons with visual impairments were not reasonably accommodated when they were informed that they could use other channels than the Internet, such as mail or the telephone, to complete their job applications.[83] The court awarded Jodhan damages, issued a declaration requiring all 106 government institutions to render their websites accessible within fifteen months, and retained jurisdiction over the case to ensure government compliance.

On appeal, the Federal Court of Appeal upheld the Federal Court's decision, found that Jodhan's equality rights were violated when she encountered these inaccessible government websites, and required the government to render its websites accessible within fifteen months. The court reiterated Justice Kelen's words that "a person is not handicapped if she does not need help. Making the government online information services accessible provided the visually impaired with 'substantive equality'. This is like the ramp to permit wheelchair access to a building. It is a ramp for the blind to access online services."[84] Jodhan was denied equal access to and equal benefit from government information and services provided online in contravention of Section 15 of the charter.[85]

However, the Federal Court of Appeal did limit the Federal Court's decision in some respects. It found that the declaration could cover only the Treasury Board and not the 106 departments mentioned by the Federal Court.[86] It also found that the government's failure to monitor and prevent deviation from its standards was not a violation of Jodhan's Section 15 rights.[87] The failure to monitor was the cause of the rights violation, not the violation itself.[88] Finally, the Federal Court of Appeal found that the Federal Court did not have jurisdiction to issue a supervisory order.[89] Nevertheless, despite these limitations, the Federal Court of Appeal decision was a victory for advocates because it held the federal government to account for its failure to render websites accessible to people with visual impairments in violation of Section 15 of the charter.

The Legal Context

The *Jodhan* case illuminates that the common law and the charter both proffer tools that can advance the rights of people with disabilities, even where disability rights legislation does not exist. The case is situated within a history of jurisprudence that has to some extent embraced the social model of disability. Section 15 of the charter distinctly seeks to promote substantive equality, not merely formal equality, and thereby it ensures equal access to and benefit of the law. Within the Canadian context, Section 15 has been used to reinforce the understanding that unconstitutional rights violations arise when barriers and stereotypes about people with disabilities impede their lives and prevent their social inclusion. Consider the *Eldridge* case, wherein claimants with hearing impairments argued that the absence of sign language interpreters in hospitals led to the claimants not being able to communicate with their physicians, which contravened their Section 15 equality rights.[90] Recognizing the historical disadvantage persons with disabilities have faced and the barriers that society constructs to perpetuate their exclusion, the Supreme Court held that if the government was going to confer a benefit (health care), it had a positive obligation to do so in a non-discriminatory manner.[91] Section 15 here was employed to protect the substantive equality of people with disabilities.

In *Via Rail*, although it was not a Section 15 case, the Supreme Court recognized again the barriers to inclusion that people with disabilities face and highlighted a need to safeguard their dignity.[92] Here, certain railway cars did not accommodate wheelchairs. Via Rail argued that modification would be too expensive and that its staff could assist people in wheelchairs with access to particular services, such as using the bathroom.⁹³ The court held that this contravened the Canada Transportation Act and noted, "It is the rail service itself that is to be accessible, not alternative transportation services such as taxis. Persons with disabilities are entitled to ride with other passengers, not consigned to separate facilities."⁹⁴ Thus both the *Eldridge* and *Via Rail* cases found that when the government or a public entity created barriers to accessibility that prevented the meaningful social inclusion of persons with disabilities, these barriers ran afoul of visions of the full embodiment of substantive equality.

Application to *Jodhan*

Applied to the *Jodhan* case, this existing case law was used to bolster the courts' findings that Jodhan faced unconstitutional discrimination. Both courts underscored the vision of substantive equality embodied in Section 15 and envisioned in *Via Rail* when they noted that mere access to the resource of the Internet was not sufficient—all channels the government provided needed to be accessible. Akin to *Eldridge*, wherein the court held that when the government conferred a benefit, it had a positive obligation to do so without discrimination, in *Jodhan*, when the government conferred access online to its resources for citizens as a benefit, it had an obligation to do so in a nondiscriminatory fashion. Failing to provide Internet access to people with visual impairments constituted discrimination. These principles were reiterated in *Via Rail*, wherein the court found that even where modifications were expensive, where a service was provided, a public entity needed to provide the tools to enable persons with disabilities to access this same service. Here, the existing jurisprudence created traction for advocates to push for more progressive reform of government websites.

Implications of *Jodhan*

The effects of the *Jodhan* decision illuminate how a progressive judicial decision can advance and protect the rights of people with visual impairments. Because the *Jodhan* decision implicated the federal government, it had an impact across Canada, even in provinces wherein disability rights legislation did not exist. The decision highlights how advocates can bring forth claims safeguarding the rights of people with visual impairments before legislation comes into existence. Even in a province such as Ontario, where legislation such as the AODA exists but where certain provisions will not come into force for a decade, the *Jodhan* case reveals how judicial decisions can ensure equality rights immediately. Here, progressive judicial decisions, such as *Jodhan*, can prove to be invaluable tools to advance the rights of people with disabilities.

Moreover, decisions such as the *Jodhan* decision can reinforce advocates' calls for stronger legislative protections. The AODA Alliance in Ontario used the *Jodhan* decision to support its call for the government "to strengthen its weak proposals for its forthcoming integrated accessibility standard, to be enacted under the AODA."[95] In essence, the decision gave citizens and advocates the traction and foundation they needed to advance a more progressive agenda that would be taken seriously by the government. However, one cautionary note should be sounded. Advocates from the blind community have recently complained that, notwithstanding the holding in *Jodhan*, internal government websites continue to be inaccessible to them. These websites are used by public servants to perform their jobs. Indeed, a government policy document drafted after *Jodhan* does not include internal government websites. This omission has the potential to seriously undermine the potential for people with print disabilities to work for the federal public service.[96] Vigilance and perhaps more litigation will be required to ensure that true accessibility is achieved.

Overall, the *Jodhan* decision reveals how courts can call the government to account for a failure to comply with human rights norms and laws. Certainly, Jodhan's case was not without its challenges, but its crucial findings and effects proffer useful tools and strategies for advocates moving forward.

Conclusion

In this chapter, we have outlined two very different approaches to addressing accessibility of ICT. The regulatory approach, embodied in the regulations promulgated under the AODA, seeks to gradually phase in increasingly stringent requirements until 2025 to ensure that people with disabilities achieve accessibility, including accessibility in the ICT sector. The commitment to training of workers and volunteers is promising and may enable a real change in attitudes toward the importance of accessibility and inclusion.

The regulatory approach, however, is vulnerable to capture by corporate interests, as indicated by the lengthy timelines. *Jodhan* provides a model for achieving access in the ICT context through litigation. However, it is unlikely that costly charter litigation, even if it is grounded in strong facts, as was the case here, is a feasible option for many. What is perhaps most needed is to combine lobbying with strategic litigation. Lobbying has the advantage of using the expert knowledge of those people with disabilities most affected by barriers. This can be transformed, on a selective basis, into test-case litigation where advocacy proves ineffective. This approach will maximize scarce resources and may often lead to informal solutions where they can be readily achieved to ensure accessibility more rapidly. Disability rights advocates would be wise to continue the long battle for accessibility on all fronts.

CHAPTER 7

Access to Justice

Fredric I. Lederer

Introduction

Access to justice is a fundamental right.[1] As the Australian Attorney General's Access to Justice Task Force declared:

> Access to justice is an essential element of the rule of law and therefore of democracy. Justice institutions enable people to protect their rights against infringement by other people or bodies in society, and allow parties to bring actions against government to limit executive power and ensure government is accountable. If people are unable to access these institutions to protect their rights, respect for the rule of law is diminished.
>
> Barriers to justice also reinforce poverty and exclusion. Maintaining a strong rule of law is a precondition to protecting disadvantaged communities and helping people leave poverty behind.
>
> Improving access to justice is therefore a key means of promoting social inclusion. Many of the issues commonly faced by people, such as family breakdown, credit and housing issues, discrimination, and exclusion from services, have a legal dimension that if not resolved can contribute to social exclusion.[2]

In his foreword to the Access to Justice Task Force report, Attorney General McClellan wisely opined that "an effective justice system must be accessible in all its parts. Without this, the system risks losing its relevance to, and the respect of, the community it serves. Accessibility is about more than ease of access to sandstone buildings or getting legal advice. It involves an appreciation and understanding of the needs of those who require the assistance of the legal system."[3] The world's legal systems differ substantially from each other, but they all embody one fundamental concept: courts exist to resolve disputes. One would also hope that in doing so, they seek to achieve just results. There are commonalities that arguably apply both to efficient dispute resolution per se and to just resolution.

For courts to be useful, members of the public must be aware of the availability of courts to resolve disputes and their basic mechanisms for dispute resolution and must also have meaningful access to court activities. Courts are complicated social mechanisms. As much as we might wish otherwise, those seeking to use the courts ordinarily should have the assistance of persons with legal expertise. The right to engage in dispute resolution is of no value unless interested persons and their representatives can participate in a meaningful fashion. Finally, those professionally engaged in dispute resolution, including decision makers, mediators, and counsel, should be highly qualified to do so, and those interested in doing so should not be constrained by unnecessary barriers to participation, such as restrictions based on perceived disabilities.

These commonalities define one aspect of "access to justice."[4] In its broadest sense, access to justice must mean not only that those aggrieved have meaningful access to dispute resolution, but also that those competent persons interested in being part of the administration of justice have a meaningful opportunity to do so.

This functional definition can be said to be broader than the United Nations Convention on the Rights of Persons with Disabilities, which provides in Article 13, "Access to Justice," that "States Parties shall ensure effective access to justice for persons with disabilities on an equal basis with others, including through the provision of procedural and age-appropriate accommodations, in order to facilitate their effective role as direct and indirect participants, including as witnesses, in all legal proceedings, including at investigative and other preliminary stages." However, Article 3 of the convention, "General Principles," declares in relevant part:

The principles of the present Convention shall be:
(a) Respect for inherent dignity, individual autonomy including the freedom to make one's own choices, and independence of persons;

(b) Non-discrimination;
(c) Full and effective participation and inclusion in society;
(d) Respect for difference and acceptance of persons with disabilities as part of human diversity and humanity;
(e) Equality of opportunity;
(f) Accessibility.

Accordingly, this chapter uses "access to justice" as pertaining not only to those who need justice but also to those who administer it.

At the same time, as noted earlier, meaningful access to justice often requires a meaningful opportunity to obtain professional legal assistance generally. That critical issue is outside the scope of this book. Instead, this chapter addresses "access to justice" as meaningful access to the courts for dispute resolution.[5] "Dispute resolution" ordinarily is the appropriate term because we now can resolve disputes via alternative dispute resolution (ADR)—mediation and arbitration—as well as by a classic trial, and although traditionally ADR was conducted outside the court structure, courts now sometimes provide ADR as well as trials.

Any discussion of access to justice from a planetary perspective is doomed to frustration because of the manifold differences among the world's legal systems, to say nothing of individual national systems. Nations using the English common-law system, for example, place great emphasis on the perceived ability of the adversarial system, in which all parties strive to present favorable evidence and discredit unfavorable evidence. Those descended from the French civil-law system likely will place greater emphasis on pretrial information gathering and less on the trial itself. It is possible, however, to evaluate any legal system from an information perspective. All legal systems consist of information gathering, information evaluation by judges, and information dissemination, if only in the form of verdicts. Accordingly, it is possible to examine how a legal system affords access to justice, but as the saying declares, "The devil is in the details." Any given court may act differently from others. Accordingly, the discussion that follows is necessarily rather general.

Modern technology has brought with it exciting opportunities to provide enhanced access to justice for all persons, but especially for those with perceived disabilities. At the same time, courts are adopting technological improvements that sometimes create new barriers to access to justice. This chapter will review briefly access to court information, to case-specific information, and to hearings, trials, and courtrooms from the perspective of those with constraints in the areas of mobility, vision, hearing, speech, and, briefly, intellectual functionality. The reader should consider that the law and culture that govern courts are jurisdiction specific, meaning that the law and culture governing a given court may be primarily local, provincial, or national or, as is more likely, a complex composite of all three. In the United States, for example, the sweeping federal Americans with Disabilities Act (ADA)[6] applies to state courts but not federal courts. States are free to supplement, although not to contradict, the statute. The federal Rehabilitation Act[7] applies to the federal courts but not the state courts unless they receive federal financial assistance. There are few, if any, binding technology standards insofar as courts specifically are concerned, although Section 508 of the Rehabilitation Act, as amended, mandates accessible information technology.[8]

Access to Court Information

Courts are repositories of large amounts of information. This includes information about the internal administrative operation of the court, including personnel, pay, and other data, as well as data related to specific cases. Traditionally, courts largely have been closed institutions understood only by lawyers and others engaged in the legal professions. Persons involved in disputes would seek legal help with little or no understanding of how dispute resolution and the courts operated. This remains true in many courts in many countries. However, courts increasingly are posting at least basic information about court functions, operations, and procedures on websites available via the Internet.[9] In the United States, one such example is the consolidated website for the three Fairfax County, Virginia, courts.[10] The circuit court's information options include jury duty, the court's dockets, marriage and divorce matters, land records, online information and services, and news, as well as links to other court and government information and activities. Some websites may include highly specific directions on how to file a civil suit without the assistance of a lawyer. In addition, many courts make available online most of their court records, including the details pertaining to individual cases. These details sometimes include not only relevant court orders and documents but even an audio recording[11] or text transcript of the proceedings. Although the move to online publication of court information should be applauded as providing increased court transparency that affords the general public the possibility of a much-enhanced understanding of the courts, online publication can be problematic for those unable to read online data.[12]

Online publication ought to be accomplished so that persons with disabilities can access the information fully. As noted earlier, Section 508 of the Rehabilitation Act and the Americans with Disabilities Act deal with this in the United States, however inadequately. This is, of course, the problem common to all electronic publication, which is addressed extensively elsewhere in this book. It may suffice to note that online text should be readable by screen readers; that online photos need adequate text captions; and that audio court records need transcripts and perhaps video recordings of sign-language interpretations for those who cannot hear them. With respect to this last point, the irony is that most digital audio court records have been made with the specific intent of avoiding costly text transcription. Whether such text transcripts (or sign language interpretations) ought to be prepared in all cases, when requested by those who are deaf or hard of hearing, or only when necessary for specific needs of those who are deaf or hard of hearing is a matter for jurisdiction-specific law.

Access to Case-Specific Information

Parties to a dispute and their legal representatives, their counsel, need to be able to review case information. In the past, that would include paper pleadings, court orders and opinions, and potentially numerous paper documents produced pretrial and at trial. Today, most case information originates in electronic form and may be shared among parties and counsel electronically. It is imperative that this information be accessible, especially to those involved in a court case. In 2014, the Ninth Judicial Circuit of Florida's Orange County Clerk of Courts entered into a settlement with the U.S. Department of Justice in just such a matter.[13] Counsel for a party in litigation was blind. The court used electronic filing that required electronic documents. A number of case documents, including a substantial number of case exhibits—pieces of evidence—were in a nonaccessible PDF format that could not be electronically read via screen readers. Despite repeated requests over a period of months to the clerk of courts, counsel did not receive accessible versions and finally had to rely on opposing counsel. Counsel filed a complaint with the Department of Justice that was resolved by the settlement, under which the clerk of courts must in the future ensure that accessible documents are provided when required. Notably, the settlement rejects the argument that having someone read the inaccessible documents to counsel would have been sufficient.

Especially in civil litigation, "electronic discovery" or "e-discovery" can involve an enormous quantity of documents and other information that is sought and disclosed. This presents two closely related problems. One is the simple number of documents. In part because of the nature of modern communications, in many cases the number of electronic documents can be vastly larger than it was when lawyers were limited to looking for paper files in file cabinets. The other, as noted earlier, is the need to be able to read the electronic documents. It is imperative that those unable to fully view images have alternative means to review them. If the material is compatible, this means screen readers or alternative technological solutions. If the material is not compatible with screen readers, scanning with text-to-voice technology might suffice for specific documents but could be vastly less efficient. In the United States, Federal Rule of Civil Procedure 34(b)(2)(E) provides that in federal cases,

> Unless otherwise stipulated or ordered by the court, these procedures apply to producing documents or electronically stored information:
> (i) A party must produce documents as they are kept in the usual course of business or must organize and label them to correspond to the categories in the request;
> (ii) If a request does not specify a form for producing electronically stored information, a party must produce it in a form or forms in which it is ordinarily maintained or in a reasonably usable form or forms; and
> (iii) A party need not produce the same electronically stored information in more than one form.

On the positive side, Rule 34 should foreclose the possibility of supplying discovery material in a form that has been intentionally chosen to be difficult to access. At the same time, it is unclear that a producing party can be required to produce material in a form necessary to accommodate the specific needs of an opposing counsel.[14]

Hearings, Trials, and Courtrooms

If a dispute is not resolved by negotiation, mediation, or arbitration, it likely will go to trial for formal adjudication. Trial procedure and evidentiary rules vary throughout the world. Nations with adjudicative systems based on the English adversarial system emphasize witness testimony with evidence presented by lawyers. The adversary system assumes that with each party trying to win, all information relevant to the case will be produced in court.[15] In contrast, nations using variations on the French civil-law system likely will emphasize an "inquisitorial" procedure that emphasizes pretrial collection of documentary information, including witness statements, with the trial judges primarily resolving the case on the basis of that information.[16] Some legal systems require or permit juries for various types of trials; others do not. However, although procedure varies greatly, the fundamental nature of trials does not. Decision makers, usually judges, decide the case on the basis of information made available to the decision maker. At present, adversarial system courts are tending to adopt courtroom technology that better enables counsel to present information and persuade the fact finder of the merits of counsels' case. European civil-law courts are more likely to emphasize courthouse data systems with data retrieval by the judges. Other forms of technology may be used regardless of the legal system. Both Australia and China, for example, use remote testimony via video conferencing.

Those present at a trial ordinarily will be the parties, the judge (or judges), counsel, witnesses, jurors, court staff, and members of the public. Let us consider how technology might assist or complicate a trial from the perspective of each of these groups. For convenience, I will use an American jury trial as the vehicle, largely because most other models likely would be less complicated, making the American jury model the best for analysis. In the model of U.S. federal court procedure, such a trial will consist of the following major components.

After a jury has been selected and the judge has given the jurors appropriate introductory information and instructions, the lawyers will make "opening statements." The opening statement is counsel's prediction of the information that counsel (and sometimes opposing counsel) will make available ("introduce") at the trial. The party with the burden of proof, plaintiff's counsel (the lawyer for the party suing) in a civil case or the prosecutor in a criminal case, presents the first opening statement.

After the opening statements, the parties through their counsel try to prove their case and disprove the other side's case. They do this by presentation of evidence, formal submission of information, the use of which ("admissibility") is subject to complex evidentiary rules.

The party with the burden of proof, the plaintiff in a civil case or the prosecution in a criminal case, presents his or her case first. Then the defense presents its case should it choose to present one. The plaintiff or prosecution may then present rebuttal evidence. In most countries using the adversarial system, counsel bring the evidence to court and present it. Only after formal receipt of evidence is the court responsible for preserving that information for verdict and possible appeal. In Australia, however, in major cases the court may require counsel to submit possible evidence to the court in advance of trial. Upon receipt, the court is then responsible for the evidence, and court personnel, or contractors, electronically will display the evidence at trial at the request of counsel.

After all the evidence has been presented, counsel will make closing arguments, or summations, trying to persuade the judge or jury to adopt their versions of the case. After that, in a jury trial, the judge will explain the law to the jury and give instructions to the jury about how to deliberate and evaluate the case. After the instructions, the jury will leave the courtroom to deliberate, to determine the verdict. After deciding a verdict, they will return to the courtroom and formally announce the verdict. Technology may play a role in all these phases.

In conducting my analysis, I will assume that the people involved may have mobility, vision, hearing, or speech issues. I will also address intellectual disabilities, primarily in dealing with witnesses or jurors.

Mobility

Ordinarily, mobility issues are or can be easily addressed in the courtroom. There usually is sufficient room at the counsel tables for parties, plaintiffs, or defendants who use mobility technology, although access to those tables can be problematic. Ramps or wheelchair lifts usually suffice to ensure that witnesses or judges who must ascend to limited spaces are able to use wheelchairs, scooters, or other devices. Depending on the courtroom configuration, access to the interior central part of the courtroom for counsel, the "well," may be problematic because the space between furniture, the "courtroom millwork," may not be wide enough. Space for jurors or members of the public with wheelchairs or scooters attending the trial may be inadequate, whether in terms of access, location, or size. People with mobility issues ought not to be treated as special and have unique locations allotted to them. Rather, they should be able to participate in the case in the same locations used by those without mobility issues. At the same time, it is critical to keep in mind individual human preferences. With Professor Michael Stein's help, many years ago, the Center for Legal and Court Technology at William and Mary Law School produced a "litigator's podium" to be used by a lawyer in a wheelchair. Counsel would roll into the podium, which consisted of a wraparound desk surface with necessary technology on the desk. The whole system rotated mechanically so counsel could question a witness or argue to judge or jury. Although the podium was quite functional, Professor Stein declined its use because he was more comfortable "pacing," rolling forward and back while speaking. Accordingly, while any specific technological effort to improve access to justice may be useful for some or even many people, it may be undesirable or unacceptable to others. Assume that a potential juror has mobility issues. There are many ways in which that juror can be accommodated in the courtroom, but it is imperative to determine the juror's personal needs and preferences.

An individual's mobility difficulty, however, might foreclose travel to the courtroom entirely. An individual might well have a condition that requires that person to remain at home or in a special medical facility. Today, such a person may appear via two-way video conferencing. Remote witness testimony is fairly common in civil cases. In the United States, because of the Sixth Amendment right to confrontation, remote prosecution testimony by other than a child-abuse victim may be unconstitutional.[17] There has been at least one case in the United Kingdom in which a remote judge presided over a trial from her hospital room.[18] In its April 2015 experimental laboratory trial, the Center for Legal and Court Technology successfully used what is believed to have been the first remote juror, an older woman who appeared in the jury box remotely from her home while using a remote-controlled camera in the jury box to be able to see the courtroom as if she were physically present. This is similar to, but not as flexible as, developing mobile "robots" who can act as a remote extension of a person.[19]

Vision

Depending on the legal system, traditional court practice is centered on witness testimony and review of evidence, customarily physical documents and physical objects such as drugs and weapons. At least in Anglo-American legal-system nations, the fact finder, judge or jury, is expected to take into consideration "demeanor evidence," the appearance and voice of a witness, in determining how much credit to give to the witness. Although I do not know of legal authority that separates hearing from vision, I suspect that the emphasis in demeanor evidence has been on the fact finder's visual observations of the witness. When a fact finder cannot fully observe the demeanor of a witness, the quality of the verdict arguably is called into question, although at least one U.S. federal court has rejected that conclusion, opining that a blind juror could rely on voice cues.[20] Fact finders with some visual ability may use technological enlargements to see the witness. Those who cannot (and there certainly have been blind judges)[21] have relied on hearing. In its 2006 experimental laboratory trial, the Center for Legal and Court Technology used a "court explicator." The explicator, a court official, described by radio-frequency headsets what the nearly blind judge (and members of the public) could not personally observe. Counsel were able to monitor the explanation and object should it have been incorrect or biased, and the description was recorded (along with the video content of courtroom proceedings) for possible appeal. This was highly effective, but it does not appear to have been replicated as of yet in a real case.

In the past, documentary or other physical evidence has been read by those concerned using either the original evidence or physical copies. Meaningful use of such documents is clearly difficult for those with limited or no vision. Those with some vision may be able to use technology that enlarges the image—customarily equipment that electronically captures the paper or object image and then makes it visible on a screen that permits significant enlargement of some or all of the image. Specialized equipment is available to assist with limited vision, permitting not just enlargement but also changing colors for ease of vision. Blind persons can use braille copies,[22] scanners with audio output, screen readers if a digital version is available for electronic devices, or an assigned reader.[23]

The defining aspect of a technology-augmented courtroom is the electronic visual display of material, primarily images of evidence, to the judge, counsel, the jury (when present), and, frequently, members of the public attending the trial. The images are displayed on large projection screens, large flat panels, or, more likely, computer monitors,[24] and sometimes, tablets. Such display is often complemented by the use of visual images during opening statements and closing arguments in adversary-system courtrooms. Visual display saves a good deal of trial time and is believed to enhance understanding of the case and fact-finder memory of details. But this shift to visual display is highly problematic for those with limited or no vision.

Because of concerns about the security of courthouse networks, displayed material ordinarily is shown by connecting notebook computers or tablets to a courtroom visual display system.[25] This means that the person viewing the information cannot enlarge it electronically, as is usually possible. Instead, the display device shows exactly what is being sent by the counsel's computer, for example, with no personal ability to focus on part of the image or to change its size. This also defeats screen readers. Accordingly, this otherwise commendable improvement in trial practice creates significant difficulties for those with limited or no sight. At present, the most obvious solution is to supply to such a person individual copies of the material in physical, braille, or electronic form as appropriate. This may not be possible in the future. Current virtual-reality developments[26] suggest that we are not far from the probable use of immersive reality in courtrooms. Indeed, in 2002, the Center for Legal and Court Technology demonstrated how witnesses could use immersive virtual reality in the context of a virtual reconstructed operating room in order to show jurors what the witnesses could have observed during a surgical procedure. In 2014, the center used 3-D technology for fact finders who donned 3-D glasses to view a brick and a baseball bat in three dimensions in a criminal case. The next step would be for jurors to be able to wear virtual-reality headsets to experience a crime scene or other location as if they were actually there. A judge or juror with limited or no vision presumably would be restricted to a verbal description of the scene.

Hearing

Witness testimony and audio evidence present obvious concerns for those who are deaf or hard of hearing. The use of real-time transcription—nearly immediate text transcription of the spoken word that can be produced by a properly trained court reporter—allows a deaf or hard-of-hearing person to read the text of testimony or audio content. However, such transcription may not be fast enough—especially for a deaf or hard-of-hearing counsel—and may also be difficult to comprehend for someone raised with sign language as the primary means of communication. As a result, the preferred solution for many deaf or hard-of-hearing persons at trial is the use of either a physically present or remote sign language interpreter. Remote sign language interpretation allows access to centralized interpreters. However, as in the case of real-time transcription, the person using a remote interpreter will be forced to look at the screen where that person appears. That might work well for a witness or juror but could interfere with a deaf counsel's witness examination.

Speech

Trial participants may be unable to speak and require resort to alternative means of communication. Witnesses, for example, might sign, provide text, or use speech-generation devices. Witnesses who are not capable of using these techniques may be able to use pictograms, potentially augmented by technological means of selecting the pictograms.[27]

Intellectual Difficulties

There are a wide variety of intellectual difficulties that can affect trial participants. Many are of no significant consequence, but some may be sufficiently severe to disqualify a person from service as a judge, counsel, or juror. Given the range of possibilities involved, the only thing that can be said is that categorical disqualifications are unacceptable, and whether technological assistance will be available or helpful may well require a case-by-case analysis. This issue is especially important for witnesses, especially testifying victims. Their evidence can be critical, and it is imperative that counsel research how best to communicate with witnesses with intellectual disabilities and solicit their testimony in a clear and useful form.

Some Research Thoughts

Access to justice could be greatly improved if more basic research were conducted. As discussed earlier, Anglo-American legal systems are highly dependent on witness testimony and, accordingly, the "demeanor evidence" presented by those witnesses. It would be very useful to determine whether judges and jurors actually can determine whether witnesses are telling the truth via how those witnesses look and sound. If we can determine truth telling via courtroom processes, are those with limited or no hearing or sight equally able—or perhaps better able—to determine who is telling the truth?

Additionally, although our societies often celebrate the opportunities brought by new technologies, their implications for access to justice tend not to be a priority. In the future, we would do well to immediately consider access to justice concerns generally and to conduct empirical research to determine effects before a technology spreads and potentially creates unforeseen problems. This could be especially important for those with disabilities. When problems are clear, we must consider solutions. If visually displayed evidence presents difficulties for those with constrained vision, we should experiment with alternative technological solutions, such as text documents displayed by networks with screen-reader enablement.

But there is a great deal we do not know today even about basic court procedures. How can we best support those who cannot hear? When is sign language imperative, and when is transcription effective? Are verdicts given by judges with perceived disabilities open to challenge, and if so, why? To what extent, if any, should persons with perceived intellectual disabilities be foreclosed from participation in the hearing or trial process? Are there situations in which jurors with some forms of intellectual disabilities would be preferred participants? More basic research might finally answer these and other important questions, and one can only hope that foundations and other funders will choose to emphasize these questions.

Conclusion

Access to justice is and should be a human right. As a matter of simple public policy, persons seeking resolution of a dispute should not be excluded because of a perceived disability. Exclusion not only is a breach of an individual's rights under a legal system but also effectively permits society to maltreat and abuse a person who cannot obtain meaningful relief in court. Legally or pragmatically barring a person from serving as a judge, counsel, juror, witness, or member of a court's staff or in some other capacity both deprives the legal system of the talent, insight, world experience, and wisdom of that person and effectively brands the excluded person as somehow less equal than others.

It is unavoidably true that when technology is useful or critical to making the legal system accessible for a person with a perceived disability, money likely will be a factor. Equipping a courthouse or courtroom with the technology necessary to assist a range of disabilities may be expensive insofar as the local budget is concerned. If the equipment goes unused because of lack of need, the expense will be painful indeed. Yet the issue is rather circular. If the technology necessary for full access is not readily and easily available, people with perceived disabilities likely will be dissuaded from participation in the search for justice.

The Old Testament book of Deuteronomy commands, "Justice, justice shall you pursue" (16:20). That is an unqualified goal, and justice should and must be available to all.

CHAPTER 8

Open Government and Digital Accessibility

Timothy Elder

Introduction

This chapter focuses on the intersection of the open-government and digital-accessibility movements. Digital accessibility concerns the ability of people with disabilities to access electronic information sources such as websites, software, mobile devices, and e-readers. The term "open government" is used interchangeably here to refer to either of two concepts. First, the traditional concept of open government reflects the principle of transparency of government information regardless of the medium of the information. Second, the modern concept of open government connotes the technology-based use of government as a platform for participation, collaboration, and innovation by crowds of citizens without limitations of geography. Under either interpretation of open government, traditional or modern, people with disabilities are greatly affected by government transparency and digital access to its information.

Plenty of writings expound on the broad implications of open government, crowd sourcing, and open data.[1] Unlike much of the existing literature, however, this chapter focuses on an often overlooked implication of the trends in the open-government movement. People with disabilities are one of the most illustrative examples of how open government might change society for better or worse.

People with Disabilities

People with disabilities have always struggled to find their place in society in the face of persecution, paternalism, segregation, discrimination, lowered expectations, and indifference. To address this problem, many societies are advancing new models of the concept of disability grounded in human rights, civil rights, rehabilitation, and social inclusion.[2] This social perspective suggests that limits are unnecessarily placed on people with disabilities because of social attitudes, conceptions, and prejudices that artificially discount their actual abilities. However, it may be premature to tout our wonderful modern progress in regard to people with disabilities because, first, the experiences of people with disabilities over the course of history in various cultures from around the world may be better than one might assume,[3] and second, it may be too early to celebrate the progress of the modern disability rights movement, given the myriad challenges ahead to full economic, political, and social inclusion.[4]

To illustrate, even if a participating seat is set at the government table for people with disabilities under modern progressive politics and concepts of disability, that participation has no guarantee of meaning or effectiveness. People with disabilities will be unable to judge and administer government programs created for their benefit if the information about the workings of those government programs is concealed from meaningful public scrutiny and accountability. Thus, however the social struggle of people with disabilities is characterized, one fundamental element of that struggle is how to access information required for meaningful participation. People with disabilities are not alone in their need for access to transparent government information. All governed peoples, including those with disabilities, struggle to increase government transparency, often referred to as the freedom of information. This universal struggle for transparency underpins almost every form of government. As transparency and access to information expand for all people as a result of the universal struggle for freedom of information, those with disabilities have an increasing opportunity to take advantage of that access to information and pull their population up through the social power strata.

Traditional Open Government

Since at least as early as the Enlightenment, writers such as John Milton expressed a value in the right to know about the laws and proceedings of government: "Give me the liberty to know, to utter, and to argue freely according to conscience, above all liberties."[5] Early open-records laws, such as the Freedom of the Press Act of 1766 in Sweden, further reflect the sentiment of the era.

Even in a democracy such as the United States, where citizens are perceived to have major power over their government, the universal civil struggle for transparency persists. The founders of the American colonies carried the values of the Enlightenment as they formed the U.S. government. James Madison described information access as an essential cornerstone of democratic governance: "A popular Government without popular information, or the means of acquiring it, is but a Prologue to a Farce or a Tragedy; or perhaps both. Knowledge will forever govern ignorance: And a people who mean to be their own Governors, must arm themselves with the power which knowledge gives."[6] Over time, the United States has gradually implemented Milton's and Madison's ideals. The U.S. Government Printing Office was established in 1861 to reliably produce and distribute official government documents for the public.[7] In 1935, the U.S. Congress created the Federal Register and legislated that presidential proclamations, executive orders, documents the president determined to have general applicability and legal effect, documents required to be published by act of Congress, and documents authorized to be published by agency regulations could not be valid against any person until they were filed at the Federal Register for public inspection.

In 1946, the Administrative Procedure Act[8] established procedures of notice and comment to ensure that the public had an opportunity to engage with federal agencies before those agencies promulgated regulations in the quasi-legislative process of executive-branch rule making. Agencies were required to publish notices of proposed rule making in the Federal Register and provide opportunity for public participation before final rules could be put into effect.

In 1966, the U.S. Congress reached an open-government milestone when it enacted the Freedom of Information Act (FOIA).[9] The FOIA establishes the right of the public to obtain records from all departments and agencies of the executive branch of the federal government, but not the Congress, the federal courts, or certain offices of the president.

Functionally, the FOIA empowers an interested person or organization to compel a specific part of the government, such as a department or commissioned agency, to search for and produce any records related to a given query. The mechanics of the FOIA include requirements and exceptions that help balance the government's interest in efficient administration and the public's interest in access to information. For example, the FOIA permits the government to charge nontrivial fees for search time and printing costs, which ensures that requesters will narrowly define their search query to the most specific records sought. Furthermore, fees for records may be waived when the requester is a nonprofit organization working toward the benefit of the public good rather than individual or commercial interests. There are also exceptions for "urgent" matters of public concern that ensure that the agency cannot deny an important request simply by delaying the request and placing it in a long waiting line. The process for requesting records can be as informal as a letter sent to the designated FOIA contact of the agency.

In practice, however, the FOIA is weakened by bureaucratic inefficiencies. Government agencies are able to skirt judicial review by refusing to allocate sufficient resources, which creates long waits and an inability to exhaust the administrative process before advancing to a court for enforcement of noncompliance. FOIA requests enter a period of indefinite suspension as they linger within a black hole of the administrative machinery.

Fortunately, some well-meaning agencies are starting to consolidate the FOIA process through a common FOIA-request website portal.[10] From the perspective of the public, the portal offers the public a single place to submit FOIA requests, track progress, communicate with the processing agency, review other similar requests, access previously released responsive documents, and file appeals. From the agency perspective, the FOIA online portal provides a secure website interface to receive, assign, and process requests, post responses, generate metrics, manage records electronically, create management reports, and electronically generate mandatory annual reporting. Unfortunately, at the time of this publication, only a minority fraction of federal agencies were participating in the common portal.

The preceding describes the FOIA process, not the substantive provisions. However, the fringes of the process can be abused to create substance: a request that is delayed does not differ from a request that is timely denied on substantive grounds. In fact, procedural abuse is worse than substantive abuse because there is no remedy for the delay within the bounds of inefficient government process.

In terms of substantive rights to information, the FOIA has expanded and contracted over its history. Members of the public and the government are engaged in a tug-of-war over the right to access information versus the need for government secrecy. Successive administrations of the executive branch have interpreted the FOIA differently, with broad implications for the information available to the public at various times.

Further, several notable amendments to the FOIA have generally pushed U.S. federal law forward to promote a more open government over time. In 1976, the U.S. Congress passed the Government in the Sunshine Act,[11] which requires certain meetings of an agency to be open to public observation with advance notice. Likewise, in 1996, the FOIA was applied to all government records regardless of format, including the large volumes of electronic records the government was generating at the time. The FOIA was amended again in 2007 to establish a central Office of Government Information Services (OGIS) to review and mediate agency compliance with the FOIA and to improve processing of FOIA requests through electronic tracking and annual reporting.

Many other governments have used the U.S. FOIA as a model. Most state and local governments in the United States have passed analogous statutes.[12] Australia's 1982 Freedom of Information Act and Canada's 1985 Access to Information Act further illustrate the trend.

Disability Advocates' Use of Open-Government Laws

Disability advocates from around the world are using traditional open-government laws to promote transparency for their civil rights. For example, in 2013, the Accessibility for Ontarians with Disabilities Act Alliance (AODA Alliance), a disability consumer advocacy group that works to support the implementation of accessibility standards, used freedom-of-information laws to request information about how the provincial government of Ontario, Canada, was implementing a plan to enforce disability access laws. The provincial government had passed a law requiring that certain private-sector businesses e-file reports on compliance with accessibility standards. Reports were due by December 2012. The government had charged the Ministry of Economic Development with enforcement of these digital-accessibility standards and allocated substantial money for enforcement.

David Lepofsky, a blind attorney and founder of the AODA Alliance, had reason to believe that the agency responsible for enforcement was not using the allocated budget as intended. The AODA Alliance filed an open-government request asking how many private-sector organizations had filed mandatory accessibility reports under the AODA, how many had not done so, what the government had done and planned to do to enforce the AODA, and how many officials had been designated under the AODA as enforcement "directors" and "inspectors." The request asked for any directions or instructions sought or obtained on how extensively the AODA would be enforced. The AODA Alliance wanted to know how many organizations had been audited or inspected under the AODA, how many had been notified that they needed to comply, and how many had been issued a compliance order or administrative penalty for noncompliance. The request also asked how much money the government budgeted for the Accessibility Directorate each year, and how much money it actually spent each year.

After the agency refused to respond to the request, the AODA Alliance was able to apply political pressure through various social media and mainstream press editorials. Eventually, the requested information was turned over. It revealed that 70 percent of businesses had not filed the required report and not one had been inspected, issued a compliance order, or fined as anticipated by the statute. The disclosed information further revealed that $24 million Canadian in government funds earmarked to oversee the law since its passage in 2005 remained unspent. A political firestorm ensued. The AODA Alliance has likewise continued to submit new open-government requests in hopes of promoting accountability and transparency of enforcement of disability access laws.

In a move similar to the AODA Alliance request, in 2012, the National Federation of the Blind (NFB), the leading advocacy organization of blind people in the United States, sent government-wide FOIA requests to every applicable U.S. federal agency. The NFB sought records related to how each agency was complying with a law that requires federal agencies to ensure that all electronic information technology procured and used by the government is accessible to government employees and members of the public who have disabilities. The government-wide request was generated after several agency websites and new mobile apps were released to the public without regard to whether that information technology was accessible in accordance with the standards of Section 508 of the Rehabilitation Act.

Unlike the AODA Alliance request, the NFB request did not target a single government agency. Rather, the NFB sent a template request to more than one hundred separate government entities seeking the same information from each. What followed was a complete cacophony of correspondence that required significant time and resources to track and synthesize.

The more than one hundred government agencies and departments interpreted the same request in a multitude of differing ways and on various timelines. Some federal agencies granted the request without delay, applied the requested public interest exception to waive any fees, and delivered responsive records. Other agencies insisted on charging for the requested documents and denied the statutory waiver for fees, notwithstanding common statutory language. Some agencies never responded. Others responded after years of delay to inquire whether the request could be closed on the assumption that there was no longer any interest in such an old request. Some agencies asserted a legal privilege for documents provided to the U.S. Department of Justice. Other agencies freely provided those same corresponding documents. The entire exercise revealed the need for a centralized U.S. FOIA process that applies to all government agencies and does away with the identical overlapping functions that exist in each agency. The current system is replete with waste and inefficiency because of a siloed approach to administrative functions.

In an ironic twist, the substantive responses obtained through the nonstandard FOIA process revealed a similar problem of nonstandard compliance with the underlying civil rights law noted in the request.[13] Agencies were using various automated website-accessibility software tools with no central comparison or intelligence and too much focus on free or low-cost tools where higher-quality tools of greater cost might have been secured for a lower price if they had been purchased in bulk by multiple agencies. Agencies were wasting effort by re-creating compliance documents on the exact same technical issues, that is, how to make PDF file formats accessible and configuration of Adobe Flash content. Moreover, many federal agency personnel had questions that could have been answered by searching a central repository of compliance materials that other agencies had already generated. Other agencies, such as the U.S. Commission of Fine Arts, revealed that they took no proactive compliance efforts and remediated only those problems that had been brought to their attention through a complaint.

Modern Open Government

Governments are increasingly collecting large quantities of electronic records and contemplating the release of such big data sets to the public. The convergence of government transparency, big data troves, and automated technologies is forcing governments to balance the kinds of interactivity that might be provided to the public.

For example, Ireland is establishing international best-practice standards for publishing and licensing open data. It will set up an Open Data platform that will facilitate feedback from citizens. The platform will enable citizens to request additional data sets, provide information about applications for which the data are being used, and provide knowledge about usability and the quality of data sets.[14]

Likewise, Brazil launched the Transparency Portal in 2004. The portal discloses real-time data on government expenditures and revenues, information on federal budget execution, salaries of national public officials, information on public officials who have been removed from office, and specific sections dedicated to the transparency of expenditures on the 2014 World Cup and the 2016 Olympic Games. In 2009, Brazil's Complementary Law No. 131 ensured that subsidiary levels of government disclosed similar financial information online subject to penalties for noncompliance.[15]

Within the United States, the proactive release of documents and data as part of the open-government initiative has increased.[16] The United States has established the data.gov website, an open online repository of thousands of data sets from many federal agencies. The website provides the data so that the public can freely develop tools, cross-reference multiple data sets, and harness the power of information for innovation, research, and collaboration.

These examples highlight a global trend to open the doors of governments so that the public can more freely access raw information in its flexible, digital form. Without this open-data movement, the public is unable to synchronize data sets from multiple sources within a government or the private sector. Further, data might be stored in proprietary databases, which would make it difficult to process those data without access to the proprietary data wrapper.

As an illustration of some of the legal tension that underlies both traditional and modern concepts of open government, U.S. courts were faced with a legal dispute over the format in which the U.S. government was required to produce records in response to a freedom-of-information request. In the National Day Laborer Organizing Network case, a coalition of community groups demanded government records consisting of electronic text records, e-mail messages, spreadsheets, and paper records. The parties litigated whether the government's production was sufficient where "(1) the data was produced in an unsearchable PDF format; (2) electronic records were stripped of all metadata; and (3) paper and electronic records were indiscriminately merged together in one PDF file."[17]

Governments are also considering to what extent they might empower citizens and colleagues from around the globe to collaborate on open records. Through the concept known as crowd sourcing, technology can make governments more communal and collective, which means inviting and encouraging everyone, regardless of geographic citizenship, to participate in new, innovative ways. For example, the U.S. Library of Congress, National Archives and Records Administration, prompts citizens to help transcribe paper archives and photo-image collections so they can be accessed in online electronic formats. When the agency posted images of Civil War letters and the 1940 census records, over 150,000 volunteers joined in electronically tagging more than 130 million records so they could be searchable on the Internet. The agency uses online technology to connect with users, who in turn codeliver government services, using the agency system as a platform for collaboration. The library uses its online technology to enable and motivate volunteer archivists to classify and categorize content, aid in appropriate retrieval of information for all users, generate metadata information, and create folksonomy (a system in which users apply public tags to online items, typically to aid them in refinding those items) to supplement expert-generated taxonomy.

To further illustrate, the U.S. Federal Transit Administration partnered with the Utah Transit Authority on the Next Stop Design project. Participants from around the world were challenged to design an ideal bus-stop shelter for a transit hub. In just a few months and with no tangible reward offered, nearly 3,200 participants registered on the site, submitting 260 high-quality architectural renderings for bus-stop shelter designs and casting more than 10,000 votes in the competition.[18] The winning design for the stop was not submitted by a U.S. resident.

The new technology-dependent trends in open government raise a number of important issues for many people with disabilities. The digitization of information is opening up unprecedented opportunities for access. The fact that the information on the Internet is contained in standardized, digital formats makes it a valuable resource for those with disabilities. Assistive software applications are designed to translate the standard code of an electronic resource, such as a website or a database, into meaningful and efficient access for users with disabilities. The standardized system of delivering machine-readable information means that the information is flexible and capable of being translated and conveyed in numerous ways. This flexibility of information makes it possible for computers and software to assist people with disabilities to adapt to the impairment of a specific sense or function. The assistive software translates the information that a person traditionally receives from a sense, whether visual, auditory, or touch, into a format that does not require the use of that sense.

For example, screen-reader applications can convert words and formatting information displayed on a computer screen into synthesized speech or refreshable braille. This can empower a user with a visual impairment to interact with complex web interfaces with the same flexibility and speed that a sighted user might exercise. Displaying a page in an inverted color scheme or with enlarged fonts may enable a person with light sensitivity to read the content. Those with manual-dexterity impairments are able to use voice-activation software to speak control and navigation commands that would normally be performed by clicking a mouse or typing on a keyboard. Audio recordings of speech dialogue can be processed to create a computer-driven transcription of dialogue in real time for persons with hearing impairments. Content layout can be automatically modified to require less cognitive overhead for those with intellectual impairments.

Government, Disability Rights, and Human Rights

Governments are increasingly recognizing the importance of digital accessibility to basic social integration. In 2015, the Colombian government entered into a four-year procurement contract to license JAWS, a popular screen-reader software program, providing free access to screen-reader technology to all visually impaired people of Colombia. This has the potential to reach up to 1.2 million users throughout the duration of the program.[19]

In addition to overcoming communications barriers, digital accessibility also tends to overcome physical barriers. Because most digital information is available for transmission over the Internet or via telecommunication networks, the peripheral, but very real, limitations of inaccessible transportation and construction that may have hindered people with mobility impairments can be reduced. In addition, the standardization of profiles and account templates using online communications channels may tend to hide or minimize the differences in physical appearance that often isolate a single person with a disability who is physically present in a group of people without disabilities.

Internationally recognized standards exist to ensure universal access to digital information for people with disabilities. The Web Content Accessibility Guidelines (WCAG) and Web Accessibility Initiative Accessible Rich Internet Applications (WAI-ARIA), published by the World Wide Web Consortium (W3C), are the leading standards for most websites and online content. These guidelines, if followed, will make content accessible to many people with disabilities, including blindness or low vision, deafness or hearing loss, learning disabilities, cognitive limitations, limited movement, speech disabilities, photosensitivity, and combinations of all these disabilities.

The global trend is to adopt accepted digital-accessibility standards as legal requirements for governments using technology. The UN General Assembly established certain obligations on signatory governments to account for digital accessibility to government information and services in the Convention on the Rights of Persons with Disabilities (CRPD).[20] Specifically, the CRPD contemplates that signatory governments will promote access for persons with disabilities to new information and communications technologies and systems, including the Internet, and promote the design, development, production, and distribution of accessible information and communications technologies and systems at an early stage so that these technologies and systems become accessible at minimum cost.

The European Union (EU), which ratified the CRPD in 2010, has pushed for digital accessibility to government information as a legal right. In 2005, the European Commission (EC) put out EU Mandate 376, which requires the three European standards organizations, the European Committee for Standardization (CEN), the European Committee for Electrotechnical Standardization (CENELEC), and the European Telecommunications Standards Institute (ETSI) to harmonize and facilitate the public procurement of accessible information and communication technology (ICT) products and services within Europe. The mandate contemplates a multiphase approach that continues today. In 2012, the EC adopted a proposal for a directive on the accessibility of the public-sector bodies' websites.[21] The directive seeks to harmonize member states' digital-accessibility requirements in line with the WCAG so that government websites are compliant with the current WCAG by 2016.

Although the United States has not ratified the CRPD as of 2016, the U.S. government is nonetheless in the process of importing the WCAG as a technical standard for measuring government compliance with existing digital-accessibility laws. Currently, Section 508 of the Rehabilitation Act, 29 U.S.C. § 794d, requires all electronic information that is used, procured, or developed by federal agencies to be compliant with certain Section 508 accessibility standards. The U.S. Access Board, which has the authority to modify these standards, proposed in February 2015 that the refreshed Section 508 technical standards should incorporate the WCAG.

Open Government and Digital Accessibility: Looking Toward the Future

Although law and policy are developing to ensure digital access to government information and services for people with disabilities, important questions remain unanswered about how these efforts will be applied to the new technology-driven open-government initiatives. Many nations have recognized that disability is an issue to consider in analyzing public participation and social inclusion. However, a far smaller number of nations are specifically recognizing the connection between digital accessibility of open data and the open-government movement.

Such connections between digital accessibility and open data, if any, will likely appear in the nation's action plan submitted to the Open Government Partnership (OGP). The Open Government Partnership is a multinational initiative that aims to secure concrete commitments from governments to promote transparency, empower citizens, fight corruption, and harness new technologies to strengthen governance. In the spirit of multistakeholder collaboration, the OGP is overseen by a steering committee including representatives of governments and civil society organizations. An increasing number of nations are joining the OGP, which was founded in 2011 by Brazil, Indonesia, Mexico, Norway, the Philippines, South Africa, the United Kingdom, and the United States.[22] More than sixty other nations have since joined. To become a member of the OGP, participating countries must deliver a country action plan developed with public consultation and commit to independent reporting on their progress going forward.

Some of these national action plans address commitments to the digital accessibility of government information for people with disabilities. However, few of the national plans each nation submits to the OGP are specifically making the connection between digital accessibility of the data provided to the public and the general level of access that people with disabilities will receive. The United States, as one of the outliers, has specifically made such a connection in its latest open-government action plan.[23]

The U.S. plan contemplates that the United States will increase accessibility of government information online for people with disabilities by taking specific steps. First, in September 2015, the U.S. Digital Service launched a set of design patterns and tools as best practices to improve design of the hundreds of websites across dozens of agencies to provide consistent, visually appealing, and easy-to-use government websites that are compliant with federal disability access requirements. Second, the United States will create software code that can assist in evaluating the accessibility of websites across the government. Third, the General Services Administration will expand the transparent reporting platform, pulse.cio.gov, to measure performance of all federal web domains against web policy requirements and industry best practices while connecting domain owners to information and resources to better ensure that their sites comply with the requirements of Section 508.

The promises of the latest U.S. plan are ambitious. One of the greatest improvements to the policy is the potential for better transparency. Under previous policy efforts, the U.S. Department of Justice was tasked with collecting survey responses every two years from every federal agency to assess the level of compliance with Section 508 requirements and report to Congress and the president on the results. The 2012 report paints a bleak picture. Among other troubling statistics, only slightly more than 50 percent of agency components had even established a general policy to implement and comply with Section 508; only about 40 percent of relevant agency components reported establishing a policy to ensure the accessibility of software; only about 30 percent of relevant agency components reported establishing a policy to ensure the accessibility of videos or multimedia productions; and only 70 percent of the agency components that maintain their own websites reported establishing formal web-accessibility policies.[24] As troubling as those statistics might be, there is little accountability because the data underlying those statistics were kept out of public view, and no agency was publicly held accountable for noncompliance.

One factor that may greatly affect the chances of an accessible nascent open-government movement is the enforcement scheme available. Some civil rights laws within the United States can be enforced through plaintiffs with private attorneys who are deputized to seek relief and recover reasonable fees from the defendant if the plaintiff prevails. This private enforcement model depends on the entrepreneurial efforts of attorneys to ensure that the supply of legal representation matches the demand of noncompliance cases. A second model of enforcing civil rights often used in the EU depends on administrative agencies with broad regulatory oversight over industry practices. These agencies pass regulations, provide guidance, and then receive and prosecute complaints. This second model depends on the effectiveness and motivation of the public entity. There are various hybrid versions that combine elements of these two approaches. Neither approach will be successful without the kind of public accountability and transparency that are needed for open government to succeed.

Conclusion

Going forward, societies must use the twin enforcement tools (private and government enforcement) coupled with the political pressure of transparency and accountability. This coupling will leverage the strengths and minimize the weaknesses of any particular approach. For example, on the one hand, there may be some digital-accessibility requirements that are best enforced through private plaintiffs on a case-by-case basis where a single regulatory body cannot adequately cover the concerns of many divergent industries and government activities. On the other hand, there may be other aspects of digital accessibility that are more efficiently enforced by promoting voluntary mass compliance in a particular industry or market through the passage of very clear technical regulations with swift public investigations rather than expensive litigation between individual parties. Governments should be structuring their legal systems to allow for both types of enforcement. Neither alone is sufficient to fully ensure that open-government efforts and the privately developed technology services and platforms that power open government will be accessible to people with disabilities in full compliance with disability access laws. Nor will the political trends toward transparency and accountability be of any use without enforcement powers to induce change.

The basic legal foundation for making the case for digital accessibility in open government exists in many jurisdictions around the globe. But how any of these open government laws will be applied to new technologies depends greatly on how we as a society embrace the concept of inclusion and integration for people with disabilities. Unless we as a global community promote effective legal enforcement regimes and liberal interpretations of old statutes to new technology, people with disabilities will never enjoy the same openness of government at the same time as citizens without disabilities. The global community must ensure that the digital-accessibility promises of the CRPD are codified in meaningful, enforceable laws. Then we must ensure that developing nations have a proven model to follow. The world will then see a whole population of people with disabilities who are empowered to contribute their talents and resources to a truly open and accessible society.

PART III

Specific Applications and Technologies

CHAPTER 9

E-Books and Human Rights

Jim Fruchterman

Introduction

Access to information is critically important to human beings. It is essential for education, livelihoods, and full participation in society. The printed book has been the primary vehicle for conveying knowledge across most human societies. Disabilities that interfere with reading books are called print disabilities. For people with print disabilities, equality of access to the information contained in books is a fundamental requirement to realize their human rights as expressed in the Universal Declaration of Human Rights, the Convention on the Rights of Persons with Disabilities, and other instruments: "We want the right to read the same book at the same time, price and place as everyone else."[1] This simple statement from the disability community sets forth the challenges of making books accessible. These challenges include the act of reading; being able to choose how to read a book; being able to read the same book without abridgment or omission; the independence and autonomy to choose when to read a book; no financial bar to reading because of disability; and portability: being able to read at home, at school, at work, under a tree, or while on a bus. The e-book offers an incredible opportunity to meet these aspirations.

Background

Book accessibility originally was thought of as a challenge to make books usable by people who were blind or visually impaired. Over time, there has been increased recognition of other disabilities that interfere with print reading. Quite a number of physical disabilities can make handling a book or turning a page difficult or impede focusing on the text on the page. Physical disabilities also include brain injuries that affect the reading process. Last, there is increased recognition of learning disabilities such as dyslexia, which, in its most severe forms, can make reading books impossible. As part of the move away from a solely medical model of disability, George Kerscher coined the term "print disability"[2] to collectively describe disabilities that functionally interfere with the reading of standard print.

Traditionally, people with print disabilities have been dependent on others for creation of books in accessible formats. Three approaches have traditionally been used to make books accessible: read them aloud, make them larger, or make them tactile. Each of these three approaches typically requires human intermediaries between the book and the consumer with a disability.

Having a human reader read a book aloud is the oldest approach, but it is highly dependent on another person, especially if that human reader is volunteering to perform the reading task. Untrained human readers will often abridge or modify the text as well. Specialized libraries that serve people with print disabilities have created high-quality versions of a select number of books using human narrators. In recent times, the affordability and portability of devices able to play audio has created a commercial market for some titles to be created as high-quality narrated audiobooks.

The creation of book editions with enlarged print has addressed the needs of many visually impaired persons, but relatively few books can justify the expense of commercially creating a separate large-print edition. Some large-print editions are also abridged versions.

Last, braille is regarded as the best format for blind people who have had the opportunity to learn it. Technology has been developed to create braille books, including braille typewriters, embossers, and printing presses. However, it has been the least commercially viable format of the three major types of accessible formats.

Before the introduction of the e-book, people with print disabilities had relatively limited options for books in their preferred formats. The availability of accessible books depended heavily on the efforts of family and friends, volunteers, and a small number of nonprofit and government groups dedicated to making a small number of books accessible.

The Advent of the E-Book

The e-book has created a huge stir in the publishing industry. The transition from paper to digital has created new mass-market opportunities that far surpass a simple change in format. Although the majority of press coverage focuses on market share among more affluent consumers, the e-book benefits much more of the global community. This is especially true of people with disabilities.

The ease of inexpensive e-book distribution creates many new possibilities. It is now possible for authors to self-publish their works and get significant readership. It becomes economically feasible to distribute far more free books because the incremental cost of an additional copy of an e-book is nearly zero. The creation of the Creative Commons open-licensing regime makes it practical for book creators to distribute books (and other works) freely. Nonprofit organizations are experimenting with e-book delivery on smartphones in the developing world, either for free or at locally affordable prices. Publishing in languages read by smaller populations may reverse long trends toward just a handful of major international languages.

The e-book has been a major technical breakthrough for people with print disabilities. In its simplest form, an e-book is the text content of a book in a word-processing file or equivalent. It is inexpensive to produce, is standardized, and can be automatically converted to many different formats. Ironically, the original digital publishing technologies that created electronic versions of books were not very accessible to people with print disabilities because they were focused heavily on making e-books look as they would appear on the printed page. However, technology advances and standards efforts have made the core commercial e-book technologies more and more accessible to people with print disabilities. The emerging dream is that all books that are born digital should be born accessible.

The production of an e-book title is quite inexpensive, even when one is starting with a print version of the book. Scanners are widely available to convert the printed pages into digital images. Optical character recognition is commonly available to convert the digital images into word-processor files, where any text-recognition errors can be quickly corrected. It is also relatively inexpensive to add important structural information about the book, such as page numbers, chapter numbers, and even descriptions of images. Depending on the complexity of a print book (from a simple novel to a science textbook), the cost of creation of a high-quality text version of the book can range from tens of dollars to the low thousands. Of course, if it is possible to have access to the original publisher-created, high-quality e-files for a book, these costs fall greatly. Automated conversion of publisher files can be accomplished for less than a dollar per book in quantity. These improvements in text-based technology make the e-book an inexpensive format to produce compared with typing the book manually or recording the book with a human narrator.

Once the e-book has been created in a high-quality digital format, it is easy to automatically convert it to all three traditional accessible formats to meet user needs. The text of an e-book can be used to generate standard audiobooks in MP3 format using voice-synthesizer technology, or it can be read aloud interactively with software on a computer or device. Large-print books can be printed out or viewed on a screen. Braille can be printed out using a specialized embosser or accessed using a braille display. The exact same source file can be used to generate all three of these formats at low cost. Some of these formats can be distributed on easily affordable devices, such as MP3 players and standard mobile phones, making it feasible to reach economically disadvantaged communities. The growing human rights consensus that people with disabilities need equal access to information, together with improved technology, means that we should be entering a world where everything born digital is born accessible.

The Policy Environment

Given the incredible accessibility advantages of the e-book, it has been a great irony that the e-book has not been very accessible. Competing social interests led to the locking up of digital content, much to the frustration of the disability community. These constraints were not aimed at people with disabilities. Instead, they experienced collateral damage from the fight against unauthorized copying and uncertainty about intellectual property rights.

Uncertainty about digital rights arose early in the digital era. Early commercial e-books provided the ability to "soundproof" books, whereby it was impossible to make the text of digital books speak aloud.³ Initially, most e-books came with technical protection mechanisms (TPMs) that disabled the ability to copy text. These digital rights management (DRM) tools were designed to make copying the books difficult in order to prevent making unauthorized copies, which was labeled "piracy" by authors and publishers. In addition, it was unclear whether allowing the text of an e-book to be read aloud infringed on the audiobook rights, since audiobook rights are typically sold separately from regular book rights.

This soundproofing of books was astounding to the community of people with print disabilities. As people who could not use the standard printed book effectively, they were the most natural customers for digital books, but they were effectively locked out of accessing this powerful resource. Luckily, the policy environment was increasingly favorable to their plight.

As discussed elsewhere in this volume, an array of civil rights legislation advanced the rights of people with disabilities to equality of access to information. In the case of e-books, copyright law and special education laws were quite critical.

Copyright exceptions make it possible to create e-book versions of print works without infringing on the copyright privileges of authors and publishers. Many countries have made the creation of accessible copies a legal activity under their copyright laws. In the United States, the creation of accessible copies was generally permitted under Section 107, commonly known as the fair-use exception. Helping the blind gain access to braille and audio versions of books on a one-off basis was a typical example of an activity that met the tests to use the fair-use exception. In the 1990s, reading systems became an important part of the technology available to people with print disabilities, enabling them to scan and create their own e-book copies of printed documents.

The production of multiple accessible copies of the same work by specialized libraries for people with print disabilities was not clearly covered by the fair-use exception. In 1996, an additional copyright exception was added to cover these specialized organizations. Section 121, also known as the Chafee Amendment after the senator who sponsored the change, permits nonprofit or government entities with a primary mission of serving people with print disabilities to make accessible copies in specialized formats, including digital text. Most of these libraries focused on the making of braille and human-narrated audio formats. In 2002, Bookshare was established as a specialized library exclusively focused on providing e-books, using the Section 121 exception as its primary legal justification.

In the United States, higher education access laws as early as 1999 started requiring publishers of print textbooks to make available e-book versions of those books.[4] There was awareness that leading publishers were creating textbooks digitally and could easily provide a digital version, even though there was no market at the time for those digital versions. This led to advocacy for a law in the United States that would address the need nationally for textbook accessibility at the primary and secondary levels.

The Individuals with Disabilities Education Act was reauthorized in 2004[5] and contained extensive provisions for e-book accessibility. To receive federal funding, local and state education agencies needed to require accessible versions of new textbooks as part of the general procurement process. A new standard for these e-books was developed, which was a subset of the DAISY disability e-book standard.[6] The National Instructional Materials Access Center was established as a central repository for these accessible e-books.[7]

These state and national laws led to an increasing flow of e-books to groups that specialized in providing accessible books to students with disabilities. These included disabled-student-services offices in higher education, braille-textbook producers, special educators, and national libraries for people with print disabilities, such as Learning Ally (then known as Recording for the Blind & Dyslexic) and Bookshare.

The commercial e-book industry came later and had limited success until the introduction of the Amazon Kindle in 2007. Initially, the Kindle was successful in the mass market but was not accessible. In 2009, Amazon started including text-to-speech options in some Kindle models, as well as introducing a larger model targeted at schools. One major authors' association campaigned against the text-to-speech option, claiming that it conflicted with audiobook licensing, and was able to persuade Amazon to make it optional.[8] Some publishers then turned off text-to-speech on their e-book titles. Disability groups demonstrated against this disabling of an accessibility feature but did not have options for legal recourse. It was difficult to pursue remedies against the makers of inaccessible technology, such as Adobe or Amazon.

However, when early-adopter schools started using e-book readers for textbooks, this created a window for disability advocates to file suit. It was possible to go after the schools employing inaccessible technology as violating the civil rights of students with disabilities. In the United States, advocacy groups have conducted an extensive campaign of litigation to enforce these civil rights.[9]

As more of the education field in the United States goes digital in delivering courses and educational materials, more issues have come up. The large Google Book scanning project, conducted in conjunction with a consortium of research libraries named the HathiTrust, led to two major lawsuits about the legality of mass digitization. The suit that actually resulted in a judgment (rather than a settlement) was *Authors Guild v. HathiTrust*. The National Federation of the Blind (NFB) successfully petitioned to be a codefendant alongside the universities because the scanned books were far more accessible than libraries full of printed books.

The HathiTrust litigation centered on two key issues. First, the universities used the database of scanned books to make it easier to find relevant books through a full-text search of their content. Faculty, staff, and students at those universities then would seek out the print version of the book in a library to consult the content. Second, faculty, staff, and students who had a print disability were able to access the digital version of that book directly. Interestingly enough, the digital version included images of full-page scans. The Authors Guild maintained that these activities represented large-scale copyright violations.

The defense was that these two uses were permitted under the two U.S. copyright exceptions already mentioned. The universities maintained that the transformative nature of the searchable full-text database use made it legal under Section 107, the fair-use exception. The NFB and the universities further maintained that the accessibility uses were permitted under both fair use and Section 121, the Chafee Amendment. HathiTrust and the NFB won strong victories at both the district-court and appellate levels, both on the general legality of mass digitization under fair-use principles in U.S. copyright law and on the legality of scanning for accessibility purposes. These court decisions not only strengthened the long-established legality of making materials accessible under fair use but also specifically extended it to full-page images, which had been an open question before the 2014 appellate decision.

Of course, these U.S. developments have occurred in the context of international human rights norms, which have established the right to access to information. The Universal Declaration of Human Rights has multiple articles that form the basis for accessibility as a human right. Article 19 speaks to the right to "seek, receive and impart information and ideas through any media." Article 26 sets forth the right to an education, and Article 27 talks about access to culture.

The Convention on the Rights of Persons with Disabilities (CRPD) builds on these three general rights to make them more specific for people with disabilities. Article 21 of the CRPD requires that parties provide "information intended for the general public to persons with disabilities in accessible formats and technologies appropriate to different kinds of disabilities in a timely manner and without additional cost" and specifically calls out braille. Article 24 talks extensively about the accommodations needed to make education accessible to people with disabilities. Article 30 on access to culture talks both about the need to make accessible forms of cultural materials and the need to balance intellectual property law (that is, copyright) with the needs of people with disabilities to avoid the creation of legal barriers to access.

These two instruments provide the broadest framework for accessibility, including access to books, by creating general rights, simply expressed. How to implement these rights is left open ended, especially in regard to books for people with disabilities.

Efforts to bridge this gap culminated in the negotiation of the Marrakesh Treaty, the full name of which is the Marrakesh Treaty to Facilitate Access to Published Works for Persons Who Are Blind, Visually Impaired, or Otherwise Print Disabled. The Marrakesh Treaty, which as of this writing has eighty-eight signatories[10] and twenty-five ratifications or accessions,[11] made the right to read much more explicit.

The World Blind Union spearheaded the advocacy for a treaty to remedy what it described as the global "book famine."[12] Notwithstanding the existing obligations under the Universal Declaration of Human Rights and the CRPD, most people with print disabilities around the world still lacked access to information, especially in the form of books for education, employment, and social inclusion. The World Blind Union did not confine its advocacy to people with blindness or vision impairments; it also advocated on behalf of any person with a print disability that interfered with book access.

Brazil, Paraguay, and Ecuador introduced a treaty draft in 2009[13] at the World Intellectual Property Organization (WIPO) after consultations with the World Blind Union and other advocacy groups. The successful completion of negotiations in Marrakesh, Morocco, in 2013 was seen as rapid by international treaty standards. The provisions of the Marrakesh Treaty are extensive, specific, and quite favorable to accessibility. The core provisions of the treaty concern national copyright exceptions and cross-border transfer of accessible materials.

Each country ratifying the treaty needs to have a domestic copyright exception, similar to the Chafee Amendment in the United States, that allows "authorized entities" to create accessible copies for people with print disabilities. It also has provisions for a small-scale exception for the production of individual copies for personal use. For example, a volunteer or family member can create an accessible version of a book for a person with a qualifying disability without violating copyright restrictions. In addition, the treaty has provisions for cross-border exchange of accessible works. This cross-border capability is expected to reduce the duplication of the work to create accessible versions of the same book title in different countries, as well as making far more materials available in countries with limited resources.

The Marrakesh Treaty reached the twenty-country ratification requirement in June 2016 and went into effect as international law on September 30. Symbolic cross-border exchanges have already occurred. The World Blind Union and disability advocates are campaigning both for additional national ratifications of the treaty and for ensuring that the provisions of the treaty are used to deliver improved access. The Marrakesh Treaty should trigger a wave of new copyright exceptions and accessibility legislation around the globe, greatly increasing accessibility of e-books.

The Accessibility Benefits from E-Book Technology

Accessibility technology before e-books was cumbersome. Specialized four-track audiotape players were created to provide audiobooks to people with print disabilities. These were incompatible with mass-market audio devices such as standard two-track audio players. Large print and braille needed to be produced in a specialized office and typically shipped via post to individuals with disabilities.

The advent of the e-book coincided with great advances in accessibility technology. Text-to-speech voice synthesizers have become increasingly human sounding, especially in widely used languages such as English and other European languages. An e-book can be quickly turned into an MP3 file and played like a music file or human-narrated audiobook on standard MP3 players, which are far less expensive than disability-specific audiobook players. In addition, free or low-cost software makes it easy to play these books on standard smartphones or tablets. The need for people with print disabilities to own or carry specialized devices is receding as these affordable mass-market devices become powerful accessible reading platforms.

It is not only possible to print out enlarged versions of books but also simple to enlarge a book on the screen of a smartphone, tablet, or personal computer. This digital presentation of large-print books saves costs and improves accessibility. Large-print books on paper are expensive to produce and generally are created in a single larger font size. Presentation on the screen of a tablet or personal computer provides a much wider range of user adaptations. The size and color of the text can be changed, including light fonts on a dark background.

The advent of electronic braille displays, devices that can pop up plastic pins representing a line of braille characters, has revolutionized the braille field for people who can afford them. Hard-copy braille books consume large quantities of paper and are quite bulky. A small memory card can now hold thousands of books, making a one-pound braille display the equivalent of a major braille book library.

For readers with a learning disability, such as dyslexia, digital presentation makes new options beyond the traditional three formats possible. One of the leading techniques in dyslexia education is multimodal presentation, engaging more than one sense at a time. E-books can be presented karaoke style, where the words are visually spotlighted as they are read aloud. This is a very powerful way to read for people whose disability interferes with the decoding of words. Seeing a word and hearing it at the same time seems to break through some of these processing difficulties.

Greater access to e-books might cause more people with relevant disabilities to identify as having them. If there are no benefits for identifying as having a hidden disability, such as dyslexia, then most people with those disabilities will not identify. However, the dynamic changes if a student with dyslexia can receive accessible books plus other accommodations, such as extended testing time, which make that student more successful in school.

The economics and convenience of digital delivery of e-books are dramatic for people without disabilities. For example, the World Reader project brings e-books to mobile-phone users in Africa. Its goal is to bring books to people who lack access to them. Pratham Books in India has the objective of putting a "book in every child's hand."[14] It does this by selling books inexpensively (typically under a dollar each) in many of India's different languages, as well as making its books freely available online. These are just two examples of what e-books make possible in terms of greater access to books for the world at large.

The economics and convenience of e-books are even greater for people with print disabilities. The incremental cost to send an e-book from an on-line repository to a personal device is tiny. The ability to be reading a new book one minute after choosing it is powerful compared with waiting days, weeks, months, or years.

These advantages make new behaviors possible for greater equality of access. For example, when the Bookshare digital library was first set up, the policy in theory was unlimited access to books. In practice, patrons were limited to downloading fifty books per month to prevent mass copying of the library. However, quite a number of Bookshare patrons were soon running into this fifty-book limit. When they were asked why they were downloading so many books, the answer was simple and familiar to people without disabilities. The readers were browsing multiple books before choosing which one to read, just as readers do in libraries or bookstores. E-books made the practice of browsing accessible where it had not been practical before.

Advances in standards have also greatly increased e-book accessibility. Originally, the DAISY Consortium, made up of the world's leading libraries for people with print disabilities, created a disability-specific e-book standard. The goal of this format was to provide the same kinds of capabilities to read and navigate a work that people without disabilities had in a printed book. This not only included the full text content of the book but also important formatting, such as page numbers, chapters, sections, footnotes, and the like. The DAISY format was much richer than early commercial e-book format standards.

However, it turned out that mass-market e-book consumers wanted many of the same book features they had when they were using printed books. Over several years, the commercial standards grew in richness until finally the disability-specific and commercial e-book format standards merged into a single standard, EPUB 3.[15] This makes the universal design of books increasingly real. Although EPUB 3 as a standard has all these capabilities, there is still a need to encourage publishers to build this rich formatting into their works to ensure that they are accessible to people with print disabilities.

As mentioned earlier, e-books are also much less expensive to produce. When a publisher supplies a well-formatted EPUB book to a specialized library (or even an individual with a disability), the automated conversion to accessible formats is essentially free. Even if a book is available only in print, or TPMs render the commercial e-book version inaccessible, the cost to scan and proofread a book is much less than a tenth of the cost of producing an audiobook with human narrators.

The digital nature of e-books also makes them much less expensive to deliver to readers. A text e-book is very small, typically less than a megabyte of data, which makes it easy to deliver quickly. Even audio e-books with human narration can be easily delivered to readers with good data connections. Cross-border sharing is also much easier if the legality of such transfers is established through permissions or international copyright norms such as those enabled by the Marrakesh Treaty.

The new technology of e-books, combined with its commercial adoption, creates new possibilities for expanded access to information for people with print disabilities. Whatever device is in a person's pocket or bag is likely to be an effective tool for accessible reading.

Conclusion

The future of books should be a "born-accessible" future. All content that is born digitally should be born accessible.[16] The ideal situation is that when a person with a disability obtains a standard commercial e-book from a book vendor or library, it should be perfectly accessible. People with disabilities should be able to use the same digital e-book just as effectively as everybody else.

This is simply universal design applied to books. The overlap of users with and without disabilities means that the best product for the mass market will be the best product for people with print disabilities. This convergence also makes securing the fundamental human rights of people with disabilities easier. Universal design of new products, services, and technologies is central to the recommendations on meeting the accessibility requirements of international human rights instruments such as the CRPD.[17]

Universal design approaches also engage the interests of authors and publishers. Authors are very interested in reaching the largest possible audiences for their works. The tone of conversations with publishers shifts dramatically when the topic moves from copyright exceptions (generally unremunerated) to increased revenues associated with a larger market. It has been estimated that the proportion of readers who might benefit from accessibility features is five or ten times larger than those who qualify under copyright exceptions.[18] The confluence of self-interest with society's commitment to accessibility makes universal design approaches particularly attractive. That is the born-accessible future.

The elements of a born-accessible future are the following:

- Digital production of richer accessible content, including images
- Better, common standards
- Reduction of DRM mechanisms
- Digital delivery on common platforms

As digital objects, e-books have new capabilities beyond those of printed books. It is possible to add images, movies, digital simulations, and links to expanded material. Dictionaries and encyclopedias can be built in. It is easier to annotate a digital work and share those annotations with other readers. Although automated translation is not near to human-quality translation, it is beginning to break down the barriers between languages. Many of these new abilities should be accessible by their very nature, but some create new accessibility challenges.

The current frontier of book accessibility is image accessibility. The cost to add rich graphics to a digital work has been falling, and authors have been taking advantage of this. Educational textbooks in the United States have become more graphics intensive, and critical parts of the educational content are now delivered partly by image.

There have been extensive efforts to expand the accessibility of images by making it easier to create image descriptions (textual descriptions of the key information in an image) or tactile versions of graphics. These efforts have traditionally been the domain of specialized groups, such as the libraries in the DAISY Consortium. The born-accessible vision would have publishers create their published images with these descriptions in the normal course of the publishing process. One major educational publisher, Wiley, committed in 2015 to provide image descriptions in the form of alt-text on its newly published books.[19] These alt-text tags not only make the images more accessible to people with print disabilities but also make searching for images easier and enrich the reading experience for all readers.

Common standards are an area of common interest for both people with print disabilities and all readers. Printed books had the benefit of being compatible with just about all people except those with print disabilities. However, e-books do not have this degree of commonality. It has been common for regular readers to be uncertain whether a given e-book will work with their device, just as print-disabled readers have wondered whether they will be able to read a given title. Common standards, such as EPUB for complete e-books or MP3 for audio files, provide assurances to consumers that they will be able to use a given book, whether or not those consumers have disabilities.

The TPMs associated with digital rights management have had a similar chilling effect on the usability of e-books. Making books difficult to copy has made them difficult to move from device to device, especially in an era where people change devices frequently. As pointed out earlier, these TPMs have frequently rendered e-books completely unusable for many people with print disabilities, especially blind people. For publishers, there has always been a question of the trade-off between preventing unauthorized copies and the reduction of sales revenue associated with a product that has TPMs that make those e-books less usable and therefore less attractive to potential buyers. More and more publishers are going DRM free and finding that revenues typically remain level or increase. The drive toward dropping TPMs serves the interests of readers with and without disabilities.

Last, common platforms also improve access to information. This applies both to major infrastructure, like the Internet, and to software and devices for individual consumers. The costs associated with technology tend to fall steadily, and this makes technology-based products more accessible to people who are economically disadvantaged, which describes many people with disabilities. With common standards, it becomes easier to access information, whether through a web search or browser or through an app on a smartphone. It also means that accessibility is being built into these common platforms, often for free. The Apple iPhone and Google Android-based smartphones both have powerful and free accessibility tools built into the platform that meet the accessibility needs of the great majority of people with print disabilities if they can afford a smartphone. It also becomes easier to add other accessibility features. The standards body for the Internet search engines approved an accessibility metadata standard that should make it easier for people with disabilities to find accessible content when they are searching the web by asking search engines to return only videos that are captioned or books that are not soundproofed. Google added text-to-speech capability in its Chrome browser, making it easy to create free e-book readers that read aloud inside the browser.

Together, these universal design capabilities will make e-books a powerful tool for equality, and not just for people with disabilities that meet the print-disability definition (blind, visually impaired, physical disabilities, and learning disabilities). Many more people with other disabilities, such as hearing impairments, attention deficits, developmental disabilities, mental health disabilities, or autism spectrum disorders, can benefit from the accessibility features that are possible with e-books.

A born-accessible future is one where the right to access information and the right to an education are realized through digital content that is affordable and accessible to all. Access to information has been frustrating for a very long time for people with disabilities because of the limitations of traditional books. The ultimate objective is to flip this dynamic. We need content that adapts to the needs of each individual user rather than the user being forced to adapt to the limitations of the content-delivery technology. Universally designed e-books will help all people with disabilities fully realize their human right of access to the information they need for education, employment, and social inclusion.

CHAPTER 10

Accessibility and Online Learning

Mary J. Ziegler and David Sloan

Introduction

Education is globally recognized as a human right. Inclusive education builds on that principle and extends the human right of education to persons with disabilities. The United Nations Human Rights Council has made clear that inclusion and inclusive education are key provisions of the UN Convention on the Rights of Persons with Disabilities (CRPD).[1] As information technologies are integrated into primary and secondary schools, colleges and universities, lifelong learning, and adult professional educational settings, accessibility to these educational offerings for people with disabilities is key to upholding inclusive education.

In this chapter, we examine (a) where education is actively incorporating technology and employing emerging technologies to deliver educational content, (b) where technology provides opportunity to learners with disabilities, (c) the legislative and standards framework relating to disability, education, and technology, (d) where technology pathways, learning-management platforms, and course content are not sufficiently accessible to learners with disabilities, and (e) what can be done to increase accessibility in technological pathways to education for persons with disabilities.

Technology supports creation and delivery of, and access to, learning experiences in many different ways. Given the dominance of use of the Internet as a delivery channel for educational experience, in this chapter we will use the term "online learning" as a generic term to cover the use of digital technology for education.

The Increasing Role of Online Learning in Education

Information and communications technologies (ICTs) are prevalent in elementary/primary schools, secondary/upper-level schools, universities, and online/remote-learning environments. Educators recognize the significant potential of emerging technologies and are rapidly integrating them into their classrooms and curricula. In higher education, there is an explosion in use of online learning, where faculty are packaging entire digital versions of their academic course instruction and content into a learning-management system (LMS). The Massive Open Online Course (MOOC) offers the promise of access to open online education regardless of geographic location or economic situation.

Instructional materials and resources are increasingly provided in digital, cloud- or web-based formats and as part of learning portals and platforms. Students are expected to engage with digital resources, including websites, electronic books, video, audio, PDF documents, interactive simulations, math games, data sets, databases, and online assessments. Laptop and desktop computers, electronic book readers, tablets, and smartphones are required for students to find, read, write, edit, and manipulate digital content, as well as to digest, communicate, share, demonstrate, and collaborate in the creation of knowledge.

Schools, colleges, and universities are actively developing technology to enhance learning, and with the increasing ubiquity of the mobile phone as a portable, location-aware, personal access device, there is a particular focus on the contribution of mobile devices to enriching the learning experience. With this technological shift, the education profession is exploring how to measure the effectiveness of technology-enhanced learning for learners. IMS Global Learning Consortium (IMS Global), a nonprofit organization that advances technology that can affordably scale and improve educational participation and attainment, gives awards each year to organizations around the world for the innovative application of technology to achieve learning impact.[2]

Even in locations where access to the Internet and educational technology may be sparse, there are significant benefits of using any technology available to create a connection among learners, learning resources, and teachers. In the majority world, where access to educational resources and services may be limited, but mobile-device ownership is high and data are cheap, online learning presents enormous potential to improve access to education. A case study of mobile learning models in Tanzanian secondary schools concluded: "Education stakeholders should consider the opportunities of technology in education in order to boost knowledge sharing among students."[3]

New technologies offer new pathways that make the experience of learning more immediate, intimate, and social. Technology implemented in classrooms, remotely, and in blended learning models gives students quick access to information, interactive ways to engage, and flexible means of communicating. Students receive immediate feedback on their progress via automatic grading and response systems. They can express themselves more freely in multiple modes, via chat and online discussions employing typing, video, and audio, which provide the potential for more effective assessment of knowledge and skills.

The Opportunities Online Learning Gives People with Disabilities

The qualities and characteristics of online learning present enormous opportunities in particular for people with disabilities to overcome barriers present in existing learning environments and receive a better-quality learning experience where the effect of their disability is minimized. The advent of the open online course (MOOCs) has particular potential to provide access to rich educational experiences for people with disabilities—a sector of society that has historically experienced discrimination in regard to education. Given the importance of education in preparing an individual to enter employment and develop a career, any shift to making education more accessible to people with disabilities should also increase their employability. The appreciation of the potential of online learning to increase social inclusion for people with disabilities is critical to understanding what mobilizes efforts to reduce or remove accessibility barriers in online learning.

Online learning has the potential to overcome physical barriers to traditional learning environments. Many schools, colleges, universities, and laboratories have physical access barriers, such as staircases that limit or prevent access to classrooms and other learning spaces, and the nature of traffic-free campuses can lead to prohibitive distances for some people with disabilities to travel to and from accessible transportation. Field learning often takes place in locations that require significant physical effort to access.

Providing an online learning environment that can be brought directly to people who have mobility impairments or medical conditions means that they can take part in learning experiences situated in environments or locations that might have otherwise been inaccessible to them. Students with mobility impairments need not travel to locations that are difficult to access. Students with medical conditions need not be exposed to environments dangerous to their health.

Online learning supports diverse learning styles. Online learning environments support content authors and instructors in creating and providing learning content in multiple digital formats, such as text, audio, video, and animation. The flexibility of digital content benefits people with various disabilities and learning preferences, who can receive and interact with content in a format that best suits their needs. For example, students who are blind or visually impaired can use options to read with text-to-speech or enlargements. Students who are deaf or hearing impaired can use visual captions, subtitles, transcripts, or video sign language interpretation of audio content. Students with dyslexia or learning disabilities can use text-to-speech output in combination with visuals to make on-screen text easier to read and comprehend. Students with attention deficit can be given the opportunity to control moving and flashing content by switching it off to reduce distraction.

Online learning encourages collaborative learning and inclusion. Accessible information, discussion, and authoring tools allow all students, including persons with disabilities, to communicate as equals in groups. This benefits a diverse set of students communicating via whatever mainstream or assistive technology they prefer or need to employ. Examples are abundant and include the following: a student who has quadriplegia and uses voice-recognition software can dictate in lieu of typing; a student with quadriplegia, cerebral palsy, or other mobility impairment can enter a discussion using a switch, head pointing, or eye-gaze input with an on-screen keyboard; and a student who is deaf can use sign language video relay services to talk via video conference sessions.

Online learning can potentially negate the need for many students to self-identify or declare that they have a disability. Online learning environments set up with known accessibility options can be used by many students with disabilities independently. Students using accessible environments may not need to request alternative formats based on their disability in advance of taking an online course, which benefits both the student and the school or university. Provision of accessible online learning resources can also help schools and universities reduce time, effort, and resources needed to provide and maintain physical copies of learning resources in alternative formats, for example, braille or large print.

There are differences between approaches to inclusion of learners with disabilities at different levels of education. At primary and secondary levels, accommodations for learners with disabilities are likely to be more personalized and provided by a human. In tertiary education, as learners grow up and learning expectations mature, learners have an increased responsibility to understand their own accessibility needs and secure the necessary accommodations. When online learning is designed with inclusion in mind, educational institutions increase the chances that a learner with disabilities can independently engage with these resources effectively, in many cases without requiring third-party intervention. Since some learners may be reluctant to disclose their disability, an accommodation strategy that does not rely on disclosure is especially effective.

Legislation and Standards

In addition to the many benefits that accessible online learning offers, the rights of people with disabilities to equal access to education are enshrined in legislation in many territories around the world. In the CRPD, the underlying value of inclusive education as a human right is encapsulated in Article 24, "Education." It sets out provisions for an inclusive education system that guarantees that children with disabilities have access to primary and secondary education without discrimination, and that suitable training and accommodations for accessibility are provided to learners and teachers alike. However, the use of technology to deliver equal access to quality learning experiences for people with disabilities is underpinned by a global legislative and standards framework that is at present inconsistent in detail and coverage. Provision of accessible online learning should therefore help educational organizations meet their legal obligations toward learners, learner family members, and contributing or supporting staff with disabilities.

Legislation on the Rights of People with Disabilities to Receive Education

Across the globe, legislation intended to protect equal access to society for people with disabilities in general includes the right to equal access to education. In the United States, Section 504 of the Rehabilitation Act of 1973 and Titles II and III of the Americans with Disabilities Act (ADA) of 1990, amended in 2008, set forth requirements for public and private schools and universities to afford students with disabilities equal opportunity to participate in programs, activities, and services. The Individuals with Disabilities Education Act (IDEA) of 1975, amended in 2004, was enacted to ensure that children with disabilities have the opportunity to receive a free appropriate public education. The National Instructional Materials Accessibility Standard (NIMAS), as part of the IDEA amendment, was published in 2006 as a standard to be used in the preparation of electronic files to be converted into specialized formats.

In 2008, the Higher Education Opportunity Act established the Advisory Commission on Accessible Instructional Materials (AIM) in Postsecondary Education for Students with Disabilities to study the state of accessible materials for students with disabilities in postsecondary education. From their recommendations to improve the quality and abundance of accessible instructional materials came the following:

- Federal guidance regarding emerging technologies: a "dear colleague" letter and accompanying list of FAQs put forth the "functional definition of accessibility" as "a person with a disability is afforded the opportunity to acquire the same information, engage in the same interactions, and enjoy the same services as a person without a disability in an equally effective and equally integrated manner, with substantially equivalent ease of use."
- In 2012, the U.S. Department of Justice (DOJ) issued an Advance Notice of Proposed Rulemaking for Web Accessibility (ARPRM) which was withdrawn in 2016, when the DOJ issued a Supplemental Advance Notice of Proposed Rulemaking (SANPRM) titled

"Nondiscrimination on the Basis of Disability: Accessibility of Web Information and Services of State and Local Government Entities."
- In 2013, the Technology, Equality, and Accessibility in College and Higher Education Act (TEACH Act) was introduced in Congress to direct the U.S. Access Board to develop accessibility guidelines for electronic instructional materials and related information technologies in institutions of higher education (IHEs).
- In 2016, the TEACH Act was superseded by introduction of the Accessible Instructional Materials in Higher Education Act (AIM-HEA) in Congress, calling for the creation of a commission to develop voluntary accessibility guidelines for electronic instructional materials and related technologies used in postsecondary education.

Also in the United States, in 1998 the Rehabilitation Act was amended to introduce Section 508, which directed the federal Access Board to establish accessibility standards for electronic and information technologies adopted by U.S. federal agencies. The resulting standards were adopted broadly by industries supplying federally funded entities and have affected many educational establishments who also use that technology and stand to benefit from improvements made to its accessibility. In addition, the Twenty-First Century Communications and Video Accessibility Act (CVAA) of 2010 does not directly apply to educational institutions, but it stipulates accessibility requirements of video content provided by television or online and of digital communication products, both of which may be used by educational organizations. Many U.S. states have additional requirements for educational technology that include accessibility requirements.

Provisions similar to the ADA exist in disability legislation in many other countries. For example, Australia's Disability Discrimination Act (1992), China's Law on the Protection of Disabled People (1990), and the Equality Act (2010) in the United Kingdom all cover to at least some extent the right to access to education for people with disabilities. Brazil has several laws and decrees, including Law No. 7853 (1989) and Law No. 12,796 (2013), that protect the rights of people with disabilities to receive education without discrimination.

Legal Developments Related to Online Learning

Although the U.S. government has not yet issued detailed guidance addressing accessible instructional materials delivered directly to students online, various U.S. universities and a provider of online learning platforms have faced complaints or investigations by the Department of Education and the Department of Justice regarding the accessibility of the online technology provided to students. The basis for these cases or investigations is a broad directive anchored in the ADA that higher education shall not discriminate on the basis of disability or deny individuals with disabilities the opportunity to participate fully in learning provided online. Many of these investigations target deficiencies in online learning accessibility and signal a watchful enforcement strategy that highlights the need for online educational providers, including the vendors who provide the means of creating online content, to prioritize accessibility for students with disabilities.

Noteworthy in many investigations are the resulting steps taken by universities to improve digital accessibility. These steps typically highlight a recognition that accessibility can be achieved only through the involvement of many stakeholders contributing to the processes that build accessible environments for learning, and that strategic planning to accommodate accessibility is necessary in addition to evaluation and repair of existing resources. At the University of Colorado at Boulder, where the DOJ closed its investigation into possible noncompliance with the ADA,[4] a new campus-wide structure was created for the continuous improvement of accessibility of ICTs. It included the appointment of a chief accessibility officer, drafting of a campus-wide digital-accessibility policy, integration of accessibility requirements into procurement practices, and remediation activities.

In the settlement agreement between the U.S. government and edX, Inc.,[5] a provider of learning-management systems and platforms, but not of learning content, edX explicitly denied being covered under or violating the ADA, but the voluntary agreement entered into by edX outlines specific provisions designed to facilitate accessibility for the parties using edX and includes a recognition that the content providers using the platform are covered and do need to be in compliance with the ADA. Provisions to increase accessibility include the following:

- Ensuring that the platform does not block or interfere with any accessibility features

- Allowing for content to be published in formats and standards that support accessibility, such as MathML, WAI-ARIA, DAISY, and EPUB3
- Providing guidance to content providers referencing the W3C web accessibility standards WCAG, ATAG, and UTAG

In this settlement, a key principle conveyed is that a learning platform, product, or tool should not interfere with the responsibility and obligation of content providers to make learning content accessible for learners with disabilities.

Legislation on Access to Copyrighted Content

Another topic that is relevant to online learning and accessibility and is covered by legislation in some jurisdictions is access to copyrighted information for educational purposes. Copyright law exists in many jurisdictions to protect the rights of content publishers and places restrictions on the ability to reproduce copyrighted content. Legislation may provide exemptions for educational use. For example, in the United States, the Technology, Education, and Copyright Harmonization Act (TEACH Act) signed into law in 2002 (not to be confused with the similarly named Technology, Equality, and Accessibility in College and Higher Education Act, a bill mentioned earlier) grants some limited rights to use copyrighted content in online teaching.

However, restrictions specified by copyright law can interfere with the need for people with print disabilities—impairments that affect an individual's ability to hold and read an item of printed literature—to receive content in an alternative format in a timely fashion. Someone who is blind will be unable to read a printed book, so an accessible alternative would be an audio version of the same book; someone who has dyslexia may have difficulty reading text that is fully justified and would benefit from the ability to customize text.

Again, some existing copyright laws include exemptions that enable reproduction of copyrighted content in an accessible format for people with disabilities, for example, copyright laws in Australia, Brazil, India, the United Kingdom, and the United States. These exemptions are usually limited in scope, with a very strict definition of disability that limits who can benefit, or can be applied only after a potentially long period of permission request and approval, which makes timely provision of material in accessible format difficult.

Globally, the World Intellectual Property Organization (WIPO) published the Marrakesh Treaty to Facilitate Access to Published Works for Persons Who Are Blind, Visually Impaired, or Otherwise Print Disabled on June 27, 2013. The intention of the Marrakesh Treaty is to reduce exclusion experienced by people with print disabilities who are unable to access the content of copyrighted content, and where the creation, reproduction, or distribution of accessible alternatives may currently be restricted or forbidden because of copyright law. It has a specific focus on supporting cross-border exchange of accessible formats—reducing the economic barrier that may exist when already-existing accessible versions of books need to be re-created when they are distributed internationally. Signatories to the Marrakesh Treaty are expected to implement the terms of the treaty by introducing or amending legislation to ensure that copyright exemptions enable people with print disabilities to receive accessible formats of protected content.

Standards and Guidelines on Accessibility of Online Learning Materials

To the best of the authors' knowledge, there is no example of accessibility requirements for online learning that are expressed directly in legislation at the time of writing. However, dialogue has recently taken place in the United States over the possibility of introducing legislation that does require online learning resources to meet a minimum technical standard for content accessibility. As noted earlier, the Technology, Equality, and Accessibility in College and Higher Education (TEACH) Act was introduced in 2013. This TEACH Act was drafted in response to the findings of the 2011 Report of the Advisory Commission on Accessible Instructional Materials in Postsecondary Education for Students with Disabilities (the AIM Report).[6]

This proposed legislation would require the Access Board to produce guidelines for accessible online learning resources, providing educational institutions with reassurance that use of technologies compliant with the TEACH Act will help them meet their existing obligations under disability-discrimination law. The terms of the TEACH Act were included in draft legislation to reauthorize the Higher Education Act, issued by Senator Tom Harkin in June 2014. Since that time, there has been substantial debate over the merits of the act. Disability organizations have given their support to the proposed legislation, while some educational organizations have voiced objections, including ones relating to the perceived influence of the Access Board over determining which educational technologies could be used in teaching and learning and the impact on adoption and use of resources that contain accessibility barriers.

Subsequently, the Accessible Instructional Materials in Higher Education Act (AIM-HEA) was introduced in Congress on September 22, 2016—the result of collaboration between disability, higher education, and industry organizations to propose a new path to voluntary guidelines that balance the interests of each stakeholder group.[7] However, until dedicated guidelines are created, online learning resource producers will look to the technical accessibility standards to which other domains conform. In particular, the suite of accessibility guidelines produced by the W3C can be applied to online learning:

- The Web Content Accessibility Guidelines (WCAG), version 2.0, provides a globally recognized standard against which learning content accessibility can be evaluated.
- The Authoring Tool Accessibility Guidelines (ATAG), version 2.0, provides a reference for support for accessibility by platforms and tools that support content creation.
- The User Agent Accessibility Guidelines (UAAG) provides a reference by which tools used to access online educational resources can be assessed for accessibility support. UAAG can be applied to tools such as web browsers, PDF viewers, and media players used by learners to access content.
- The Accessible Rich Internet Applications (WAI-ARIA) specification provides a standard means to add additional accessibility information to dynamic web content and applications for learning in order to enable them to be successfully used with assistive technologies.

The Section 508 Standard, referred to by Section 508 of the Rehabilitation Act in the United States, presents a set of technical accessibility requirements for web and software applications, among other technologies. A new final rule for Section 508 was issued in January 2017, with implementation in 2018. The new 508 Standard incorporates WCAG 2.0 by reference, thereby harmonizing with other international accessibility standards.[8]

Additional general accessibility standards of relevance to online learning accessibility include the following:

- The PDF UA (Universal Accessibility) standard includes accessibility requirements for online educational resources published in PDF format.
- ISO 9241-171 2008 is a standard for software accessibility, which could be applied to nonweb educational software interfaces.
- European Standard 301-549 specifies functional accessibility requirements for ICT products and services, as well as test procedures and evaluation methodologies to assess whether requirements have been met.
- British Standard 8878 was published in 2010 as a definition of a process by which organizations can procure, create, and provide accessible web products and experiences. It could be applied by educational organizations to procurement, commissioning, and internal development processes for online learning.

Accessibility Standards and Guidelines with a Learning Focus

Following the general standards described in the previous section will help ensure that online learning resources meet a high level of accessibility in terms of content. There are also some guidelines that focus more specifically on accessibility and online learning resources, recognizing that there are some unique contextual characteristics of online learning resources that affect how accessibility is approached, most notably that their purpose is to support and evaluate the learning process.

Some organizations have issued guidelines specifically focused on online learning accessibility. For example:

- The UK Open University, where many learners study remotely, has been a pioneer in the use of learning technology and has published

a set of accessibility guidelines to support creation of online educational resources.[9]
- The Center on Accessible Distance Learning (AccessDL), part of University of Washington DO-IT (Disabilities, Opportunities, Internetworking, and Technology), shares guidance on making distance learning courses and programs accessible to both students and instructors with disabilities.[10]
- The National Center for Accessible Media (NCAM) has published guidelines on creation of accessible test items.[11]

The IMS Global Learning Consortium has been particularly active in the area of defining metadata standards for accessibility for learner and learning resource profiling, and how these profiles can be used to tailor learning content to suit a learner's accessibility needs. IMS standards include the following:

- Access for All 3.0, a public draft of which was made available in 2012 (http://www.imsglobal.org/accessibility/index.html), is the latest in a series of specifications supporting provision of metadata that describe a learner's accessibility needs and the accessibility features of a learning resource. With these two profiles, the potential exists for a capable LMS to automatically adapt a learning resource to suit a learner's needs.
- Accessible Portable Item Protocol (APIP, http://www.imsglobal.org/apip/), published in 2014, is a data model intended for the creation of test items that can be adapted to suit a learner's accessibility needs and that are also interoperable across different test systems.
- In 2002, IMS Global also published Guidelines for Developing Accessible Online Learning Applications,[12] in which the guidelines are organized by type of educational content and tool.

Current Approaches to Accessibility in Education

As ICTs become extensively integrated into the fabric of each student's educational and learning experience, it is vital that learners with disabilities be provided direct and seamless access to these technologies. As with other digital experiences, integrating accessibility considerations into the design and delivery of online learning experience is critical to an equitable experience for learners with disabilities.

Making Online Learning More Accessible

Educators employ various approaches to consider accessibility for students with disabilities in the planning, design, and use of online learning. In some cases, drivers and motivators for improvements come from policy requirements, government investigations, or litigation, but there is also a more holistic movement that sees accessibility within the larger context of enhancing access to and quality of the educational experience.

Many organizations support research and strategies focused on inclusive classroom instruction and accessible course materials. Most of this focus is on adopting a universal design for learning (UDL) approach to using technology, which is promoted as applying an evidence-based approach to designing learning experiences that can be tailored to people with a range of learning styles. This approach extends the focus of accessibility on people with disabilities to a wider recognition of human diversity and implies that basing teaching on a single approach to learning will be less effective than one that recognizes and supports different learning styles.

The Center for Applied Special Technology (CAST) published Version 2.0 of the UDL Guidelines in 2011.[13] These guidelines are structured around three principles of UDL: provide multiple means of representation, provide multiple means of action and expression, and provide multiple means of engagement. Although technology is not a prerequisite for implementing UDL, "powerful digital technologies applied using UDL principles enable easier and more effective customization of curricula for learners."[14] The University of Washington Do-IT Center provides a resource on universal design in education, including principles, training resources, and case studies.[15]

The topic of accessibility and online learning has received substantial attention from practitioners and researchers from both the technology-accessibility perspective and the educational perspective. Various online communities exist to discuss the topic of online learning accessibility, and dedicated conferences are devoted to the subject, such as the Accessing Higher Ground (AHG) conference held annually in Colorado.

Teaching Accessibility as a Digital Skill

In addition, some initiatives are under way to make accessibility a core educational competency and digital literacy skill for the next generation of digital product and service developers, designers, managers, and users. In the disciplines of computing science and digital media design, accessibility is emerging as a subject of importance, especially within the subject of human-computer interaction and user-experience design; there is a slow but growing demand for professional skills in this area, marked by the establishment of a professional society, the International Association of Accessibility Professionals (IAAP) in late 2013. In July 2015, the Teaching Accessibility initiative was launched[16] as a consortium including representatives from the technology industry, academia, and disability advocacy organizations, set up to raise awareness and activity in teaching accessibility as a skill in higher education.

However, the ubiquity of technology means that the majority of the digital content creators of the future, the people responsible for buying and managing digital products and services, are unlikely to have a formal education in computer science, so accessibility and inclusive communication need to become a core part of digital literacy. For the next generation of learners, who have grown up in a digital world and in a world that increasingly recognizes the normality of diversity, the importance of understanding and applying principles of inclusive design will become even more significant.

Barriers and Challenges in Accessibility for Online Learning

Types of Accessibility Barriers for Students and Teachers

Technology is introducing new pathways to learning—how students interact with information, how they collaborate and communicate, how they receive feedback, and how their knowledge is assessed. For learners and teachers with disabilities, technology is capable of improving existing pathways or providing pathways where none previously existed. However, despite recognition of the importance of accessibility in delivering online learning, the reality is often that online learning platforms, tools, and content contain roadblocks for students with disabilities. Online learning resources and the tools and platforms used to create and provide access to them do not meet the needs of many learners with disabilities.[17]

Some barriers are present because of an absence of additional information necessary to ensure accessibility for people with sensory impairment, for example:

- A diagram of a key process lacks a text equivalent, so the stages of the process are not available to people who cannot see the diagram.
- A video of a lecture is not captioned, so any deaf or hard-of-hearing student is prevented from accessing information in the audio portion of the video.
- A video of a teacher giving a demonstration but without oral description lacks an audio description of the visual portion of the content, so a blind or visually impaired student is prevented from learning from the visual elements of the video.
- Discussion boards, key to social interactions and communication, are not structured to allow a student requiring a screen reader to effectively navigate threaded discussions and thus create a barrier to participation for students who are blind or visually impaired.

Some barriers are present because of the visual design of the resource:

- Colored text is used to indicate a correct answer to a question in a formative test. The correct answer is not accessible to students with a visual impairment that affects their ability to distinguish the color.
- A resource is presented as a graphic of text, but it is not possible for a learner with dyslexia to change the appearance of the text to make it easier to read.

Some barriers are present because of shortcomings in the underlying behavior of the resource, in the way it supports interaction or navigation. For example:

- Interactive simulations typically require the ability to use a mouse or other equivalent pointing device to manipulate the interaction and thus leave any student with a physical impairment that limits mouse usage unable to interact and learn from the simulation.
- The complexity of navigation structure and interactions make it difficult for learners with attention deficit, short-term memory issues, or cognitive limitations to locate learning material.

Teachers, faculty, and other instructors, the authors of educational content, are also experiencing barriers to creating accessible content in a realm that is not completely under their control. Even teachers with a long history of practice in teaching students with disabilities in a traditional classroom setting may find it challenging to create curricula in a technical, remote realm with constraints imposed on them by learning-management platforms developed by third parties. The technical-standards approach of a one-size-fits-all accessible curriculum module has in some instances removed an otherwise personal and effective approach to access. For example, students and teachers who are accustomed to relying on live interpreters such as sign language or deaf-blind tactile signing to communicate must learn new means to provide the same level of communication access. Entirely new technical competencies and solutions may need to be scoped out and implemented.

Why Barriers to Accessibility Exist

Why might such barriers exist in online learning resources and tools and the platforms used to provide access to and interaction with these resources and tools? Fundamentally, digital-accessibility barriers exist because of a lack of technical quality in a resource or tool, but this quality is typically absent because of a weak or ineffectual process that led to the creation and use of the digital tool or resource in question. The weakness of the process is in failing to identify responsibility for accessibility and to support each stakeholder in meeting his or her responsibilities.

Stakeholders in online learning systems who have responsibilities include the following:

- Vendors: the people or organizations who create and make available digital platforms, tools, and resources used for online learning
- Central services: the people or organizations within an educational organization who have responsibility for procuring and administering tools that will be used for teaching and learning purposes, including organizations such as IT services, the library, learning technology centers, disability support, and web development
- Teachers: the people who select and use tools and resources supplied to construct a learning experience, which may have been provided for them by the educational organization, or which they may have chosen independently
- Staff and professional developers: people who support the development of teaching skills
- Learners: the people taking part in the learning experience, who will be using platforms, tools, and resources to learn, and who are also very likely to be creating digital content as part of a learning activity or for formative or summative assessment purposes
- Standards, policy, and legislation creators: the people, organizations, or governments that define rules and guidance applicable to online learning
- Researchers: the people who introduce new innovations in online learning or conduct research and collect empirical data on the effectiveness of learning implementations and innovations

Accessibility barriers arise when stakeholders do not recognize, understand, or have a process to enact responsibilities for accessibility. Vendors, for example, may not have considered accessibility sufficiently in the design and construction of platforms and tools, perhaps inadvertently because of lack of knowledge of accessible design, perhaps as a deliberate decision influenced by the need to meet other business goals and the perception that accessibility can legitimately be sacrificed despite the related legal obligations or market opportunities. Alternatively, accessibility may have been addressed during design and development, but to an insufficiently high level of quality or thoroughness. This may be due to factors such as a lack of accessibility knowledge and skills in the design and development team, misapplication of technical accessibility standards in an educational context, and ineffective consideration of accessibility in quality-assurance testing. The result is that while some areas of the product are highly accessible, certain user tasks may remain impossible for people with disabilities to complete. For example, consider an online assessment application that supports creation of tests with a range of question types. Some, such as free-text questions, have been designed with accessibility in mind, so that a visually impaired learner who uses a screen reader or a learner with cerebral palsy who uses a switch device to control her or his computer can independently answer the question. But if other questions, such as grid-based Likert-type ranking questions or drag-and-drop questions, have not been provided with the necessary keyboard support and accessibility information needed by screen-reader users and switch users, these question types cannot be independently used by all learners.

Central services personnel, who are likely to have responsibility for procuring or specifying systems that will support learning and teaching, may not have the process, authority, or expertise to ensure that, first, suitable accessibility provisions are included in contractual or product specifications; second, quality influences selection of third-party solutions; and third, requirements specified in contractual agreements are delivered. In addition, organizations may express accessibility demands that are vague or idiosyncratic or may fail to push back when promised accessibility is not delivered, decreasing the likelihood that the vendor will respond to any demands for more accessible features.

Teachers and learners also cannot be assumed to have in-depth knowledge of accessibility or educational tools that support accessible digital content creation or consumption. Educational resources in formats such as video, animation, or PDF can provide particular challenges for learners with disabilities when there is an absence of essential features such as synchronized captions for video or tags to provide PDF documents with structural information. Adding these features can, in many cases, take time and expert knowledge. If an educational institution places limited value on accessibility awareness as a professional teaching quality and does not recognize competence in this area, there is less motivation for teachers to develop their skills and knowledge in inclusive teaching.

If processes do not exist that identify responsibility for accessibility, if content-creation tools lack easy support for addition of accessibility features, if supporting services such as video-captioning services do not exist or are difficult to find and use, if training is not provided to teachers, and if a learning experience involves interaction with peer-generated content, learners who have disabilities are often placed at a disadvantage.

Building Responsibility to Support Accessible Outcomes

Shared Responsibility

Responsibility across stakeholder groups hinges on a unified commitment to, and practice of, accessibility.[18] Each stakeholder group, whether motivated by policy, legislation, market competition, or the value of inclusive design, shares responsibility for collaborating across stakeholder groups with a common goal of accessible outcomes for persons with disabilities. Although specific responsibilities can be delineated for each stakeholder group, a fluid and flexible understanding of the interplay across stakeholder groups is required to achieve accessible outcomes. Each stakeholder has responsibility to evaluate and adjust how his or her contributions affect the ability of other groups to achieve accessibility. Ideally, responsibilities cascade from one stakeholder to the next; each recognizes the opportunity to design, develop, or influence elements that support, interoperate with, or integrate with other stakeholder contributions.

Vendors, Providers, and Product Developers

As the stakeholder group responsible for the majority of provisions of technologies used for online learning, vendors have immediate and foundational responsibility for the accessibility of these technologies. Vendors may be commercial organizations creating products for sale to third parties, or they may be providing or adapting free and open-source products. Vendors of digital platforms, tools, and resources provide the framework, structure, or pathways for sharing accessible information, content, and communications.

Although the legal obligation for accessibility may fall on the schools and universities providing online learning, vendors may lose customers if they fail to consider accessibility. In addition, there is growing evidence that vendors who incorporate accessibility and inclusive design into their product lines increase customer loyalty and improve usability and the user experience for all users.[19]

Vendors developing products and services can exercise their responsibility by employing systematic processes or approaches to integrating existing industry standards, guidelines, and emerging trends applicable to their business that affect accessibility. The WAI-Engage Community Group has created Accessibility Responsibility Breakdown (ARB) matrices, where organizational responsibilities for meeting the Web Accessibility Initiatives Web Content Accessibility Guidelines (WCAG 2.0) success criteria are mapped to project-management, research, design, content, and development roles.[20]

Vendors' responsibility also must include an understanding of their customer base and the responsibilities that their customers in the education sector have to their users, with an avenue to adapt and change to meet that need. Vendors must recognize that an accessible platform, LMS, or tool employed by central services or teachers to post content that is accessible to learners involves more than just ensuring that their product meets website-accessibility standards. They must ensure that their products do not interfere with central services and teachers' ability to provide content that is accessible to their learners in standard accessible formats, that they provide avenues for feedback from all stakeholders regarding accessibility, and that a process exists to improve any identified obstacles to customers meeting their legal obligations for accessibility.

Central Services

Central services in schools and universities have core responsibility for the selection, integration, and support of the technology that forms the online learning experience for teachers and learners. Information technology, student services, and academic professionals all influence the procurement, development, and maintenance of learning platforms, systems of record, and learning tools and materials employed by teachers and learners.

In the central-services stakeholder group, responsibility for accessibility lies primarily in the decision-making processes. As each technology is procured, developed, or implemented, part of the decision-making process must include a review of the technology's accessibility qualities and the impact of its use on accessible learning experiences. To uphold this responsibility, institutions or schools can create internal policies that support the review process and name an authoritative entity to be in charge of the review.

In addition to a review process for technology decisions, central services hold responsibility for developing a process for other stakeholders, specifically teachers, learners, researchers, and policy makers, to bring forward an immediate or long-term accessibility issue or consideration. When educational organizations collectively make similar accessibility demands, vendors are more likely to respond in a positive manner.

Parallel and important trends are occurring to support central services in their accessibility responsibility. IT leaders and professionals are actively recognizing and responding to a need for enabling connected and integrated IT architectures based on open standards for all central services, including learning environments. Such architectures can more easily incorporate accessible and inclusive design standards and decisions, resulting in a review process that is not siloed for each implementation.[21]

Teachers

Teachers, instructors, and faculty are the authors and facilitators of online learning experiences. They have essential responsibility in the creation and implementation of learning tools and materials that convey knowledge, engage learners in discussion, and assess skills. Therefore, teachers need to be engaged in the relationship of good teaching practice to accessible online learning. This is essentially not a new responsibility for teachers—what is new is the technology. As early adopters of online learning, they are experimenting with each implementation to figure out its strengths and weaknesses in comparison to traditional instructional pathways to learning. Therefore, along with researchers and central services, teachers need to be part of the process of evaluating the effectiveness of technology tools for all learners, including those with disabilities.

Learning platforms need to engage educators in the process of creating digital environments with the flexibility to embrace UDL principles. Instructors who are able to customize the use of technology in the classroom to create learning experiences that are flexible and accessible will reduce the burden of making content accessible through remediation.[22]

To meet their responsibility, teachers and faculty may require resources to acquire digital skills that build on their teaching expertise and allow them to apply it flexibly via technology for all learners. UDL, for example, may need to become an approach to learning applied by teachers who recognize that providing flexible means to convey, engage with, and assess knowledge meets the needs of most learners. This means that staff and professional developers also have a responsibility to recognize and support teachers in acquiring knowledge and skills of inclusive teaching, so that it becomes a core professional skill expected of teaching staff.

Learners

Learners, as consumers of online learning, also have responsibility for accessible outcomes. Learners with disabilities will independently or in conjunction with assistance provided by central services or teachers be directly exposed to the accessibility options or assistive technologies available to them to access online learning and will have the responsibility of actively choosing the web browser or assistive technology that works most effectively for them. When vendors, central services, and teachers have provided robust[23] and flexible options to learners, they tend to independently find pathways to engage with content and communicate with other participants or teachers. When, however, these options provided are not sufficiently accessible to learners, they also hold responsibility for making teachers and central services aware of any obstacles to accessibility.

Researchers

Researchers with expertise in the design and development of technology and in education hold the innovative responsibility for exploring new accessible online learning pathways. Researchers exist in each and every stakeholder group. Vendors invest in research to improve their product, teachers develop new solutions to convey their materials, and very often learners are researchers for solutions. In addition, researchers can provide more empirical evidence of the effectiveness of UDL.[24]

Standards, Policy, and Legislation Creators

Standards, policy, and legislation creators hold the guiding responsibility for providing stakeholders with the framework or process for understanding their obligations toward people with disabilities, as well as the means to meet those obligations. A guiding framework that focuses on accessible outcomes without dictating implementation detail that has the potential to impede technological progress and innovations sets up pathways for equal opportunity. There are many existing accessibility standards that can be applied to online learning, for example, W3C WCAG, but as technology evolves and knowledge grows about how it can best serve people with disabilities, guidelines, standards, and their supporting resources need to be updated to reflect this evolution. The importance of process standards for accessibility in helping organizations define and apply effective processes for acquiring accessible learning technology will also grow.

Conclusion

Disruptive growth in online learning and emerging educational technologies is changing how educational content is delivered globally, and this growth provides enormous potential to reduce exclusion for people with disabilities by making learning experiences more accessible. The existing legal and standards framework provides a solid platform for educational organizations to understand and meet their obligations toward learners with disabilities, although there is potential scope for more specific accessibility requirements to be defined for online learning resources. Process standards for procurement and development of accessible technology exist but need greater adoption by educational institutions in order to increase the chances of acquiring accessible technology with minimal need for retrofitting or providing workarounds for accessibility barriers present. The wide and growing array of online learning platforms, tools, and resources presents some accessibility challenges, and research continues into improving the use of technology to enhance learning for everyone, including people with disabilities, while now there is a substantial and growing body of knowledge to support accessible design. When all stakeholders involved in the education process, from those involved in providing the experience to those doing the learning, understand and meet their responsibilities, the chances of a universally accessible educational experience are maximized.

CHAPTER 11

Who Owns Captioning?

Raja Kushalnagar

Introduction

Captions, which can also be referred to as subtitles, are the synchronized text representation of audio in audiovisuals, such as television programming. People who cannot hear the dialogue (Deaf), those who have difficulty in understanding the dialogue (hard of hearing), and those who do not know the language (hearing speakers of other languages) have the option of turning on closed captions in their preferred language and reading the text representation of the audio instead of trying to listen or understand the audio.

Around 5 percent of people worldwide, that is, 360 million, have disabling hearing loss.[1] This percentage grows with age: nearly 25 percent of those aged sixty-five to seventy-four and 50 percent of those seventy-five and older have disabling hearing loss.[2] To be accessible, the speech has to be transformed into a visual representation that can either wholly substitute for the aural representation or supplement it, depending on the viewer's hearing abilities and language fluency.

There are two main visual representations of speech. One representation is sign language, in which a human or computer-animated avatar translates the speech into signs; the signs closely parallel speech characteristics and are usually preferred by people who are conversant with sign language. Another visual representation of speech is the textual representation of the audio, which can be shown line by line, synchronized with the visual representation, or as a scrolling transcript next to the video. Both representations are considered to be accessible to people who are literate in that language. Furthermore, the subtitling can be shown either in the same language (same-language subtitling) or in a different language (foreign-language subtitling).

The term "captioning" encompasses the entire process of converting the audio content to its equivalent synchronized text representation. The democratization and resulting widespread availability of captioning technology through cheaper and easier-to-use software have enabled more people, including creators, distributors, and consumers, to create captions for audiovisuals. The multiplication of possible captioners at each stage can enhance accessibility and caption value-added features for audiovisual content if the captioners have time or money or detract from it if they do not. When a captioner between the content creator and the consumer adds captions, it is not clear how to allocate the property rights for captions. It is also not clear how the captioner's property rights in captions may interfere with the temporary monopoly awarded to the copyright owner. Under copyright law in most jurisdictions around the world, this is a technical, fact-specific legal question that is usually resolved through application of well-established precepts of copyright law; in most cases, the owner of the programming will own the copyright in the captions through ownership of the copyright in the underlying video programming, except in cases where the secondary producer adds some original, separately copyrightable element in the captions, or when the two parties specify alternate arrangements by contract. Whether that ownership operates to exclude others then depends on the applicability of copyright exceptions and limitations.

In most countries, including the United States, accessibility is viewed either as a public good or as a human right whose cost is borne by those providing products and services that must be accessible, including the government. Those costs, in turn, can be passed on through higher prices or taxes. Whenever these generalized accessibility-law mandates focus on the copyright owner's responsibilities to add captioning access, there is no real conflict between copyright and accessibility laws. On the other hand, for pragmatic reasons, these mandates usually exempt individuals and small organizations who do not have the time or money to add captioning to their content. In such cases, there is no recourse for distributors or consumers who wish to add caption access because they have no copyright ownership stake. The mandates can also be influenced by the national governments' enforcement agencies' jurisdiction. For example, in the United States, the laws and regulations for captioning audiovisuals often depend on delivery format or content type.

The scope and breadth of accessibility law continues to grow as it evolves over time to respond to societal expectations in meeting the needs of people with sensory differences. Accessibility law updates can interact with copyright-law updates, especially in connection with the copyright limitations for people with sensory differences. The impetus for change in accessibility and copyright laws often occurs because of the introduction of new understandings of human rights or changes in technology. For example, there was no need for movie accessibility for Deaf and hard-of-hearing viewers before the 1930s, when all movies were silent. The introduction of audio in the movies from 1927 onward created an abrupt accessibility gap for Deaf and hard-of-hearing viewers. The resulting need for an accessible representation of the audio component led to the introduction and evolution of closed captioning, in which captions are not visible until the viewer activates them through program interaction.

There are multiple stakeholders in the ownership and use of captions: producers, copyright holders, disabled consumers, and all consumers, and not all share the same goals. This chapter examines intellectual property issues associated with captioning.

History

The earliest movies or audiovisuals, starting from the early 1900s to the late 1920s, could display only visuals and not audio. Audio content was conveyed through intertitles: texts drawn or printed on paper, filmed, and placed between sequences of the movies. These "silent" movies were accessible to hearing and Deaf consumers, although not to blind or low-vision consumers. At the end of the 1920s, advances in movie technology could convey both video and audio, ushering in the talkies era. As a result, Deaf consumers could no longer get full access to movies, and some of them foresaw captions as a means to access the audio component.[3]

The lack of automated technology to create alternate representations of the audio meant that the process of adding captions or dubbing was a long and expensive process[4] whose cost could be recovered only if the market was large enough to justify it. In dubbing, employees add speech dialogue in the native language; in subtitling, employees type the synchronized speech dialogue in the native language and display it as captions.[5] Subtitling is distinct from captioning in that subtitling does not convey non-speech information and sounds that are important to Deaf and hard-of-hearing people, such as the absence of sound to convey suspense, a doorbell ringing, or speaker identification; this distinction between captioning for Deaf and hard-of-hearing viewers and subtitling for hearing viewers is enshrined both in practice and in the law in many countries, including the United States.[6]

Ironically, movies are far more likely to be shown with alternate audio representations in countries with small markets for their native language than in countries with large markets for their native language. The reason is that entertainment companies in small markets for the native language found it cheaper to import foreign movies and adapt them with alternate representations of audio content in their movies than it was to make their own movies; they would not likely be able to recover the cost of making high-quality movies. Producers felt it was safer to import movies and to dub, subtitle, or caption these movies, as the cost of the dubbing or subtitling could be spread over the entire pool of consumers in the country. On the other hand, in large countries, such as the United States, the entertainment companies had a large-enough market to support the cost of making movies in their native language, and the market that needed captions or subtitles was far smaller. Without a legal mandate or economic rationale, entertainment companies would not create accessible movies or audiovisuals in large markets for those who cannot hear or understand the audio component.

When television was introduced in the late 1930s, there was no provision for captioning or subtitling at all, whether edited or in real time. There was little awareness of accessibility needs until the passage of the Universal Declaration of Human Rights at the United Nations in 1948. Over the next two decades, the view of accessibility for movies and television programming as a public good or human right gained traction in most countries. The continuing evolution of accessibility resulted in official government support and funding of captioning for movies, such as the Captioned Films for the Deaf program[7] in the United States by the 1950s. The movies were made accessible by adding text etched onto film print and circulated among Deaf clubs and social groups. These films were captioned with the explicit permission of the content or copyright owner and were funded by the U.S. government for the benefit of Deaf consumers' access to theater shows.[8] The success of captioned movies did not carry over to television right away, but the increased social expectations from the film-captioning law and the presence of captioning agencies accelerated the process. By the 1970s, television producers were able to create open-captioned versions of television programs, where the text that conveyed the audio content of a program was visible to all viewers of the program.[9] Soon thereafter, they were able to develop techniques to display the captions as closed captioning in the United States and as teletext in many European countries.[10]

In 1980, closed-captioning encoding on television was standardized as a protocol by the government broadcasting regulatory agency in the United States, the Federal Communications Commission (FCC). Soon afterward, the encoding of closed captioning (also called subtitles) on television was standardized as the World System Teletext protocol by the broadcasting regulatory agencies in many European countries.[11]

In the United States, at first, captioning services were available only from two not-for-profit entities, WGBH's Caption Center and the National Captioning Institute. The relatively high cost of captioning services initially limited the growth of available hours and types of captioned television. To help spur captioning growth, funding partnerships were established between the public and private sectors. In a natural extension of the captioned-films program, the United States Department of Education awarded grants to caption news, sports, children's, prime-time, and daytime programming, which resulted in volume and variety of captioned programs. Over time, funding also came from other sources, including the broadcast and cable television networks, foundations, and advertisers.

As the marketplace grew, so did the emergence of for-profit captioning agencies, which have vastly increased the depth and expertise of the market in providing captioning services and coverage. This in turn led to the growth of captioning throughout the 1980s and into the early 1990s, resulting in nearly universal captioning of traditional over-the-air broadcast television on a voluntary basis.

In 1993, there was a dramatic leap in audiovisual accessibility in the United States when the federal government mandated closed captioning on all television sets with screen size over thirteen inches through the Television Decoder Circuitry Act of 1990. The act mandated, as of July 1, 1993, "that apparatus designed to receive television pictures broadcast simultaneously with sound be equipped with built-in decoder circuitry designed to display closed-captioned television transmissions when such apparatus is manufactured in the United States or imported for use in the United States, and its television picture screen is 13 inches or greater in size." Before the act, over one million closed-caption set-top decoders and specially equipped televisions were sold during the first decade of closed captioning, while over twenty million new televisions with built-in captions were sold in the United States during the first year of the mandate. A decade later, virtually every TV in America had the capability to display captions. Captions had made the leap from obscure to the mainstream, visible and recognized on televisions everywhere in the United States, from homes to airports, eating establishments, and public spaces, virtually anywhere in America television programming was watched or exhibited. The cycle was repeated for online media in the early years of the twenty-first century; again, it took about a decade for the laws to catch up through the passage of the Twenty-First Century Communications and Video Accessibility Act[12] in the United States.

Accessibility Law

In most countries, accessibility has consistently been regarded as a public good the market cannot provide; therefore, the cost of providing accessibility must be borne by the entities providing the products and services, including the government. Those costs, in turn, may ultimately be passed through to other consumers in the form of higher prices or to the public at large through taxes.

The rights of people with disabilities at the UN can be viewed as an indicator of the state of accessibility laws in many countries worldwide. Over the past several decades, the UN has passed several international legal agreements on disabilities. The goal of these agreements is to ensure equalization of opportunities for people with disabilities. The agreements over time reveal a gradual sharpening of the focus on their rights, including the right to audiovisual access.

The earliest agreement on disabilities focused on those with mental retardation in 1971,[13] followed by agreement on rights for persons with disabilities in 1975.[14] The UN General Assembly proclaimed 1981 the International Year of Disabled Persons and called for aspirational programs of action. Subsequently, the General Assembly proclaimed 1983 to 1992 the Decade of Disabled Persons, during which governments and organizations could implement activities recommended in the World Programme of Action Concerning Disabled Persons, culminating in the 1994 Vienna Declaration and Programme of Action, which was endorsed by both the General Assembly and the UN Standard Rules on the Equalization of Opportunities for Persons with Disabilities. The Standard Rules represents a strong moral obligation and a political commitment of governments to take appropriate action to ensure equalization of opportunities; the ideal is full equalization of, participation in, and enjoyment of all human rights by persons with disabilities. Toward this goal, the Standard Rules specifies accommodation models and rules for political decision making. Standard Rule 5 recommends the use of appropriate technologies to provide access to spoken information. In 2006, the UN passed the Convention on the Rights of Persons with Disabilities (CRPD), which included several specific regulations and mandates for Deaf and hard-of-hearing consumers. In particular, Article 9 covers captioning for Deaf and hard-of-hearing consumers through the statement that "States Parties shall take appropriate measures to ensure to persons with disabilities access, on an equal basis with others, to . . . information, communications and other services, including electronic services and emergency services. . . . States Parties shall also take appropriate measures to . . . promote access for persons with disabilities to new information and communications technologies and systems, including the Internet."

Audiovisual captioning grew rapidly in the 1990s and the early years of the twenty-first century in developed countries. such as the United States and the United Kingdom, because of the early adoption of accessibility and captioning laws and technical advances. The success of these acts led to the adoption of similar accessibility laws by other countries. Many countries implemented their accessibility laws through legislation, evolution of human rights, or directives and ordinances by regulatory agencies. For example, in the United Kingdom, legislation has been backed by a national regulatory agency (Ofcom), which has resulted in mandated levels of captioned content on free-to-air and subscription television close to 100 percent.

There has been no clear pattern in which countries have adopted mandates for the production and dissemination of accessible audiovisuals other than that most have been developed countries, presumably because they have the legal and technical infrastructure that the Deaf and hard-of-hearing communities can tap into. Most countries worldwide are slowly adding rules or regulations for adding captions to audiovisuals, and citizens in these countries have limited access to audiovisuals.

For example, Brazil has a strong and robust legal and technical infrastructure, but it is a large developing country with a population of over 200 million people, of whom about 2.5 percent, that is, about 5 million, are Deaf or hard of hearing or have recognized, serious hearing impairments. In 1989, the federal government passed the Equal Opportunities for People with Disabilities Act, which preceded the U.S. Americans with Disabilities Act.[15] Many Latin American countries, such as Costa Rica, followed suit in passing similar disability laws.[16] Brazil's law required an increasing percentage of programs to be captioned, and subsequent amendments added coverage for Internet streaming, cable programs, and, in some cases, intranet programs must be captioned in Portuguese, and mandated quality to be 98.5 percent or above for real-time captions. At first some broadcasters embraced captioning as a way to reach an underserved sector of the population, but the majority tried to ignore the law. After some time, the Deaf community organized and began putting pressure on broadcasters and bringing complaints to the government to make captioning universal. As the Brazil example shows, there is a trend toward harmonization of standards through liberal borrowing of policies and guidelines worldwide. This helps not only in regard to cost effectiveness but also in delivering access to captioning.

Another significant barrier to audiovisuals can be found in the form of digital rights management (DRM) and technological protection measures (TPMs). Articles 11 and 12 of the WIPO Copyright Treaty (WCT) and Articles 18 and 19 of the World Intellectual Property Organization (WIPO) Performances and Phonograms Treaty (WPPT) have made it possible for member states to oblige the setting in place of a DRM regime. DRM regimes are undesirable because they grant copyright owners digital rights that go far beyond property rights that are the subject matter of copyright. DRM regimes also extend control to ideas and works in the public domain. Furthermore, since DRMs can trace users, they raise serious concerns of data protection and privacy. Today, DRMs are usually exercised by intermediaries, such as distributors, and not necessarily the authors of works. Hence, many times, authors are unable to access their own works in different formats or by using different devices because of the DRMs placed by the distributor.

However, the trend of providing more accessibility mandates or rights for people with disabilities has not translated into a corresponding increase in funding by most countries. Although most national governments often fund the technological development of captions when a new medium emerges, they do not typically increase the funding for growth in audiovisual content through broadcast or through the Internet on a proportional basis. Similarly, most national governments limit the caption mandate for content producers to large producers and do not include individuals or small providers because they typically do not have the financial or technical resources.

In the United States, accessibility mandates are embedded in a variety of federal laws, primarily the Americans with Disabilities Act, which makes "places of public accommodation" responsible for making their premises accessible, and the Rehabilitation Act, which makes the federal government and entities receiving federal funding responsible for making their programs and services accessible. Similarly, the Telecommunications Act of 1996[17] and the Twenty-First Century Communications and Video Accessibility Act of 2010 assign captioning responsibility to content creators in the video-programming creation and distribution chain. During the early days of captioning, the federal government was the primary funder for development of captioning processes and the resulting creation of captions for television and cinematic programming, with the explicit permission of the program owner. As the technology matured, the captioning costs were increasingly viewed as a social good that was to be covered by the program owner rather than the government. These mandates, however, do not take into account recent advances in captioning technology, such as crowd sourcing or automatic speech recognition, that enable third parties and consumers to add accessibility themselves. The captioning rights of third parties and consumers conflict with the rights of the audiovisual content owner, primarily under copyright law. In general, though, it is not easy to separate the layered enhancements of a creator's work by other parties, whether known or unknown. Normally, the separation between creators is clearly allowable only when explicit licensing and permissions are granted. Nor are there clear precedents for a successful claim of any kind of fair-use exemption for an individual or group to alter a third party's content in order to make it accessible to people with disabilities.

Copyright Law

Copyright law grants a temporary monopoly on the property rights of the content to the author of a creative expression and derivatives thereof, so as to provide an incentive for the author not only to create the expression but also to make it widely available to the public. Copyright law can be regarded as an adjunct to disability law that encourages authors to make their creative works accessible to society through property-like rights and market forces. In the United States, this premise is embedded in the progress clause of the

Constitution, which permits Congress to enact copyright legislation only for the purpose of "promot[ing] the Progress of Science and useful Arts."

In the United States, copyright law entitles the copyright holder to an enumerated set of exclusive rights. Copyright protection extends to "original works of authorship fixed in any tangible medium of expression" (17 U.S.C. § 102(a)). The primary section of copyright law is codified at Title 17 of the U.S. Code, specifically, Sections 106 and 106(2), which grant exclusive rights in copyrighted works. Section 106 provides that, subject to Sections (limitations) 107 through 122, the owner of a copyright under this title has the exclusive rights to reproduce it, prepare derivative works, distribute copies, and perform or display. If it were not for the limitations, the copyright owner's "monopoly" would be a hardship on persons whose use of the works Congress deems desirable as a function of its constitutional empowerment to "promote the Progress of Science." The laws relevant to the growth and acceptance of captioning and video description include the TV Decoder Circuitry Act (1990), the Telecommunications Act (1996) and the Twenty-First Century Communications and Video Accessibility Act (2010), the Digital Millennium Copyright Act (1998), and the Chafee Amendment (Section 121 of the Copyright Act, 1996).

Through one lens, the very existence of laws that require accessibility for copyrighted works suggests that copyright laws do not completely serve the needs of society. In other words, the exclusive rights granted to the creators of websites, videos, and books stimulate so little activity to make those works accessible to people with disabilities, even though doing so is a right exclusively afforded the copyright holder, that the government must step in with prescriptive measures.

Furthermore, in today's globalized world, copies are sold worldwide, but copyright and attached limitations are national. For example, U.S. copyright law has no extraterritorial effect. The Berne Convention for the Protection of Literary and Artistic Works vests the exclusive right to authorize the reproduction of such works in their authors. Authors may and almost invariably do transfer most of those rights to their publishers. However, the Berne Convention permits states to enact statutory exceptions. It provides as follows: "It shall be a matter for legislation in the countries of the Union to permit the reproduction of such works in certain special cases, provided that such reproduction does not conflict with a normal exploitation of the work and does not unreasonably prejudice the legitimate interests of the author."

This Berne Convention clause acknowledges the fact that there are classes of people whose ability to enjoy protected works is hindered because of copyright protection, because the work, as published, is inaccessible to them. Making a previously inaccessible work accessible is consistent with the normal exploitation of that work. As long as the statutory exceptions ensure that the reproductions do not unreasonably prejudice the interests of copyright holders, these reproductions are permissible under the Berne Convention. However, parties to the Berne Convention are states, and individuals do not derive rights from international treaties.

The Berne Convention, along with the World International Property Organization Copyright Treaty, forms the basis for international copyright protection. It requires all participating states not to treat authors from other states worse than their own authors. In the context of copyright exceptions, it is acceptable, though not required, to enact such exceptions and thereby in effect to expropriate copyright in special cases, as long as the normal exploitation of authors' work remains the same and their interests are not prejudiced. These exceptions permit the production of accessible materials without recourse to copyright holders. That is, they prevent copyright holders from asserting their statutory monopoly to prohibit the reproduction of the objects of their copyright in alternative formats. It is clear, though, that countries that do not enact such statutory exceptions do not violate their obligations under international law.

In all countries where statutory exceptions have been enacted, these countries have kept the exceptions narrow so that permissible reproductions do not hurt the interests of copyright holders. As a result, the legislation tends to be very specific about the institutions authorized to undertake permitted reproductions, and care is taken to permit such activities by bodies conducted on a not-for-profit basis, or designated government agencies, or specially registered agencies with a licensing authority.[18]

Currently, most exceptions or limitations to copyright law have been for print accessibility and are typically national in scope. For example, in the United States, the Chafee Amendment permits distribution of print-accessible materials to blind and low-vision consumers. However, the amendment does not provide access to print-accessible materials for a library for the blind outside the United States or a blind reader outside the United States. Therefore, accessible copies are often limited to residents within the national boundaries. In the absence of international agreements, someone who has made an accessible copy in one country may not be entitled to provide a copy to someone in another country.

In response to the need for an international agreement on cross-border sharing of print-accessible resources, the individual country members of the World Intellectual Property Organization (WIPO) met in Marrakesh, Morocco, in 2010. The goal was to develop a treaty that addressed the need for a comprehensive transnational solution that balanced the needs of print-disabled consumers and copyright holders of print materials. The resulting Marrakesh Treaty provides minimum standards for limitations and exceptions regarding the making and distribution of accessible-format works and allows for cross-border sharing of these formats. Furthermore, the treaty permits authorized entities to import and export accessible-format works for beneficiary persons, allowing entities to share resources. In addition to international treaties, many developed countries also have comprehensive accessibility laws, including the United States, which has the Chafee Amendment, the fair-use doctrine, and exceptions to the rules governing import and export, but if another country does not allow export of accessible print materials, print-disabled consumers in the United States will not be able to access it. The Marrakesh Treaty indicates that there is a worldwide consensus on balancing the needs of print-disabled consumers and copyright holders by permitting cross-border sharing of accessible print for print-disabled consumers. The social and technical trends that led to the Marrakesh Treaty suggest that there can be significant support for a similar initiative at the national and international levels for creation and sharing of accessible media, for example, captioned media, for auditory-disabled consumers, including those who are Deaf or hard of hearing. In addition to national legislation, there is also a need for international agreements to assure international sharing and access to cross-border repositories of accessible copies. This is vital for third-party providers of captioning, consumers, and those who provide services to them

The Intersection of Copyright Law and Accessibility Law on Captioning

As noted earlier, in most countries, the owner of the video likely will own the copyright in the captions by virtue of his or her ownership of the copyright in the underlying video, except where the entity that adds the captions adds some original, separately copyrightable element in the captions, or if the parties specify some different arrangement by contract. In all countries that have signed on to the international copyright conventions, the copyright ownership vests automatically when a video is created. Whether that ownership operates to exclude others then revolves around the applicability of exceptions and limitations.

Generally, copyright vests in the author of the audiovisual, but audiovisual companies usually enter into agreements with the authors whose work they disseminate that provide, among other things, for the transfer of copyright in the audiovisual to the company on certain terms. To the extent that those terms require a license to be granted both by the author and the company, the company can and mostly does act as an intermediary for consumers. The application process can become very complex in cases where the original company transfers those rights after mergers or if they are wound up and the rights are not disposed of in a manner that makes it possible to trace the current holder, especially in developing countries. There is no limitation or exception to the copyright act for adding captions to copyrighted content.

Economic Incentives

Despite the tension between accessibility through captioning and copyright law, there are possible economic incentives that can promote third-party captioning. Copyright law in the United States serves as an incentive for authors and distributors to create new works by protecting their ability to economically exploit the works after the fact. On the other hand, they have long been resistant to calls from the Deaf and hard-of-hearing community to provide captions on the grounds that doing so is too expensive and uneconomical. This resistance is likely to continue as the circle of copyright holders expands beyond video producers to include individuals and small businesses with fewer resources and potentially limited legal captioning requirements leveraging the Internet to distribute video.

Finally, technological developments are poised not only to lower the cost of captions but also to allow the extraction of revenue from captions for nonaccessibility purposes. Captions can provide high temporal resolution, finely grained content information, and searchable metadata about videos.

This additional information can facilitate search-engine optimizations that funnel more viewers to a video and inclusion of more accurate and more profitable targeted advertising alongside videos. Captions can also be used to facilitate searching and provision of television news archives for use by journalists, researchers, librarians, students, and others.

These trends will likely create new financial conflicts between video distributors and copyright holders. Ironically, copyright holders have used captions of videos owned by others in order to help facilitate parody or other fair uses. For example, popular comedy shows like *The Daily Show* and *The Colbert Report* have been using closed-caption indexes to enable writers to search for particular keywords and to cue videos to the proper spot by using the timing data included with captions.[19]

Solutions for Copyright Versus Accessibility

There are multiple approaches to resolving the conflict between copyright law and accessibility law—for example, copyright exemptions, fair use, or a captioning mandate backed with funds. In regard to legal mandates with funding, in the early years, the government was the primary funder for captioning, and ownership was rarely an issue because copyright owners generally did not have to pay for captioning. However, over time, as accessibility mandates moved the funding mechanism from the public realm to the private realm, the exclusivity provided by copyright law became a significant barrier, and funding creators is no longer easy to justify. The trend toward smaller, more personal production, distribution, and consumption has also added multiple layers of responsibility.

These multiple layers of responsibility make it harder to identify who can give permission to add captions or related accessibility features, such as video descriptions, commentary, subtitles, ASL, language dubs, and script rewrites, even under the fair-use exception. It also becomes harder to identify the parties who can give permission to extract and use the audiovisual metadata index, search, locate, archive, repurpose, resell, and sell ads.

In regard to copyright accessibility for audiovisuals, there is no accessibility-specific exemption or limitation in U.S. law, unlike print accessibility. Even for print accessibility, the Copyright Act's Chafee Amendment limits exclusive rights only for certain types of books, for certain types of entities, and for certain types of disabilities.

Often one entity in the chain might want to assign exclusive rights in the accessibility feature to someone else in an effort to avoid the mandate or attempt to make some other party responsible for compliance. For example, in the United States, video distributors attempted to avoid some terms of the Federal Communications Commission's captioning rules by arguing that complying with them would violate the exclusive rights of the copyright in the video, which was generally held by some other party. The question of ownership can arise in negotiations between the copyright owner and a contracted accessibility provider, such as the captioning company.

Similarly, other exceptions to national copyright laws could be used. For example, in the United States, the fair-use exception allows creators of new content to make certain types of uses of a copyrighted work without infringing the exclusive rights of the copyright holder. The potential creator of new content does not have to ask permission to engage in fair use, so, if copyright holders cannot be contacted or identified, permission is not required. On the other hand, invoking the fair-use exception continues to be uncertain because it is a multifactor test, and there is no case directly on point for captions. In a related accessibility case for print accessibility, the HathiTrust case,[20] a federal court held that books could be digitized, in part to provide accessibility to blind and low-vision consumers, which strongly supports the fair-use doctrine in the United States for accessibility. One of the major factors considered is the purpose and character of fair use: accessibility purposes are considered to be fair use, even though they are not clearly transformative. The court in the HathiTrust case noted that books were not transformed merely by being in alternate formats. Another factor is the effect of the market. Typically, the market for closed captions that copyright holders are interested in serving is very small. If this was a market that copyright holders were strongly compelled to serve and they felt that they wanted to do so anyway, most copyright holders would be incentivized to add captioning. Collectively, these factors strongly suggest that captioning would fall under fair use, but unfortunately there has been no case law on this issue. A further caveat about using the fair-use exemption is that many countries do not have this kind of exemption or an equivalent.

The tension between copyright law and accessibility mandates and the absence of a clear exception can also affect third parties, such as consumers or libraries. They are neither subject to an accessibility mandate nor hold the copyright, so they cannot make it accessible without being held liable under copyright law. This kind of tension between copyright law and accessibility mandates can also affect intermediaries who make or run accessibility programs, for example, those who provide crowd-sourced captioning and description systems. These intermediaries could be held secondarily liable for inducing or contributing to copyright infringement. In general, the exceptions and limitations in copyright law usually obviate any questions of ownership that might arise in each of these situations.

Conclusion

Although national copyright laws strive to balance the rights and interests of various stakeholder groups in society, copyright limitations tend to be very conservative and are updated very slowly, if at all. Instead, national accessibility laws and mandates have been far more effective in making audiovisuals accessible to people who are Deaf or hard of hearing. However, national accessibility laws are not well equipped to handle the question of ownership of captions by third parties and consumers. It is becoming urgent to address this issue of caption ownership because more and more consumers and third-party providers are able to add captions themselves through new technology approaches, such as crowd sourcing and automatic speech recognition. Fair use under copyright law could be extended to handle accessibility through legislation, which might be necessary in the context of the anti-circumvention measures of the Digital Millennium Copyright Act, which does not accommodate fair use.

Technical advances in search and indexing capabilities raise the possibility that captions can have some independent, non-accessibility use, primarily related to data aggregation and searching. For example, a provider of streaming audiovisual content could use captions and transcribed descriptions of a video as metadata against which to sell ads or optimize search functionality. Similarly, reporters could use captions of video to search for particular clips, perform data analysis, and so on, while services could use captions to automatically generate foreign-language translations. In each of these cases, where these features can result in external revenue possibilities, content and caption owners' financial interests could compel them to raise questions about ownership of the accessible content. For example, copyright owners and caption producers would have to analyze the fair-use calculus as they sought to apportion the resulting benefits among themselves.

If the economic benefit flowing from external benefits is less than the cost of creating the accessibility feature, an audiovisual's copyright holder might not add captions even if he or she could extract substantial revenue from ad sales or search-engine optimization. To address this issue, it is important to apportion responsibility and ownership in a way that maximizes accessibility while minimizing overall costs and taking advantage of the positive externalities. If the economic benefit from the external benefits is greater than the cost of providing the accessibility feature, then economic incentives should make it easier to promote equal access nationwide. A holistic approach that considers both copyright and accessibility law is vital to support copyright holders' stake in captioning.

National and international agencies need to provide an effective balance between copyright owners' interests as reflected in copyright laws and Deaf and hard-of-hearing users' interests as reflected in accessibility laws. Given that technology changes rapidly, copyright-related acts such as copyright limitations and exceptions should be format and technically neutral. Conversely, accessibility laws should take into account externalities that can influence a copyright owner's captioning access incentives. Finally, because copyright laws are national, the stakeholders from each country should be encouraged to work with their international counterparts to promote and manage the captions for the benefit of all stakeholders worldwide, toward the goal that all citizens should be able to participate in society and access information, whether through print or audiovisuals.

CHAPTER 12

Information Privacy and Security as a Human Right for People with Disabilities

Jonathan Lazar, Brian Wentz, and Marco Winckler

Introduction

Providing personal data online is generally a requirement for participation in the information society in which we live today. Many users share personal data with other people or organizations via a multitude of applications, such as social networks, e-commerce websites, recruitment portals, online insurance and banking applications, and e-government web portals, to mention a few.[1] Often, people have no choice but to share some data if they want to access services provided by such applications. The data typically include personal identification information (including name, address, document IDs, and e-mail address) and also might include a personally identifiable aspect of users' identity (such as an IP address or geolocation). Personal data are diverse, but they can be characterized as being data owned by me, about me, directed toward me, sent or posted by me, experienced by me, and relevant to me.[2] Therefore, owning or having access to someone's personal data provides a means for discovering the person's identity, which has direct implications for privacy. Although some data are more sensitive in terms of data protection than others, any personal data may be perceived as sensitive if they are combined with other data, even though any one element may not be seen as sensitive in isolation.

Collecting and sharing information about others is part of human nature, but problems of privacy can arise when personal data are collected or disclosed without proper consent, potentially affecting some aspect of people's lives, for example, damage to their reputation, material and financial losses, or preventing people from access to rights, opportunities, and benefits they deserve. People with disabilities often rely on technology devices to compensate for their disabilities. However, this reliance on technical devices may mean that more data are being collected about them than about the typical citizen (without their knowledge), or that they are more susceptible to threats related to privacy and security. Furthermore, if data are collected without an individual's knowledge that document that an individual has a disability, this information, a violation of his or her privacy, could potentially be used to discriminate against the individual. This chapter will start by defining the terms "privacy" and "security," relating the topics to human rights, and will then provide a detailed discussion of the implications of information-technology privacy and security for people with disabilities.

Security and Privacy

This book focuses on frontiers at the intersection of technology accessibility and human rights for people with disabilities. In many ways, the topic of information security and privacy is a frontier because both the legal side and the technical side are unsolved, so to speak. The topics of security and privacy are complex for the general population, not just for people with disabilities. When new security features are introduced, they are often hard to use and in fact may not actually improve security. Breaches of personal data continue to make the news headlines. Many countries do not have adequate data-privacy protections enshrined in policy or law. And when it comes to information privacy and security for people with disabilities, there is not a great base of literature. There are not yet existing best practices that others should be encouraged to follow. It is a complex area that is in no way solved or close to being solved.

It is important to note that there are two closely related topics: privacy and security. Dourish and Anderson, in their seminal 2006 article, describe some of the differences:

> In the information-technology domain, security describes, first, the ways in which information systems may be vulnerable to a range of conscious attacks in which the effectiveness of a system or the integ-

rity of its operation might be compromised and, second, the technical countermeasures that can be used to detect, respond to, and protect a system from these attacks. Privacy, on the other hand, is something of a catch-all term that refers primarily to the ways in which individuals or organizations might lose control of access to information and to individuals. It embodies a number of different aspects, including solitude (the right to be left alone), confidentiality (the right to control one's own information), and autonomy (the right to control self-preservation).[3]

Dourish and Anderson discuss security in terms of attacks on information systems. However, because our focus is on humans (often referred to in human-computer interaction as "users"), our discussion of security will focus instead on how users help protect against attacks. The typical approaches for users are to use some form of authentication—passwords, security questions, human-interaction proofs, or biometrics (all discussed in later sections of this chapter). All of these allow users to demonstrate that they indeed are who they claim to be and therefore should be allowed access to sensitive data.

Designing for security is inherently challenging because unlike usability, which no one is actually working against, there are always people who are trying to hack existing security features, and therefore the security landscape is always changing. The ever-changing security requirements make the situation more complex and confusing for users. Furthermore, users are rarely focused on security. A user's goal is to complete a task, and security just gets in the way of the user attempting to complete a task. Users are typically focused on their own goals, not on the goal of keeping an information system secure.[4] Security features need to be secure enough to avoid being compromised, but at the same time, they need to be usable enough that users can successfully use them.[5] The term "usable security" is often discussed, under which security can be implemented in a way that users find easy to use, so that they do not give up and do workarounds that are inherently insecure (such as writing their passwords, which they no longer can remember, on a sticky note placed on their display monitor or under their keyboard).

From a user's point of view, security and privacy are very closely related because the user's goal is keeping his or her data private, and security (whether in the form of passwords, biometrics, or something else) is simply the mechanism for keeping the data private. For that reason, the two topics are often discussed together, and in the user's mind, they often are considered the same, since a breach in security will inevitably lead to a breach in privacy. Although there is a complex relationship between privacy and security, in this chapter, we will not delve into that complex relationship and will simply be viewing security as a mechanism for supporting privacy.

Privacy and Security as a Human Right

The UN Convention on the Rights of Persons with Disabilities (CRPD) has two articles, Articles 22 and 31, that specifically relate to privacy of data and information for persons with disabilities. Article 22 states, "States Parties shall protect the privacy of personal, health and rehabilitation information of persons with disabilities on an equal basis with others." Article 31 states that there should be compliance "with legally established safeguards, including legislation on data protection, to ensure confidentiality and respect for the privacy of persons with disabilities." Combined with other articles of the CRPD focusing on technology accessibility (Articles 9 and 21, discussed in other chapters throughout this book), these articles of the CRPD clearly provide a basis for describing information-technology privacy and security (as a technical mechanism for ensuring privacy) as a human right. Even before the advent of digital information technology and the Internet, privacy as a concept was present in many older human rights documents, such as the International Covenant on Civil and Political Rights (ICCPR). Article 17 (subsection 1) of the ICCPR states that "no one shall be subjected to arbitrary or unlawful interference with his privacy, family, home or correspondence, nor to unlawful attacks on his honour and reputation." The Universal Declaration of Human Rights (UDHR), proclaimed by the United Nations in 1948, is often considered the core foundation of human rights law, and it includes the same text in Article 12 as that in Article 17 of the ICCPR.

There are many trends that increase the amount of personal data being collected and stored in large databases. These trends include the increased use of sensors, more people shopping on e-commerce, mobile-phone apps that often collect personal data, and the full computerization of health-care records. As more personal data continue to be collected and stored on electronic data systems, this human right to information privacy and security is critical for persons with disabilities.[6] Data are being collected in many ways about all individuals, sometimes in an automated manner and sometimes by an individual providing her or his information. These data are stored, shared, and compared with other existing data, often to create profiles of individuals.[7] People with disabilities should have the ability to control the data about themselves, especially because (as discussed later in the chapter) information about an individual's disability status may potentially be used to discriminate against that individual. What happens if data collected, stored, and shared are incorrect? How can individuals with disabilities control those data and ensure that they are corrected? The existing work on privacy and security of data for people with disabilities is limited, but this is a growing area that needs more attention.

Information-Technology Security for People with Disabilities

There are many challenges to privacy and security of data and information technology for people with disabilities. The challenges can be illustrated with a common question asked by university students who are studying the topic of computer interface design for people with disabilities. Students often ask why a drive-up automated teller machine (ATM) needs to have an option for blind users (braille or audio). A blind user will not be driving a car, right? This question and the misunderstanding of the technology need help illustrate multiple points about privacy and security for people with disabilities because there are multiple reasons for having accessibility features on a drive-up ATM. The first reason is that often, there will be a blind person as a passenger in the car who wants to use the ATM machine. If the ATM is not accessible for blind users, the blind user will be forced to give his or her personal identification number (PIN) to another individual, potentially compromising both privacy and security. Imagine that the blind individual is in a taxicab. Would the blind individual want to provide a PIN to the taxicab driver? Of course not. The blind passenger in the taxicab will want to interact with the machine independently. There is another reason drive-up ATMs should have braille and audio options. There should be one standard ATM with accessibility features rather than multiple ATMs, some for drive-up, some for walk-up, some with accessibility features, and some without accessibility features, which cost more for manufacturers (because they must build multiple versions) and add unpredictability for blind users, who are never sure which type of ATM they will be approaching and whether it will have accessibility features. Inaccessibility of banking applications poses challenges for people with disabilities because the privacy and security of banking data are so important. Branham and Kane describe how blind individuals who are in a committed relationship sometimes have their partner perform online banking tasks on their behalf because the banking applications are inaccessible.[8]

Various forms of information-technology security often pose great challenges for people with disabilities. The most common forms of information-technology security include passwords, security questions, human-interaction proofs, token-based authentication (such as bank cards and smart cards), and biometrics. Generally, the authentication mechanisms can be organized into three categories: something you know (knowledge-based mechanisms, such as passwords or security questions), something you have (token-based mechanisms, such as a smart card or chip-based card), or something you are (biometric-based mechanisms, such as fingerprints or voice recognition). Each type of authentication method poses challenges for people with specific disabilities. A 2015 study illustrated the frustrations of users with visual impairments when trying to use and verify authentication techniques commonly used on web interfaces.[9] Typical password-formatting techniques that might cause mild frustration to most users can create instances of extreme frustration and wasted time for users with disabilities.

The most common form of authentication is password-based, requiring a login ID (username) and a password. Passwords are generally accessible for people who are blind, people who are Deaf, and people with motor impairments. However, as passwords are increasingly required to be more complex (a minimum number of characters and a mix of uppercase and lowercase letters, numbers, and symbols), they pose challenges for people with cognitive impairments (due both to remembering the complex password and the complexity in data entry) and perhaps for people with motor impairments, especially those using primarily speech recognition.[10] Security questions (such as "What was your first street address as a child?" or "What was the name of the first school that you attended?") pose similar challenges for people with cognitive or motor impairments. Graphic passwords, where users must either recognize a series of graphic objects or select points on a screen, might be easier for some users, but they are inherently inaccessible for blind users, and despite the visual strengths of people with Down syndrome, the graphic passwords are more difficult than traditional alphanumeric passwords for them.[11]

Human-interaction proofs (HIPs) are a form of authentication that is particularly challenging for people with disabilities. HIPs are most commonly seen in the form of a Completely Automated Public Turing Test to Tell Computers and Humans Apart (CAPTCHA). Visual CAPTCHAs often appear as letters or numbers that are distorted, the idea being that humans can interpret them, whereas computers cannot. In reality, CAPTCHAs are hard for most users to interpret (although people with Down syndrome seem to complete visual CAPTCHAs at a very high rate of success,[12] unlike other people with cognitive impairments). Of course, visual CAPTCHAs are inherently inaccessible for people who are blind or low vision, and many websites (but hardly enough) offer audio CAPTCHAs, where there is distorted audio of letters or numbers. Although these audio CAPTCHAs may be theoretically accessible for blind users, in reality, they are often very hard to complete, with success rates below 50 percent for blind users.[13] For instance, one website has an audio CAPTCHA where distorted words are presented in audio, but the user is expected to enter only the first letter of each word, although the instructions do not indicate that in any way, making the CAPTCHA virtually impossible to use. The reality is that most users, with or without disabilities, do not like CAPTCHAs.

The increasing use of two-factor authentication also remains a challenge. Token authentication, such as smart cards and chip cards, may pose the most challenges for people with motor impairment, who may have trouble physically manipulating them into devices.[14]

Biometrics are increasing in popularity. However, it is important to note that usually, people with at least one type of disability are shut out of each type of biometric. For example, blind people can interact with fingerprint recognition and voice recognition just fine as long as the prompts (for where and when to place a finger or speak) are accessible. Retina or iris scanning, on the other hand, is likely to be problematic for blind people, who may have deformed or missing eyes or no ability to open their eyelids. Similarly, voice recognition will work for most users, except for Deaf users who may not use speech as their primary communication method. Fingerprint scanning can work for both blind and deaf users as long as the prompts are accessible; however, it may pose challenges for people with motor impairments, who are unable to place their fingers in the proper location or may have fingers deformed or missing.

Inaccessible security features will lead to one of two scenarios: either the user with a disability will be unable to access the various information, applications, and opportunities, or, toward the goal of accessing that information, the user with a disability will allow another person to complete the security process on his or her behalf, in the process potentially compromising security and definitely compromising independence. For all these reasons, people with disabilities are often concerned about privacy and security in the context of eavesdropping, passwords, social media, and technical support.[15]

Information Privacy for People with Disabilities

People with disabilities are rightfully concerned about the privacy of their personal information for a number of reasons. This section discusses some of the emerging topics of interest in information privacy for people with disabilities: (1) privacy of disability status, (2) privacy of geolocation data, and (3) privacy policies and terms of service.

Privacy of Disability Status

Whether someone has a disability is often considered private information. Some people with disabilities are sensitive to sharing in public that they have a disability. Someone who observes a person with a white cane or in a wheelchair, for instance, might immediately identify that person as having a disability, but there are many disabilities that are not immediately obvious to an observer, including cognitive disabilities, neurological disorders, and mental health challenges. Even if a disability would be obvious to an observer, people with disabilities may not necessarily want the classification of disability listed within their personal data. Why? Personal information describing someone's unique disabilities might sometimes be used as a reason for discriminating against a person with a disability. For example, people with disabilities are often subjected to diverse forms of discrimination at work.[16] The concern is that knowing that an individual has a disability might lead to unfair treatment in an employment position or even unfair treatment in applying for a job.[17] Because of the often high rate of unemployment for persons with disabilities,[18] disclosure of personal information regarding a disability during the job-search and hiring process can be of particular concern. One study indicated that persons with disabilities were more likely not to receive a callback from a potential employer once their disability status was known.[19] Furthermore, people with disabilities often face other forms of discrimination, such as pricing discrimination and limited access to online markets.

One increasing concern is that individuals with disabilities no longer have control over whether data about their disability status are collected. Current technologies offer the potential to collect, store, and share personal information about an individual's disability status without the user's consent. Many software applications collect lots of information about their users because such information is extremely valuable for marketing purposes: the more information organizations have, the more they can customize their marketing and make it more effective. Some of the ways this can occur can be disturbing. For instance, Elgan illustrates the potential problem of having a new class of smartphone applications that use the microphone built into your phone as a covert listening device, monitoring the sounds in your office, kitchen, living room, and bedroom.[20] Such applications use ambient sounds to figure out what you are paying attention to.

A real risk for people with disabilities is that their disability status could automatically be discovered and then stored alongside other personal data about them. As users peruse web applications, they leave traces (such as previously visited websites or the characteristics of the web browser they are using) that can be used as "fingerprints" to identify and track the users' behavior. Kendria Alt describes a situation where browser detection can be used to automatically identify who, visiting a website, has a disability.[21] Other authors have written about how users can be identified by their typing patterns,[22] and it seems likely that such approaches could be used to identify whether a user has a cognitive or motor impairment. Indeed, every time a user visits a website, he or she provides, even without knowing it, lots of information about his or her browser configuration. Web browsers are programmed to transmit such data so that the website can format the content sent back to users according to the device capabilities. Thus it is quite easy for a website being requested by a user to detect the web browser, the software version, the device's screen size and color depth, system fonts, whether cookies are enabled, and the presence of a screen reader or any possible installed add-ons or browser enhancers. This type of data can be used by a company, university, or nonprofit organization to infer a user's disability, even without asking the user to explicitly disclose that information. For example, it is possible to infer whether the user is blind by detecting whether the user is using a screen reader or accessibility-related plug-ins. If a user is using a specialized browser, such as HearSay, that has been specifically designed for people who are blind, or an add-on, such as Chrome Daltonize (for color-blind users) or Firefox FoxVox (for blind users), either one of these situations will lead to an easy identification that the user has a disability. Many add-ons have been specifically designed to cover a large set of disabilities, and many people depend on them to get proper access to web content. Such add-ons are installed only by those people who are in need of an assistive technology, so their presence is often a good indication of users' disabilities. There is a parallel in the social context, where using a specific assistive technology may identify an individual as having a disability when that disability would otherwise not be obvious to an observer.[23] This is an emerging topic that requires increased research in the future to counteract a potential threat to privacy for people with disabilities.

Privacy of Geolocation Data

Modern societies rely on a variety of navigation devices on a daily basis. Originally, this would simply have involved the use of portable GPS devices, including those used in motor vehicles. Today, however, most mobile devices, including smartphones and tablets, have built-in GPS capabilities, leverage mobile or wireless networks to determine location, or use a combination of both techniques to determine location. Many individuals with disabilities rely heavily on the use of such devices for navigation on a daily basis, perhaps even more than the general population. There are many benefits, including assisting with finding directions or the right place to obtain assistance, helping with memory problems, and helping in emergency situations. Using radio-frequency identification (RFID) tags and other technologies, individuals can easily keep track of items that otherwise might get lost.[24] On the other hand, there is the potential that such geolocation data that are generated from the use of location-enabled devices might also be exploited for either malicious purposes or might present a general disclosure of privacy-related data without the knowledge or awareness of the individual.[25] This privacy challenge affects the entire population of users, but it especially affects people with disabilities since they rely very heavily on GPS for navigation and independence.

The benefits of geolocation on mobile devices for people with disabilities have been widely discussed by researchers,[26] and the potential pitfalls of such data are evident in the daily news in stories such as John McAfee's geolocation data from a digital photo posted online giving away his location and leading to his deportation.[27] Another common concern is that the use of geolocation data could allow an individual to be the victim of some type of criminal activity.[28] It is clear that there are potential benefits of geolocation that should be made available to people with disabilities, but there must be disclosure, awareness, and safeguard mechanisms with such technology that protect the rights of those same individuals. More work certainly needs to be done, investigating the emerging concerns for people with disabilities and geolocation tracking.

Privacy Policies and People with Disabilities

It seems simple to solve: if personal data are being collected without users' consent, the solution is to clearly inform the users about what data are being collected, stored, and shared about them. These descriptions of what data are being collected can usually be found in a privacy policy. Not all websites and applications offer privacy policies, and sometimes the privacy policies are embedded within a larger agreement, the terms-of-service (ToS) policies. These policies, provided by applications and websites, should clearly inform users about what types of data are being collected. Such policies would enable users to make informed privacy decisions, but current notice and choice mechanisms, such as publicly posted policies and ToS agreements, are generally ineffective because they are neither usable nor useful and are therefore ignored by users.[29] To place this statement in context, researchers determined that reading all the privacy policies users might encounter in a year would take seventy-six work days.[30] Indeed, ToS agreements are often considered too long to be read and too complex to be understood. Often, these ToSs are provided in a dialogue box that is superimposed on the screen (sometime in graphics-only format) in a very small font size. This combination of small font, long and complex text descriptions, and solely graphic format may make it impossible for people with various disabilities to read and comprehend ToSs.

In some countries and geographic regions, there are requirements for websites to provide a privacy policy and limits on what types of data can be collected. What is considered an appropriate level of privacy is often culturally determined. For instance, France has had a data privacy law (N. 78-17) since 1978. The law applies to public and private organizations and forbids gathering sensitive data about persons, and this has expanded to include collection of data via websites and applications. This encourages privacy protection, but by in essence discouraging the development of centralized databases, the Commission Nationale de l'Informatique et des Libertés (CNIL), a council that supervises privacy, potentially hinders the government's attempts at fraud prevention. For example, until recently, students applying for a public university in France had to repeatedly fill in the forms with high school grades. By adding grades manually, users could make errors that could not be verified by automated tools comparing new data to the original. Privacy policies are also reinforced by regulations such as the EU Directive for personal data protection,[31] often called "the cookie law" because it explicitly refers to a user's right to allow or disable the storage of cookies in the user's browser. A cookie is a small piece of data that a website asks your browser to store on your computer or mobile device. The cookie allows the website to track users' actions or preferences over time. Originally, the cookie technology was designed to track users' behavior inside a single website. However, a website owner may (and often does) contract with another website to allow that site to share or access the cookie data. This has been widely used as a technique for sharing personal data for marketing and advertisement purposes.[32] The cookie law allows users the right to refuse to permit the website to collect personal data using cookies. In other words, website owners must ask users whether they agree to most cookies and similar technologies (for example, web beacons and Flash cookies) before the site starts to use them. Moreover, if users allow cookies, they must be informed about how cookies will be used by the website, for example, why the cookies are requested and for how long they will be kept on the web browser. It is interesting to note that the United States has not been a leader in this area and does not have any broad federal-level information-privacy laws. Laws that do exist related to information privacy are limited by sector (such as the Health Insurance Portability and Accountability Act for health care) or population (such as the Children's Online Privacy Protection Act). The Federal Trade Commission (FTC) has been the primary actor in the area of web tracking and privacy in the United States.[33]

Conclusion

Often, individuals, policy makers, and society do not immediately identify that people with disabilities deserve or need information privacy. Part of this may be cultural—often, people with disabilities are seen getting help from others for transportation, transactions, or learning, so the assumption is then made that people with disabilities are comfortable sharing their personal data with others. That is a misleading and incorrect assumption. People with disabilities do indeed need the same privacy and security protections that all individuals need, and they actually need these privacy and security protections more than the typical user because of their reliance on technology. People with disabilities are likely to have more personal information stored in their accounts or devices than the average citizen does. For instance, blind people are more likely than the average citizen without a disability to receive and pay bills online (because it is a format more useful to them than paper bills). Deaf people may text-message personal information in situations where other citizens might simply make a phone call to discuss personal data where no permanent record will be made. Those who rely on voice-recognition input (speech-to-text) to run their computer (often, people with motor impairments) may be more susceptible to others overhearing their information being inputted (blind users overcome this same privacy concern on voice output, text-to-speech, by using headphones). Privacy and security are paramount concerns for people with disabilities when they interact with digital technology, and this is a topic that needs further investigation.

CHAPTER 13

How Does Inaccessible Gaming Lead to Social Exclusion?

Joyram Chakraborty

Introduction

Modern-day video games provide great entertainment for the masses. From the latest first-person-shooter (FSP) games with ultrahigh-definition graphic engines to the most cutting-edge 3-D real-time-strategy (RTS) games, there is a video game for everyone. Or is there? Most video games gain popularity based on features such as graphics, level of skill required, and just plain word of mouth from friends or social media. But what happens to those gaming enthusiasts with disabilities who simply cannot access the game? What are the societal effects of excluding people with disabilities from the world of computer gaming? Exclusion of people with disabilities from video gaming because of inaccessible interfaces can lead to exclusion in important areas such as employment, education, health care, and socializing; therefore, equal access to gaming can be viewed as a human right. It is imperative that gaming developers and other stakeholders take a human rights approach in the design, testing, and marketing of video games to ensure the enjoyment of those human rights by all.

How Does Gaming Relate to Accessibility?

Video gaming may be perceived by some as a pastime of limited interest, limited usefulness, and a limited population of users. However, research and various statistics have indicated that games are increasingly used for other purposes than entertainment.[1] Gamers are turning toward video gaming as sources of income by engaging in e-gaming. Portals such as online poker and betting against computer-generated algorithms allow the masses to generate income as well as entertainment. When people gather for recreation, they often do so by playing various games, such as Dance Dance Revolution, Guitar Hero, Grand Theft Auto, NFL, FIFA, or World of War Craft, to name just a few. Over the past thirty years, gaming has moved from being an esoteric activity in arcades and basements to a mainstream societal activity. Gaming is no longer only an individual activity where people play against "the computer." Rather, gaming is now a core part of social interaction and recreation for the masses in multiple ways. In many ways, gaming needs to become like unified sports, where teams consist of people both with and without disabilities. Unified sports are no longer restricted to the basketball court or soccer field. Instead, increasing numbers of video gamers with disabilities are being engaged through local-area-networked and Internet-based gaming sessions.[2] Preliminary research findings have demonstrated the significant inclusive potential of "video gaming unified sports."[3]

The designs of video games contain some similarities. Some games may include complex algorithms designed to create obstacles or challenging situations that the player must overcome, while others may simply require acclimatizing to a second life environment. However, all games require a degree of interaction from the gamer or end user. These interactions may be in the form of direct or indirect input and may produce consequentially direct or indirect output. Typically, these input devices take the form of controllers such as keyboards, joy sticks, or mice. Some of the next generation of input instruments, including motion and sonic devices, are designed to capture gamers' physiological responses through nontraditional methods, thereby increasing gamer satisfaction. Output from most video games is indicated in some form of a monitor or screen. Some next-generation output devices, such as haptic and virtual reality, produce stimuli designed to trigger other physiological responses from the gamers. These are proving to be increasingly popular with the gaming community.

But what happens when the controls are not accessible, for example, input devices that can be described only by using words (such as "Using the BlackWidow Tournament Edition in front of you") but cannot be seen, output responses that cannot be heard, or complex gaming algorithms that cannot be interacted with? This inaccessibility arises because the tools for interaction are not designed to be inclusive. In other instances, the games might require separate controllers or multilevel controls, such as those on the PlayStation Network, to play multiplayer games. The positioning of the buttons, levers, or joystick on the input devices makes the controllers inaccessible. As a result of the impasse, gamers with disabilities simply give up. Arcade-based video games, such as racing using a driving wheel or martial arts using joystick controllers, have been commonly replicated for various consoles like Sony PlayStation or Microsoft Xbox to huge success. The expectation, from a firm's sales perspective, is to sell as many units of the game as possible. This demand on the game-development supply chain implies that very few customizations of the games or the consoles are possible. As a result, gamers with disabilities often have to seek out creative ways to remain included. These may involve seeking out patches of open-source code, often riddled with bugs and malware, or investing in additional hardware, such as surround-sound speakers. Even after all these additional modifications to the gamer controls, there are significant limitations to the gamers' satisfaction for individuals with disabilities.

Gaming would be important even if the only issue was to ensure that people with disabilities were included in recreation. However, the use of video games applies to more than just recreation. The fields of education, employee training, job application, and health care use video games as a part of their routine activities. However, all these fields have gaming-accessibility challenges that result in exclusions for differently abled persons. Inaccessible controls, navigational difficulties, and readability challenges are just some of the features of video games that make them out of reach. Yet findings from several bodies of accessibility research have indicated significant benefits of inclusive game design in the fields of education, employment, and various types of health care.

It is important to place gaming in the context of human rights. At first thought, the connection between gaming and human rights may appear to be tenuous. People often associate human rights with the basic necessities, such as access to clean water and food, and freedom of speech. How can gaming be a human right when people think of gaming as being for individuals with free time and money? On closer inspection, the right for people with disabilities to have equal access to technology and information is established in both national governmental laws, like the Americans with Disabilities Act, and core human rights treaties, such as the UN Convention on the Rights of Persons with Disabilities (CRPD). When a person cannot be included in social activities because that person has a disability, and the social activity uses technology that is inaccessible, that leads to social exclusion. But as will be documented in this chapter, gaming is used not only for recreation but also for employment, education, health care, and rehabilitation. Researchers often talk about "gamification," which is application of game elements in a nongaming context. For example, parts of a lesson may be conveyed through interactive animations that teach or illustrate a particular concept. Therefore, through gamification, the learning may become more effective. However, if the gamification is not inclusive, the lesson is not taught to everyone. Therefore, being excluded from gaming can actually lead to exclusion from education (as well as other areas, such as employment and health care). That explains why access to gaming, in some senses, can be viewed as a fundamental human right, because exclusion from gaming can lead to exclusion from major parts of society.

Existing Solutions and the CRPD

Research studies in the area of human-computer interaction (HCI) and accessibility have been undertaken to highlight this accessibility challenge and to propose solutions as an incremental fix. Several studies have been carried out to examine ways to creatively use existing gaming infrastructure to create accessible solutions for very specific disabilities. Although these studies highlight the possibilities of success using user-centered approaches to accessibility, very few empirical studies have been carried out to test these solutions. The link between human rights and computer gaming may become clearer by performing a "mapping" of how specific articles of the CRPD directly relate to gaming and then by providing existing technical examples of how access to gaming can be implemented (Tables 13.1, 13.2, 13.3, and 13.4). The technical examples are included from some of the top publication outlets in HCI and accessibility: *ACM Transactions on Accessible Computing Journal* (*TACCESS*), the ACM SIGACCESS Conference on Assistive Technologies (ASSETS), the Cambridge Workshop on Universal Access and Assistive Technology (CWUAAT), and the ACM Conference on Human Factors in Computing Systems (CHI).

Table 13.1. Gaming and Accessibility

CRPD Article 9—*Accessibility*	*Research Examples*
Information, communications, and other services, including electronic services and emergency services.	Chakraborty et al. 2014.[1] Carried out a usability study of six blind gamers using a PC-based re-creation of a console video game to understand the accessibility requirements of blind users.
Promote access for persons with disabilities to new information and communications technologies and systems, including the Internet.	Sporka et al. 2006.[2] Tested the design of an input system using nonspeech (any sound other than clear words) and speech recognition to control the trajectory of the game Tetris for users with motor impairments.

Relevant literature from 2005 to 2015 mapped to the UNCRPD, Enable: UN Convention on the Rights of Persons with Disabilities, 2006, accessed January 17, 2013, www.un.org/disabilities/documents/convention/convoptprote.pdf.

[1] J. Chakraborty, J. Hritz, and J. Dehlinger, "Preliminary Results in the Understanding of Accessibility Challenges in Computer Gaming for the Visually Impaired," in *Inclusive Designing: Joining Usability, Accessibility, and Inclusion*, ed. P. M. Langdon, J. Lazar, A. Heylighen, and H. Dong (New York: Springer, 2014), 83–92.

[2] Adam J. Sporka, Sri H. Kurniawan, Murni Mahmud, and Pavel Slavik, "Non-speech Input and Speech Recognition for Real-Time Control of Computer Games," in *Proceedings of the 8th International ACM SIGACCESS Conference on Computers and Accessibility* (New York: ACM, 2006), 213–20.

Accessibility Challenges in Education, Employment, and Health Care

What makes gaming especially important as a human rights issue is that gaming is not just for enjoyment anymore but is now often used for learning exercises in education, for qualifications testing for employment, and for health care.

Gaming and Education

The appeal of video games in education is widespread.[4] An increasing number of institutions, from early elementary education providers to postgraduate studies, are applying gaming-based education systems.[5] The value of these interactive and innovative game-based learning programs is widely

Table 13.2. Gaming and Education

CRPD Article 24—Education	Research Examples
Facilitating the learning of braille, alternative script, augmentative and alternative modes, means and formats of communication, and orientation and mobility skills and facilitating peer support and mentoring.	Sanchez and Espinoza 2011.[1] Designed a study to determine the effect of audio and haptic-based videogames on orientation and navigation skills.
Ensuring that the education of persons, and in particular children who are blind, deaf, or deafblind is delivered in the most appropriate languages and modes and means of communication for the individual and in environments that maximize academic and social development.	Hussaan, Sehaba, and Mille 2011.[2] Developed a serious game to support learning for children and adolescents with intellectual disabilities related to perception, attention, memory, oral language, written language, logical reasoning, visual-spatial, and transverse competencies.
	Madeo 2011.[3] A prototype game of hangman was created for deaf children using Brazilian Sign Language. A graphic interface that recognized the Latin alphabet was used to record and process visual signs for the deaf users.

[1] Jaime Sánchez and Matias Espinoza, "Audio Haptic Videogaming for Navigation Skills in Learners Who Are Blind," in *ASSETS 2011: Proceedings of the 13th International ACM SIGACCESS Conference on Computers and Accessibility* (New York: ACM, 2011), 227–28.

[2] Aarij M. Hussaan, Karim Sehaba, and Alain Mille, "Helping Children with Cognitive Disabilities Through Serious Games: Project CLES," in *ASSETS 2011: Proceedings of the 13th International ACM SIGACCESS Conference on Computers and Accessibility*, 251–52.

[3] Renata Cristina Barros Madeo, "Brazilian Sign Language Multimedia Hangman Game: A Prototype of an Educational and Inclusive Application," in *ASSETS 2011: Proceedings of the 13th International ACM SIGACCESS Conference on Computers and Accessibility*, 311–12.

acknowledged by parents and adults alike. Together with faster computers and Internet connections, these programs have thrived, bringing education to new frontiers across the world.[6] However, significant challenges exist for persons with disabilities for whom these gaming system remain inaccessible.

Gaming in education is typically interactive. Designers of educational games will create in-game scenarios where input from end users leads to permutations of output with an educational theme. This interactivity serves as

Table 13.3. Gaming and Health Care

CRPD Article 26—Habilitation and Rehabilitation	Research Examples
States Parties shall promote the availability, knowledge, and use of assistive devices and technologies, designed for persons with disabilities, as they relate to habilitation and rehabilitation.	Waddington et al. 2015.[1] Presented design requirements for the video game Eyelander as a part of a game-based therapy program to improve functional vision for neurological vision impairment (NVI) users.
	Hernandez et al. 2012.[2] Designed a gaming station using a standard Xbox 360 and a pedaling mechanism to allow eight children with cerebral palsy input control.

[1] Jonathan Waddington et al., "Participatory Design of Therapeutic Video Games for Young People with Neurological Vision Impairment," in *CHI 2015: Proceedings of the 33rd Annual ACM Conference on Human Factors in Computing Systems* (New York: ACM, 2015), 3533–42.

[2] Hamilton A. Hernandez et al., "Design of an Exergaming Station for Children with Cerebral Palsy," in *Proceedings of the SIGCHI Conference on Human Factors in Computing Systems* (New York: ACM, 2012), 2619–28.

a training tool to teach the concept that the educator has planned. However, if the student cannot engage the system through the available mouse or keyboard and cannot interpret output through the available monitor or visual effects, the game-based education cannot support the needs of the end user. This inaccessibility not only prevents equal opportunity to education for all but also leads to social exclusion for those who are left out.

Gaming in education would be more inclusive if the systems had accessibility features.[7] This would directly affect the various social interactions that go with education: friendships made with colleagues and peers over the network; trials and tribulations from the learning process resulting in shared experiences; and cross-cultural learning through engagements with others in the education system.

Gaming and Employment

The use of electronic games has made significant inroads in several industries as a training tool for employees.[8] These game-based training methods

Table 13.4. Gaming for Recreation

CRPD Article 30—Participation in Cultural Life, Recreation, Leisure, and Sport	Research Examples
To encourage and promote the participation, to the fullest extent possible, of persons with disabilities in mainstream sporting activities at all levels.	Rector, Bennett, and Kientz 2013.[1] Reported the findings of a controlled study of sixteen people who are blind or have low vision engaging with an exergame, Eye-Free Yoga.
To ensure that persons with disabilities have an opportunity to organize, develop, and participate in disability-specific sporting and recreational activities and, to this end, encourage the provision, on an equal basis with others, of appropriate instruction, training, and resources.	Gerling, Mandryk, and Kalyn 2013.[2] Reported the findings of a wheelchair-accessible, motion-based game where the motion of a wheel chair, captured through a KINECT Wheel tool kit, and Cupcake Heaven, a wheelchair-based video game, were used to engage older adults.
To ensure that persons with disabilities have access to sporting, recreational, and tourism venues.	Vickers, Istance, and Hyrskykari 2013.[3] Designed a gaze-only method to control locomotion using eye-tracking equipment and tested it on users with cerebral palsy and muscular dystrophy playing World of War Craft and Snap Clutch on a PC.
To ensure that children with disabilities have equal access with other children to participation in play, recreation, and leisure and sporting activities, including those activities in the school system.	
To ensure that persons with disabilities have access to services from those involved in the organization of recreational, tourism, leisure, and sporting activities.	Ye et al. 2012.[4] Designed a multiplayer exercise video game using a novel cycling-based exergaming station to allow children with cerebral palsy to perform vigorous exercise together.

[1] Kyle Rector, Cynthia L. Bennett, and Julie A. Kientz, "Eyes-Free Yoga: An Exergame Using Depth Cameras for Blind and Low Vision Exercise," in *Proceedings of the 15th International ACM SIGACCESS Conference on Computers and Accessibility* (New York: ACM, 2013), DOI: 10.1145/2513383.2513392.

[2] Kathrin M. Gerling, Regan L. Mandryk, and Michael R. Kalyn, "Wheelchair-Based Game Design for Older Adults," in *Proceedings of the 15th International ACM SIGACCESS Conference on Computers and Accessibility* (New York: ACM, 2013), DOI: 10.1145/2513383.2513436.

[3] Stephen Vickers, Howell Istance, and Aulikki Hyrskykari, "Performing Locomotion Tasks in Immersive Computer Games with an Adapted Eye-Tracking Interface," *ACM Transactions on Accessible Computing (TACCESS)* 5, no. 1 (2013): 1–33.

[4] Zi Ye et al., "Liberi and the Racer Bike: Exergaming Technology for Children with Cerebral Palsy," in *Proceedings of the 14th International ACM SIGACCESS Conference on Computers and Accessibility* (New York: ACM, 2012), 225–26.

have proved to be effective replacements for human training in certain instances, such as operating simple machinery or gadgets and performing organizational tasks using the firm's intranet.[9] In other cases, complex and highly interactive skill sets may be offered through training using virtual reality or simulators.[10] Unfortunately, very few training facilities make significant modifications for people with disabilities, and those that do not thereby make these game-based training methods inaccessible. As a result of a lack of training, these individuals are left ill equipped to seek employment opportunities in these types of organizations.

Talented employees with skill sets in demand should not be hampered by a lack of accessible tools in the workplace to accommodate their needs. Unfortunately, for-profit organizations face a perceived conflict between making customized accommodations and achieving cost effectiveness. In order to remain competitive, most firms use off-the-shelf equipment with few costly modifications for the majority of their employees. The bar to justify the need for customized tools is set considerably higher, and in most cases, such customization must be approved by authority much higher in the organizational hierarchy. This combination of bureaucratic requirements and the need to appease shareholders results in potential new hires with disabilities being refused an equal opportunity to be employed and trained properly.

Gaming and Health Care

A number of studies have shown the potential benefits of interactive video games in the care of the elderly, the long-term rehabilitation of specific illnesses, and improving fitness for persons with disabilities.[11]

Studies of the elderly have found significant benefits from increased motivation to engage in physical activities as a result of playing interactive video games.[12] These studies have shown that with minor modifications to the gaming interface to account for the learning curve, there was an increase in user acceptance and user satisfaction rates within the elderly population engaged in gaming. These studies also reported significant reductions in resting systolic blood pressure and other improvements in the overall health-related physical fitness of the elderly who were engaged in video gaming. This body of research noted minimal negative side effects and found that accessible gaming promotes social inclusion for the elderly.[13]

The benefits of interactive gaming have also been identified for some long-term rehabilitation programs, such as those for cerebral palsy, brain injuries, and cognitive and motor skills.[14] Several prominent studies of these programs have noted significant benefits from the intervention of video gaming using specially modified interfaces to accommodate the participants. In these studies of interventions for cerebral palsy and brain injuries, specially designed user interfaces for existing off-the-shelf games or newly designed simple video games created opportunities for user participation. Some of these modifications included cycling-based inputs for PC-environment games, while others included haptic sensor gloves for a virtual-reality environment. Some of the benefits identified in these studies included increased motivation to engage or remain in therapy, increased awareness, improved muscle coordination, and better balance. However, the costs involved in increasing the gaming accessibility are perceived to be prohibitive.[15] As a result, very few of these accessibility-modified video games are commercially available, and this lack of availability leads to social exclusion.

Legal Cases Related to Video-Game Inaccessibility

Accessibility in society is a right. Laws ensuring equal opportunity, such as the Americans with Disabilities Act (ADA), the Twenty-First Century Communications and Video Accessibility Act (CVAA), and similar laws, were written to mandate equal access and to prohibit discrimination, like the Civil Rights Act of 1964.[16] Unfortunately, the laws have not kept up with the technology, and the ADA has not been interpreted to include video games. In *Stern v. Sony Corp.* (2010), a plaintiff with a learning disability brought a suit claiming that Sony violated Title III of the ADA by failing "to accommodate his disability by modifying ... video games ... to provide visual and auditory cues" to make them more accessible. The plaintiff tried to argue that he was being denied access to Sony's conventions tied to their games as a result of his disability. The court found no evidence of this alleged inaccessibility to Sony's products, nor did it find any evidence to support that the plaintiff sought out any auxiliary aids to allow him to enjoy the convention. As a result, the court dismissed the case against Sony.

The primary laws and regulations within the video-game industry are generally considered to relate to the following topics:

1. Digital Millennium Copyright Act: prohibiting unlawful copy of electronic media[17]
2. Gaming censorship and addiction according to cultural norms in the country[18]
3. Classification and regulation of strong pornographic content according to the national laws[19]
4. Restrictions on the sale of rated content, such as violent video games[20]

The movement toward gaming accessibility now relies on two versions of a set of guidelines that were developed as a free resource to assist game developers. One, called Game Accessibility Guidelines, was developed by a collection of game developers and accessibility experts with a list of resources outlining how to design video games in an accessible manner. The second, a document titled *Includification*, which contains guidelines on making games accessible for those with physical, visual, cognitive, and hearing disabilities, was developed by the public charity Ablegamers.[21]

The Game Accessibility Guidelines are divided into three sets of instructions—basic, intermediate, and advanced—for developers designing video games for the following disabilities: motor, cognitive, vision, hearing, and speech. Each of these disability-specific instructions at the level of design intervention contains explanations, best-practice examples, and tools for further assistance in designing accessible video games.[22] Although somewhat similar in the language applied, the list of game-accessibility guidelines does not contain any specific technical guidelines, tools for testing, or a comprehensive list of solutions, such as those found in the Web Content Accessibility Guidelines (WCAG).[23] Both guideline documents are suggested as best practices in the gaming-accessibility design community. However, limited empirical research using end users with disabilities has been carried out to determine the usefulness of the documents. As a result, most video games from the industry rely on in-house technical expertise for all end-user requirements, including accessibility.

Conclusion

Modern-day video games have extensive potential beyond simply entertainment. They have the potential to extend education beyond paper-based classroom settings with limited seating and timings. The application of video games in rehabilitation has the potential to increase patient motivation and interest while serving as a tool in the recovery process. The use of video games in elderly care can serve as the focal point of increasing social interactions. Video games using virtual-reality tools can enhance future employee training modules and current employee skill sets. The potential for video games is immense. However, as technology advances, there is a responsibility to design tools more carefully to ensure that everyone can participate. Inclusion in all activities is a human right. No longer should any individual be left out of gaming for fun, entertainment, education, employment, or health care simply because he or she has a disability. As accessibility research in the area of video games increases, the requirements for making video games more inclusive become easier to understand, manage, and develop. With minor modifications to the gaming interface, the modern-day video game has the potential to be inclusive for everyone.

PART IV

International Development

CHAPTER 14

The Pivot Model of Policy Entrepreneurship: An Application of European Ideas in the Global South

G. Anthony Giannoumis, Mirriam Nthenge, and Jorge Manhique

Introduction

Previous research has attempted to explain the influence of social institutions—that is, formal and informal norms, values, and procedures—on the behavior of policy actors. This chapter refers to social institutions as the relatively enduring norms, values, and procedures important to a society. For example, democratic norms and values such as political representation and government accountability influence whether, how, and to what extent interest groups and other policy actors can participate in the design and implementation of public policy. Theorists have argued that interdependent networks of policy actors contribute to the stability and perpetuation of social institutions. Political scientists have demonstrated that "advocacy coalitions"[1] or informal networks of policy actors structure policy design. In contrast, other scholars[2] have argued that "policy entrepreneurs" embedded in networks of policy actors can support institutional change by introducing new ideas into policy processes. However, previous research has not examined fully the processes by which policy entrepreneurs, embedded in networks of interdependent actors, contribute to institutional change. This chapter asks, "How can policy networks provide an opportunity for policy entrepreneurs to contribute to institutional change?"

We aim to examine the social institutions that structure the behavior of policy actors involved in promoting the accessibility of information and communication technology (ICT) for persons with disabilities in the European Union (EU). Interest organizations, advocating for disability rights in the EU, have supported the introduction of antidiscrimination legislation and ICT-accessibility policies. For example, the European Disability Forum, a pan-European disabled persons' organization (DPO), has called for the introduction of EU legislation aimed at ensuring the accessibility of ICT, among other things.[3]

However, the abilities of national interest organizations to promote policy change in the EU have been limited because of what previous research argues is a "democratic deficit."[4] Essentially, in the EU, as a supranational government, the principal actors are member-state governments.[5] Despite the democratic deficit in the EU, scholars have pointed out that recent trends have increased the channels for participatory processes and enabled interest organizations and other policy actors to contribute to policy design.

The EU ratified the Convention on the Rights of Persons with Disabilities (CRPD) in December 2010. The CRPD is the first treaty to be ratified and endorsed by the EU. The CRPD obliges states parties to undertake, among other actions, proactive steps "including legislative, administrative and other measures for the implementation of the rights recognized in CRPD" (Article 4, section 1, paragraph a). The CRPD makes it clear that "in the development and implementation of legislation and policies to implement the Convention, and in other decision-making processes concerning issues relating to persons with disabilities, States Parties shall closely consult with and actively involve persons with disabilities" (Article 4, paragraph 3). Thus, as a normative instrument, the CRPD is a valuable tool to mitigate the democratic deficit in the EU member states and to increase the participation of persons with disabilities and their representative organizations. Participatory processes relate to the implementation of the CRPD and the role of persons with disabilities and representative organizations in decision-making processes, including the design and implementation of legislation affecting the enjoyment of their fundamental rights (Article 4, section 3).

At the same time, policy entrepreneurs have contributed to institutional change by promoting ICT accessibility in public procurement standards. Despite institutional constraints in the EU that have limited the ability of interest organizations to promote EU legislation, policy entrepreneurs, embedded in networks of policy actors, have successfully contributed to institutional change by introducing a European standard for public procurement, which aims to promote, among other things, ICT accessibility. This chapter argues that interest organizations in the EU have, in part, redirected advocacy efforts from promoting EU legislation to promoting European standards for public procurement. It uses the concept of a "pivot"—adopted from the literature on business and entrepreneurship—to characterize the strategic redirection of advocacy efforts and aims to illustrate and apply the pivot concept in the Global South, using Mozambique and Kenya as examples.

First, this chapter introduces a theoretical framework that provides different analytic perspectives for examining the social institutions and institutional changes that have occurred in the EU, the networks of interdependent policy actors that operate in the EU, and the use of social regulations to coerce and persuade service providers to ensure ICT accessibility. Second, it analyzes the institutional constraints and participatory processes in the EU. Third, it examines the EU's policy approach to regulating ICT accessibility. Fourth, it discusses the results in the context of ICT accessibility in the Global South, using Kenya and Mozambique as illustrative cases. Fifth, it concludes by summarizing the results.

Analytic Framework

This section presents different analytic perspectives for examining the role of policy networks in promoting ICT accessibility in the EU and reviews research on social institutions, policy networks, and social regulation.

Social Institutions

Although the academic literature provides multiple definitions of institutions, scholars largely concur that institutions act as structural features of society, and they refer to an "enduring collection of rules and organizational practices."[6] Some authors[7] differentiate between rational-choice and sociological models for examining institutions and argue that rational-choice institutionalism emphasizes the strategic and analytic choices of policy actors in determining policy outcomes. From a rational-choice perspective, institutions structure the interactions among policy actors by constraining the choices and responses of policy actors. These authors often contrast rational-choice institutionalism with sociological institutionalism, which emphasizes the cultural attitudes and values in determining organizational practices. From a sociological approach, institutions influence the choices of policy actors by structuring the expectations of policy actors and the possibilities for action. Although previous research has often retained the distinction between rational-choice and sociological institutionalism, some scholars[8] argue for combining institutional perspectives.

While scholars characterize social institutions as resilient and enduring, research on policy transfer has attempted to explain institutional change. According to some researchers, policy transfer refers to "knowledge about policies, administrative arrangements, institutions and ideas in one political setting" that are used in another. Authors argue that policy transfer involves "lesson-drawing" where policy actors will actively search for "policy solutions to new or changing problems."[9]

This chapter combines rational-choice and sociological institutionalism to examine the social institutions that structure both the interactions and expectations of policy actors and the possibilities for participating in the design of ICT-accessibility policies in the EU. In addition, it uses research on social institutions as a basis for considering the role of policy entrepreneurs and policy networks in facilitating and contributing to institutional change.

Policy Networks

Previous research has examined the influence of interdependent networks of policy actors on institutional stability and has referred to informal "networks among important policy participants" as advocacy coalitions. Scholars have argued that advocacy coalitions structure policy design by translating "components of their belief systems into actual policy."[10] As belief systems among policy networks remain relatively stable, policy change becomes difficult. Similarly, other authors argue that networks of policy actors develop a "common definition of appropriate practice," which gives actors the "same views on the effectiveness of policy alternatives."[11]

Scholars have extended the advocacy-coalition framework[12] in order to explain institutional change and argue that policy entrepreneurs, like business entrepreneurs, function to "discover unfulfilled needs and suggest innovative means to satisfy them," "bear the reputational . . . financial and emotional risks involved in pursuing actions that have uncertain consequences," and assemble and coordinate "networks of individuals and organizations that have the talents and resources necessary to undertake change."[13] Similarly, previous research demonstrates that policy entrepreneurs act as a mechanism of institutional change. "Institutional entrepreneurs" or "high-level public and private decision makers" such as "key policymakers in the legislative and executive branches of government" or "top corporate managers" introduce new ideas that "enable or facilitate decision making and institutional change by specifying for decision makers how to solve specific problems."[14]

Research has demonstrated that policy networks in the EU have acted as a mechanism of governance.[15] The EU's policy approach "promotes networks, participation, and inclusion . . . as means to . . . find effective policy solutions to major problems and overcome popular distrust of governing institutions."[16] Some scholars have argued that an "intricate global network of public, private and mixed institutions and norms, partially orchestrated by [international organizations] and states," has contributed to "the promulgation and implementation of non-legally-binding standards of behavior, applicable directly to private actors rather than to states, in settings that have traditionally called for mandatory regulation."[17]

This chapter uses scholarship on policy networks as a basis for examining the multitude of policy actors and interests involved in promoting ICT accessibility in the EU. In addition, it uses this research to examine the role of DPOs and policy entrepreneurs in designing ICT-accessibility policies in the EU.

Social Regulation

The academic literature has characterized social regulation as the use of legislative, financial, or persuasive policies to coerce or persuade market actors to achieve social outcomes.[18] Social regulation includes "co-regulation, where responsibility for regulatory design or regulatory enforcement is shared by the regulator and the regulatees, often state and civil actors."[19] Some scholars have examined coregulatory processes from a top-down perspective in the EU and have argued that the EU "has made participation of civil society in the decision making process a key objective."[20]

This chapter argues that coregulation involves engaging nonstate actors in participatory processes that contribute to policy design. Inspired by approaches used by entrepreneurs in business, we use the concept of a pivot from research on entrepreneurship. In an examination of entrepreneurial experiences in the ICT industry, some scholars conceptualize a pivot as "a different method for achieving your vision."[21] These authors have argued that entrepreneurs should consider whether to pivot when they experience a lack of progress, and the success of a pivot is measured by whether the business experiences a post hoc increase in productivity. Other scholars have provided a complementary definition of the pivot concept, stating that "a pivot is not a failure."[22] According to these authors, a pivot is "a substantive change" enacted by an entrepreneurial leader that is "driven by . . . learnings and insight[s]" from customers.

An analysis of regional educational policy in the United States provides a useful illustration of the pivot concept in policy design. According to the authors, the "policy entrepreneur and his allies decided to change their strategy." While retaining "their longer-term goal of constitutional change," they "decided first to seek a shorter term goal" by introducing a new program that took into account institutionalized norms and values.[23]

This chapter refers to a pivot as the strategic use of participatory processes that contribute to institutional change. It examines the pivot concept in relation to policy networks and social institutions and argues that policy entrepreneurs can provide the opportunity for interest organizations, embedded in networks of policy actors, to pivot by strategically redirecting advocacy efforts to support institutional change.

Institutional Constraints and Participatory Processes in the EU

The previous section identified several analytic dimensions of examining the institutional constraints and policy networks involved in ICT accessibility. The EU provides a useful case for examining ICT accessibility because the European Commission (EC) has attempted to use a variety of policy instruments to regulate ICT accessibility. In addition, policy networks within the

EU have participated in the design and implementation of ICT-accessibility policies. This section examines the networks within EU member states and the institutional changes that have occurred on both the national and the supranational level. It uses qualitative data from policy documents to support the analysis.

Some scholars[24] have characterized the EU as an "economic and political partnership . . . based on a series of treaties."[25] However, several researchers have debated whether and to what extent the delegation of power to the EU by member states has resulted in a "democratic deficit."[26] Scholars have yet to converge on a single definition or conceptualization of the EU's democratic deficit, and because previous research has posed a variety of sometimes competing analyses of the EU's democratic deficit, a comprehensive review of the literature is beyond the scope of this chapter. It examines in particular the EU's democratic deficit as the result of institutional constraints that limit the participation of policy actors in policy design.

Democratic Deficit

Researchers have argued that "the shortcomings of [the EU's] institutional arrangements" have resulted in a democratic deficit.[27] In other words, while representatives in the European Parliament are directly elected, membership in the European Commission and the Council of Ministers is not subject to direct election and thus produces a democratic deficit. Thus authors have suggested that the EU's democratic deficit results from the formal and informal norms, values, and procedures of the EU institutions that constrain the ability of the electorate to hold those institutions accountable.

One author argues that "public interest–orientated" proponents have characterized the democratic deficit as unproblematic, since "democratic accountability plays a diminished role in the operation of most states."[28] Ultimately the author argues that "means need to be found for enhancing the democratic accountability of EU decision-makers" and concludes that "the current limitations of EU democracy place democratic limits on what the EU should do—even in the name of rights or the public interest."

Other scholars have provided a useful counterargument to these claims. While some scholars recognize the EU's democratic deficit as a disjunction between the EU's "power and electoral accountability,"[29] others provide a more nuanced analysis and characterize the democratic deficit as "a lack of procedural ... or 'input legitimacy.'"[30] One scholar who has examined input legitimacy in the EU relates the EU's democratic deficit to participatory processes, stating that "those who are affected by a norm have somehow been included (and have the right to be included) in the process of its formulation." The author argues further that input legitimacy "depends on mechanisms and procedures that are able to include the will of the people in decision-making and then translate it into political decisions." The author has also analyzed several formal and informal "channels" where civil society actors may contribute to policy design as advisers and consultants. Thus, according to these authors, participatory processes may mitigate the EU's democratic deficit.

In the context of the CRPD, the EU could apply two approaches to mitigate the democratic deficit. First, since members of the EU, like those in many other regional economic bodies, are not elected, the appointments should consider representation of persons with disabilities. Second, persons with disabilities and their representative organizations should be consulted throughout the process of drafting policy and legislation. This chapter focuses on the participation of persons with disabilities and their representative organizations. Therefore, the next section analyzes the participatory processes that have influenced policy design in ICT accessibility for persons with disabilities.

Participatory Processes

The previous section has demonstrated that the EU's democratic deficit has resulted in institutional constraints that have limited, in part, the participation of policy actors in policy design. However, previous research has shown that participatory processes provide a useful mechanism for mitigating the EU's democratic deficit and can act as a basis for policy actors to contribute to policy design.[31] One scholar has examined, among other things, consultation processes as a mechanism for policy actors to participate in EU decision making.[32] According to the author, "Consultations are soft tools mainly used by the Commission to receive technical knowledge and identify interests and needs of interested parties before developing legislative proposals." The author states that consultations are "open to stakeholders, interested parties and the wider public," which allows "for a wide range of actors . . . includ[ing] public authorities, business, associations of different kinds as well as individual citizens to participate."

However, consultations may also represent a superficial means for participation. As one scholar has pointed out, consultations are often used when "the Commission demands approval for decisions which have been already taken, without offering adequate space and time to give meaningful input."[33] In addition, consultations often involve only a select group of policy actors. According to the author, "The composition of civil society that participates [in] consultations at the EU level is largely dictated by which groups and associations the Commission chooses to fund and, often, creates." For example, the author argues that the "European 'platforms' . . . are collective subjects composed of umbrella organizations, which constitute fora for discussion and provide a synthesis among different positions of different actors in a specific field on a named topic." The author further argues, "Platforms are not participatory tools. . . . They are networks of [civil society organizations] . . . not directly funded by the EU, but heavily incentivised by the EU and the CSOs that are part of them are heavily subsidized through EU funds."

One such platform, the European Social Platform, "was created . . . with a direct remit to campaign for a European civil dialogue" and includes the European Disability Forum (EDF).[34] The EDF is a pan-European disability advocacy organization, funded in part by the EU and made up of DPOs from throughout Europe. The participation of persons with disabilities also relates to the ability of these groups to participate meaningfully in decision-making processes. The Committee on the Rights of Persons with Disabilities issued the General Comment on Article 9, based on state reports from developing and developed countries. The committee noted "the lack of involvement of persons with disabilities and their representative organizations in the design, implementation and monitoring of accessibility standards, and absence of effective complaint and remedy mechanisms." Despite the existence of forums for participation, the ability to participate meaningfully in these forums is limited in many contexts, particularly in developing countries. Persons with disabilities and their representative organizations sometimes lack the knowledge and expertise on issues of ICT accessibility required to participate in standardization.

The next section examines the EU's approach to regulating ICT accessibility where advocates such as the EDF have encountered institutional constraints in lobbying for EU legislation and where national policy actors have used participatory processes in standardization to engage in policy design.

Regulating ICT Accessibility in the EU

The EU has a tradition of promoting ICT accessibility through persuasive policies. In 2010, the EU published the European Disability Strategy 2010–2020, which aimed to promote the rights of persons with disabilities in many areas, including access to ICT. As part of the European Disability Strategy 2010–2020, the EU proposed to use legislative and other policy instruments, including standardization, to promote ICT accessibility. In 2011, the EC issued a consultation and roadmap for the European Accessibility Act (EAA)—a legislative initiative that aims to improve "both from the demand and supply side, the markets for goods and services that are accessible for persons with disabilities." However, despite efforts by the EDF and DPOs in Europe to lobby in support of the EAA, the EU has yet to legislate.[35]

Although the EU's democratic deficit has, in part, limited the influence of national interest organizations in promoting the EAA, participatory processes have allowed national policy actors to participate as coregulators in the design of European ICT-accessibility standards. The EU uses standards as an instrument of social regulation.[36] Standardization in the EU typically involves a variety of civil society actors, including businesses and interest organizations, as both consultants and coregulators. Thus EU standardization provides a mechanism for civil society actors to participate in policy design.

In 2005, the EU issued a standardization mandate (M 376) to the European Standards Organizations (ESO)[37] in support of ICT-accessibility requirements for public procurement.[38] According to the European Commission, Inmaculada Placencia-Porrero sponsored the standardization mandate. Placencia-Porrero has promoted the rights of persons with disabilities in the EU since the 1990s by initiating policy reforms to promote ICT accessibility, among other things. Although the EU is not formally involved in the design of standards beyond issuing a mandate to the ESO, the EDF acted as a consultant throughout the process. Nonetheless, the development of the M 376 standards principally involved national standards organizations, interest organizations, and businesses. AENOR, the Spanish national standards organization, led the development of the M 376 standard, and among the interest organizations involved, two Spanish interest organizations, Fundación ONCE and its subsidiary Technosite, participated directly in the design of the M 376 standard. Both Fundación ONCE and Technosite were also involved in the design of ICT-accessibility standards in Spain, which were used to justify the enactment of ICT-accessibility legislation.

ICT Accessibility in the Global South

How can institutional constraints in the EU inform the promotion of ICT accessibility in the Global South? This chapter argues that the salience of the pivot concept is further emphasized when it is applied to interest organizations in the Global South, where financial resource constraints combine with institutional constraints to limit the opportunities for both state and nonstate actors to participate in policy design and support institutional change. It argues that although an enabling normative framework at the national level exists in both Mozambique and Kenya, in practice, effective and meaningful participation of persons with disabilities and representative organizations remains a challenge.

This section attempts to probe the application of the pivot model by applying it to the Global South. It examines not only whether the model may be useful for explaining the participation and influence of DPOs in ICT-related policies in the EU but also, when applied to countries in the Global South, whether it may be used to examine both ICT-accessibility and social development efforts. This section broadens the application of the pivot model by addressing social development factors in the Global South, including affordability of ICT-related products, Global South power relations as recipients of technology, and elements of international cooperation.

Although the EU is an economic body, it has made substantial legislative efforts to promote and protect human rights. In contrast, most regional economic bodies in the Global South focus primarily on economic and political integration.[39] Human rights issues are considered social issues and thus remain at the periphery.

In East Africa, for example, where Kenya is a member state of the East African Community (EAC), the treaty of establishment of the EAC in Article 120c calls on states to "closely cooperate themselves in social welfare with respect to among others the development and adoption of a common approach towards disadvantaged and marginalized groups including . . . persons with disabilities." Article 39 further places individual responsibilities on member states to "harmonise social policies in areas including promotion of equal opportunities and gender equality." Regarding accessibility, the EAC policy on persons with disabilities (2012), which was formulated as part of the collective responsibility to provide welfare to marginalized groups, provides that the EAC shall ensure the development of disability-friendly facilities and infrastructure, promote the use of sign language and braille, and establish a tax-free provision for all equipment that promotes access for persons with disabilities, including equipment and motor vehicles (Section 6.4). In addition, the policy recognizes the participation of persons with disabilities in the decision-making process, including policy design, implementation, and monitoring. However, this remains only a policy reference because there is marginal implementation.[40]

Further, a closer analysis of the treaty of establishment indicates that it encourages a voluntary approach, where partner states "closely cooperate" on social issues. In the absence of a mandatory requirement on issues of human rights in the regional framework, governing economic bodies can be seen as one of the reasons that partner states mainly refer to international, regional, and national laws and policies on human rights issues as opposed to a regional framework.[41] The analysis of institutional constraints therefore shifts from regional to national, where most decision-making processes in relation to issues of persons with disabilities occur. It is vital to note that in both Kenya and Mozambique, the right to information and accessibility is recognized constitutionally[42] and in specific legislation or policies on human rights for persons with disabilities.[43] Regarding participation, the Constitution of Kenya provides an opportunity to ensure the participation of persons with disabilities in key decision-making processes, including ICT-accessibility issues. Under Article 10 on national values and principles of governance, the constitution binds state organs, state officers, public officers, and all persons whenever applying the constitution or making or implementing public policy decisions to ensure participation of people and protection of the marginalized, including persons with disabilities. The constitution further requires that persons with disabilities make up 5 percent of elective and appointive positions in public bodies (Article 54(2)) and elective posts (Articles 97(1)(c) and 98(1)(c) and (d)). This quota system presents persons with disabilities the opportunity to participate in policy design as legislators, as well as in public bodies such as standards organizations and advisory commissions. However, although normatively the law safeguards participation of persons with disabilities and their representative organizations in key decision-making processes, including ICT-accessibility policies, in practice, the implementation of the law is limited. In response to a review by the Committee on the Rights of Persons with Disabilities,[44] DPOs in Kenya described consultation processes as "ad hoc episodic interfacing meetings and consultations with DPOs umbrella bodies including the Kenya National Association of the Deaf, United Disabled Persons of Kenya and the Association of the Physically Disabled of Kenya; but whose outcomes are not binding on participants, including policy makers; and in most cases remain un-implemented or enforceable with no accountability."

In Mozambique, the Policy for Persons with Disabilities recognizes the right of individuals and organizations to influence all decision-making processes that affect the life of persons with disabilities. Further, the strategy on employment in the public sector for persons with disabilities provides for the gradual adoption of employment quotas for employment of persons with disabilities in the public sector. In addition, the Federation of People with Disabilities in Mozambique (FAMOD)[45] acts as a representative of all DPOs and is a member of the National Council for Persons with Disabilities (CNAD). The CNAD coordinates governmental programs across all relevant governmental departments and is led by the Ministry of Women and Social Affairs, the entity responsible for the implementation of disability law and policy.

The challenge, however, is that although Kenya and Mozambique have established this mechanism of participation, there are structural factors that limit the participation of DPOs in the decision-making process related to ICT. For instance, in Mozambique, previous research suggests that civil society has marginal influence on law and policy-design processes concerning ICT.[46] Because the state budget is financed, in part, via direct budget support[47] and democratic institutions are insufficiently developed, the government tends to be accountable to donors rather than civil society and other institutional actors, such as the Mozambican Parliament. Therefore, involvement of persons with disabilities in ICT policy design is limited. Some authors recommend establishing specific participation mechanisms for civil society in decision-making processes for ICT policy and law, including monitoring and implementation.

Further, while in EU member states consumer adoption of ICT is high, in Mozambique ICT is still an emerging market. In general, there are few, if any, civil society organizations (CSOs) working on issues of ICT. Among

DPOs, there is limited understanding of accessibility as prescribed in the CRPD. Law and policy typically address accessibility in the built environment and neglect ICT accessibility.[48] DPOs lack expertise on law and policy reform concerning ICT accessibility, and therefore, there is an urgent need to develop the capacity of DPOs at the local and national level.[49] The situation is similar for Kenya.[50]

The lack of a welfare state in Kenya and Mozambique, like other countries in the Global South, means that these countries offer only minimal protections to their citizens, and persons with disabilities receive limited state support, if any.[51] Ensuring ICT accessibility requires both consultative and participatory processes whose goals are to achieve norms and standards that promote accessible ICT and a user population that is able to afford the services and hence experience the benefits.[52] For instance, despite recent positive economic performance, the World Bank still considers Mozambique a low-income country, where more than half the population lives on less than a dollar per day.[53] Further, the National Institute of Statistics estimated that only 26 percent of the Mozambican population has access to electricity.[54] Thus a large proportion of the population cannot afford the costs of ICT, such as computers and Internet services.

In cases where citizens can afford ICT, constraints associated with lack of infrastructure further limit access to ICT. The Research ICT in Mabila study, part of the Research Africa Initiative, provides data that support this argument. For instance, the percentage of people with access to fixed telephones (teledensity) is estimated at 0.4 percent and with access to mobile penetration at 33.1 percent, while for Internet users it is fixed around 4.8 percent.[55] In addition, evidence suggests that the initial state strategy on ICT was mainly focused on the state apparatus (e-government, the State Financial Management System) and expanding ICT services to communities in rural areas (telecenters).[56] However, these investments have yet to address issues of ICT accessibility for persons with disabilities. In such a scenario, economic empowerment programs and opportunities are vital. Access to gainful education and employment is a key contributor to promoting accessible ICT. This implies that discussions about ICT accessibility in the Global South must go beyond participation in policy design and must involve persons with disabilities in social development programs.

As recipients of technology produced by companies based in the Global North, the governments of Kenya and Mozambique enjoy less influence over global ICT markets, and thus consumers have less choice in purchasing ICT products and services. This translates to less power to negotiate terms of ICT policies. Because consumer products are imported from the Global North, consumers living in states in the Global South can purchase only products made available to their market. For example, Apple products are often considered to have high-quality accessibility features. However, the average cost of an Apple iPhone is around three hundred euros, which is typically not affordable for many persons with disabilities in Kenya who may be unemployed and living in poverty. Income per capita is one of the factors that affect supply of mobile phones.[57] The supply of iPhones on the Kenyan market will therefore be lower than that of other mobile phones, which may not have similarly high-quality accessibility features. As a result, people who rely on accessibility features to use their mobile phones, such as the blind or partially sighted, do not have access to consumer technology on an equal basis with others.

From the preceding discussion, it is evident that there are a number of challenges to ensuring ICT accessibility that specifically affect the Global South. The CRPD as a tool for achieving human rights of persons with disabilities presents an innovative solution to resolving these challenges. Article 32 of the CRPD requires states parties to cooperate internationally, and Article 33 requires the establishment of national monitoring mechanisms. National efforts to achieve ICT accessibility can be promoted through exchange programs and information sharing, as well as through the provision of technical and economic assistance. CSOs may influence international partners to adopt ICT-accessibility law and policy, for instance, by using donor agreements with the governments in the Global South to ensure the acquisition of accessible products and services. Through Article 33(2), national human rights institutions can be used as an agenda-setting tool by emphasizing the need to prioritize ICT accessibility through their key role of promotion, protection, and monitoring of human rights of persons with disabilities.

Thus, although both Kenya and Mozambique ensure that participatory processes exist that enable DPOs to contribute to decision making in ICT-accessibility policy, the experiences of DPOs suggest that these processes may not ensure meaningful participation. The pivot model suggests that DPOs in Kenya and Mozambique could strategically redirect their efforts from existing participatory forums to new or more meaningful efforts to ensure ICT accessibility. This section suggests that DPOs could pivot by focusing on structural factors that limit participation in five ways. First, DPOs could strategically redirect their efforts to promoting government accountability. Second, DPOs could support capacity building and competence in ICT accessibility among civil society organizations. Third, DPOs could support social development programs that promote ICT infrastructure investment. Fourth, DPOs could support the importation of low-cost accessible ICT. Fifth, DPOs could help ensure that international development programs promote ICT accessibility by requiring accessibility in donor agreements. Although each of these efforts requires investment and comes with differing costs and benefits, DPOs could nonetheless strategically redirect their efforts to take advantage of these opportunities for further promoting ICT accessibility in Kenya and Mozambique.

Conclusion

This chapter argues that social institutions constrain the behaviors of interest organizations in the EU. Policy entrepreneurs supported institutional change by providing opportunities for interest organizations to introduce ICT accessibility into public procurement standards. However, to participate in standardization, interest organizations must leverage the interdependent relations within policy networks, which enabled Fundación ONCE and Technosite to pivot by redirecting advocacy efforts to promoting institutional change in the EU.

We further argue that policy entrepreneurs provide opportunities for interest organizations to pivot by leveraging network relationships to participate in policy design and support institutional change. Although the EU's democratic deficit has, in part, limited advocacy efforts by the EDF to promote EU legislation for ICT accessibility, participatory processes provided an opportunity to enhance ICT accessibility through standardization. As a policy entrepreneur, Inmaculada Placencia-Porrero prompted institutional change by initiating the development of the M 376 standards. National interest organizations, including Fundación ONCE and Technosite, participated in the development of the M 376 standards. This chapter argues that these actors pivoted from the broader strategy to legislate for ICT accessibility to promoting ICT accessibility through standardization.

In addition, the Global South presents a unique scenario where, at the moment, a national focus on ICT accessibility will be a more viable strategy than regional advocacy efforts. Therefore, ICT accessibility in the Global

South will to some extent depend on the level of regulation and efficacy of ICT law and policy in the Global North. Although on paper, opportunities for participation of CSOs and persons with disabilities in policy design may be clear, ultimately such participation depends on how well versed the key state institutions (legislative, executive, and judicial) are on the rights of persons with disabilities, including ICT accessibility, and on the ability and capacity of DPOs to meaningfully and effectively influence decision-making processes.

Furthermore, development efforts in the Global South are typically financed by international organizations. This chapter argues that ICT-accessibility advocates in the Global South could pivot by redirecting efforts to advocating for socially responsible use of donor funding. International cooperation is required by the CRPD, and international donors are part of a global network of policy actors. With support from policy entrepreneurs within international development organizations, national interest organizations in the Global South could support institutional change by participating in the design of an organizational policy that requires all technology-based funding be subject to an accessibility review.

CHAPTER 15

The Accessibility Infrastructure and the Global South

Joyojeet Pal

Introduction

The coming of the UN Convention on the Rights of Persons with Disabilities (CRPD) and its exceptional success in bringing together nation-states to sign and ratify it signaled a new hope for greater accessibility for people with disabilities in much of the Global South. Since the UN adopted the convention in 2006, there has indeed been significant activity in disability-related policy making, but inaccessibility in architectural, economic, social, and digital realms remains the rule rather than the exception in much of the world.

As several scholars have noted, nation-states have signed the convention but have not acted resolutely on it.[1] Part of the challenge in several regions lies in reengineering the existing infrastructure and practices to achieve greater accessibility. This has presented two problems: first, ensuring the political and social will to act on legislative reform and accessible practices, and second, meeting the costs involved in upgrading the infrastructure. As is true with reengineering physical infrastructure, massive challenges hinder the reframing of policies and legislative structures made without consideration for accessibility. Although much work exists on the framing of new policy, comparatively little exists on evaluating present policy.[2]

Accessible digital technologies represent a small part of the overall accessibility pie but have been at the center of much attention because of the perceived promise of digital technologies to rearrange some of the structural imbalances that stack social and economic possibilities against people with disabilities. Ideas of technology reframing relationships of structural inequity are not specific to issues of disability and inaccessibility alone. Similar notions of technology correcting long-standing social issues of marginality have been proposed in discussions about the digital divide in much of the West and more recently in the continuing debate about the role of technology in global development.

The fundamental idea of technology as a personal, controllable artifact has gained strength in recent years with the proliferation of mobile devices worldwide. The idea of millions of the world's poorest people competently using mobile technologies has contributed to the widespread notion that change is not only possible but also is within the reach of those largely considered to be the most excluded from global wealth and attainment.[3] In turn, the very same ideas have furthered the belief that access to technology artifacts in and of itself represents a pathway to a global digital future.

For people with disabilities, there is little doubt that assistive technologies (ATs) within an accessible environment are critical to most forms of effective participation in a digital society. Yet too strong a focus on the affordances of technology can lead to rejection of individuals and their abilities, as well as the environment they exist in. Very little work has examined the gap between policy pronouncements—often driven at an international level by representatives of nation-states—and the complex on-the-ground realities of disability and access to services. Thus, although the CRPD does represent a massive global initiative in expanding accessibility, the practicalities of creating accessible physical and digital spaces require a closer look at the social and human infrastructure surrounding the people at stake.

Related Work

The idea of an enabling environment, which I refer to as an "accessibility infrastructure," is defined here as the sum of technological, social, and economic facilities that underlie the use of AT in a given ecosystem. Technological facilities include elements related to the network environment, information infrastructure, and human support that enable the individual to operate the AT to achieve its intended technical goals. Social and economic facilities, on the other hand, include elements related to the social environment of awareness of disability issues and support for the economic opportunities enabled by effective AT use.

The idea of an infrastructure has been extended beyond the core elements that support a function within a specific domain. The idea of an "entrepreneurial infrastructure," for instance, argues for linking physical resources with leadership and community development.[4] Within the domain of learning technologies, the idea of a social infrastructure goes a step further and argues that the use of technology for learning extends past the functional elements of technology to cultural beliefs, practices, sociotechnical relations, and interactions between the learning environment and the outside world.[5]

In human-computer interaction (HCI), this idea of infrastructure has been applied to the need for HCI to extend beyond methodological toolboxes relating primarily to an individual-system relationship to broader thought processes about the interactions involved in the building of technical systems.[6] Likewise, including social and economic factors in the definition of accessibility infrastructure helps in the consideration of elements that are fundamental enough to the usability of AT that they cannot be decoupled from the technology's functional use.

The idea of an accessibility infrastructure further borrows from work in sociotechnical studies that turns away from a black-box approach to artifacts that sees technologies as stand-alone items that interact with life situations toward a more nuanced view of interdependences.[7] This has long been an area of concern in organization theory, where scholars have called for package views of technology as existing within an ecosystem.[8] Such a view tempers the existing "techie triumphalism"—the thinking that technology offers a solution to any and all problems related to social and economic marginalization[9]—that has marked much of the past two decades.

Research has looked at areas where social infrastructure can be a barrier to AT use, such as lack of social support,[10] stigma associated with being an AT user,[11] negative attitudes of service providers or AT trainers, and lack of appropriate training.[12] There is also significant discontinuation of the use of ATs that are initially adopted, and one of the biggest factors in such discontinuation is individual disenchantment with technology.[13]

The Accessibility Infrastructure

In her introduction to the first special issue on assistive technology for the journal *Disability and Rehabilitation*, accessibility scholar Marcia Scherer marked what she then saw as a transition from a 20th-century "focus on people and their needs as a population" to one that was more about individuals, given that in the twenty-first century we have "largely succeeded in building our service infrastructure, and because we have the legislation and policies in place to protect our health, safety and rights, we can focus on the person."[14] Scherer's argument was related more centrally to the idea of technology customizability, but it hinged on a central premise of a solid service infrastructure, supported in turn by legislative and policy frameworks that enable the technology. Scherer revisited her position a little more than a decade later, turning back to a one-size-fits-all paradigm of the collective rather than the individual just as AT choices were increasingly being driven by affordability and speed to market.[15]

Scherer's precondition of a reliable framework within which AT entered the lives of users is largely unviable in much of the Global South. Unlike the situation in much of the West, where technology has largely followed or moved alongside developments in policy, a key difference in many of the recent signatory nations to the CRPD has been that AT has preceded relatively unprepared legal, political, and social environments. The possibilities that AT allows for people with disabilities in much of the world where architectural, economic, and social infrastructures have been built or refitted for accessibility are drastically different from those possibilities where the support structure is not available.

Over the past seven years, I and my colleagues have conducted mixed-method studies in urban areas of several countries around the world, mostly examinations of AT use in low- and middle-income regions, including Costa Rica, Ecuador, Guatemala, India, Jordan, Malawi, Mexico, Peru, Rwanda, Sierra Leone, and Venezuela.[16] Each of the countries had signed and ratified the CRPD, and all the Latin American sites and Rwanda had also ratified the optional protocol. The studies had distinct findings, many specific to the location and type of AT studied; however, themes of the accessibility infrastructure appeared consistently. Here I look at these distinctions under technical, economic, and social facilities, each of which is a part of my definition of the accessibility infrastructure.

Accessibility Overview of the Nations Studied

Although the nations studied are all broadly low- and middle-income countries, they range widely in size, level of economic development, access to technology, and policy history on disability issues. There are elements of infrastructure relevant to accessibility across the physical, virtual, and legal spaces. An overview of the basic legal and communications environment helps craft the settings in which this research was undertaken (Table 15.1). Technological indicators such as mobile and Internet access are important in terms of people's access to information, especially with mobile devices becoming accessibility tools. The rate of urbanization is important because of the concentration of accessibility-related services in urban areas.

Malawi

Malawi's Handicapped Persons Act (1971) is generally considered charity-based legislation. This policy was to be replaced by the National Policy on the Equalisation of Persons with Disabilities, which has not been ratified. Malawians have constitutional nondiscrimination protection under Section 20(1); however, the movement to a more rights-based approach to disability has been slow.[17] Malawi is among the countries that have not ratified the CRPD. Our research in Malawi, conducted in 2013, found that both architectural accessibility and access to AT in urban hubs of Malawi were poor. Multicountry studies have shown that access to assistive devices and vocational training is extremely low.[18]

Ecuador

Ecuador has had a national agency for people with disabilities (Consejo Nacional de Discapacidades, CONADIS) since 1996 alongside a periodic collection of disability-related statistics. A 2001 Ecuadorian law, Ley Vigente Sobre Discapacidades, contains protections for personal rights, coverage,

Table 15.1. Demographics of the Countries Studied

	Demographic overview			Technology infrastructure		Disability in society	
Country	Population (millions, 2014 est.)	GNI US$ (per capita)[1]	Percent Population Urban	Mobile Access[2]	Internet Access[3]	UNCRPD Status[4]	YLD[5]
Costa Rica	4.7	9,750	76%	143.83%	49.4%	OP ratified (Oct 2008)	7.9
Ecuador	16.0	6,040	64%	103.90%	43.0%	OP ratified (Apr 2008)	9.2
Guatemala	16.2	3,340	51%	106.63%	23.4%	OP ratified (Apr 2009)	10.0
India	1,252.4	1,610	32%	74.48%	18.0%	Con ratified (Oct 2007)	10.5
Jordan	7.6	4,940	83%	147.80%	44.0%	Con ratified (Mar 2007)	7.9
Malawi	16.3	250	16%	30.50%	5.8%	Signed only (Sep 2007)	13.1
Mexico	121.7	9,880	79%	82.54%	44.4%	OP ratified (Dec 2007)	8.2
Peru	31.1	6,270	78%	102.92%	40.2%	OP ratified (Jan 2008)	9.4
Rwanda	11.3	650	28%	64.02%	10.6%	OP ratified (Dec 2008)	13.3
Sierra Leone	6.5	720	40%	76.66%	2.1%	Con ratified (Mar 2007)	14.7
Venezuela	30.6	12,820	89%	98.95%	57.0%	OP ratified (Sep 2013)	9.1

[1] World Bank 2014 estimates of gross national income per capita.
[2] ITU.int 2014 estimates, active mobile connection as percentage of population; this number can be greater than 100% if people own more than one SIM card.
[3] World Bank 2014 estimates (http://data.worldbank.org/indicator/IT.NET.USER.P).
[4] OP ratified: optional protocol ratified; Con ratified: basic convention ratified.
[5] Years lost due to disability per 100 persons according to World Report on Disability. WHO defines YLD as the per capita aggregated years lost due to a health condition or its consequences. It is a component of disability-adjusted life year (DALY), which also includes years of life lost due to premature mortality.

and benefits. In 2008 the government of Rafael Correa instituted an initiative called Ecuador sin Barreras, bringing to national attention the issues around inaccessibility in society, with a key champion in Lenin Moreno, the vice president, himself a wheelchair user. Although studies have cited the lack of architectural accessibility, particularly in the highlands,[19] there have been important advances, such as the creation of an accessible rapid transit system and access to mobile technology across the population.

Costa Rica

In addition to its ratification of the optional protocol of the CRPD, Costa Rica has amended a number of legacy laws, including a law that specifies equal rights to education, access to work and hiring, social services, rehabilitation, and access to information and libraries. As a middle-income country, Costa Rica has a fairly well developed technology infrastructure and relatively good access to mobile devices. Among the Latin American regions studied, Costa Rica has the lowest rate of years lost to disability (YLD), indicating fewer challenges to the well-being of people with disabilities.

India

India's 2011 census estimated a disability prevalence of 2.2 percent in the country, among the lowest official estimates in the world because of issues with data collection and the lack of legal recognition of specific impairments or conditions as resulting in disablement. India has had the Persons with Disabilities Act since 1995, but efforts have been under way to update it. Accessibility for people with disabilities has been a major challenge, both in architectural access in rapidly urbanizing cities and in technological accessibility. There is a high degree of dependence on nonstate actors for access to accessible technologies.

Venezuela

Venezuela has had the Law for the Integration of Persons with Disabilities since 1993, which covers work, personal rights, health-care access, telecommunications access, and architectural accessibility. Since 2006, Venezuela has also had laws specifying employment quotas for people with disabilities, and in 2014 the Presidential Council for People with Disabilities was created to eliminate discrimination and increase disability awareness. However, despite its high telecommunications access and a high per capita income relative to the rest of Latin America, the rate of YLD remains high in Venezuela.

Sierra Leone

Although Sierra Leone ratified the CRPD within its first year, poverty and civil war have posed significant challenges to accessibility. These challenges include continuing debate about segregation versus integration of people with disabilities, a cycle of disability poverty,[20] and an Ebola epidemic, which has had an uneven impact on people without social safeguards. Sierra Leone has had constitutional provisions for nondiscrimination and welfare, but studies have shown greater exclusion from public health among people with disabilities.[21] Access to assistive technologies, such as screen readers, is extremely low.

Guatemala

After ratification of the CRPD, Guatemala designated the National Council for the Care of Persons with Disabilities as the government agency responsible for addressing issues relating to compliance. However, because of the recent history of violence in Guatemalan urban centers, with rates among the highest in the world, safety and access to services for people with disabilities have been major issues. Our work in Guatemala focused on the role of technology centers for people with disabilities as "safe spaces" in Guatemala City.

Mexico

Mexico expanded legal provisions for the inclusion of people with disabilities with a 2011 law that bans discrimination, in a historic act in which the president decried the country's paternalistic treatment of people with disabilities. The country also has local and regional discrimination laws. In addition, the National System for Integral Family Development works to provide services to people with disabilities. Mexico's size and diversity have led to significant variance in services, and the capital remains the primary locus of accessibility.

Jordan

After ratifying the CRPD in 2007, Jordan adopted the Law on the Rights of Persons with Disabilities. The Jordanian government, unlike that of a number of other countries, supervises all institutions offering welfare, rehabilitation, and relief. Although access to accessible mobile devices was found to be relatively easier in Jordan than in other sites, challenges to digital accessibility remain because of the lack of content in Arabic.

Peru

Peru has had a general law protecting the rights of persons with disabilities since 1999, as well as a disability commission (CONADIS) to connect with the disability community. Peru's Plan for Equal Opportunities defines disability as the relationship of people with their surroundings, a move away from the medical approach in many low- and middle-income countries. Peru was also among the first countries to specify the need for AT training centers through a 2005 law for the promotion of Internet access and physical accessibility of public Internet facilities for people with disabilities.

Rwanda

Rwanda has extremely high levels of exclusion from schooling[22] and shortages of accessible technologies and access to care.[23] Rwanda has not had an inclusive legal framework around disability; it did, however, create the National Council for People with Disabilities in 2010 to mainstream disability across government services. Despite the impressive gains in technology infrastructure in the country, Rwanda lags in providing access to quality accessible technologies for people with disabilities, such as vision impairments.

Technical Facilities

A common set of technical infrastructure challenges that we found across all sites was the lack of training support. Community service organizations (CSOs) such as disabled people's organizations (DPOs) were overwhelmingly important in the ecosystem of service providers regarding both access to and training in AT use. The extent of acquisition of AT through nonprofit organizations differed depending on the nature of the disability (people who needed screen readers, for instance, were consistently more likely to obtain these through CSO contacts than people who needed wheelchairs), and there were also regional differences (in Jordan, for instance, more people depended on state sources for AT than in India). The consistent factor, however, was the centrality of CSOs to the technology use environment. "There's no institution that teaches us [web applications]," said a fifty-one-year-old man from Peru. "We have to find shortcuts with the keyboard; we have to check compatibilities among the programs, and those things we learn by practice."[24]

Training for technology and access to appropriate technology were frequently noted themes across sites. For instance, our study in Mexico, which focused on empowerment within the community of wheelchair users, showed that access to and training in the use of active wheelchairs, which are better suited for uneven roads, was a challenge, whereas in Jordan, Peru, and India, where we examined desktop environments for people with visual impairments, we found that training in use of screen readers was a challenge. The common thread was the need for independent and constantly evolving forms of training, particularly in an accessibility environment that evolved rapidly with new technologies and infrastructures alike.

Research participants across the sites who used nonvisual interfaces, in particular, reported the lack of access to training in step with the evolution of the technology. In countries with limited social networks for people with disabilities, the transition out of educational institutions often meant that people had no social infrastructure to share experiences on AT or other technology use. A twenty-year-old Jordanian man emphasized the importance of online social networks for this purpose: "It became the main source to

[stay] connected with old friends.... Also, it allowed me to know how the SR works better since these require special scripts.... Many of the people with low vision cannot make use of the FB because they do not know about the scripts that come along with JAWS, but have to be added separately."[25]

Online social media helped fill the gap left by the lack of posteducational social infrastructure in many locations, but they also played an important role in building a support structure for technology use and a means for independent access to training resources. However, the first step in setting up basic access remains a challenge in much of the world. In the case of people with vision impairments, for instance, the initial cost of a computing device was compounded by the cost of expensive software. Falling prices alongside rising computing capabilities on mobile devices have improved the situation in many parts of the Global South, but because of the lack of an accessibility infrastructure, such as accessible public libraries, informal networks of citizens continue to drive technology choices.

The reliance on market forces for choices of technology may seem a priori a good means to validate the quality of new technologies, but it also indicates that people without access are likely to be excluded from these networks. In countries with fairly well developed networks of AT users, such as India, these online networks have increasingly become the norm, whereas in poorer nations, such as Malawi and Sierra Leone, these support networks do not exist online. Likewise, access to language resources is a significant accessibility-infrastructure barrier. In the case of screen-reading technology, Spanish-speaking individuals in Latin America and English-educated populations in other regions could access large amounts of data using screen readers that functioned well on roman script. However, language itself can be a barrier, as told by a twenty-four-year-old Amman, Jordan, man: "Once you start using Arabic, the problems increase substantially. Sometimes, there are buttons that are not accessible.... We use TTS [text-to-speech] that is installed on its own.... The [screen reader] I am using is actually cracked [pirated]; I installed it from the Internet. I got this link from one of my friends. We usually tell each other once we know if there is anything new."[26]

Studying the use of AT also makes clear that the elements of daily technology use that have become ubiquitous for much of the population can be additionally disabling because of the lack of supporting infrastructure. The increasing prevalence of web-based on-demand video content (and in some cases required video-based job-training content) meant that the average person with hearing had much better access to information than someone who relied on captioning, which is rarely available outside a small number of languages.

The increasing use of location-based services offered a different set of challenges for both wheelchair users and people with vision impairments. On the one hand, these offered new means of way finding, but on the other, the lack of accompanying architectural infrastructure meant that relying on these services posed other risks. A twenty-nine-year-old man from India illustrated this point: "Although we have GPS and although we have maps, Bombay is not a place which you can rely on maps. I mean, I had a terrible experience. Even if I am using maps, I am not sure it is giving me right direction."[27]

A wheelchair user may have no clear indication of the quality of flat pavement access in directions offered by a global positioning system (GPS); likewise, an individual relying on a screen reader may not have the same good sense of control over his or her environment as a sighted person combining GPS with visual perceptions. As social media technologies become the standard means of selecting locations for social occasions, such as hotels or restaurants, there is an obvious increase in the possibility of accessibility-related information, but there are accompanying risks with the accuracy of such information and individuals' control over verifiability.

That individuals have better accessibility information through social media is clearly a good thing, and where individuals or groups could create networks of reliable information, these were extremely valuable. However, the challenge emerges when networks become the norm, part of the general expectation of how people interact in society, without the legal and social infrastructures that govern such information. The increase in online information did not necessarily equate to an increase in a culture of individuals adding to the requisite metainformation—such information was not truly accessible to everyone.

Economic Facilities

The up-front cost of accessibility in workplaces emerged consistently as a challenge people faced in getting a job interview. On the one hand, computing in the workplace made certain kinds of office jobs much more accessible to people with disabilities, but on the other, it created new forms of channeling people with disabilities toward certain jobs, as described by a twenty-six-year-old Caracas man: "They place us, more than anything, in the area of informatics, because you will be in a chair, you go in your wheelchair if you are in a wheelchair, and the whole time you will be there at your computer, you don't have to move or anything."[28]

As with the respondent in Venezuela, we came across many cases where the focus of workplace access was on the specifics of the job function rather than the ecosystem for work. In the absence of structured options that allowed for more broad-based entry into the workforce, people with visual impairments in India were offered training in business-process outsourcing tasks such as medical transcription, and that type of training was incorporated into basic screen-reader training. Such training clearly had benefits for workplace skill development but provided training so specific that it had no transferability to other occupations, as in the case of a thirty-three-year-old medical transcriptionist from Bangalore who found herself redundant once transcription jobs started reducing in number: "[My] entire basic [computer] course involved in medical transcription. . . . I was very proud to say that I know medical transcription because it is a way for overall improvement in terms of communication, language, computer usage, everything, and also you get a stature by earning," she said. "In the beginning, it was a very high salary; these days it is nothing."[29]

The experiences of people coming out of training centers enabling screen-reader access in India are comparable in some ways to experiences in parts of Latin America. With the lack of functioning state-run employment exchanges, nonprofit screen-reading training centers were typically part of DPOs or CSOs that provided services for people with disabilities. Consequently, these locations doubled as channels to employers. Convincing employers who had never hired a person with a specific disability that a prospective employee had the skills to perform relevant work was a challenge across locations. A consistent illustration of this was employers' reluctance to invest in licensed screen-reader software. Software such as JAWS (Job Access with Speech) or WindowEyes, industry-standard screen readers, typically cost roughly US$1,000 per license, prohibitive for individuals and significant for small companies.

The lack of stable alternatives to JAWS or WindowEyes (the open-source software Non Visual Desktop Access [NVDA], while widely installed by users across locations, was considered significantly less powerful as an enterprise tool) meant that users had to deal with demo versions, which were particularly problematic in workplaces where the network needed to be restarted to boot up JAWS. A man from Lima, fifty-four, described a case in point: "In that time there was no license and we had to restart the computer every 40 minutes. So imagine, you're preparing the text and the machine tells you that you have to restart it, otherwise your JAWS turns off."[30] In several countries, the problem with pirated screen readers appeared repeatedly—people had a copy of AT on a personal machine, but companies were often unwilling to allow them to use it on company networks if it meant using unlicensed software.

With the lack of accessible work environments being the standard rather than the exception, participants in the research frequently noted being more embarrassed about the costs incurred by their employers than expectant that this would be a standard of practice. Consequently, when people with disabilities were employed at certain firms that were accessible and made available the requisite AT for people to be effective at work, word got around. These firms came to be known as "champion firms" and became popular among job candidates.

Beyond such champion firms, the existence of champion organizations such as CSOs was a more important concern, especially for people who found that their access to economic opportunities was mediated through these organizations. As stated by a forty-four-year-old man from Quito: "One never knows when the program [Ecuador Sin Barreras] funding will be cut, by the next government, for example, and these opportunities won't exist."[31]

Social Facilities

A consistent theme of our research on AT across all locations was the gap between the theoretical possibilities that the technology allowed and what the workplace believed a person with a disability could do. The issues with workplace opportunities found in the technical and economic challenges are closely related to the underlying social and cultural attitudes toward disability that we found across locations.

The first and most common cultural attitude is that of charity. This attitude is problematic because of the ways in which it infantilizes individuals with disabilities, such that those individuals are not seen as capable of managing their own affairs and are instead expected to be dependent economically and socially on others. This attitude by extension implies that accessibility is not the responsibility of the state but of charitable individuals. As a

Jordanian man summarized, "You can have all the tech you want, but people think still that a VI [person with a vision impairment] should remain a 'blind' person working and living in a mosque.... [When I went job hunting,] I would be thrown out of some places by the security. There are others who would give me money as though I am a beggar. He only looks at me as though I am someone in need and a conduit to get to heaven."[32]

The charity-oriented view of technology reinforces the idea that the individual employment seeker with a disability is necessarily at the workplace as an act of charity by the employers rather than for the skills that person brings to the workplace, as would be true for any other employee. A thirty-one-year-old woman from San José, Costa Rica, explained it this way: "People think that every disabled person is a 'pobrecita' [poor little thing]. That word has destroyed this country. The 'pobrecita' is conception that the [person with a disability] is useless, that depends on charity . . . so when people see that you can do something . . . they are amazed!"[33]

A broader cross-regional pattern was that of an urban-rural distinction in access to resources. People with disabilities who were from villages and who had the means to relocate often moved to urban areas to find better access to accessible services. In much of the Global South, lack of adequate transportation and education infrastructure in rural areas has meant that community resources for people with disabilities are relatively limited.

This creates exclusions that are driven by information asymmetry. We found that people living in rural areas had far less awareness of accessibility services than those in urban areas. "I come from a rural background; through some of the friends who had moved to city, I came to know that even VI can use computers with the help of a talking button," said a twenty-four-year-old man in Chennai, India. "My parents also encouraged me to go to the nearby town to study and get introduced to computers. So I completed my 12th grade and moved to Chennai to join a college. While attending the college, I actually started to operate computers with AT."[34]

The social infrastructure for people with disabilities extends beyond the logistics of access to services to a more fundamental issue of social networks. Although people who had congenital disabilities or who had acquired disabilities at a young age were relatively aware of AT, those who had acquired disabilities later in life had a hard time finding out about AT options and in some cases went years without access to basic information. We also found here the impacts of an underdeveloped educational infrastructure, which leads to the segregation of people with disabilities, and consequently a lack of awareness of AT in the mainstream population outside of those with disabilities, because those who acquire disabilities later in life often do not have people with those impairments in their immediate economic and social circles. A sixty-year-old from India described the experience of losing sight later in life: "Though I was staying in an [affluent] area and I was surrounded by highly educated people, . . . I remained at home for 10 years without knowing that I could be independent. But I feel even now the situation is the same; whenever people see me carrying a laptop or working on the computers, they ask what it is that I am doing with a computer when I can't see."[35]

Social inhibitors related to job-market outcomes extended beyond factors such as charity or tradition-driven attitudes toward the care of people with disabilities. A separate set of beliefs contributes to perceptions of why individuals have disabilities, such as transgressions in past lives,[36] curses,[37] or demonic possession.[38] Such beliefs, far from being the exception, were common among people without disabilities as they explained the causes for their impairments.[39] Individuals subjected to multiple forms of social exclusion driven by such beliefs had less social capital and consequently comparatively fewer pathways into services or employment.[40]

As with the centrality of CSOs in ensuring economic and technical resources for people with disabilities, these organizations offered both social connections and a safe space for interaction; in several study locations, these organizations were seen as places devoid of beliefs and exclusions that were otherwise markers of peoples' public experiences. A thirty-year-old woman from Campeche, Mexico, described her experience with a CSO: "For me it [the CSO] was like a club, like a club where we all spoke the same language because we all had a disability. What was different, what was strange, was not having a disability, not the person who has one. . . . In addition to preparing us in computers it was like a community in which we felt understood. And beyond that it was one of the first things that I did that motivated me more as a person."[41]

Conclusion

Accessibility has been a complex debate in much of the Global South in the years since the UN CRPD. The global consciousness on signing the convention created formal state-level recognition of issues related to disabilities, but our work over the past several years has shown the very same issues repeated across various regions. In much of the Global South, we found lingering economic and social inequalities that have led to the creation of subclasses of exclusion among AT users in these regions. And even when individuals with economic means in countries like Peru, Mexico, India, and Jordan could afford to avail themselves of the latest personal AT, these technologies invariably fell short of their full use potential given the larger infrastructure within which they were operated.

Framing accessibility from the perspective of individuals and their relationship with technology overestimates the affordances of the artifact itself without the supporting infrastructure. The vision of what a well-stocked mobile or desktop device can do for the social and economic participation of a person with a disability in the West has long dominated the discourse of accessibility, which places at its center of its analysis the individual and the transformative technology. That accessible technology exists and that international conventions such as the CRPD explicitly recommend their representation in national disability policy approaches are largely separate from states parties grasping or making available the conditions necessary for these technologies to be usable.

Yet it is important to go beyond stating the obvious. There is no doubt that mobiles are playing an enhancing the quality of individuals' exchanges with their surroundings and economies, even in those societies least equipped with accessible digital or architectural publics. Indeed, important trends have the potential to raise consciousness of accessibility. The falling prices of mobile devices and the relatively lesser requirement for training in their use are reduced cost and training barriers in comparison with the desktop environment, particularly for people with visual impairments. Device manufacturers and content producers who need to make their products accessible and aligned with the legal strictures of Western markets likewise end up benefiting the world as a whole. Multilingual systems, crowd-sourced efforts, such as accessibility ratings for businesses, restaurants, travel, and medical services, and captions for video content similarly expand the realm of accessible information.

Despite the fact that some of these expanding accessibility options exist already, we still find severe limitations to the use of accessible devices—people with disabilities often find that the purchase of technology needs to be accompanied by justifications of financial benefit. In societies where people with disabilities are not expected to contribute to economic resources and are often excluded from control of household expenditure decisions, the problem is arguably generational in that the history of disability in society becomes an important indicator of the possibilities the state or family alike affords the individual. We saw this to be true in the workplace in the reluctance of companies to invest in AT for computing devices. Collectives, be they families or units of governance, frequently measure their welfare in short-term assessments of the economic benefit of investing in accessibility. Here, the disability community plays a role both as the exemplar, making accessible technology visible in public places, and as a support structure for those seeking knowledge and support as potential AT users. This underlines the need for an accessibility-infrastructure approach to thinking about AT that includes educating a range of stakeholders about the need for AT.

This chapter recognizes the need for rethinking the accessibility infrastructure in three specific ways: technical infrastructure, economic infrastructure, and social infrastructure. Regarding technical infrastructure, in order for AT to be usable in individual and community settings, nation-states must invest in a range of technical support options. These include annual surveys of AT users to understand typical blocks to effective use of technology; access to AT information and training at existing institutions, such as public libraries and colleges, included within the purview of Article 24 of the CRPD; encouragement of online social groups for the exchange of technical support; language-specific resources, such as support for captioning for digital content and local languages for screen readers; and engagement with AT producers to negotiate bulk rates for low-cost technology.

Improvements in the economic infrastructure will require implementation of the CRPD's requisite steps to functionally ensure reasonable accommodation at the workplace. The first step is ensuring the use of surveys directly through state means or through public-private partnerships, such as crowd-sourced building surveys of architectural infrastructure for AT access, including wheelchair ramps and braille signage, per Articles 9 and 20. Other steps will be the creation of nondiscrimination training materials; implementation of nondiscrimination laws in the job-selection process, per Article 5; creation of information resources for individuals to report workplace conditions; and enforcement of the requirement that major service providers ensure that their materials are available in accessible formats, per Article 21.

Social infrastructure would be enhanced if nation-states provided educational campaigns through popular media on disability issues. In this regard, detailed surveys should first be conducted of the prevalent cultural attitudes toward disability, per Article 31 of the CRPD. In response, mass-media campaigns should be conducted to resolve misunderstandings about disability issues, per Article 8. The use of AT and the workplace equity of people with disabilities should be highlighted in such campaigns. Finally, disability studies should be incorporated into school curricula by taking further the spirit of Article 8.

The purpose of this work is not to undermine the successes of legislative gains and the consciousness of disability from a rights perspective that the CRPD has arguably had an important role in furthering. Our goal, rather, is to closely examine accessibility, and specifically digital accessibility, since the adoption of the CRPD. As more nation-states implement their own accessibility agendas, it is imperative that thought be applied to the technical, economic, and social infrastructures that enable or disable the technology itself to function.

CHAPTER 16

ICT Access, Disability Human Rights, and Social Inclusion in India

Sanjay S. Jain

Introduction

Unless societies embrace principles of accessibility and universal design[1] across all sectors, including information and communication technology (ICT), the normative goal of full participation and social inclusion[2] of disabled persons[3] is merely a distant dream. This is true for all states, including India. Examining accessibility for disabled persons in India reveals a strange paradox. On the one hand, India is making headway generally in the arena of science and technology, including the development, dissemination, and use of ICTs. On the other, little progress has been made in the evolution of accessible and enabling environments for disabled persons. This chapter surveys the status of disabled persons and their access to ICT in India, assesses progress undertaken by the Indian government and the private sector, and considers future avenues for improvements in the sector.

The Relationship of Disability, Technology, and Society

Estimates of the number of disabled persons in India vary depending on the source. The World Bank estimated that disabled persons constituted 4 to 8 percent of the country's population, or some 40 to 90 million persons, in 2007. However, the 2011 national census, which used a different methodology and definition of disability, estimated 2.13 percent of the Indian population, about 22 million individuals, to have some form of disability. Both estimates are well under the global average of 15 percent, but the relevant point is that even the lower figure is drastically above the 0.0009 percent of the national budget directly spent by India on the disability sector.[4] With such limited resource allocation, it is questionable how India can fulfill its obligations to persons with disabilities. The situation regarding accessible ICT is no different.

The interaction and encounters of disabled persons in the technosphere of Indian society overemphasize a medical model of disability. Some disability rights advocates, for example, Fiona Kumari Campbell, view technological interventions as devaluing the experience of disability because they seek to adapt and repair deficiencies of disabled bodies through the use of technical gadgets. According to Campbell, this in turn has the capacity "to redefine disability as being provisional or tentative"[5] and in consequence also causes disabled persons themselves to internalize an "ableist" view of disabled persons. However, Campbell does not adopt the simplistic assumption "that technologies are inherently dangerous or implicitly beneficial"[6] and instead emphasizes that all human life is now pervaded by technology. Like Campbell, I do not accept an exaggerated and suspicious outlook regarding the relationship of disability and technology at its face value. Instead, I endorse her point of view that adoption and acceptance of technology should not make any disabled person believe that she or he is no longer disabled. In other words, embracing technology cannot and should not be perceived as a movement toward restoration of normality.

At the same time, the role of technology as an enabling or disabling factor cannot be viewed in isolation. Rather, the issue must be examined through the lens of social informatics. According to Mark Warschauer, social informatics implies that the goal of providing access to ICT cannot proceed without socioeconomic development. He argues that realizing this objective involves not only providing computers and Internet links or shifting to online platforms but also developing relevant content in diverse languages, promoting literacy and education, and mobilizing community and institutional support toward achieving community goals. In this way, technology becomes a means, and often a powerful one, rather than an end in itself.[7] Warschauer's approach very vividly exposes the simplistic paradigm underlining the so-called mainstream digital divide that, according to Vandana Chaudhary and her colleagues, "overlooks the relationship between disability, technology, and society, and offers unsophisticated digital solutions to complex problems." Notably, "digital solutions" in India and the United States "disregard the economic, technological, social, and cultural factors that underpin the complex reality of the digital divide."[8] Thus it is not possible to remedy the right of disabled persons to access ICT across the world merely by focusing on economic resources and by supplying them with technogadgets, because doing so does not fully manifest the complexities of the digital divide.

Chaudhary and colleagues illustrate the relevance of context by comparing inaccessible formal informational structures in the United States with informal information sources in India. They reach the startling conclusion that "in India, digital scarcity excludes visually disabled people from access to formal information." This makes them "info poor" in relation to technology access vis-à-vis disabled persons in the United States. However, the relative ease of accessing informal information and the ability to maneuver informational spaces through the support of social networks make them "info rich" in comparison with their American counterparts. In other words, we have to transcend the binary of info rich and info poor and adopt a cross-cultural and sociopolitical perspective to address the issue of informational inequity in civilization.[9]

Toward a Normative International Regime of Accessibility as a Right

Internationally, the importance of accessibility got real momentum with the commemoration of the International Year of Disabled Persons in 1981. Although the World Programme of Action concerning Disabled Persons 1982[10] emphasized the importance of access to various systems of society, the United Nations Standard Rules on the Equalization of Opportunities for Persons with Disabilities[11] targeted ICT accessibility as an area of priority for states.[12] Rights-based claims of accessibility, universal design, and reasonable accommodation transformed into legal obligations on states parties with the entry into force of the United Nations Convention on the Rights of Persons with Disabilities (CRPD).[13] The CRPD explicitly incorporates the principles of rights to accessibility and universal design as legal norms by adopting a twin-track approach. These rights are conceived as overarching principles under Article 3 and as specific obligations under Article 9, which addresses access, and Article 21, which relates to freedom of expression; these rights are raised implicitly in a number of other articles, including Article 30, which relates to participation in social, cultural, and leisure activities. Notably, the experts elected by states to monitor the CRPD issued a general comment on accessibility in 2014. The comment is categorical in articulating the significant role of accessibility in empowering disabled persons and highlights the significance of accessible ICT for enabling the full participation of disabled persons in all walks of life.

It is interesting to examine the question whether the obligation to provide reasonable accommodation stands on higher footing than the obligation to provide accessibility and promote universal design. However, this question should be answered in light of the contexts of these obligations. The former is case sensitive to particular circumstances and can succeed only if it does not impose "disproportionate and undue burden" on its providers.[14] Thus a duty to provide reasonable accommodation could also cover certain aspects of a right to accessibility, for example, where an inaccessible website does not allow disabled persons to obtain information or use a service on an equal basis with others. In consequence, the operation of principles of reasonable accommodation and accessibility may have a symbiotic relationship with the reasonable-accommodation mandate in a way that breaks new ground for judicial review and rights conceptualizing. Imprints of these international developments are also visible in the Incheon Strategy[15] adopted by states of the Asia-Pacific region, to which India is a party. India is, foremost for this subject, likewise a state party to the CRPD, through which it is obligated to provide accessible and barrier-free environments to its disabled citizens.

India's Legal Landscape

The CRPD has the potential to transform the Constitution of India. Unlike the constitutions of South Africa,[16] Canada,[17] or other states, the Indian Constitution does not explicitly enjoin disability-based discrimination. It nevertheless echoes the principle of accessibility in a number of fundamental rights, including rights to equal protection of the law,[18] freedom of speech and expression and freedom of movement,[19] and human dignity.[20] Further, a reading of Article 14, which enshrines the principles of equality before the law and equal protection of the law, in conjunction with Articles 15 and 16, which impose antidiscrimination obligations on the state and its citizens, and alongside Articles 3, 5, and 9 of the CRPD is imperative as an aftermath of CRPD ratification. Doing so results in a categorical inference that discrimination on the ground of disability amounts to unequal treatment and denial of equal protection of the law. This point is further strengthened by the fact that just as social disabilities are combated in the Indian Constitution on the grounds of race, caste, sex, and other status-based identities, by analogy, discrimination on the ground of disability must also be prohibited. The proposition may be stated from another angle: if citizens with social disabilities can redress discrimination, the constitution cannot deny redress for discrimination on the ground of disability. In fact, Indian courts have held in several cases that disability-based discrimination violates the right to equality under the constitution.[21] Accessible ICT creates opportunities to access information and enhance the socioeconomic and political mobility of disabled citizens. Conversely, its denial amounts to violation of equal protection of the law, a fundamental constitutional right. Recognition and protection of a right to accessible ICT by disabled persons similarly promote the social model of disability, which is at the core of the CRPD.[22]

Before CRPD ratification, the enactment of the Persons with Disabilities (Equal Opportunities, Protection of Rights and Full Participation) Act, 1995, was the first major step taken by the Parliament of India toward the recognition and protection of certain de facto interests of disabled persons. Although this act does not recognize or explicitly protect the right to accessibility, it incorporates this principle by implication in Section 42, which requires appropriate schemes to provide aids and appliances to persons with disabilities. The national policy on persons with disabilities adopted by India in 2006 continued the focus on assistive devices by procurement of learning equipment such as braille-writing machines, dictaphones, CD players and tape recorders, communication aids, and assistive and alerting devices. Curiously, it does not mention computers or accessibility-enhancing software, nor is there any attempt to shed light on the need for accessible websites.[23] Perturbed by the accessibility deficit in this policy, a large number of nongovernmental organizations (NGOs) in the disability sectors, such as the DAISY Forum of India, the Inclusive Planet Centre for Disability Law and Policy, Xavier's Resource Centre for the Visually Challenged, the Centre for Internet and Society, the National Federation of the Blind, and the National Association for the Blind (NAB), formed an alliance to press India on this issue. This coalition also lobbied for adoption of a draft consultation paper by the Ministry of Electronic and Information Technology, New Delhi (MEITY), on a National Policy on Universal Electronic Accessibility (NPOUEA) in March 2010.[24] The Indian government released this policy in revised form in October 2013.

The National Policy on Universal Electronic Accessibility

The NPOUEA is a forward-looking document that emphasizes and articulates the rights of "disabled persons" as they might be envisioned in the preamble to the Indian Constitution, which is silent about disability.[25] The policy covers electronics and ICT products (both hardware and software), assistive technology, and independent-living aids and advocates for the adoption of the principle of universal design.[26] It ensures justice, equality, liberty and fraternity, individual dignity, and equal status and opportunity to all citizens, including disabled persons. One of the major aspirations of this policy is to facilitate equal, unhindered, and universal access to electronics and ICT products and services, with local language support to disabled persons. In doing so, it emphasizes that electronics and ICT can mitigate barriers faced by individuals with disabilities and enable them to participate independently in day-to-day life. The NPOUEA also recognizes the need to eliminate discrimination on the basis of disability and to facilitate equal access to electronics and ICT.[27] Therefore, the NPOUEA is the first policy document in which the government of India explicitly links reasonable accommodation with disability-based discrimination; it achieves this goal by adopting verbatim the definition of "discrimination on the basis of disability and universal design" from the CRPD.[28]

The NPOUEA places important stakeholders—including central government ministries, states, union territories, departments and agencies, publicly funded entities, civil society organizations, and service providers—under an obligation to raise awareness about this policy and assist in its implementation. The policy attaches particular importance to the role of disabled people's organizations (DPOs) in the promotion of electronics and ICT products and services among disabled persons. Educational and vocational training institutes are similarly called on "to impart training on usage of electronics and ICTs products and services for PWDs [persons with disabilities]."[29]

A number of strategies have been conceived for the effective implementation of this policy, including raising awareness about universal electronics accessibility and the adoption of universal design, capacity building and infrastructure development, setting up of model electronics and ICT centers for providing training and demonstrations to special educators and physically or mentally disabled persons, conducting research and development, developing programs and schemes with greater emphasis on disabled women and children, and developing government procurement guidelines for electronics and ICTs in the light of accessibility and assistive needs.[30] Another aspect is informing the electronics and ICT curricula in programs like computer science and engineering about accessibility standards and guidelines and universal design.[31]

The policy likewise calls for the implementation and monitoring of progress toward these goals, with strong emphasis on the participation of rehabilitation professionals and disabled persons.[32] The NPOUEA calls for adherence to all contemporary accessibility standards, including Authoring Tools Accessibility Guidelines (ATAG), Web Content Accessibility Guidelines (WCAG), and User Agent Accessibility Guidelines (UAAG). The policy mandates that content in electronic format, including publications, periodicals, journals, multimedia, and educational materials like textbooks, be produced in accessible format with local language support.[33]

E-educational initiatives like Inflibnet, EPG Pathshala,[34] and EduSAT[35]— e-platforms for students and teachers at graduate and postgraduate levels that provide multimedia access to a number of world-famous databases and e-resources nearly free of charge—and ePathshala[36] are noteworthy in this connection. These initiatives have been found to be quite useful and reasonably accessible for disabled persons, including myself. Two more recent initiatives seeking to increase access for persons with disabilities to ICT are set forth in the following sections.

The New Delhi Declaration on Inclusive ICTs for Persons with Disabilities

With a view to include disability-related ICT issues in the forthcoming United Nations Sustainable Development Goals (SDGs), an international conference titled "From Exclusion to Empowerment: Role of Information and Communication Technologies for Persons with Disabilities" was convened in November 2014 in New Delhi by the government of India in cooperation with UNESCO, UN member states (especially Kuwait), and international, regional, and national public and private partners. The conference adopted a vital outcome document, "The New Delhi Declaration on Inclusive ICTs for Persons with Disabilities: Making Empowerment a Reality."[37] This declaration calls on all states to use their energies and abilities to "utilize advice and experience" from disabled people "in the design and production of mainstream and assistive products and services from the outset rather than as an afterthought,"[38] to do so by applying universal design and open-access principles,[39] and, moreover, to make disability accessibility "a required part of every procurement procedure" and best practice both within state services and "when negotiating with private sector partners."[40] To ensure the efficacy of this declaration, states are called on to "adopt, implement and monitor national accessibility standards and measures including subsidies or fiscal relief to families which have people with disabilities,"[41] and "to assure them full participation in knowledge societies."[42] Similarly, corporations in the sphere of ICT are called on to recognize the needs and perspectives of persons with disabilities both as a rights obligation and as a potential customer base[43] and therefore to apply universal design principles and to include disabled persons in developing "accessible, affordable and inclusive products and services."[44]

Accessible India Campaign

The Accessible India Campaign is the most concrete action by the Indian government to materialize the goals set forth in the NPOUEA, the New Delhi Declaration, the Incheon Strategy, the CRPD, and General Comment 2 of the CRPD committee. It was launched on the occasion of the International Day of Persons with Disabilities, December 3, 2015. Its vision statement recognizes the human rights obligations arising in connection with accessible ICT[45] and commits the government of India to adopt a multipronged strategy consisting of "leadership endorsements," "mass awareness," "capacity building through workshops," legal interventions, technology solutions, resource generation, and encouraging public-private collaborations.[46] One of the focus areas of the Accessible India Campaign is to identify the interface of ICT with universal accessibility by increasing the percentage of accessible public documents and websites.[47] To attain this objective, India will conduct an accessibility audit of 50 percent of all government websites, both central and state, and convert them into fully accessible websites by

July 2019.[48] India will also ensure that at least 50 percent of all public documents issued by both central and state governments meet accessibility standards by July 2019.[49] Regrettably, the campaign does not target or sanction privately operated websites and servers that are dedicated for public use, even to the extent of WCAG-standard compliance, and instead leaves the private realm to self-regulation.[50]

Additional Initiatives by the Indian Government

The Indian government has proposed national disability rights legislation to be in compliance with the CRPD. The Rights of Persons with Disabilities Bill, 2014,[51] lays great emphasis on principles of accessibility and would impose duties on the National Commission for Persons with Disability (NCPD) to formulate regulations addressing aspects of accessibility[52] and on appropriate levels of government to provide all audio, print, and electronic media in accessible format, equal access to electronic media, and electronic goods and services in universal design format.[53] The bill similarly promotes the development, production, and distribution of universally designed consumer products for disabled persons[54] and would require all service providers to adhere to accessibility regulations within two years of notification. However, the central government, following consultations with the NCPD, could grant further extensions in respect to certain services.[55] The central and state governments would also be obligated to initiate sensitization and awareness-raising programs and research and development to enhance habilitation and rehabilitation services. All universities would be mandated to promote teaching and research in disability studies.[56] Although these provisions are salutary, the duties and responsibilities cast on the NCPD and relevant governments are fairly general, without specific time frames or mechanisms for noncompliance, and so courts may find it extremely difficult to affix responsibility for their implementation.

For the first time in India, a government has attempted to address the issue of accessible television to persons with disabilities. The Accessible India Campaign provides for the enhancement of "the proportion of daily captioning and sign language interpretation" of public television programs, including news, supported by the government.[57] The campaign aimed at the development and adoption of national standards on captioning and sign language interpretation in consultation with national media authorities by July 2016[58] and ensuring that 25 percent of all public television programs aired by government channels meet these standards by July 2019.[59] This initiative, while groundbreaking, is nevertheless perfunctory because it brings into its coverage only two types of disability groups and limits its scope to news programs. Moreover, by being limited to the public realm, it ignores the mandate of the CRPD, the New Delhi Declaration, and General Comment 2 vis-à-vis public-private partnerships. Worse still, the campaign does not emphasize the need to comply with international television-accessibility standards evolved by the International Television Union and others.

Some progress has been made in mandating the provision of educational content in accessible formats with the amendment of the Indian Copyrights Act 1957 to enable the alteration of copyrighted materials in accessible formats for disabled persons.[60] However, these rights come with substantial riders and exceptions.[61] Interestingly, these loopholes are not applicable to the alteration of copyrighted materials in any accessible formats by any person to facilitate the ability of disabled persons to access the same, including sharing with any person with a disability for private or personal use, educational purposes, or research.[62]

The Ministry of Electronics and Information Technology (MEITY) of the government of India, through the e-Governance Group, has issued a notification that all government procurements[63] be compliant with Government of India Guidance for Websites[64] and must adhere to access-specification templates evolved by MEITY and National Informatics Centre Services Incorporated. Thus, when the government is procuring ICT equipment like computers and scanners, it must be certain that the technology procured is accessible. The coordinating committee (constituted specially by MEITY to implement NPOUEA) also emphasized the need for an accessibility audit of all government websites, as well as researching the status of existing text-to-speech (TTS) tools in regional languages for disabled persons and investigating the development of TTS software in the five Indian languages (with financial support from MEITY).[65] The major weakness of all these actions is that there is no specific timeline, so their implementation is uncertain.

A number of other initiatives by the Indian government to improve the inclusion of disabled persons in civic life by improving accessibility of ICT are worth mentioning. These include the issuance of smart cards to disabled persons to enable access to online ticket-booking facilities of the Indian Railways;[66] provision for audio-video announcement of stops in some Mumbai

Local trains and in all metro trains and sign language training of customer relation assistants (CRAs) to help hearing- and vocally impaired commuters by the Delhi Metro and Chennai Metro corporations;[67] provision of financial assistance by the University Grant Commission, India, to universities and colleges to undertake accessibility audits, to establish enabling cells, and to buy accessibility-enhancing software and gadgets;[68] availability of accessible mobile phones by all major mobile companies; the State of Maharashtra providing financial assistance to all its employees with disabilities to buy, among other things, accessibility-enhancing software and equipment; the National Handicapped Development and Finance Corporation providing loans at low interest rates to PWDs to purchase computers and software;[69] some domestic and international airlines providing safety manuals in braille; lifts with braille keypads and audio announcements being installed in many public and private buildings; and the availability of remote controls for television with accessible features, such as keys with dots and various shapes to facilitate tactile sensation.

Since the issuance of circulars by the Reserve Bank of India[70] and the Indian Bank Association (IBA),[71] some positive developments have taken place in making banking accessible to disabled persons. These include taking steps to install voice-guided and braille-keypad-enabled ATMs with ramps for wheelchairs and providing information, via a dedicated website, about accessible ATMs throughout India.[72] To provide one example, the State Bank of India removed the requirement of a Completely Automated Public Turing Test to Tell Computers and Humans Apart (CAPTCHA) by heeding the protests of its visually challenged customers and reverting to the use only of passwords. Banks are particularly concerned about the legal capacity of persons with disabilities when it comes to establishing identity by way of thumb impression (from personal experience, the author has received continuous denial for issuance of a credit card from all the major banks of India, including the State Bank of India, because he is blind and cannot put his signature). There is vast potential to enhance accessible banking services for persons with disabilities. First, banks need to evolve sensitization programs to train their staff. Second, it is important to note that a package of accessible banking services should not adopt a one-size-fits-all approach and must be sensitive to disability-specific needs. For example, persons with cognitive disabilities would not be able to use ATMs if the steps involved in using an ATM or completing other physical transactions are not logical and simple, even if the ATMs are accessible for blind users. Similarly, customers with autism or other physical disabilities may have hand-function issues that can cause their signatures not to match the ones on record.[73] Such issues need to be addressed sensitively and by resorting to universal design. Thus, although progress on accessibility has been slow, overall, it is being made.

Civil Society Initiatives

A close look at the work of various NGOs reveals that efforts are being made by civil society to use ICT as a disability human rights enabler. However, major advocacy initiatives instituting litigation against inaccessible websites, television, or other electronic goods have not yet been launched. This section briefly highlights some of the enabling initiatives.

The DAISY Forum of India,[74] in collaboration with Tata Consultancy Services, has established an electronic library of books in DAISY format for people with print disabilities. Saksham Trust Noida (Saksham), Worth Trust Digitization, Chennai, and Xavier's Resource Centre for the Visually Challenged, Mumbai (XRCVC), in collaboration with Benetech USA, have initiated a Book Share project in India. This is an online library of documents that can be downloaded and read by visually impaired persons using a computer or a mobile phone. The individual subscription for this library is provided at nominal cost.[75] Additionally, Saksham, in collaboration with Intel, Equal Opportunity Cell, Delhi University, and the Industrial Finance Corporation of India, has developed an accessible netbook called Samarth for persons who are blind or have low vision. The netbooks come equipped with free and open-source software installed and tested and are distributed to users at subsidized cost. In a related venture, the National Association for the Blind Delhi and Saksham are training children with visual impairments to use computers with accessible software. Under this initiative, children with visual impairments use laptops at school and by doing so have reduced their dependence on human readers for reading and writing—now they do their in-school and homework assignments and write exams independently.

Such efforts should be financed by the government at both central and state levels in the light of the NPOUEA policy. Particularly in rural areas, the Indian government needs to strengthen NGOs working for the uplift of disabled persons and involve them with initiatives like the Sarvashiksha

Abhiyan (Education for All Mission)[76] to provide accessible educational material to students with disabilities and resource teachers in multimedia formats.

The work of NGOs goes beyond the education sector and includes collaboration with corporate as well as educational institutions (for example, the Indian Institute of Technology [IIT], Delhi) in making headway in other areas. For instance, Accessibility Consulting Services, a wing of Tata Consultancy Services (TCS),[77] is a giant in the ICT sector. It is providing cutting-edge accessibility solutions, such as the TCS Accessibility Compliance Assessment Tool (an automated tool for web-accessibility testing with the ability to crawl an entire website and validate dynamic content to diagnose pages automatically, report violations, and suggest remedies); the TCS Accessibility Toolbar (a browser plug-in tool for quick and visual evaluation of all relevant information at a single click); Accessibility Certifications (to assist in obtaining multiple types of accessibility statements and WCAG 2.0 conformance claims); and the TCS Accessible Content Publisher (a file-conversion tool that converts files from diverse formats into accessible formats).

The NGO Centre for Internet and Society has launched an innovative initiative, the Access to Knowledge Project, to work toward catalyzing the growth of the open-knowledge movement in South Asian and Indic languages. One of the missions of this project is to bring more content under free license. The current focus of this project is on five local Indic-language areas (Kannada, Konkani, Marathi, Odia, and Telugu). Students with disabilities are also being trained to use resources under this project.[78] This scheme is also engaged in strengthening NVDA, a free screen-reading software, to provide Indian local languages support for visually impaired persons.[79]

UNESCO, Saksham, PrasarBharati (the agency that regulates the state television network), MEITY, and a local manufacturer of set-top boxes have collaborated to initiate a pilot project to provide accessible programs on television for visually challenged and speech-impaired persons. Initially, this group is focusing on Doordarshan (a national television network), and some programs are being enabled with features of closed captioning and audio description. The programs will be telecast through an enabling set-top box with a switch-on and switch-off interface for these features. Users are being invited to buy these set-top boxes and participate in a pilot project.[80]

The IIT, Delhi, has established the Assist Tech Lab to promote research and development in the manufacturing of assistive technology and devices. The lab is engaged in a number of projects, such as the Centre of Excellence in Tactile Graphics funded by the Ministry of Communication and Information Technology. Applications developed in this center include the creation of accessible diagrams for class IX/X math and science textbooks and diagrams explaining functionality, training resources for assistive technologies, and the "smart cane," an affordable obstacle-detection system.

In addition, Saksham initiated a project to develop audio descriptions of movies, beginning with four famous Bollywood Hindi films, *Black*, *Fanna*, *Munnabhai Mbbs*, and *Lage Raho Munnabhai*, as a noncommercial venture wherein the movies are distributed free of cost throughout India. The NAB, in collaboration with a Pune-based software firm, Extentia Information Technology, is engaged in the development of an app called Easy Access that will help the visually impaired operate their Android cellphones through text-to-speech features. The app will be made available for download on Google Play Station.[81] Students and researchers at IIT, Delhi, are demonstrating extraordinary interest in promoting cutting-edge assistive technology by organizing seminars and conferences[82] and presenting papers[83] on the topic.

Nongovernmental organizations, including DPOs, have also undertaken programs to help persons with disabilities access ICT, including offering related training to ensure digital literacy and skills. For example, the New Delhi branch of the Indian National Association for the Blind established a computer training and technology center with accessible and affordable ICT for blind people and has been running initial and update courses for free since 1993. Courseware was developed in braille, audio, large-print, and electronic-text formats to cater to people with visual impairment. Projects included developing braille-transcription software, search engines, and text-to-speech software in Hindi. Visually impaired students became trainees at the computer company sponsoring the center.[84]

In summation, a fair amount of work is being done by NGOs. Nonetheless, NGOs are not as sensitive to a cross-disability, inclusive perspective as they ought to be, and in consequence, universal design is not always incorporated into their strategies. Further, better coordination among NGOs and government entities would avoid duplication of effort. It is striking that as of yet, no watchdog has arisen from the NGO sector in India to expose inaccessibility in the public domain. It is hoped that affected parties will bring these issues of inaccessibility to the fore by reporting them to concerned authorities through the mobile app made available on the website of the Accessible India Campaign.

Conclusion

In sharp contrast to countries like the United States where issues of accessibility are extensively legislated,[85] in India there are no corresponding legal standards. Soft-law instruments like the NPOUEA and initiatives like the Accessible India Campaign cannot substitute for cohesive legal enforcement. The high-level committee mechanism provided in the NPOUEA is simply not equivalent to the type of monitoring mechanism and national focal point suggested by the CRPD committee.[86] The Indian Parliament and the central government must take urgent steps to constitute a National Access Board with offices in each of the twenty-eight states and seven union territories of India to initiate serious consultations with disability rights groups regarding the enforcement and implementation of the right to accessibility, including carrying out access audits.

From the perspective of disability studies, the Indian scenario is far from sanguine because there is too much focus on addressing digital scarcity and provision of software and technogadgets. Rather, the Indian digital divide can be effectively addressed only from the perspective of socioinformatics, that is, using ICT to promote the sociopolitical and economic inclusion of disabled persons by opening avenues of education, entrepreneurship, health, and political participation. For countrywide application, these ICT solutions must also have local language support. Policy makers must adopt a holistic perspective on empowering disabled persons and be inclusive of all disability groups, whereas the present mechanisms mostly address those individuals with sensory and physical disabilities. The Indian government must also cease leaving the private sector unregulated and become more sensitive to issues of affordability, which raises a secondary barrier to access. If these concerns are not taken seriously by the government, it will find it extremely difficult to defend itself before the CRPD committee. Despite all these shortcomings, the work done by DPOs and NGOs in collaboration with the corporate sector raises optimism as they make constant efforts to eliminate barriers by resorting to cutting-edge assistive technology. Banks and financial institutions must likewise encourage start-ups and young entrepreneurs by providing capital and finance on easy conditions to promote further research and development in the area of accessible ICTs.

NOTES

Foreword

1. "CRPD ICT Accessibility Progress Report 2013," http://g3ict.org/resource_center/CRPD_2013_ICT_Accessibility_Progress.

2. "CRPD Implementation: Promoting Global Digital Inclusion Through ICT Procurement Policies & Accessibility Standards," http://g3ict.org/resource_center/publications_and_reports/p/productCategory_whitepapers/subCat_7/id_339/.

Introduction

1. "About the FTC," Federal Trade Commission, https://www.ftc.gov/about-ftc.

2. A related topic, addressed by several contributors in this volume, is the effect of exceptions to intellectual property law and regimes as exemplified by the Marrakesh Treaty and also required by the CRPD.

1. Standards Bodies, Access to Information Technology, and Human Rights

1. "World Wide Web Consortium (W3C)," last modified January 5, 2016, http://www.w3.org/.

2. "Web Accessibility Initiative (WAI)," accessed January 9, 2016, http://www.w3.org/WAI/.

3. "Accessible Platform Architecture Working (APA) WG," last modified December 9, 2015, http://www.w3.org/WAI/APA/.

4. "Internet.org," accessed January 9, 2016, https://info.internet.org/en/mission/.

5. "[CRPD] Article 9—Accessibility," accessed January 9, 2016, http://www.ohchr.org/EN/HRBodies/CRPD/Pages/ConventionRightsPersonsWithDisabilities.aspx#9.

6. "[CRPD] Article 21—Freedom of Expression and Opinion, and Access to Information," accessed January 9, 2016, http://www.ohchr.org/EN/HRBodies/CRPD/Pages/ConventionRightsPersonsWithDisabilities.aspx#21.

7. "Section 508 Standards—Background," accessed January 9, 2016, http://www.access-board.gov/guidelines-and-standards/communications-and-it/about-the-section-508-standards/background.

8. "Standard—EN 301 549," accessed January 9, 2016, http://mandate376.standards.eu/standard.

9. "Web Accessibility and Older People: Meeting the Needs of Ageing Web Users," accessed January 9, 2016, http://www.w3.org/WAI/older-users/.

10. "Authoring Tool Accessibility Guidelines (ATAG) 2.0," W3C World Wide Web Consortium Recommendation, ed. Jan Richards, Jeanne Spellman, and Jutta Treviranus, September 24, 2015, https://www.w3.org/TR/2015/REC-ATAG20-20150924/. Latest version at http://www.w3.org/TR/ATAG20/.

11. "Open Stand: Joint Statement of Affirmation," accessed January 9, 2016, https://open-stand.org/about-us/affirmation/.

12. "Open Stand: Principles," accessed January 9, 2016, https://open-stand.org/about-us/principles/.

13. "W3C Patent Policy," last modified February 5, 2004, http://www.w3.org/Consortium/Patent-Policy-20040205/.

14. "World Wide Web Consortium Process Document," last modified September 1, 2015, http://www.w3.org/2015/Process-20150901/.

15. "World Wide Web Consortium Process Document: Technical Reports," last modified September 1, 2015, http://www.w3.org/2015/Process-20150901/#Reports.

16. "W3C Open Web Testing Plan," last modified April 3, 2013, http://www.w3.org/wiki/Testing; "Test the Web Forward: W3C's One Stop Shop for Open Web Platform Testing," accessed January 9, 2016, http://testthewebforward.org/.

17. "W3C Web Content Accessibility Guidelines 2.0 Approved as ISO/IEC International Standard," last modified October 15, 2012, http://www.w3.org/2012/07/wcag2pas-pr.html.

18. "Web Accessibility Infrastructure Committee," accessed January 9, 2016, http://waic.jp/.

19. "WCAG 2.0 Translations," accessed January 9, 2016, http://www.w3.org/WAI/WCAG20/translations.html.

20. "Policy for Authorized W3C Translations," accessed October 16, 2013, http://www.w3.org/2005/02/TranslationPolicy.html.

21. "Web Content Accessibility Guidelines (WCAG) 2.0," W3C World Wide Web Consortium Recommendation, ed. Ben Caldwell, Michael Cooper, Loretta Guarino Reid, and Gregg Vanderheiden, December 11, 2008, https://www.w3.org/TR/2008/REC-WCAG20-20081211/. Latest version at https://www.w3.org/TR/WCAG20/.

22. "Introduction to Understanding WCAG 2.0," last modified February 26, 2015, http://www.w3.org/TR/UNDERSTANDING-WCAG20/intro.html.

23. "WCAG 2.0 Layers of Guidance," last modified December 11, 2008, http://www.w3.org/TR/WCAG20/#intro-layers-guidance.

24. "Requirements for WCAG 2.0 Extensions: First Public Working Draft," last modified January 5, 2016, http://www.w3.org/TR/wcag2-ext-req/.

25. "Guidance on Applying WCAG 2.0 to Non-Web Information and Communications Technologies (WCAG2ICT)," last modified September 5, 2013, http://www.w3.org/TR/wcag2ict/.

26. "User Agent Accessibility Guidelines (UAAG) 2.0," W3C World Wide Web Consortium Recommendation, ed. James Allan, Greg Lowney, Kim Patch, and Jeanne Spellman, December 15, 2015, https://www.w3.org/TR/2015/NOTE-UAAG20-20151215/. Latest version at https://www.w3.org/TR/UAAG20/.

27. "Web Technology Accessibility Guidelines: Editor's Draft," accessed March 3, 2015, https://w3c.github.io/pfwg/wtag/wtag.html.

28. "Media Accessibility User Requirements," last modified December 3, 2015, http://www.w3.org/TR/media-accessibility-reqs/.

29. "Easy Checks: A First Review of Web Accessibility," last modified March 2014, http://www.w3.org/WAI/eval/preliminary.

30. "Web Accessibility Evaluation Tools List," accessed January 9, 2016, http://www.w3.org/WAI/ER/tools/.

31. "Diagram Center: Making It Easier, Cheaper, and Faster to Create and Use Accessible Digital Images," accessed January 9, 2016, http://diagramcenter.org/.

32. "Cognitive and Learning Disabilities Accessibility Task Force," accessed January 9, 2016, http://www.w3.org/WAI/PF/cognitive-a11y-tf/.

33. "Web Accessibility Initiative Home Page," accessed January 9, 2016, http://www.w3.org/WAI/.

2. Accessible ICTs and the Opening of Political Space for Persons with Disabilities

1. As used in this chapter, the term "ICT" refers to the ascribed meaning set forth in the Convention on the Rights of Persons with Disabilities, Articles 2 and 9.

2. Humphrey Taylor, "How the Internet Is Improving the Lives of Americans with Disabilities," *Harris Interactive, Inc.*, June 7, 2000, http://www.harrisinteractive.com/harris_poll/index.asp?pid=93.

3. G3ict, "Convention on the Rights of Persons with Disabilities, 2013 ICT Accessibility Progress Report," accessed August 25, 2015, http://g3ict.org/design/js/tinymce/filemanager/userfiles/File/CRPD2013/CRPD%202013%20ICT%20Accessibility%20Report.pdf.

4. U.S. Presidential Commission on Election Administration, "The American Voting Experience: Report and Recommendations of the Presidential Commission on Election Administration," January 2014, accessed August 25, 2015, https://www.supportthevoter.gov/ files/2014/01/Amer-Voting-Exper-final-draft-01-09-14-508.pdf.

5. See, e.g., Michael A. Stein and Jan Fiala, "Democratic Life of the Union: Toward Equal Voting Participation for People with Disabilities," *Harvard Journal of International Law* 55 (Winter 2014): 71.

6. Peter Blanck, *eQuality: The Struggle for Web Accessibility by Persons with Cognitive Disabilities* (Cambridge: Cambridge University Press, 2014).

7. These ideas are reflected in political philosophy, for instance, in Judith Shklar's work. Of particular note, she emphasizes the critical importance of citizens being able

to participate meaningfully in life decisions. See Judith Shklar, *American Citizenship: The Quest for Inclusion* (Cambridge, Mass.: Harvard University Press, 1991).

8. For more on disability human rights, see Michael Ashley Stein, "Disability Human Rights," *California Law Review* 95, no. 75 (February 2007): 111.

9. Michael Ashley Stein and Janet E. Lord, "The Domestic Incorporation of Human Rights Law and the United Nations Convention on the Rights of Persons with Disabilities," *University of Washington Law Review* 83 (2008): 449.

10. ITU and G3ict, "e-Accessibility Toolkit for Policy Makers," accessed August 15, 2015, www.e-accessibilitytoolkit.org.

11. Elise Ackerman, "Blind Voters Rip E-Machines," *San Jose Mercury News*, May 15, 2004.

12. Aleda Davis, "Touch Screen Not Best Choice for Disabled Voters," *Daytona Beach News-Journal*, June 22, 2005, http://www.votersunite.org/article.asp?id=5588.

13. CRPD, arts. 3 and 9.

14. CRPD, art. 21.

15. CRPD, art. 31; see also art. 32.

16. ITU and G3ict, "e-Accessibility Policy Toolkit for Persons with Disabilities G3ict," accessed August 30, 2015, http://www.e-accessibilitytoolkit.org/toolkit.

17. For discussion of this tripartite schema, see ITU, G3ict, and Center for Internet and Society, "e-Accessibility Policy Handbook for Persons with Disabilities," undated, accessed November 3, 2016, http://g3ict.org/resource_center/e-Accessibility%20Policy%20Handbook.

18. For more on capturing user perspectives effectively, see G3ict, *User Driven e-Accessibility*, 2015, accessed November 3, 2016, http://g3ict.org/resource_center/e-Accessibility%20Policy%20Handbook.

19. Victorian Electoral Commission, "Improving Access to the Victoria Electoral System: A Disability Action Plan for 2016–2019" (hereafter cited as "Disability Action Plan for 2016–2019"), July 2015, https://www.vec.vic.gov.au/files/DisabilityPlan.pdf.

20. Help America Vote Act of 2002 (HAVA), Pub. L. 107-252, 116 Stat. 1666–1730 (2002), codified at 42 U.S.C. §§ 15301–15545.

21. Victoria Electoral Commission, "Improving Access to the Victoria Electoral System: A Disability Action Plan for 2011–2015" (hereafter cited as "Disability Action Plan for 2011–2015"), undated, accessed November 1, 2016, https://www.vec.vic.gov.au/files/DisabilityPlan.pdf.

22. See Janet E. Lord, Michael Ashley Stein, and Janos Fiala, "Facilitating an Equal Right to Vote for Persons with Disabilities," *Journal of Human Rights Practice* 6, no. 1 (2014): 115–39.

23. Ibid.

24. Specifically, democracy-assistance efforts pay little or no attention to enfranchising persons with disabilities, notwithstanding the fact that many targeted countries have substantial populations of disabled persons on account of poverty, armed conflict, and other factors.

25. See Ace Project, web discussion, "Social Media and Voter Education," October 8, 2012, http://aceproject.org/electoral-advice/archive/questions/replies/7941 84390.

26. See Janet E. Lord and Michael Ashley Stein, "Deaf Identity and Rights in Africa: Advancing Equality Through the Convention on the Rights of Persons with Disabilities," in *Citizenship, Politics and Difference*, ed. Audrey C. Cooper and Khadijat K. Rashid (Washington, D.C.: Gallaudet University Press, 2015): 220–20.

27. See Victorian Electoral Commission, "Disability Action Plan for 2011–2015."

28. Sarah Burd-Sharps and Patrick Guyer, "The Cost of Modernizing Voter Registration Systems: A Case Study of California and Arizona," Social Science Research Council, January 2014, ACLU-Voter Reg Costs Online 2015_0224%20(1).pdf.

29. For more on elections and ICTs generally, see International Democracy Education IDEA, http://aceproject.org/ace-en/topics/et/topic_index.

30. Susan Mizner and Eric Smith, "Access Denied: Barriers to Online Voter Registration for Citizens with Disabilities," ACLU and Center for Accessible Technology, February 2015, https://www.aclu.org/sites/default/files/field_document/021915-aclu-voterregonline_0.pdf.

31. Ibid.

32. See European Union Fundamental Rights Agency, "Are Websites That Give Information on Voting and Candidates Accessible?," accessed November 1, 2016, http://fra.europa.eu/en/publications-and-resources/data-and-maps/comparative-data/political-participation/accessible-websites.

33. Beyond e-voting machines, examples of electronic kiosks include ATMs and airport check-in machines, among others.

34. See Dónal Rice, ed., "Electronic Kiosks," in G3ict, "eAccessibility Policy Toolkit for Persons with Disabilities," accessed August 15, 2015, http://www.e-accessibilitytoolkit.org/toolkit/technology_areas/electronic_kiosks. For guidelines covering all information and services delivered by means of electronic kiosks, including e-voting machines, see Centre for Excellence in Universal Design at the National Disability Authority, Ireland, "Public Access Terminal Guidelines," undated, accessed August 15, 2015, http://www.universaldesign.ie/it-accessibility-guidelines/public-access-terminals.

35. For additional information on accessibility design of electronic voting machines, vote-by-phone systems, and web-based voting systems, see National Federation of the Blind, "Nonvisual Access Election Technology Guide," accessed November 1, 2016, https://nfb.org/purchasing-voting-machine.

36. For voting machine manufacturers and manufacturers' video demonstrations for accessibility functions, see National Federation of the Blind, "Help America Vote Act Training Videos," accessed November 1, 2016, https://nfb.org/hava-training-video.

37. For more information on the system used in Massachusetts, see AutoMARK Voter Assist Terminal, http://www.sec.state.ma.us/ele/eleaccessible/accessibleidx.htm.

38. GAO, "Elections: Federal Efforts to Improve Security and Reliability of Electronic Voting Systems Are Under Way, but Key Activities Need to Be Completed" (Washington, D.C.: October 2005). For an instructional video on how to use one example of sip-and-puff voting technology, see http://sos.iowa.gov/elections/voterinformation/accessibility.html. For more on e-voting (electronic ballot delivery) deployed for voters with disabilities, U.S. military, and overseas voters, see Democracy Live, "Live Ballot," accessed on November 3, 2016, http://democracylive.com/our-products/liveballot-online.

39. *National Federation of the Blind v. Lamone*, U.S. District Court for Maryland, September 14, 2014. See also Andy Jones, "Court Orders Maryland to Use Accessible Absentee Voting System," September 16, 2014, http://www.rootedinrights.org/court-orders-maryland-to-use-accessible-absentee-voting-system/.

40. Center for Excellence in Universal Design and National Disability Authority, "Measures to Improve Accessibility of Public Website in Europe," accessed August 15, 2015, http://universaldesign.ie/Technology-ICT/Measures-to-Improve-Accessibility-of-Public-Websites-in-Europe/.

41. See Janet E. Lord, Deepti Samant Raja, and Peter Blanck, "Beyond the Orthodoxy of Rule of Law and Justice Sector Reform: A Framework for Legal Empowerment and Innovation Through the Convention on the Rights of Persons with Disabilities," *World Bank Legal Review* 4 (2012): 85.

42. Council on Access to Information for Print-Disabled Canadians, "Fulfilling the Promise:Report of the Task Force on Access to Information for Print-Disabled Canadians," Ottawa, October 31, 2000, http://www.collectionscanada.gc.ca/accessinfo/005003-4300-e.html.

43. See Center for Excellence in Universal Design, "ICT Procurement Toolkit," accessed August 15, 2015, http://www.universaldesign.ie/useandapply/ict/itprocurementtoolkit.

44. U.S. Agency for International Development, "Disability Policy," 2004, accessed August 15, 2015, http://www.usaid.gov/about_usaid/disability/.

45. See "Project Vote, Elements of a Successful Pollworker Training Program," Policy Brief no. 9, February 8, 2007, https://www.supportthevoter.gov/files/2013/08/Project_Vote_Policy_Brief_9_Elements_of_Successful_Poll_Worker_Training.pdf.

46. Victorian Electoral Commission, Disability Action Plan for 2011–2015.

47. Government of Canada Task Force on Access, "Fulfilling the Promise: The Report of the Task Force on Access to Information for Print-Disabled Canadians," October 2000, https://www.collectionscanada.gc.ca/accessinfo/005003-4300-e.html.

48. Down Syndrome Ireland, "My Opinion My Vote!," accessed October 15, 2015, http://www.downsyndrome.ie/campaigns-and-projects/my-opinion-my-vote/.

49. Advocacy Center, "Creating an Accessible Political Campaign: Practical Tips to Include People with Disabilities and Win More Votes!," January 2001, http://www.advocacyla.org/tl_files/publications/AccessibleCampaignforWeb.pdf.

50. "Reč na reč: Debata kandidata za predsednika Srbije 2012," Radio-Televizija Srbije, June 16, 2012.

51. See Lord and Stein, "Deaf Identity and Rights in Africa."

52. NDI and IFES, "Equal Access: How to Include People with Disabilities in Elections and Political Processes," 2014, accessed August 15, 2015, https://www.ndi.org/files/Equal-Access_How-to-include-PWD-in-elections-political-processes.pdf.

53. Down Syndrome Ireland, "A Lot Done but More to Do," accessed August 15, 2015, http://www.downsyndrome.ie/campaigns-and-projects/my-opinion-my-vote/a-lot-done-but-more-to-do/.

54. Interview with Steven Estey, July 22, 2015.

55. ITU, G3ict, IDA, UNESCO, and Microsoft, "The ICT Opportunity for Persons with Disabilities," 2014, accessed August 31, 2015, http://unesco-ci.org/cmscore/files/FINAL_ICT_Disability_Dev_Report_ACCESSIBLE_2013_09_18.docx.

56. For more on enabling ICTs in the context of disability generally, see UNESCO, "Global Report: Opening New Avenues for Empowerment—ICTs to Access Information and Knowledge for Persons with Disabilities," accessed August 15, 2015, http://www.unesco.org/new/en/communication-and-information/resources/publications-and-communication-materials/publications/full-list/unesco-global-report-opening-new-avenues-for-empowerment-icts-to-access-information-and-knowledge-for-persons-with-disabilities/.

3. Web Accessibility for People with Cognitive Disabilities

1. Peter Blanck, *eQuality: The Struggle for Web Accessibility by Persons with Cognitive Disabilities* (Cambridge: Cambridge University Press, 2014).

2. Stephen Wicker and Stephanie Santoso, "Access to the Internet Is a Human Right," *Communications of the ACM* 56, no. 6 (2013): 45–46.

3. Peter Blanck and Jonathan Martinis, "The Right to Make Choices," National Resource Center for Supported Decision-Making, *Inclusion* 3, no. 1 (2015): 24–33; Ivan Illich, *Tools for Conviviality*, accessed January 13, 2015, http://www.preservenet.com/theory/Illich/IllichTools.html; Michelle Putnam, "Bridging Network Divides: Building Capacity to Support Aging with Disability Populations Through Research," *Disability and Health Journal* 7, no. 1 (2014): S51–S59.

4. Rune Halvorsen and Bjorn Hvinden, *Active Citizenship for Persons with Disabilities—Current Knowledge and Analytical Framework*, 2013, DISCIT, accessed December, 6, 2016, https://blogg.hioa.no/discit/publications/.

5. Peter Blanck, *eQuality*, 245.

6. Eli Pariser, *The Filter Bubble: What the Internet Is Hiding from You* (New York: Penguin, 2011).

7. Americans with Disabilities Act of 1990, ADA Amendments Act of 2008, 42 U.S.C. § 12101(a)(8) (2008); Michael Morris, Christopher Rodriguez, and Peter Blanck, "ABLE Accounts: A Down Payment on Freedom," *Inclusion*, 4, no. 1 (2016): 21–29.

8. Rob Imrie, "Universalism, Universal Design and Equitable Access to the Built Environment," *Disability and Rehabilitation* 34, no. 10 (2012): 873–82; Lisa Schur, Peter Blanck, and Douglas Kruse, *People with Disabilities: Sidelined or Mainstreamed?* (Cambridge: Cambridge University Press, 2013).

9. W3C, "[DRAFT] Basic Glossary for WAI Documents," August 9, 2005, http://www.w3.org/WAI/lexicon/#equiv.

10. Internet World Stats, http://www.internetworldstats.com/stats.htm.

11. Henry Blodget, "The Future of Digital: 2014," accessed January 13, 2015, http://www.businessinsider.com/the-future-of-digital-2014-slide-deck-2014-12#-70.

12. Natasha Lomas, "1.2 Billion Smartphones, Tablets to Be Bought Worldwide in 2013; 821 Million This Year: 70% Of Total Device Sales," AOL Tech, November 6, 2012, http://techcrunch.com/2012/11/06/gartner-1-2-billion-smartphones-tablets-to-be-bought-worldwide-in-2013-821-million-this-year-70-of-total-device-sales/; Jun Yang, "Smartphones in Use Surpass 1 Billion, Will Double by 2015," Bloomberg, October 17, 2012, http://www.bloomberg.com/news/2012-10-17/smartphones-in-use-surpass-1-billion-will-double-by-2015.html.

13. European Commission, "Proposal for a Directive of the European Parliament and of the Council on the Accessibility of Public Sector Bodies' Websites," accessed January 15, 2015, http://ec.europa.eu/digital-agenda/en/news/proposal-directive-european-parliament-and-council-accessibility-public-sector-bodies-websites.

14. W3C, "[DRAFT] Basic Glossary for WAI Documents."

15. Paul Baker, John Bricout, Nathan Moon, Barry Coughlan, and Jessica Pater, "Communities of Participation: A Comparison of Disability and Aging Identified Groups on Facebook and LinkedIn," *Telematics and Informatics* 30 (2012): 22–34.

16. Lee Feigenbaum, Ivan Herman, Tonya Hongsermeier, Eric Neumann, and Susie Stephens, "The Semantic Web in Action," *Scientific American* 297 (2007): 90–97.

17. Amrish Chourasia, Dan Nordstrom, and Gregg Vanderheiden, "State of the Science on the Cloud, Accessibility, and the Future," *Universal Access in the Information Society* 13, no. 4 (2014): 483–95.

18. Jonathan Lazar, Libby Kumin, and Jinjuan Feng, "Understanding the Computer Skills of Adult Expert Users with Down Syndrome: An Exploratory Study," in *Proceedings of the 13th International ACM SIGACCESS Conference on Computers and Accessibility* (New York: ACM, 2011), 51–58.

19. Elizabeth Ellcessor, "Captions On, Off, on TV, Online: Accessibility and Search Engine Optimization in Online Closed Captioning," *Television New Media* 13 (2012): 329–52.

20. W3C, "[DRAFT] Basic Glossary for WAI Documents."

21. Yao Ma, Jinjuan Feng, Libby Kumin, and Jonathan Lazar, "Investigating User Behavior for Authentication Methods: A Comparison Between Individuals with Down Syndrome and Neurotypical Users," *ACM Transactions on Accessible Computing (TACCESS)* 4, no. 4 (2013): 15.

22. "Cognitive and Learning Disabilities Accessibility Task Force (Cognitive A11Y TF)," Web Accessibility Initiative, 2016, accessed February 15, 2016, https://www.w3.org/WAI/PF/cognitive-a11y-tf/.

23. David Braddock, Mary Rizzolo, Micah Thompson, and Rodney Bell, "Emerging Technologies and Cognitive Disability," *Journal of Special Education Technology* 19, no. 4 (2004): 49–56.

24. Aisling de Paor, Gerard Quinn, and Peter Blanck, eds., *Genetic Discrimination: Transatlantic Perspectives on the Case for a European-level Legal Response* (New York: Routledge, 2015).

25. David Braddock, Richard Hemp, Mary Rizzolo, Emily Tanis, Laura Haffer, Amie Lulinski, and Jiang Wu, *State of the States in Developmental Disabilities* (Washington, D.C.: AAIDD, 2013).

26. John Sweller, Paul Chandler, Paul Tierney, and Martin Cooper, "Cognitive Load as a Factor in the Structuring of Technical Material," *Journal of Experimental Psychology: General* 119, no. 2 (1990): 176–92.

27. Tony Schwartz, "Faced with Overload, a Need to Find Focus, Life@Work," *New York Times*, May 17, 2013.

28. Yury Puzis, Yevgen Borodin, Faisal Ahmed, and I. V. Ramakrishnan, "An Intuitive Accessible Web Automation User Interface," in *Proceedings of the International Cross-Disciplinary Conference on Web Accessibility* (Stony Brook, N.Y.: Stony Brook University, 2012), 41–44.

29. Jamie Knight, "Cognitive Accessibility 101—Part 1: What Is Cognitive Accessibility?," accessed March 13, 2015, http://jkg3.com/Journal/cognitive-accessibility-101-part-1-what-is-cognitive-accessibility; Jamie Knight, "Cognitive Accessibility 101—Part 2: How It Effects Me and the Tools I Use," accessed March 13, 2015, http://jkg3.com/Journal/cognitive-accessibility-101-part-2-how-it-effects-me-the-tools-i-use.

30. Peter G. Fairweather, "How Older and Younger Adults Differ in Their Approach to Problem Solving on a Complex Website," *ACM ASSETS'08* (October 13–15, 2008): 67; Simon Harper and Yeliz Yesilada, "Web Accessibility: Current Trends," in *Handbook of Research on Personal Autonomy Technologies and Disability Informatics*, ed. Jose Pereira (Madrid: IGI Global, 2011), 172–90.

31. Shawn L. Henry, Shadi Abou-Zahra, and Judy Brewer, "The Role of Accessibility in a Universal Web," in *Proceedings of the 11th Web for All Conference* (New York: ACM, 2014), http://dl.acm.org/citation.cfm?id=2596695&picked=prox.

32. Emily Tanis, Susan Palmer, Michael L. Wehmeyer, Danial K. Davies, Steven E. Stock, Kathy Lobb, and Barbara Bishop, "Self-Report Computer-Based Survey of Technology Use by People with Intellectual and Developmental Disabilities," *Intellectual and Developmental Disabilities* 50, no. 1 (2012): 53–68.

33. G. Anthony Giannoumis, "Regulating Web Content: The Nexus of Legislation and Performance Standards in the United Kingdom and Norway," *Behavioral Sciences and the Law* 32, no. 1 (2014): 52–75.

34. Kasper Hornbaek, "Current Practice in Measuring Usability: Challenges to Studies and Research," *International Journal of Human-Computer Studies* 64, no. 2 (2006): 79–102.

35. Fairweather, "How Older and Younger Adults Differ," 71.

36. Micah Mazurek, Paul Shattuck, Mary Wagner, and Benjamin P. Cooper, "Prevalence and Correlates of Screen-Based Media Use Among Youths with Autism Spectrum Disorders," *Journal of Autism and Developmental Disorders* 42, no. 8 (2011): 1757–67.

37. Melissa Dawe, "Desperately Seeking Simplicity: How Young Adults with Cognitive Disabilities and Their Families Adopt Assistive Technologies," in *Proceedings of the SIGCHI Conference on Human Factors in Computing Systems* (New York: ACM, 2006), 1143–52; Gregg Vanderheiden, "Fundamental Principles and Priority Setting for Universal Usability," in *CUU '00 Proceedings of the 2000 Conference on Universal Usability* (New York: ACM, 2000), 32–38.

38. Gary Heil, Tom Parker, and Deborah C. Stephens, *One Size Fits One: Building Relationships One Customer and One Employee at a Time* (New York: Wiley, 1999); Jutta Treviranus, "You Say Tomato, I Say Tomato, Let's *Not* Call the Whole Thing Off: The Challenge of User Experience Design in Distributed Learning Environments," *eLiterate*, July 1, 2008, http://mfeldstein.com/you-say-tomato-i-say-tomato-let%E2%80%99s-not-call-the-whole-thing-off-the-challenge-of-user-experience-design-in-distributed-learning-environments/; WebAIM, "Design Considerations: One Size Fits All?," 2013, accessed April 19, 2015, http://webaim.org/articles/design/.

39. Timothy Berners-Lee, *Weaving the Web: The Original Design and Ultimate Destiny of the World Wide Web by Its Inventor* (New York: HarperOne, 1999).

40. Evan Brown, "Best Practices for Providers of Goods and Services on the Internet of Things," accessed February 15, 2015, http://blog.internetcases.com/2015/01/27/best-practices-for-providers-of-goods-and-services-on-the-internet-of-things/.

41. Gregg Vanderheiden, Jutta Treviranus, Marie Gemou, Evangelos Bekiaris, and Kasper Markus, "The Evolving Global Public Inclusive Infrastructure (GPII), in *Universal Access in Human-Computer Interaction: Design Methods, Tools, and Interaction Techniques for eInclusion*, Lecture Notes in Computer Science 8009 (Heidelberg: Springer-Verlag Berlin, 2013): 107–16.

42. Harper and Yesilada, "Web Accessibility."

43. Tim Berners-Lee, "Testimony Before the United States House of Representatives Committee on Energy and Commerce Subcommittee on Telecommunications and the Internet Hearing on the 'Digital Future of the United States: Part I—The Future of the World Wide Web,'" March 1, 2007.

44. Mark Greaves and Peter Mika, "Semantic Web and Web 2.0," *Web Semantics: Science, Services and Agents on the World Wide Web* 6 (2008): 1–3.

45. W3C, "OWL Working Group," 2012, accessed January 15, 2015, http://www.w3.org/2007/OWL/wiki/OWL_Working_Group.

46. National Council on Disability, *The Power of Digital Inclusion: Technology's Impact on Employment and Opportunities for People with Disabilities* (Washington, D.C.: National Council on Disability, 2011).

47. Global Public Inclusive Infrastructure, accessed February 15, 2016, http://www.gpii.net/; Gregg Vanderheiden and Jutta Treviranus, "Creating a Global Public Inclusive Infrastructure," in *Proceedings of the 6th International Conference on Universal Access in Human-Computer Interaction: Design for All and eInclusion*, vol. 1 (Berlin: Springer, 2011), 517–26.

48. "Raising the Floor: One-Size-Fits-One Digital Inclusion," Raising the Floor, 2016, accessed February 17, 2016, http://raisingthefloor.org/.

49. Colin Gibbs, "Challenges and Opportunities Abound in the Fragmented IoT," October 8, 2014, http://research.gigaom.com/2014/10/challenges-and-opportunities-abound-in-the-fragmented-iot/.

50. Catherine Easton, "The Web Content Accessibility Guidelines 2.0: An Analysis of Industry Self-Regulation," *International Journal of Law and Information Technology* 19, no. 1 (2010): 74–93; Steven E. Stock, Daniel K. Davies, Michael L. Wehmeyer, and Yves Lachapelle, "Emerging New Practices in Technology to Support Independent Community Access for People with Intellectual and Cognitive Disabilities," *Neurorehabilitation* 28 (2011): 1–9.

51. Peter Blanck, "Americans with Disabilities and Their Civil Rights: Past, Present, Future," *University of Pittsburgh Law Review* 66 (2005): 687–719; Peter Blanck, "The Struggle for Web Accessibility by Persons with Cognitive Disabilities," *Behavioral Sciences and the Law* 32, no. 1 (2014): 4–32.

52. Peter Blanck, Eve Hill, Charles Siegal, and Michael Waterstone, *Disability, Civil Rights Law, and Policy: Cases and Materials*, 3rd ed. (London: Thomson/West, 2014).

53. NAD, "NAD Sues Harvard and MIT for Discrimination in Public Online Content," February 12, 2015, http://nad.org/news/2015/2/nad-sues-harvard-and-mit-discrimination-public-online-content; *National Association of the Deaf v. Harvard University*, Class Action Complaint for Declaratory and Injunctive Relief (West. Div. D. Mass., Feb. 12, 2015); *National Association of the Deaf v. Massachusetts Institute of Technology*, Class Action Complaint for Declaratory and Injunctive Relief (West. Div. D. Mass., Feb. 12, 2015).

54. Casey Fabris, "Technology: As High-Tech Teaching Catches On, Students with Disabilities Can Be Left Behind," *Chronicle of Higher Education*, February 25, 2015.

55. U.S. Department of Justice Office of Public Affairs, "Justice Department Reaches Settlement with edX Inc., Provider of Massive Open Online Courses, to Make Its Website, Online Platform and Mobile Applications Accessible Under the Americans with Disabilities Act," April 2, 2015, http://www.justice.gov/opa/pr/justice-department-reaches-settlement-edx-inc-provider-massive-open-online-courses-make-its; U.S.

Department of Justice, "Settlement Agreement Between the United States of America and edX Inc., Under the Americans with Disabilities Act, DJ No. 202-36-255," April 2, 2015, http://www.justice.gov/sites/default/files/opa/press-releases/attachments/2015/04/02/edx_settlement_agreement.pdf.

56. *National Federation of the Blind v. Scribd*, Case No. 2015 WL 1263336 (D. Ct. D. Vermont, Mar. 19, 2015).

57. Blanck, "Americans with Disabilities and Their Civil Rights."

58. European Disability Forum, "80 Million Persons with Disabilities Call for Accessible Information & Communication Technologies," February 21, 2015, http://www.edf-feph.org/Page_Generale.asp?DocID=13855&thebloc=34202.

59. Stock et al., "Emerging New Practices in Technology."

60. Michael Waterstone and Michael Stein, "Disabling Prejudice," *Northwestern Law Review* 102 (2008): 1351–78.

4. The Intersection of Human Rights, Social Justice, the Internet, and Accessibility in Libraries

1. Özlem Sensoy and Robin DiAngelo, *Is Everyone Really Equal? An Introduction to Key Concepts in Social Justice Education* (New York: Teachers College Press, 2015).

2. Olaf Cramme and Patrick Diamond, *Social Justice in the Global Age* (Cambridge, UK: Polity, 2009); Sonia Nieto, foreword to *Social Justice Pedagogy Across the Curriculum: The Practice of Freedom*, ed. Thandeka K. Chapman and Nikola Hobbel (New York: Routledge, 2010), 3–20.

3. Eleanor Frances Brown, *Library Service to the Disadvantaged* (Metuchen, N.J.: Scarecrow, 1971); Eunice Lovejoy, "History and Standards," in *That All May Read: Library Service for Blind and Handicapped People*, ed. Frank Kurt Cykle (Washington, D.C.: Library of Congress, 1983), 1–24.

4. Wayne Wiegand and Marija Dalbello, introduction to *A History of Modern Librarianship: Constructing the Heritage of Western Cultures*, ed. Pamela Richards, Wayne Wiegand, and Marija Dalbello (Santa Barbara, Calif.: Libraries Unlimited, 2015), xv–xix.

5. Donna Dziedzic, "Public Libraries," in Cykle, *That All May Read*, 309–26.

6. Wayne Wiegand, "United States and Canada," in Richards, Wiegand, and Dalbello, *History of Modern Librarianship*, 69–142.

7. American Library Association, "Library Services for People with Disabilities Policy," Association of Specialized and Cooperative Library Agencies (ASCLA) (2001).

8. Tom McNulty, "Libraries, Media Centers, Online Resources, and the Research Process," in *A Guide to High School Success for Students with Disabilities*, ed. Cynthia Ann Bowman and Paul T. Jaeger (Westport, Conn.: Greenwood Press, 2004), 117–31.

9. Wiegand, "United States and Canada," 69–142.

10. Paul T. Jaeger, *Disability and the Internet: Confronting a Digital Divide* (Boulder, Colo.: Lynne Rienner, 2012); Jonathan Lazar, Paul T. Jaeger, and John Carlo Bertot,

"Persons with Disabilities and Physical and Virtual Public Library Settings," *Public Libraries and the Internet: Roles, Perspectives, and Implications*, ed. John Carlo Bertot, Paul T. Jaeger, and Charles R. McClure (Westport, CT: Greenwood, 2011), 177–89.

11. Ursula Gorham, Natalie Greene Taylor, and Paul T. Jaeger, eds., *Perspectives on Libraries as Institutions of Human Rights and Social Justice* (London: Emerald Group, 2016); Paul T. Jaeger, Natalie Greene Taylor, and Ursula Gorham, *Libraries, Human Rights, and Social Justice: Enabling Access and Promoting Inclusion* (Lanham, Md.: Rowman and Littlefield, 2015).

12. Anthony Woodiwiss, *Human Rights* (New York: Routledge, 2005).

13. William K. Frankena, "The Concept of Social Justice," *Social Justice* 1 (1962): 17.

14. Jaeger, Taylor, and Gorham, *Libraries, Human Rights, and Social Justice*.

15. Ibid.

16. John Carlo Bertot, "Public Access Technologies in Public Libraries: Effects and Implications," *Information Technology and Libraries* 28, no. 2 (2009): 81; Terence M. Duffy, "Museums of 'Human Suffering' and the Struggle for Human Rights," *Museum International* 53, no. 1 (2001): 10–16; Marci Hoffman, "Developing an Electronic Collection: The University of Minnesota Human Rights Library," *Legal Reference Services Quarterly* 19, nos. 3–4 (2001): 143–55; Paul T. Jaeger, John Carlo Bertot, and Ursula Gorham, "Wake Up the Nation: Public Libraries, Policy Making, and Political Discourse," *Library* 83, no. 1 (2013): 61–72; Paul T. Jaeger, John Carlo Bertot, Kim M. Thompson, S. M. Katz, and E. J. DeCoster, "Digital Divides, Digital Literacy, Digital Inclusion, and Public Libraries: The Intersection of Public Policy and Public Access," *Public Library Quarterly* 31, no. 1 (2012): 1–20; Jaeger, Taylor, and Gorham, *Libraries, Human Rights, and Social Justice*; Kathleen de la Peña McCook and Katharine J. Phenix, "Public Libraries and Human Rights." *Public Library Quarterly* 25, nos. 1–2 (2007): 57–73; Brian Real, John Carlo Bertot, and Paul T. Jaeger, "Rural Public Libraries and Digital Inclusion: Issues and Challenges," *Information Technology and Libraries (Online)* 33, no. 1 (2014): 6; Graham Stinnett, "Archival Landscape: Archives and Human Rights," *Progressive Librarian* 32 (2009): 10; David Suárez, "Education Professionals and the Construction of Human Rights Education," *Comparative Education Review* 51, no. 1 (2007): 48–70; Kim M. Thompson, Paul T. Jaeger, Natalie Greene Taylor, Mega Subramaniam, and John Carlo Bertot, *Digital Literacy and Digital Inclusion: Information Policy and the Public Library* (Lanham, Md.: Rowman and Littlefield, 2014).

17. Kofi Annan, comments at Telecomm 99+Interactive 99, accessed August 24, 2015, www.itu.int/itunews/issue/1999/09/telec99.html.

18. Edward F. Halpin, Steven Hick, and Eric Hoskins, introduction to *Human Rights and the Internet*, ed. Steven Hick, Edward F. Halpin, and Eric Hoskins (London: Macmillan, 2000), 3–15.

19. Woodiwiss, *Human Rights*.

20. Rikke Frank Jørgensen, ed., *Human Rights in the Global Information Society* (Cambridge, Mass.: MIT Press, 2006).

21. Kay Mathiesen, "The Human Right to Internet Access: A Philosophical Defense," *New ICTs and Social Media: Revolution, Counter-revolution and Social Change* 18, no. 9 (2012), http://www.i-r-i-e.net/inhalt/018/Mathiesen.pdf; Mathiesen, "The Human Right to a Public Library," *Journal of Information Ethics* 22 (2013): 60–79; Mathiesen, "Human Rights for the Digital Age," *Journal of Mass Media Ethics* 29, no. 1 (2014): 2–18.

22. Abid Hussain, preface to Hick, Halpin, and Hoskins, *Human Rights and the Internet*, x.

23. David Banisar, "The Right to Information in the Information Age," in Jørgensen, *Human Rights in the Global Information Society*, 73–90.

24. Jaeger, Taylor, and Gorham, *Libraries, Human Rights, and Social Justice*.

25. Peter Brophy and Edward Halpin, "Through the Net to Freedom: Information, the Internet and Human Rights," *Journal of Information Science* 25, no. 5 (1999): 351–64; Leah A. Lievrouw and Sharon E. Farb, "Information and Equity," *Annual Review of Information Science and Technology* 37, no. 1 (2003): 499–540; Susan Nevelow Mart, "The Right to Receive Information," *Law Library Journal* 95 (2003): 175–89; William McIver, William Birdsall, and Merrilee Rasmussen, "The Internet and the Right to Communicate," *First Monday* 8, no. 12 (2003), http://firstmonday.org/article/view/1102/1022; Taylor L. Willingham, "Libraries as Civic Agents," *Public Library Quarterly* 27, no. 2 (2008): 97–110.

26. UNESCO, International Federation of Library Associations and Institutions, and National Forum on Information Literacy, *Beacons of the Information Society: The Alexandria Proclamation on Information Literacy and Lifelong Learning*, last updated June 1, 2006, http://portal.unesco.org/ci/en/ev.php-URL_ID=20891&URL_DO=DO_TOPIC&URL_SECTION=201.html.

27. World Intellectual Property Organization (WIPO), "Marrakesh Treaty to Facilitate Access to Published Works for Persons Who Are Blind, Visually Impaired, or Otherwise Print Disabled," last updated June 27, 2013, http://www.wipo.int/treaties/en/text.jsp?file_id=301016.

28. Halpin, Hick, and Hoskins, introduction to *Human Rights and the Internet*.

29. Jaeger, "Internet Justice: Reconceptualizing the Legal Rights of Persons with Disabilities to Promote Equal Access in the Age of Rapid Technological Change," *Review of Disability Studies: An International Journal* 9, no. 1 (2014): 39–59; Jaeger, Taylor, and Gorham, *Libraries, Human Rights, and Social Justice*; Jes A. Koepfler, Christopher Mascaro, and Paul T. Jaeger, "Homelessness, Wirelessness, and (In)Visibility," *First Monday* 19, no. 3 (2014), http://firstmonday.org/ojs/index.php/fm/article/view/4846; Lucy Eleonore Lyons, "Human Rights: A Universal Declaration," *College and Research Libraries News* 72, no. 5 (2011): 290–93; Paul Sturges and Almuth Gastinger, "Information Literacy as a Human Right," *Libri* 60 (2010): 195–202; Thompson et al., *Digital Literacy and Digital Inclusion*.

30. Human Rights Council, *Report of the Special Rapporteur on the Promotion and Protection of the Right to Freedom of Opinion and Expression, Frank La Rue*, United

Nations, last updated May 16, 2011, http://www2.ohchr.org/english/bodies/hrcouncil/docs/17session/A.HRC.17.27_en.pdf.

31. Lyons, "Human Rights," 290–93; UNESCO, *Beacons of the Information Society*.

32. Kara Sprague, Ferry Grijpink, James Manyika, Lohini Moodley, Bertil Chappuis, Kanaka Pattabiraman, and Jacques Bughin, "Offline and Falling Behind: Barriers to Internet Adoption," McKinsey & Company, September 2014, http://www.mckinsey.com/industries/high-tech/our-insights/offline-and-falling-behind-barriers-to-internet-adoption.

33. Duffy, "Museums of 'Human Suffering' and the Struggle for Human Rights"; Hoffman, "Developing an Electronic Collection"; Jaeger, Taylor, and Gorham, *Libraries, Human Rights, and Social Justice*; McCook and Phenix, "Public Libraries and Human Rights"; Katharine J. Phenix and Kathleen de la Peña McCook, "Human Rights and Librarians," *Reference and User Services Quarterly* 45, no. 1 (2005): 23–26; Stinnett, "Archival Landscape"; Suárez, "Education Professionals and the Construction of Human Rights Education"; Mega Subramaniam, Rebecca Oxley, and Christie Kodama, "School Librarians as Ambassadors of Inclusive Information Access for Students with Disabilities," *School Library Research* 16 (2013); 1–34; Thompson et al., *Digital Literacy and Digital Inclusion*.

34. Kathleen de la Peña McCook, *Introduction to Public Librarianship* (New York: Neal-Schuman, 2011).

35. P. Fessler, "Why Disability and Poverty Still Go Hand in Hand 25 Years After Landmark Law," accessed August 20, 2015, http://www.npr.org/sections/health-shots/2015/07/23/424990474/why-disability-and-poverty-still-go-hand-in-hand-25-years-after-landmark-law?sc=tw.

36. Mathiesen, "Human Right to a Public Library."

37. Lua Gregory and Shana Higgins, eds., Information Literacy and Social Justice: Radical Professional Praxis (Sacramento, Calif.: Library Justice, 2013); Melissa Morrone, ed., *Informed Agitation: Library and Information Skills in Social Justice Movements and Beyond* (Sacramento, Calif.: Library Justice, 2014).

38. Jaeger, *Disability and the Internet*; Jaeger, "Internet Justice"; Paul T. Jaeger, "Disability, Human Rights, and Social Justice: The Ongoing Struggle for Online Accessibility and Equality," *First Monday* 20, no. 9 (2015), http://firstmonday.org/ojs/index.php/fm/article/view/6164/4898.

39. Jaeger, "Disability, Human Rights, and Social Justice."

40. Jaeger, *Disability and the Internet*; Lazar, Jaeger, and Bertot, "Persons with Disabilities and Physical and Virtual Public Library Settings."

41. John Carlo Bertot, Paul T. Jaeger, Jean Lee, Kristofer Dubbels, Abigail J. McDermott, and Brian Real, *Digital Inclusion Survey: Survey Findings and Results* (College Park, Md.: Information Policy & Access Center, 2013).

42. Ibid.

43. Susannah Fox, *Older Americans and the Internet*, Pew Internet and American Life Project (Washington, D.C.: Pew Research Center, 2004); Susannah Fox and Mary Madden, "Generations Online (Demographic Report)," Pew Internet and American Life Project, 2006; Paul T. Jaeger and Cynthia Ann Bowman, *Understanding Disability: Inclusion, Access, Diversity, and Civil Rights* (Westport, Conn.: Greenwood Press, 2005); University of California at Los Angeles, *UCLA Internet Report: Surveying the Digital Future* (Los Angeles: Anderson Graduate School of Management, last updated February 2003), http://images.forbes.com/fdc/mediaresourcecenter/UCLA03.pdf.

44. Kerry Dobransky and Eszter Hargittai, "The Disability Divide in Internet Access and Use," *Information, Communication and Society* 9, no. 3 (2006): 313–34.

45. Jaeger, *Disability and the Internet*.

46. Elfreda V. Blue and Darra Pace, "UD and UDL: Paving the Way toward Inclusion and Independence in the School Library," *Knowledge Quest* 39, no. 3 (2011): 48; Subramaniam, Oxley, and Kodama, "School Librarians as Ambassadors of Inclusive Information Access."

47. Bertot et al., *Digital Inclusion Survey*.

48. Ibid.

49. Jaeger, *Disability and the Internet*.

50. Lazar, Jaeger, and Bertot, "Persons with Disabilities and Physical and Virtual Public Library Settings."

51. Thompson et al., *Digital Literacy and Digital Inclusion*.

52. Kathryn Zickuhr, "Innovative Library Services 'in the Wild,'" Pew Research Center, *Libraries in the Digital Age* (blog), 2013, http://libraries.pewinternet.org/2013/01/29/innovative-library-services-in-the-wild/.

53. HathiTrust. "Welcome to the Shared Digital Future," accessed June 25, 2015, http://www.hathitrust.org/about.

54. American Library Association, "Library Services for People with Disabilities Policy."

55. District of Columbia Public Library, "Accessibility Hackathon 2," accessed August 22, 2015, http://dclibrary.org/node/32540.

56. Tara Brady, Camille Salas, Ayah Nuriddin, Walter Rodgers, and Mega Subramaniam, "MakeAbility: Creating Accessible Makerspace Events in a Public Library," *Public Library Quarterly* 33, no. 4 (2014): 330–47.

57. District of Columbia Public Library, "Adaptive Services," accessed August 22, 2015, http://dclibrary.org/services/lbph#ATP.

58. Jill Lewis, "Information Equality for Individuals with Disabilities: Does It Exist?," *Library* 83, no. 3 (2013): 229–35.

59. Lyons, "Human Rights," 290–93

60. McCook, *Introduction to Public Librarianship*.

61. Wiegand and Dalbello, introduction to Richards, Wiegand, and Dalbello, *History of Modern Librarianship*.

62. Richards, Wiegand, and Dalbello, *History of Modern Librarianship*.
63. Jaeger, *Disability and the Internet*.

5. Public Financing of Information Technology and Human Rights for People with Disabilities

1. Elizabeth R. Petrick, *Making Computers Accessible: Disability Rights and Digital Technology* (Baltimore: Johns Hopkins University Press, 2015).

2. U.S. Access Board, "About the Section 508 Standard-Regulatory Assessment," http://www.access-board.gov/guidelines-and-standards/communications-and-it/about-the-section-508-standards/background/regulatory-assessment/chapter-1-background.

3. Deborah Kaplan and John DeWitt, "Telecommunications and Persons with Disabilities: Building the Framework," Blue Ribbon Panel on National Communications Policy, 2nd report, World Institute on Disability, 1993, 25–26.

4. U.S. Access Board, "About the Section 508 Standards/Background," http://www.access-board.gov/guidelines-and-standards/communications-and-it/about-the-section-508-standards/background.

5. Section 508, 29 U.S.C. § 794d (a) (2) (B): "The Access Board shall periodically review and, as appropriate, amend the standards required under subparagraph (A) to reflect technological advances or changes in electronic and information technology."

6. 29 U.S.C. § 794d (d).

7. General Services Administration, http://section508.gov/.

8. Section 508.gov, "Best Practice Library," http://www.section508.gov/content/learn/best-practice-library.

9. Section 508.gov, "OMB Strategic Plan," http://www.section508.gov/document/strategic-plan.

10. 29 U.S.C. § 794d (f).

11. "Cal State's Strong Push for Accessibility Gets Results," *Chronicle of Higher Education*, December 12, 2010.

12. "Chapter 3: General Effective Communication Requirements Under Title II of the ADA," ADA Best Practices Tool Kit for State and Local Governments, U.S. Department of Justice, 2007, www.ada.gov/pcatoolkit/ch3_toolkit.pdf.

13. Section508.gov, GSA Government-Wide Section 508 Accessibility Program, "Create Accessible Electronic Documents," http://www.section508.gov/content/build/create-accessible-documents; WebAIM: Web Accessibility in Mind, "Create Accessible Word Documents," http://webaim.org/techniques/word/; "Acrobat Pro DC PDF Accessibility Repair Workflow," http://www.adobe.com/accessibility/products/acrobat/acrobat-pro-dc-pdf-accessibility-repair-workflow.html.

14. World Wide Web Consortium, Web Accessibility Initiative, wiki, "Accessibility Testing," http://www.w3.org/wiki/Accessibility_testing.

15. U.S. Department of Homeland Security, "DHS Section 508 Compliance Test Processes," http://www.dhs.gov/compliance-test-processes.

16. Information Technology Industry Council, "Accessibility," http://www.itic.org/policy/accessibility/.

17. EN 301 549 Accessible ICT Procurement Toolkit, "Conformity Assessments and Attestations," http://mandate376.standards.eu/planning-procurement/conformity-assessment-and-attestations.

18. NASCIO, "Accessibility in State Procurement," http://www.nascio.org/PDAA.

19. Undue burden is defined and discussed at 36 Code of Federal Regulations §§ 1194.2 (a), (a)(1), and 1194.4.

20. 29 U.S.C. § 794d (a) (5).

21. 36 Code of Federal Regulations § 1194.3.

22. 36 Code of Federal Regulations § 1194.31.

23. 36 Code of Federal Regulations § 1194.41.

24. U.S. Access Board, "Proposed Information and Communications Technology (ICT) Standards and Guidelines," http://www.access-board.gov/guidelines-and-standards/communications-and-it/about-the-ict-refresh/final-rule.

25. "Action 64: Ensure the Accessibility of Public Sector Websites," European Commission, Digital Single Market, accessed December 8, 2016, https://ec.europa.eu/digital-single-market/en/pillar-vi-enhancing-digital-literacy-skills-and-inclusion/action-64-ensure-accessibility-public.

26. G3ict, "CRPD 2013 ICT Accessibility Progress Report," http://www.g3ict.org/resource_center/CRPD_2013_ICT_Accessibility_Summary_Tables_12-_26#tables22-25.

27. United Nations Enable, http://www.un.org/disabilities/default.asp?navid=15&pid=150.

28. Cynthia Waddell, "Worldwide Accessibility Laws and Policies," in *Web Accessibility: Web Standards and Regulatory Compliance*, ed. Jim Thatcher et al. (New York: Springer-Verlag, 2006), 547–79.

29. Gunela Astbrink and William Tibben, "Public Procurement and ICT Accessibility," University of Wollongong, Research Online, 2013, ro.now.edu.au/cgi/viewcontent.cgi?article=3308&context=eispapers.

30. ETSI, http://www.etsi.org/technologies-clusters/technologies/human-factors?tab=2.

31. "Accessible ICT Procurement Toolkit," http://mandate376.standards.eu/.

32. National Disability Authority of Ireland, "Procurement and Accessibility," 2013, http://www.procurement.ie/publications.

33. Centre for Excellence in Universal Design, "IT Procurement Toolkit," http://universaldesign.ie/Technology-ICT/IT-Procurement-Toolkit/.

34. G3ict, "CRPD Implementation: Promoting Global Digital Inclusion Through ICT Procurement Policies & Accessibility Standards," 2015, http://g3ict.org

/resource_center/publications_and_ reports/p/productCategory_whitepapers/subCat_7/id_339/.

6. Using Provincial Laws to Drive a National Agenda

Thanks to Professors Michael Stein and Jonathan Lazar for inviting us to contribute and to David Baker for his tireless advocacy on these issues. We also wish to thank Barry Sookman, Jeffrey Stark, John Rae, and April D'Aubin for their helpful insights.

1. *Attorney General of Canada v. Jodhan*, 2012 FCA 161 [*Jodhan II*]; *Jodhan v. Attorney General of Canada*, 2010 FC 1197 [*Jodhan I*].

2. See Scott E. Hollier, "The Disability Divide: A Study into the Impact of Computing and Internet-Related Technologies on People Who Are Blind or Vision Impaired," Curtin University of Technology, 2007, http://digitalcommons.ilr.cornell.edu/gladnetcollect/340/.

3. The original language was "handicap." See Human Rights Code, SO, 1981, chap. 53 (coming into force June 15, 1982). See also David Lepofsky, "The Long, Arduous Road to a Barrier-Free Ontario for People with Disabilities," *National Journal of Constitutional Law* 15 (2004): 140–44 (describing campaign to amend the Ontario Human Rights Code). For an interesting if polemical discussion, see Ian Hunter, "Liberty and Equality: A Tale of Two Codes," *McGill Law Journal* 29 (1983): 1–23.

4. In most other provinces and in the federal system, the human rights commissions still play the role of gatekeeper and determine whether to refer a specific complaint to the respective tribunal. For a good overview, see Pearl Eliadis, *Speaking Out on Human Rights: Debating Canada's Human Rights System* (Montréal: McGill-Queen's University Press, 2014).

5. See secs. 91–92, Constitution Act, 1867, 30 & 31 Victoria, chap. 3.

6. See, e.g., *Alberta Government Telephones v. Canadian Radio-Television and Telecommunications Commission*, [1989] 2 SCR 225 (finding that the telephone company is an interprovincial undertaking within the meaning of s. 92(10)(a) of the Constitution Act, 1867).

7. Melanie D. McNaught and Heather Power, *What's New in Human Rights: The Pinto Report and Other Updates* (Toronto: Filion Wakely Thorup Angeletti, 2013). Most disability discrimination claims in Ontario have to do with employment.

8. Colleen Watters, "History of Advocacy Organizations of the Blind in Canada: Two Stories," in *Making Equality: History of Advocacy and Persons with Disabilities in Canada*, ed. Deborah Steinstra and Aileen Wight-Felske (Concord, Ont.: Captus Press, 2003), 163–77.

9. Harold Hongju Koh, "Transnational Legal Process," *Nebraska Law Review* 75 (1996): 182–84. See also Melissa Waters, "Mediating Norms and Identity: The Role of Transnational Judicial Dialogue in Creating and Enforcing International Law," *Georgetown Law Journal* 93 (2005): 487. Ravi Malhotra has written about the theories of Koh and Waters in the context of the Convention on the Rights of Persons with

Disabilities (CRPD). See Ravi Malhotra, "The United Nations Convention on Rights of Persons with Disabilities in Canadian and American Jurisprudence," *Windsor Yearbook of Access to Justice* 32, no. 2 (2015): 1–18.

10. For a more in-depth treatment of the impact of disability rights law on social norms, see Michael A. Stein, "Under the Empirical Radar: An Initial Expressive Law Analysis of the ADA," *Virginia Law Review* 90 (2004): 1151–91. Of course, one also has to bear in mind that the disability rights movement is global.

11. Ontarians with Disabilities Act, RSO 2001, chap. 32 [ODA]. For discussions, see Phyllis Gordon, Harry Beatty, and Bill Holder, "An Analysis of the Ontarians with Disabilities Act, 2001," *Journal of Law and Social Policy* 17 (2002): 15–38; Lepofsky, "Long, Arduous Road" (recounting the history of the campaign to enact the ODA). The ODA has yet to be repealed.

12. Lepofsky, "Long, Arduous Road."

13. Gordon, Beatty, and Holder, "Analysis of the Ontarians with Disabilities Act," 18.

14. Ibid., 18–19.

15. Lepofsky, "Long, Arduous Road," 157–59. In the Canadian parliamentary system, a private member's bill does not typically have the support of the government and rarely is enacted into law.

16. See generally Stein, "Under the Empirical Radar."

17. Lepofsky, "Long, Arduous Road," 223–26.

18. Ontarians with Disabilities Act, sec. 6.

19. Gordon, Beatty, and Holder, "Analysis of the Ontarians with Disabilities Act," 21; Mayo Moran, *Second Legislative Review of the Accessibility for Ontarians with Disabilities Act, 2005* (Toronto: Queen's Printer, 2014), 7.

20. See generally David Mullan and Antonella Ceddia, "The Impact of Public Law on Privatization, Deregulation, Outsourcing and Downsizing: A Canadian Perspective," *Indiana Journal of Global Legal Studies* 10 (2003): 199–246.

21. Gordon, Beatty, and Holder, "Analysis of the Ontarians with Disabilities Act," 21. One of the positive aspects of the ODA, however, was that it did require municipalities to have accessibility advisory committees that are staffed by a majority of people with disabilities. See ibid., 26.

22. Accessibility for Ontarians with Disabilities Act, 2005, SO 2005, chap. 11 [AODA].

23. There is a very skeletal law in one other province, Manitoba, but the accessibility standards are still being formulated. The Customer Service Standard Regulation in Manitoba came into force in November, 2015. For discussion of some of the developments leading to this, see Karine Levasseur, "Unnecessary Delay? Bill 47, the Accessibility Advisory Council Act and Amendments to the Government Purchases Act," *Manitoba Law Journal* 35, no. 2 (2012): 221. Nova Scotia is about to introduce accessibility legislation at the time of writing.

24. Accessibility Standards for Customer Service, O Reg 429/07.

25. Moran, *Second Legislative Review*, 12–13.

26. See Integrated Accessibility Standards (IASR), O Reg 191/11, sec. 7.

27. See, e.g., ibid., sec. 14.

28. See, e.g., Citizens with Disabilities–Ontario, *Submission Paper to Moran Legislative Review* (Toronto: CWD-O, 2014), 4–5 (arguing for an amendment to clarify vague language respecting timelines for enforcement of ICT regulations relating to the provision of materials in accessible formats and emergency procedures).

29. For a discussion of the issue in the financial services industry, see Lawrence G. Baxter, "Understanding Regulatory Capture: An Academic Perspective from the United States," in *The Making of Good Financial Regulation: Towards a Policy Response to Regulatory Capture*, ed. Stefano Pagliari (Guildford: Grosvenor House, 2012), 53–69.

30. IASR, sec. 83. There appears to be no intent to systematically audit obligated authorities for violations.

31. For a full discussion of this point, see Ravi Malhotra and Robin Hansen, "The United Nations Convention on the Rights of Persons with Disabilities and Its Implications for the Equality Rights of Canadians with Disabilities: The Case of Education," *Windsor Yearbook of Access to Justice* 29 (2011): 73–106.

32. IASR, sec. 9.

33. Ibid., sec. 9(3).

34. CRPD, G.A. Res. 61/106, U.N. Doc. A/RES/61/106, Art. 9.

35. Ibid., Art. 9(1)(b).

36. Ibid., Art. 21.

37. Ibid., Art. 30.

38. IASR, sec. 10.

39. Ibid., sec. 11.

40. Ibid., sec. 12.

41. Ibid., sec. 12(3).

42. Citizens with Disabilities–Ontario, *Submission Paper*, 4–5.

43. IASR, sec. 12(1)(a).

44. Ibid., sec. 12(5).

45. Ibid., sec. 13.

46. Ibid.

47. IASR, sec. 14.

48. Ibid., sec. 14(4).

49. Ibid., sec. 15.

50. Ibid., sec. 16.

51. Ibid., sec. 17.

52. Ibid., sec. 17(3).

53. Ibid., sec. 18.

54. Ibid., sec. 18(3).

55. Ibid., sec. 19.

56. Ibid., sec. 26. Similarly, the IASR requires conventional and specialized transportation providers to make information on their vehicles, routes, and services available in alternative formats; see sec. 34.

57. Geof Collis, "Site Check: New Durham Region Transit Website Not Accessible Despite Claims," November 16, 2012, http://enforcement.aoda.ca/site-check-new-durham-region-transit-website-not-accessible-despite-claims/.

58. Ibid.

59. Alliance for Equality of Blind Canadians, "Strengthening the Proposed Integrated Accessibility Regulation Under the Accessibility for Ontarians with Disabilities Act (2005)," http://www.blindcanadians.ca/publications/briefs/2011-strengthening-proposed-integrated-accessibility-regulation-under-accessibil. For an account of the potential impact of the CRPD in the context of ICT, see Axel Leblois, "Implementing the Digital Accessibility Agenda of the UN Convention on the Rights of Persons with Disabilities: Challenges and Opportunities," in *European Yearbook of Disability Law*, vol. 1, ed. Gerard Quinn and Lisa Waddington (Antwerp: Intersentia, 2009), 139–45.

60. Barry Sookman, "Canada to Accede to Marrakesh Treaty and Extend Copyright Term in Sound Recordings," http://www.barrysookman.com/2015/04/21/canada-to-accede-to-marrakesh-treaty-and-extend-copyright-term-in-sound-recordings/.

61. Amitra V. Singh, "Bill C-65: Amending the Copyright Act to Comply with the Marrakesh Treaty," http://www.bereskinparr.com/Doc/id592.

62. Barry Sookman, personal communications with Malhotra.

63. Singh, "Bill C-65."

64. "2009 CCD Award Recipient: Chris and Marie Laporte Stark," http://www.blindcanadians.ca/participate/awards/104-chris-marie-laporte-stark-2009. We thank Jeffrey Stark for drawing our attention to this.

65. "Brief to CRTC Phase 3 of Let's Talk TV," June 25, 2014, http://www.ccdonline.ca/en/technology/Lets-Talk%20-TV25June2014; April D'Aubin, "CCD and the Access to Technology Issue" (unpublished paper on file with the authors, 2015), 1.

66. "Brief to CRTC Phase 3."

67. CRPD, Art. 30.

68. D'Aubin, "CCD and the Access to Technology Issue," 2.

69. Donna Jodhan, "About the Author," May 17, 2015, http://www.donnajodhan.com/about-the-author.html.

70. Ibid.

71. Donna Jodhan, "An Update to My Charter Challenge," *Accessibility News*, http://www.accessibilitynews.ca/acnews/editorials/commentary.php?donna=68.

72. Ibid.

73. *Jodhan II*, paras. 9–14.

74. Ibid., para. 4.

75. See generally Merly Zisman Gary, Cara Wilkie, and David Baker, "The Law as It Affects People with Disabilities: A Case Study Paper on Rights to Supports Prepared for the Law Commission of Ontario," July 2010, http://www.lco-cdo.org/disabilities/bakerlaw.pdf; David Baker and Erin Hallock, "The Relationship Between Long-Term Disability Benefits and the Duty to Accommodate: The Plaintiff's Perspective," 2010, http://www.bakerlaw.ca/wp-content/uploads/LTDandDTA.pdf.

76. CCD Online, "Jodhan Decision Advances Access to Web Sites for Person with Vision Impairment," http://www.ccdonline.ca/en/blog/jodhan.

77. *Jodhan II*, para. 18.

78. Ibid., para, 19.

79. *Jodhan I*, para, 100.

80. Ibid.

81. Ibid.

82. Ibid.

83. Ibid.

84. *Jodhan II*, para, 8.

85. Ibid., para. 1.

86. Ibid., para. 108.

87. Ibid., para. 134.

88. Ibid.

89. Ibid., para. 186.

90. *Eldridge v. British Columbia* (Attorney General), [1997] 3 SCR 624.

91. Ibid.

92. *Council of Canadians with Disabilities v. Via Rail Canada Inc.*, [2007] 1 SCR 650.

93. Ibid.

94. Ibid.

95. AODA Alliance, "United for a Barrier-Free Ontario," http://www.aodaalliance.org/strong-effective-aoda/06012012.asp. The AODA Alliance continues the work of previous disability rights groups.

96. Julie Ireton, "Public Servants with Visual Impairments Say Government Failing Them," July 2, 2015, http://www.cbc.ca/news/canada/ottawa/public-servants-with-visual-impairments-say-government-failing-them-1.3126588.

7. Access to Justice

1. See, e.g., UN Convention on the Rights of Persons with Disabilities, Article 13, Access to Justice, § 1; and *United States v. Lane*, 541 U.S. 509 (2004).

2. Access to Justice Taskforce, Attorney-General's Department [Australia], "A Strategic Framework for Access to Justice in the Federal Civil Justice System: A Guide for Future Action" (footnote omitted), September 2009, https://www.ag.gov.au/LegalSystem/Documents/A%20Strategic%20Framework%20for%20Access%20to%20Justice%20in%20the%20Federal%20Civil%20Justice%20System.pdf.

3. Ibid.

4. "Access to justice" can be a far larger concept, of course. Lawyers regularly provide advice and assistance to enable people to accomplish personal, family, business, and organizational goals, and access to legal assistance can be said to be a fundamental part of "access to justice." This chapter, however, deals only with dispute resolution in the form of courts.

5. Courts may be responsible for functions other than dispute resolution. In the United States, for example, state courts may be responsible for land records, estate administration, and marriages, to mention only a few. See the Fairfax County, Virginia, website, http://www.fairfaxcounty.gov/courts/.

6. For general information and news, see the United States Department of Justice, Civil Rights Division, http://www.ada.gov.

7. 29 U.S.C. 701.

8. See the World Wide Web Consortium, "Techniques for WCAG 2.0," http://www.w3.org/TR/2012/NOTE-WCAG20-TECHS-20120103/pdf.html, for accessible PDF documents.

9. Court data related to internal functions, such as personnel records, likely will not be available to the public.

10. Fairfax County, Virginia, http://www.fairfaxcounty.gov/courts/ (a site on behalf of the circuit court, the court of general jurisdiction; the district court, a court that handles lesser matters, including traffic matters; and the juvenile and domestic relations court, handling family matters).

11. In the United States, the federal courts' PACER (Public Access to Court Electronic Records) court information database, https://www.pacer.gov/, includes digital audio court record recordings.

12. Although online access to court information is outside the scope of this chapter, the reader should note that it can create tension between the public's right to know and personal privacy. In the past, many personal data were effectively shielded from public exposure by what has been called the doctrine of practical obscurity—the fact that an average person did not know that the records existed, and even if a person did know of their existence, he or she customarily did not know how to access them. Online access potentially makes information easily searchable and available.

13. *Settlement Agreement Between the United States of America and the Orange County Clerk of Courts Under the Americans with Disabilities Act*, Department of Justice Complaint #204-17M-440 (July 17, 2014), http://www.ada.gov/occ.htm.

14. See Fed. R. Civ. P. 26(b)(2)(C)(iii) (court must limit discovery if "the burden or expense of the proposed discovery outweighs its likely benefit, considering the needs of the case, the amount in controversy, the parties' resources, the importance of the issues at stake in the action, and the importance of the discovery in resolving the issues").

15. That will be true, at best, only if counsel are at least competent, which they may not be, and, ideally, evenly matched in ability. Further, the emphasis on courtroom battle can obscure important information.

16. Although the inquisitorial model lacks the uncertainties of the potentially mismatched adversarial-legal-battle system, it is heavily dependent on the judges and investigating police or magistrate. Depending on the country, inquisitorial nations often have incorporated aspects of the adversarial model, including an increased role for lawyers.

17. Compare *United States v. Yates*, 438 F.3d 1307 (11th Cir. 2006) (en banc) (unconstitutional) with *United States v. Abu Ali*, 528 F.3d 210 (4th Cir. 2008) (remote deposition testimony constitutional) and *Harrell v. State*, 709 So. 2d 1364 (Fla. 1998); cert. denied, 525 U.S. 903 (1998) (constitutional).

18. See "UK Internet First for Injured Judge," *BBC News*, July 30, 1999.

19. See, e.g., Krishnaswamy Kavita, *Attending Conferences via Robots*, accessed August 3, 2015, https://www.washington.edu/doit/attending-conferences-robots (discussing the Beam Telepresence Robot); and Jon Kelvey, "A Quick Reminder That Technology Can Be Wonderful," *Slate*, July 22, 2014.

20. *Galloway v. Superior Ct.*, 816 F. Supp. 12 (D.D.C. 1993) (holding Washington, D.C., Superior Court prohibition on blind persons serving as jurors as violative of federal statutes). In *Galloway*, the court opined that the "plaintiff has offered uncontradicted testimony that blind individuals, like sighted jurors, weigh the content of the testimony given and examine speech patterns, intonation, and syntax in assessing credibility. Thus, 'the nervous tic or darting glance, the uneasy shifting or revealing gesture is almost always accompanied by auditory correlates[, including, inter alia,] clearing the throat, pausing to swallow, voice quavering or inaudibility due to stress or looking downward' (Kaiser, 'Juries, Blindness and the Juror Function,' *Chicago-Kent Law Review* 60 (1984): 191–200), and permits a blind juror to make credibility assessments just as the juror's sighted counterparts do. Interestingly, at least ten states—Oklahoma, California, Virginia, Oregon, Texas, South Carolina, Washington, Massachusetts, Wisconsin, and New York—have enacted statutes that forbid exclusion of blind persons from jury pools solely because of their disability." *Galloway*, 16–17 (footnote omitted).

21. *Galloway*, 17.

22. See, e.g., *United States v. Scheur*, 547 F. Supp. 2d 580 (E.D. La. 2008).

23. Ibid.

24. Members of the public today usually see such images on large flat panels.

25. In 2015 and 2016, both simulated and real court proceedings tested jury tablet displays that were connected wirelessly to counsel's tablet or phone. It is unclear at this time whether tablet display use would permit enlargement for both technical and legal reasons.

26. See, e.g., Christopher Mims, "Virtual Reality Isn't Just About Games," *Wall Street Journal*, August 3, 2015, B1, col. 1.

27. "The Right to Be Heard," Haruv Institute, Hebrew University, Israel, https://www.youtube.com/watch?v=Bgmli_aElYY.

8. Open Government and Digital Accessibility

1. Daniel Lathrop and Laurel Ruma, *Open Government: Collaboration, Transparency, and Participation in Practice* (Sebastopol, Calif.: O'Reilly Media, 2010), https://github.com/oreillymedia/open_government.

2. David Wasserman, Adrienne Asch, Jeffrey Blustein, and Daniel Putnam "Disability: Definitions, Models, Experience," in *Stanford Encyclopedia of Philosophy* (Winter 2015), ed. Edward N. Zalta (Stanford, CA: Stanford University, 2015), http://plato.stanford.edu/archives/win2015/entries/disability/.

3. Sara Scalenghe, *Disability in the Ottoman Arab World, 1500–1800* (New York: Cambridge University Press, 2014); Martha L. Rose, *The Staff of Oedipus: Transforming Disability in Ancient Greece* (Ann Arbor: University of Michigan Press, 2003).

4. Lisa Schur, Douglas Kruse, and Peter Blanck, *People with Disabilities: Sidelined or Mainstreamed?* (New York: Cambridge University Press, 2013).

5. John Milton, *Areopagitica; A Speech of Mr. John Milton: For the Liberty of Unlicenc'd Printing, To the Parlament [sic] of England* (London: n.p., 1644), 35.

6. James Madison to W.T. Barry, August 4, 1822, in *The Writings of James Madison*, vol. 9, ed. Gaillard Hunt (New York: G. P. Putnam's Sons, 1910), 103.

7. *Keeping America Informed: The United States Government Printing Office: 150 Years of Service to the Nation* (Washington, D.C.: U.S. Government Printing Office, 2011).

8. Administrative Procedure Act of 1946, 5 U.S.C. § 552.

9. Freedom of Administration Act of 1966, 5 U.S.C. § 552.

10. "FOIAonline," accessed November 9, 2015, https://foiaonline.regulations.gov/foia/action/public/home.

11. The Government in the Sunshine Act of 1976, 5 U.S.C. § 552(b).

12. "Open Government Guide," Reporters Committee for the Freedom of the Press, accessed June 17, 2015, http://www.rcfp.org/open-government-guide.

13. Jonathan Lazar, Daniel Goldstein, and Anne Taylor, *Ensuring Digital Accessibility Through Process and Policy* (Waltham, Mass.: Morgan Kaufmann, 2015), 164.

14. Open Government Partnership, "What's in the New OGP National Action Plans? An Overview of Commitments from 35 OGP Countries," 2014, http://www.opengovpartnership.org/sites/default/files/OGP-Whats-in-the-New-OGP-NAPs-report-web.pdf.

15. Open Government Partnership, "Brazil's Second OGP Action Plan (English Version)," 2013, http://www.opengovpartnership.org/sites/default/files/BR-PlanoDeAcao-ActionPlan-revisado_ago-13.docx.

16. "Freedom of Information Act: Memorandum for the Heads of Executive Departments and Agencies," 74 Fed. Reg. 4681 (January 26, 2009); Executive Office of the

President, Office of Management and Budget, "Open Data Policy—Managing Information as an Asset," May 9, 2013, https://www.whitehouse.gov/sites/default/files/omb/memoranda/2013/m-13-13.pdf.

17. Jonathan Lazar, Timothy Elder, and Michael Stein, "Understanding the Connection Between HCI and Freedom of Information and Access Laws," *ACM Interactions* 20, no. 6 (2013): 60–63.

18. Daren C. Brabham, "Motivations for Participation in a Crowdsourcing Application to Improve Public Engagement in Transit Planning," *Journal of Applied Communication Research* 40, no. 3 (2012): 307–28.

19. "JAWS and MAGic Selected by the Ministry for Information and Communications Technologies (MinTIC) for the Visually Impaired of Colombia," Freedom Scientific, March 13, 2014, http://www.freedomscientific.com/About/News/Article/13.

20. "Convention on the Rights of Persons with Disabilities," December 13, 2006, Treaties and Other International Acts Series 2515, no. 44910 (2011): 3.

21. "Proposal for a DIRECTIVE OF THE EUROPEAN PARLIAMENT AND OF THE COUNCIL on the Accessibility of Public Sector Bodies' Websites," European Commission, COD 2012/0340, accessed June 15, 2015, http://eur-lex.europa.eu/legal-content/EN/TXT/?uri=COM:2012:0721:FIN.

22. "What is the Open Government Partnership?" Open Government Partnership, accessed December 27, 2015, http://www.opengovpartnership.org/about.

23. Open Government Partnership, "Third Open Government National Action Plan for the United States of America," 2015, http://www.opengovpartnership.org/sites/default/files/final_us_open_government_national_action_plan_3_0.pdf.

24. "Section 508 Report to the President and Congress: Accessibility of Federal Electronic and Information Technology," United States Department of Justice, Civil Rights Division, September 2012, https://www.ada.gov/508/508_Report.htm.

9. E-Books and Human Rights

1. Stephen King, "The Daisy Consortium Global Partnership: Working with the NFB to End the Book Famine," Braille Monitor, accessed October 20, 2016, https://nfb.org/images/nfb/publications/bm/bm12/bm1210/bm121005.htm.

2. "George Kerscher, Ph.D," accessed October 23, 2016, http://kerscher.montana.com/vita-2016-august.html.

3. James Fruchterman and George Kerscher, "The Soundproof Book: Exploration of Rights Conflict and Access to Commercial EBooks for People with Disabilities," *First Monday* 7, no. 6 (June 2002), http://firstmonday.org/ojs/index.php/fm/article/viewArticle/959/.

4. Assem. Bill 422, 1999–2000 Reg. Sess. (Cal. 1999), http://www.leginfo.ca.gov/pub/99-00/bill/asm/ab_0401-0450/ab_422_bill_19990915_chaptered.html.

5. Individuals with Disabilities Education Act (IDEA), as amended in 2004, PL 108-446, 20 United States Code (USC) 1400 et seq.

6. "Accessible Standards for Publishing," Daisy Consortium, http://www.daisy.org/publishers.

7. 34 CFR 300.172(e)(2) [20 USC 1412(a)(23)(E), 1474(e)(3)(A)].

8. Jack Schofield, "Amazon Caves to Authors Guild over Kindle's Text-to-Speech Reading," *Guardian*, March 1, 2009.

9. Settlement Agreement, *National Federation of the Blind v. Arizona Board of Regents*, CV09-01359, January 8, 2010, http://www.ada.gov/arizona_state_university.htm.

10. Contracting Parties: Marrakesh Treaty to Facilitate Access to Published Works for Persons Who Are Blind, Visually Impaired, or Otherwise Print Disabled, accessed October 20, 2016, http://www.wipo.int/treaties/en/ShowResults.jsp?treaty_id=843.

11. Ratifications and Accessions: Marrakesh Treaty to Facilitate Access to Published Works for Persons Who Are Blind, Visually Impaired, or Otherwise Print Disabled, accessed October 20, 2016, http://www.wipo.int/treaties/en/ShowResults.jsp?search_what=N&treaty_id=843.

12. "Speech by WBU President Dr. William Rowland in Amsterdam on Wednesday 23rd April 2008 on the Occasion of WBU's Press Conference Launching Its Global Right to Read Campaign," accessed October 20, 2016, g3ict.org/download/p/fileId_783/productId_124.

13. SCCR/18/5—Proposal by Brazil, Ecuador and Paraguay, Relating to Limitations and Exceptions: Treaty Proposed by the World Blind Union (WBU), http://www.wipo.int/meetings/en/doc_details.jsp?doc_id=133353.

14. "About Us," Pratham Books, accessed October 23, 2016, http://prathambooks.org/about-us.

15. International Digital Publishing Forum, EPUB 3, http://idpf.org/epub/30.

16. Betsy Beaumon, "Born Accessible and the New Golden Age of Inclusive Education," keynote address at the 52nd Annual Learning Disabilities Association of America Conference, Chicago, February 2015, http://benetech.org/2015/02/25/born-accessible-and-the-new-golden-age-of-inclusive-education/.

17. Committee on the Rights of Persons with Disabilities, General Comment 2, http://daccess-dds-ny.un.org/doc/UNDOC/GEN/G14/033/13/PDF/G1403313.pdf?OpenElement.

18. James Fruchterman, "Making the Book Truly Accessible," keynote address at the O'Reilly Tools of Change Conference, New York, February 2011, https://www.youtube.com/watch?v=uUu8CkQ3DJU.

19. Kim Sugeno, "Wiley Incorporates Alt Text to Make Content More accessible," Wiley Exchange, May 5, 2015, http://exchanges.wiley.com/blog/2015/05/05/wiley-incorporates-alt-text-to-make-content-more-accessible/.

10. Accessibility and Online Learning

1. Article 24 of the CRPD, http://www.un.org/disabilities/default.asp?id=284, states: "States Parties to recognize the right of persons with disabilities to education.

With a view to realizing this right without discrimination and on the basis of equal opportunity, States Parties shall ensure an inclusive education system at all levels and lifelong learning."

2. IMS Global Learning Consortium, http://imsglobal.org.

3. Fideo F. Chambo et al., "Mobile Learning Model for Tanzania Secondary Schools: Case Study of Kilimanjaro Region," *Journal of Emerging Trends in Computing and Information Sciences* 4, no. 9 (September 2013): 698–701.

4. University of Colorado Boulder, "Digital Accessibility Initiative Update: Department of Justice Inquiry Closed," May 27, 2015.

5. Settlement Agreement Between the United States of America and EdX, Inc. Under Americans with Disabilities Act, DJ No. 202-36-255, 2015, http://www.justice.gov/sites/default/ files/opa/press-releases/attachments/2015/04/02/edx_settlement_agreement.pdf.

6. Report of the Advisory Commission on Accessible Instructional Materials in Postsecondary Education for Students with Disabilities (AIM Report), 2011, http://www2.ed.gov/about/bdscomm/list/aim/meeting/aim-report.pdf.

7. AIM HEA Act, Accessible Instructional Materials in Higher Education Act, https://www.congress.gov/bill/114th-congress/house-bill/6122]

8. "Proposed Information and Communication Technology (ICT) Standards and Guidelines: Published in the *Federal Register* on February 27, 2015 (80 FR 10880)," United States Access Board, https://www.access-board.gov/guidelines-and-standards/communications-and-it/about-the-ict-refresh/proposed-rule.

9. "Accessibility Guidelines," Open University Web Standards, http://www.open.ac.uk/about/web-standards/standards/accessibility-standards/accessibility.

10. Access DL: The Center on Accessible Distance Learning, http://www.washington.edu/doit/programs/accessdl.

11. NCAM Item Writer Guidelines, http://ncam.wgbh.org/experience_learn/educational_ media/accessible-assessments/item-writer-guidelines.

12. "IMS Guidelines for Developing Accessible Learning Applications," IMS Global Learning Consortium, http://www.imsglobal.org/accessibility/accessiblevers/.

13. CAST [Center for Applied Special Technology], Universal Design for Learning Guidelines, Version 2.0, Wakefield, Mass., 2011, http://www.udlcenter.org/aboutudl/udlguidelines.

14. "UDL and Technology," National Center on Universal Design for Learning, http://www.udlcenter.org/aboutudl/udltechnology.

15. "Introduction to Universal Design in Education," The Center for Universal Design in Education, http://www.washington.edu/doit/programs/center-universal-design-education/introduction-universal-design-education.

16. Teaching Accessibility, http://teachingaccessibility.com/.

17. Hadi Rangin, "A Comparison of Learning Management System Accessibility," *Hadi Rangin's Blog*, March 11, 2013, http://blog.bargirangin.com/2013/03/a-comparison-of-learning-management.html.

18. Jane Seale, *E-Learning and Disability in Higher Education: Accessibility Research and Practice* (New York: Routledge, 2014).

19. Sarah Horton and W. Quesenbery, *A Web for Everyone: Designing Accessible User Experiences* (Brooklyn, N.Y.: Rosenfeld Media, 2014).

20. WAI-engage, "Accessibility Responsibility Breakdown," http://www.w3.org/community/wai-engage/wiki/Accessibility_Responsibility_Breakdown; Sarah Horton and D. Sloan, "Accessibility in Practice: A Process-Driven Approach to Accessibility," in *Inclusive Designing*, ed. Patrick Langdon et al. (New York: Springer, 2014), 105–15.

21. Rob Abel, M. Brown, and J. Seuss, "A New Architecture for Learning," *EDUCAUSE Review* 48, no. 5 (September–October 2013), 88–102.

22. CAST, Universal Design for Learning Guidelines, version 2.0.

23. WCAG Principle 4, "Robust—Content must be robust enough that it can be interpreted reliably by a wide variety of user agents, including assistive technologies," http://www.w3.org/TR/WCAG20/#robust.

24. Seale, *E-Learning and Disability in Higher Education*.

11. Who Owns Captioning?

1. World Health Organization, "Deafness and Hearing Loss," Fact Sheet Nº300, 2015. http://www.who.int/mediacentre/factsheets/fs300/en/.

2. National Institute on Deafness and Other Communication Disorders, "Quick Statistics," *Quick Health Statistics*, 2015, http://www.nidcd.nih.gov/health/statistics/pages/quick.aspx.

3. Emil S. Ladner, "Silent Talkies," *American Annals of the Deaf* 76 (1931): 323–25.

4. Malcolm J. Norwood, "Captioning for Deaf People: An Historical Overview," in *Speech to Text: Today and Tomorrow. Proceedings of a Conference at Gallaudet University*, ed. J. E. Harkins and B. M. Virvan (Washington, D.C., September 1988), 134.

5. Hussayam Safar, "Study on Use of Subtitling," accessed January 9, 2015, http://www.mcu.es/cine/docs/Novedades/Study_on_use_subtitling.pdf.

6. Federal Communications Commission, "IP Closed Captioning Order on Reconsideration and FNPRM," 2013.

7. U.S. Congress, Public Law 85-905, 1958.

8. Norwood, "Captioning for Deaf People."

9. Ibid.

10. British Broadcasting Corporation, "History of Teletext," 2014, http://main.wgbh.org/wgbh/pages/ncam_old/archives/teltexhist.html.

11. Ibid.

12. U.S. Congress, Twenty-First Century Communications and Video Accessibility Act of 2010, Public Law 111–260, 124 Stat. 2751 (2010).

13. United Nations General Assembly (UNGA), Declaration on the Rights of Mentally Retarded Persons, *World Medical Journal* 25 (1971), http://www2.ohchr.org/english/law/res2856.htm.

14. United Nations General Assembly (UNGA), Declaration on the Rights of Disabled Persons, 1975, http://www.ohchr.org/EN/ProfessionalInterest/Pages/RightsOfDisabledPersons.aspx.

15. Costa Rica, Ley de Igualdad de Oportunidades para las Personas con Discapacidad (Law of Equal Opportunities for Persons with Disabilities), 1996.

16. Organization of American States, Inter-American Convention on the Elimination of All Forms of Discrimination Against Persons with Disabilities, 1999.

17. U.S. Congress, Telecommunications Act of 1996, Public Law 104-104, 110 Stat. 56 (1996).

18. J. W. Roos, "Copyright Protection as Access Barrier for People Who Read Differently: The Case for an International Approach," *IFLA Journal* 31, no 1 (2005): 52–67.

19. Rakesh Agrawal, "Inside the Jokes: TV Search Technology Yields Creative, Comedic Screenwriting," in *SMPTE Annual Tech Conference & Expo* (Hollywood, Calif., 2010), 1–6, http://ieeexplore.ieee.org/document/7269105/.

20. *Authors Guild v. HathiTrust*, 755 F.3d 87 (2d Cir. 2014)

12. Information Privacy and Security as a Human Right for People with Disabilities

We appreciate the constructive feedback from Harry Hochheiser on an earlier draft.

1. Gaëlle Calvary, Audrey Serna, Joëlle Coutaz, Dominique Scapin, Florence Pontico, and Marco Winckler, "Envisioning Advanced User Interfaces for E-Government Applications: A Case Study," in *Practical Studies in E-Government*, ed. Saïd Assar, Imed Boughzala, and Isabelle Boydens (New York: Springer, 2011), 205–28.

2. William Jones, *Keeping Found Things Found: The Study and Practice of Personal Information Management* (Amsterdam: Morgan Kaufmann, 2010).

3. Paul Dourish and Ken Anderson, "Collective Information Practice: Exploring Privacy and Security as Social and Cultural Phenomena," *Human-Computer Interaction* 21, no. 3 (2006): 319–42.

4. Claire-Marie Karat, Carolyn Brodie, and John Karat, "Usability Design and Evaluation for Privacy and Security Solutions," in *Security and Usability: Designing Secure Systems That People Can Use*, ed. L. Cranor and S. Garfinkel (Sebastopol, Calif.: O'Reilly, 2005), 47–74.

5. M. A. Sasse and I. Flechais, "Usable Security: Why Do We Need It? How Do We Get it?," in Cranor and Garfinkel, *Security and Usability*, 13–30.

6. Omer Tene and Julie Polonetsky, "Privacy in the Age of Big Data: A Time for Big Decisions," *Stanford Law Review Online* 64 (February 2012), https://www.stanfordlawreview.org/online/privacy-paradox-privacy-and-big-data/.

7. Maurits Kaptein, Dean Eckles, and Janet Davis, "Envisioning Persuasion Profiles: Challenges for Public Policy and Ethical Practice," *Interactions* 18, no. 5 (2011): 66–69.

8. Stacey Branham and Shaun Kane, "Collaborative Accessibility: How Blind and Sighted Companions Co-create Accessible Home Spaces," in *Proceedings of the 33rd Annual ACM Conference on Human Factors in Computing Systems* (New York: ACM, 2015), 2373–82.

9. Bryan Dosono, Jordan Hayes, and Yang Wang, "'I'm Stuck!': A Contextual Inquiry of People with Visual Impairments in Authentication," in *SOUPS 2015: Proceedings of the Eleventh Symposium on Usable Privacy and Security* (USENIX, 2015), 151–68, https://www.usenix.org/conference/soups2015/proceedings.

10. Shaojian Zhu, Yao Ma, Jinjuan Feng, and Andrew Sears, "Don't Listen! I Am Dictating My Password!," in *Proceedings of the 11th International ACM SIGACCESS Conference on Computers and Accessibility* (New York: ACM, 2009), 229–30.

11. Yao Ma, Jinjuan Feng, Libby Kumin, and Jonathan Lazar, "Investigating User Behavior for Authentication Methods: A Comparison Between Individuals with Down Syndrome and Neurotypical Users," *ACM Transactions on Accessible Computing (TACCESS)* 4, no. 4 (2013): 1–15.

12. Jonathan Lazar, Libby Kumin, and Jinjuan Feng, "Understanding the Computer Skills of Adult Expert Users with Down Syndrome: An Exploratory Study," in *Proceedings of the 13th International ACM SIGACCESS Conference on Computers and Accessibility* (New York: ACM, 2011), 51–58.

13. Graig Sauer, Jonathan Lazar, Harry Hochheiser, and Jinjuan Feng, "Towards a Universally Usable Human Interaction Proof: Evaluation of Task Completion Strategies," *ACM Transactions on Accessible Computing* 2, no. 4 (2010): 1–32; J. Bigham and A. Cavender, "Evaluating Existing Audio CAPTCHAs and an Interface Optimized for Non-visual Use," *Proceedings of the SIGCHI Conference on Human Factors in Computing Systems* (New York: ACM, 2009), 1829–38.

14. K. Helkala, "Disabilities and Authentication Methods: Usability and Security," in *ARES 2012: 2012 Seventh International Conference on Availability, Reliability and Security* (Piscataway, N.J.: Institute of Electrical and Electronics Engineers, 2012), 327–34.

15. T. Ahmed, R. Hoyle, K. Connelly, D. Crandall, and A. Kapadia, "Privacy Concerns and Behaviors of People with Visual Impairments," in *Proceedings of the 33rd Annual ACM Conference on Human Factors in Computing Systems*, 3523–32.

16. M. C. Weber, *Disability Harassment* (New York: New York University Press, 2007).

17. J. Lazar, A. Olalere, and B. Wentz, "Investigating the Accessibility and Usability of Job Application Web Sites for Blind Users," *Journal of Usability Studies* 7, no. 2 (2012): 68–87.

18. Bureau of Labor Statistics, "Persons with a Disability: Labor Force Characteristics Summary," 2015, http://www.bls.gov/news.release/disabl.nr0.htm.

19. M. Ameri, L. Schur, M. Adya, S. Bentley, P. McKay, D. Kruse, and K. Sullivan, "The Disability Employment Puzzle: A Field Experiment on Employer Hiring Behav-

ior," *Proceedings of the 2015 Labor and Employment Relations Association Conference*, 2015, https://www.aeaweb.org/aea/2015conference/program/retrieve.php?pdfid=1211.

20. M. Elgan, "Snooping: It's Not a Crime, It's a Feature," *Computerworld*, April 16, 2011.

21. K. Alt, "Browser Enhancer Detection by Employers and Insurance Companies," *Journal on Telecommunications and High Technology Law* 10 (2012): 445–92.

22. A. Peacock, X. Ke, and M. Wilkerson, "Identifying Users from Their Typing Patterns," in Cranor and Garfinkel, *Security and Usability*, 199–220.

23. K. Shinohara and J. Wobbrock, "In the Shadow of Misperception: Assistive Technology Use and Social Interactions," in *Proceedings of the SIGCHI Conference on Human Factors in Computing Systems* (New York: ACM, 2011), 705–14.

24. J. A. Kientz, S. N. Patel, A. Z. Tyebkhan, B. Gane, J. Wiley, and G. D. Abowd, "Where's My Stuff? Design and Evaluation of a Mobile System for Locating Lost Items for the Visually Impaired," in *Proceedings of the 8th International ACM SIGACCESS Conference on Computers and Accessibility* (New York: ACM, 2006), 10310.

25. M. Damiani, "Third Party Geolocation Services in LBS: Privacy Requirements and Research Issues," *Transactions on Data Privacy* 4, no. 2 (2011): 55–72.

26. Mike Wu, Ronald Baecker, and Brian Richards, "Field Evaluation of a Collaborative Memory Aid for Persons with Amnesia and Their Family Members," in *Proceedings of the 12th International ACM SIGACCESS Conference on Computers and Accessibility* (New York: ACM, 2010), 51–58; Jason Behmer and Stillman Knox, "LocalEyes: Accessible GPS and Points of Interest," *Proceedings of the 12th International ACM SIGACCESS Conference*, 323–24; A. An, H.-D. J. Jeong, J. Lim, and W. Hyun, "Design and Implementation of Location-Based SNS Smartphone Application for the Disabled Population," in *Proceedings of the 2012 Sixth International Conference on Innovative Mobile and Internet Services in Ubiquitous Computing* (Washington DC: IEEE Computer Society, 2012), 365–70.

27. B. Weitzenkorn, "McAfee's Rookie Mistake Gives Away His Location," *Scientific American*, December 2012, 1.

28. B. Acohido, "Why Geolocation Apps Can Be Dangerous," *USA Today*, September 27, 2011.

29. Florian Schaub, Rebecca Balebako, Adam L. Durity, and Lorrie Faith Cranor, "A Design Space for Effective Privacy Notices," in *SOUPS 2015: Proceedings of the Eleventh Symposium on Usable Privacy and Security*, 1–18, https://www.usenix.org/sites/default/files/soups15_full_proceedings.pdf.

30. A. Madrigal, "Reading the Privacy Policies You Encounter in a Year Would Take 76 Work Days," *Atlantic*, March 1, 2012.

31. European Union, "Reform of the Data Protection Legal Framework in the EU," 2015, http://ec.europa.eu/justice/data-protection/reform/index_en.htm.

32. D. Bergemann and A. Bonatti, "Selling Cookies," *American Economic Journal: Microeconomics* 7, no. 3 (2015): 259–94.

33. Jonathan R. Mayer and John C. Mitchell, "Third-Party Web Tracking: Policy and Technology," in *Proceedings of the 2012 IEEE Computer Society Symposium on Security and Privacy* (IEEE 2012), 413–27.

13. How Does Inaccessible Gaming Lead to Social Exclusion?

1. Bei Yuan, Eelke Folmer, and Frederick C. Harris Jr., "Game Accessibility: A Survey," *Universal Access in the Information Society* 10, no. 1 (2011): 81–100;

Kurt Squire, *Video Games and Learning: Teaching and Participatory Culture in the Digital Age* (New York: Teachers College Press, 2011).

2. Roy McConkey, Sandra Dowling, David Hassan, and Sabine Menke, "Promoting Social Inclusion Through Unified Sports for Youth with Intellectual Disabilities: A Five-Nation Study," *Journal of Intellectual Disability Research* 57, no. 10 (2013): 923–35; David Hassan, Sandra Dowling, Roy McConkey, and Sabine Menke, "The Inclusion of People with Intellectual Disabilities in Team Sports: Lessons from the Youth Unified Sports Programme of Special Olympics," *Sport in Society* 15, no. 9 (2012): 1275–90.

3. Adam J. Sporka, Sri H. Kumiawan, Murmi Mahmud, and Pavle Slavik, "Non-speech Input and Speech Recognition for Real-Time Control of Computer Games," in *Proceedings of the 8th International ACM SIGACCESS Conference on Computers and Accessibility* (New York: ACM, 2006), 213–20. Zi Ye, Hamilton A. Hernandez, T. C. Graham, Darcy Fehlings, Lauren Switzer, Md Ameer Hamza, and Irina Schumann, "Liberi and the Racer Bike: Exergaming Technology for Children with Cerebral Palsy," in *Proceedings of the 14th International ACM SIGACCESS Conference on Computers and Accessibility* (New York: ACM, 2012), 225–26.

Kyle Rector, Cynthia L. Bennett, and Julie A. Kientz, "Eyes-Free Yoga: An Exergame Using Depth Cameras for Blind and Low Vision Exercise," in *Proceedings of the 15th International ACM SIGACCESS Conference on Computers and Accessibility* (New York: ACM, 2013), 12.

Kathrin M. Gerling, Regan L. Mandryk, and Michael R. Kalyn, "Wheelchair-Based Game Design for Older Adults," in *Proceedings of the 15th International ACM SIGACCESS Conference on Computers and Accessibility*, 27. Joyram Chakraborty, Joseph Hritz, and Josh Dehlinger, "Preliminary Results in the Understanding of Accessibility Challenges in Computer Gaming for the Visually Impaired," in *Inclusive Designing*, ed. P. M. Langdon, J. Lazar, A. Heylighen, and H. Dong (New York: Springer, 2014), 83–92.

4. Katie Larsen McClarty, Aline Orr, Peter M. Frey, Robert P. Dolan, Victoria Vassileva, and Aaron McVay, "A Literature Review of Gaming in Education," *Gaming in Education*, 2012.

5. Alice Mitchell and Carol Savill-Smith, *The Use of Computer and Video Games for Learning: A Review of the Literature* (London: LSDA Agency, 2004).

6. Michael F. Young, Stephen Slota, Andrew B. Cutter, Gerard Jalette, Greg Mullin, Benedict Lai, Zeus Simeoni, Matthew Tran, and Mariya Yukhymenko, "Our Prin-

cess Is in Another Castle: A Review of Trends in Serious Gaming for Education," *Review of Educational Research* 82, no. 1 (2012): 61–89.

7. Elaine Pearson and Chris Bailey, "Evaluating the Potential of the Nintendo Wii to Support Disabled Students in Education," *ICT: Providing Choices for Learning. Proceedings Ascilite Singapore*, 2007, 833–36.

8. David R. Michael and Sandra L. Chen, *Serious Games: Games That Educate, Train, and Inform* (Cengage, Ohio: Muska and Lipman/Premier-Trade, 2005).

9. Kevin Corti, "Games-Based Learning: A Serious Business Application," *Informe de PixelLearning* 34, no. 6 (2006): 1–20.

10. Michael Zyda, "From Visual Simulation to Virtual Reality to Games," *Computer* 38, no. 9 (2005): 25–32.

11. Pamela M. Kato, "Video Games in Health Care: Closing the Gap," *Review of General Psychology* 14, no. 2 (2010): 113.

12. Katherin M. Gerling, Regan Mandryk, and Conor Linehan, "Long-Term Use of Motion-Based Video Games in Care Home Settings," in *Proceedings of the 33rd Annual ACM Conference on Human Factors in Computing Systems*, (New York: ACM, 2015), 1573–82.

13. Darren E. R. Warburton, Shannon S. D. Bredin, Leslie T. L. Horita, Dominik Zbogar, Jessica M. Scott, Ben A Esch, and Ryan E. Rhodes, "The Health Benefits of Interactive Video Game Exercise,' *Applied Physiology, Nutrition, and Metabolism* 32, no. 4 (2007): 655–63

Belinda S. Lange, Requejo, Sandra Marie Flynn, A. A. Rizzo, F. J. Valero-Cuevas, Lisa Baker, and C. Winstein, "The Potential of Virtual Reality and Gaming to Assist Successful Aging with Disability," *Physical Medicine and Rehabilitation Clinics of North America* 21, no. 2 (2010): 339–56.

14. Cynthia Putnam and Jinghui Cheng, "Motion-Games in Brain Injury Rehabilitation: An In-situ Multi-method Study of Inpatient Care," in *Proceedings of the 15th International ACM SIGACCESS Conference on Computers and Accessibility*, 58; B. Biel Moyà Alcover, Antoni Jaume-i-Capo, Javier Varona, Pau Martinez-Bueso, and Alejandro Mesejo Chiong, "Use of Serious Games for Motivational Balance Rehabilitation of Cerebral Palsy Patients," in *Proceedings of the 13th International ACM SIGACCESS Conference on Computers and Accessibility* (New York: ACM, 2011), 297–98; Karina Caro, Ana I. Martinez-Garcia, Monica Tentori, and Ivan Zavala-lbara, "Designing Exergames Combining the Use of Fine and Gross Motor Exercises to Support Self-Care Activities," in *Proceedings of the 16th International ACM SIGACCESS Conference on Computers and Accessibility* (New York: ACM, 2014), 247–48.

15. Brannon Zahand, "Making Video Games Accessible: Business Justifications and Design Considerations," MSDN Library Technical Articles, 2007, https://msdn.microsoft.com/en-us/library/windows/desktop/ee415219(v=vs.85).aspx.

16. Gary Powers, Vinh Nguyen, and Lex Frieden, "Video Game Accessibility: A Legal Approach," *Disability Studies Quarterly* 35, no. 1 (2015): n.p.

17. U.S. Digital Millennium Copyright Act, Public Law 1998 (105–304), 112.

18. Antonius J. Van Rooij, Gert-Jan Meerkerk, Tim M. Schoenmakers, Mark Griffiths, and Dike Van De Mheen, "Video Game Addiction and Social Responsibility," *Addiction Research and Theory* 18, no. 5 (2010): 489–93.

19. Daithí Mac Síthigh, "The Regulation of Video Games: Past, Present and Future," *Entertainment Law Review* 21, no. 8 (2010): 298–303.

20. Frederick Schauer, "Harm(s) and the First Amendment," *Supreme Court Review* 1 (2011): 81–111.

21. Mark C. Barlet and Steven D. Spohn, *Includification: A Practical Guide to Game Accessibility* (Charles Town, W.Va.: Ablegamers Foundation, 2012).

22. Barrie Ellis, G. Ford-Williams, L. Graham, D. Grammenos, I. Hamilton, E. Lee, J. Manion, and T. Westin, *Game Accessibility Guidelines: A Straightforward Reference for Inclusive Game Design*, 2013, http://gameaccessibilityguidelines.com/.

23. Shawn L. Henry, Web Content Accessibility Guidelines (WCAG), 2008, https://www.w3.org/TR/WCAG20/.

14. The Pivot Model of Policy Entrepreneurship

1. Paul A. Sabatier and Christopher M. Weible, "The Advocacy Coalition Framework: Innovations and Clarifications," in *Theories of the Policy Process*, ed. Paul A. Sabatier (Boulder, Colo.: Westview, 2007): 189–220.

2. Michael Mintrom and Sandra Vergari, "Advocacy Coalitions, Policy Entrepreneurs, and Policy Change," *Policy Studies Journal* 24, no. 3 (1996): 420–34.

3. European Disability Forum, "Draft EDF Response to the Public Consultation with a View to a European Accessibility Act," 2012, http://cms.horus.be/files/99909/MediaArchive/EDF%20response%20to%20the%20EAA%20consultation_FINAL.doc.

4. Richard Bellamy, "Still in Deficit: Rights, Regulation, and Democracy in the EU," *European Law Journal* 12, no. 6 (2006): 725–42; Delia Ferri, "Participation in EU Governance: A 'Multi-level' Perspective and a 'Multifold' Approach," in *Citizen Participation in Multi-level Democracies*, vol. 5, ed. Cristina Fraenkel-Haeberle, Sabine Kropp, Francesco Palermo, and Karl-Peter Sommermann (Brill Online, 2015), 334–67, http://booksandjournals.brillonline.com/content/books/b9789004287945s020; Andreas Follesdal and Simon Hix, "Why There Is a Democratic Deficit in the EU: A Response to Majone and Moravcsik," *JCMS: Journal of Common Market Studies* 44, no. 3 (2006): 533–62; Justin Greenwood, "Organized Civil Society and Input Legitimacy in the EU," in *Democratic Dilemmas of Multilevel Governance: Legitimacy, Representation and Accountability in the European Union*, ed. Joan DeBardeleben and Achim Hurrelmann (New York: Palgrave Macmillan, 2007), 177–94; Giandomenico Majone, "Europe's 'Democratic Deficit': The Question of Standards," *European Law Journal* 4, no. 1 (1998): 5–28.

5. Ferri, "Participation in EU Governance."

6. James G. March and Johan P. Olsen, "Elaborating the 'New Institutionalism,'" in *The Oxford Handbook of Political Institutions*, ed. R. A. W. Rhodes, S. A. Binder, and B. A. Rockman (New York: Oxford University Press, 2006), 3.

7. Peter A. Hall and Rosemary C. R. Taylor, "Political Science and the Three New Institutionalisms," *Political Studies* 44, no. 5 (1996): 936–57.

8. Peter A. Hall, "Historical Institutionalism in Rationalist and Sociological Perspective," in *Explaining Institutional Change: Ambiguity, Agency, and Power*, ed. J. Mahoney and K. A. Thelen (New York: Cambridge University Press, 2010), 204–23.

9. David Dolowitz and David Marsh, "Learning from Abroad: The Role of Policy Transfer in Contemporary Policy-Making," *Governance* 13, no. 1 (2000): 5, 21.

10. Sabatier and Weible, "The Advocacy Coalition Framework," 196.

11. Dietmar Braun and Fabrizio Gilardi, "Taking 'Galton's Problem' Seriously," *Journal of Theoretical Politics* 18, no. 3 (2006): 310.

12. Paul A. Sabatier, "An Advocacy Coalition Framework of Policy Change and the Role of Policy-Oriented Learning Therein," *Policy Sciences* 21, nos. 2–3 (1988): 129–68.

13. Mintrom and Vergari, "Advocacy Coalitions, Policy Entrepreneurs, and Policy Change," 422.

14. John L. Campbell, *Institutional Change and Globalization* (Princeton, N.J.: Princeton University Press, 2004), 98–101.

15. Kenneth Abbott and Duncan Snidal, "International Regulation Without International Government: Improving IO Performance Through Orchestration," *Review of International Organizations* 5, no. 3 (2010): 315–44

16. Mark Bevir, *Democratic Governance* (Princeton, N.J.: Princeton University Press, 2010), 119.

17. Abbott and Snidal, "International Regulation Without International Government," 315.

18. Marie-Louise Bemelmans-Videc, Roy C. Rist, and Evert Vedung, *Carrots, Sticks and Sermons: Policy Instruments and Their Evaluation* (New Brunswick, N.J.: Transaction, 1998).

19. David Levi-Faur, "Regulation and Regulatory Governance," in *Handbook on the Politics of Regulation*, ed. David Levi-Faur (Cheltenham: Edward Elgar, 2011), 10.

20. Ferri, "Participation in Eu Governance," 337.

21. Eric Reis, *The Lean Startup* (New York: Crown Business, 2011), 113.

22. Steve G. Blank and Bob Dorf, *The Startup Owner's Manual: The Step-by-Step Guide for Building a Great Company* (Pescadero, Calif.: K&S Ranch, 2012), chap. 2.

23. Mintrom and Vergari, "Advocacy Coalitions, Policy Entrepreneurs, and Policy Change," 429.

24. Lisa Waddington and Gerard Quinn, eds., *European Yearbook of Disability Law*, vol. 2 (Antwerp: Intersentia, 2010).

25. Ibid., 163.

26. Pippa Norris, "Representation and the Democratic Deficit," *European Journal of Political Research* 32, no. 2 (1997): 273–82.

27. Bellamy, "Still in Deficit," 725.

28. Ibid., 726–27.

29. See, for example, Ferri, "Participation in Eu Governance," 334.

30. See, for example, Greenwood, "Organized Civil Society," 177.

31. Ibid.

32. Ferri, "Participation in Eu Governance," 346–47.

33. Ibid., 346.

34. Ibid., 348.

35. The EU has mainstreamed ICT accessibility as a requirement in certain policies and programs. However, the EU has yet to establish a legal obligation for private-sector enterprises to ensure ICT accessibility. For more information, see Delia Ferri and G. Anthony Giannoumis, "A Revaluation of the Cultural Dimension of Disability Policy in the European Union: The Impact of Digitization and Web Accessibility," *Behavioral Sciences and the Law* 32, no. 1 (2014): 33–51.

36. Michelle P. Egan, *Constructing a European Market: Standards, Regulation, and Governance* (New York: Oxford University Press, 2001).

37. The ESO consists of three pan-European standards organizations.

38. European Commission, "Standardisation Mandate to CEN, CENELEC and ETSI in Support of European Accessibility Requirements for Public Procurement of Products and Services in the ICT Domain M 376-EN," December 7, 2005, http://ec.europa.eu/growth/tools-databases/mandates/index.cfm?fuseaction=search.detail&id=333.

39. René N. G. Kouassi, "The Itinerary of the African Integration Process: An Overview of the Historical Landmarks," *African Integration Review* 1, no. 2 (2007): 1–23.

40. According to personal communication between one of the authors and an individual who participated in formulation of the policy, "Since the formulation of the policy in 2012, there is no evidence of subsequent plans to ensure the operationalization of specific clauses," which, this chapter argues, is due to lack of funds and support staff within the EAC to drive the disability agenda and the emphasis of individual member states to responsibly implement the policy at the national level. Moreover, the effort to harmonize disability issues within the region is currently being conducted by the Eastern Africa Federation of the Disabled (EAFOD), which is a DPO.

41. For example, in submitting its initial state report to the Committee on Rights of Persons with Disabilities, Kenya listed all the international and regional treaties and conventions but did not mention the East African Community Policy on Persons with Disabilities (2012), which forms part of its disability policies as a member state of the East African Community.

42. See Constitution of Kenya 2010, Article 54, and Mozambique Constitution, Section 154.

43. See Politica da Pessoa Portadora de Deficiencia, 1999; and Lei do Acesso a Informação, 2014.

44. Committee on the Rights of Persons with Disabilities, Replies of Kenya to the List of Issues, information from civil societies organizations, CRPD/C/KEN/Q/1, 2015, accessed August 22, 2015, http://tbinternet.ohchr.org/_layouts/treatybodyexternal/SessionDetails1.aspx?SessionID=995&Lang=en; Committee on the Rights of Persons with Disabilities, Initial Reports of States Parties Due in 2010–Kenya, 2014, CRPD/C/KEN/1, http://tbinternet.ohchr.org/_layouts/treatybodyexternal/Download.aspx?symbolno=CRPD%2fC%2fKEN%2f1&Lang=en.

45. FAMOD, "Position Document on Revision of Mozambican Constitution," submitted to Ad-Hoc Commission for revision on Mozambican Constitution, August 2013; FAMOD, "Access Audit Report," submitted to Ministry of Women and Social Affairs, May 2014.

46. Polly Gaster et al., *Inclusão digital em Moçambique: Um desafio para todos* (Maputo: CIUEM, 2009).

47. "A Method of Financing a Partner Country's Budget Through Transfer of Resources from a Donor to a Partner Government's Treasury," Memorandum of Understanding Between Government of Mozambique and the Provision of General Budget Support, May 2009.

48. Jorge Manhique, "Accessibility Decree in Mozambique: Weaknesses and Opportunity to Improve the Implementation (unpublished paper, 2015).

49. Open Society Initiative for Southern Africa (OSISA), *Country Report, Mozambique*, 2012, 35–40, http://www.osisa.org/keywords/mozambique.

50. Kenya National Commission on Human Rights, *From Norm to Practice: A Status Report on Implementation of Rights of Persons with Disabilities*, 2014, http://www.knchr.org/Portals/0/Reports/Disability%20Report.pdf.

51. Elizabeth Kamundia, "Choice, Support and Inclusion: Implementing Article 19 of the CRPD in Kenya" (LLM thesis, National University of Galway–Ireland, 2012).

52. Mirriam Nthenge, "Right to Accessibility for Persons with Disabilities in Kenya: Exploring Legislative Framework on Accessibility; A Means to an End?" (unpublished paper, 2015).

53. World Bank, *Mozambique*, May 24, 2015, http://data.worldbank.org/country/mozambique.

54. Instituto Nacional de Estatistica, *Caderno de Informal Rapida*, 2014, http://www.ine.gov.mz/estatisticas/publicacoes/copy_of_caderno-de-informacao-rapida.

55. F. Mabila, "Understanding What Happens in ICT in Mozambique: A Supply- and Demand-Side Analysis of the ICT Sector," 2013, http://www.researchictafrica.net/publications/ Evidence_for_ICT_Policy_Action/Policy_Paper_10_Understanding_what_is_happening_in_ICT_in_Mozambique.pdf.

56. CPInfo, *Estratégia de governo electrónico de Moçambique: Colocar os serviços públicos junto do cidadão* (Maputo: UTICT, 2005).

57. Jenny C. Aker and Isaac M. Mbiti, "Mobile Phones and Economic Development in Africa" (Center for Global Development Working Paper 211, 2010).

15. The Accessibility Infrastructure and the Global South

1. Raymond Lang, "The United Nations Convention on the Right and Dignities for Persons with Disability: A Panacea for Ending Disability Discrimination?," *ALTER—European Journal of Disability Research/Revue Européenne de Recherche sur le Handicap* 3 (2009): 266–85.

2. Hasheem Mannan et al., "Core Concepts of Human Rights and Inclusion of Vulnerable Groups in the Disability and Rehabilitation Policies of Malawi, Namibia, Sudan, and South Africa," *Journal of Disability Policy Studies* 23, no. 2 (2012): 67.

3. Jonathan Donner, "Blurring Livelihoods and Lives: The Social Uses of Mobile Phones and Socioeconomic Development," *Innovations* 4 (2009): 91–101.

4. Cornelia Butler Flora and Jan L. Flora, "Entrepreneurial Social Infrastructure: A Necessary Ingredient," *Annals of the American Academy of Political and Social Science* 529 (1993): 48–58.

5. Katerine Bielaczyc, "Designing Social Infrastructure: Critical Issues in Creating Learning Environments with Technology," *Journal of the Learning Sciences* 15 (2006): 301–29.

6. W. Keith Edwards et al., "The Infrastructure Problem in HCI," in *Proceedings of the SIGCHI Conference on Human Factors in Computing Systems* (New York: ACM, 2010), 423–32.

7. Bruno Latour, *Science in Action: How to Follow Scientists and Engineers Through Society* (Cambridge, Mass.: Harvard University Press, 1987).

8. Rob Kling and William H. Dutton, "The Computer Package: Dynamic Complexity," in *Computers and Politics: High Technology in American Local Governments*, ed. J. N. Danziger and W. H. Dutton (New York: Columbia University Press, 1982), 22–50.

9. Kentaro Toyama, *Geek Heresy: Rescuing Social Change from the Cult of Technology* (New York: PublicAffairs, 2015).

10. Marcia J. Scherer, *Living in the State of Stuck: How Technology Impacts the Lives of Persons with Disabilities* (Cambridge, Mass.: Brookline, 1996).

11. Phil Parette and Marcia Scherer, "Assistive Technology Use and Stigma," *Education and Training in Developmental Disabilities* 39 (2004): 217–26.

12. Jodie A. Copley and Jenny Ziviani, "Barriers to the Use of Assistive Technology for Children with Multiple Disabilities," *Occupational Therapy International* 11 (2004): 229–43.

13. Marti L. Riemer-Reiss and Robbyn R. Wacker, "Factors Associated with Assistive Technology Discontinuance Among Individuals with Disabilities," *Journal of Rehabilitation* 66 (2000): 44.

14. Marcia J. Scherer, "The Change in Emphasis from People to Person: Introduction to the Special Issue on Assistive Technology," *Disability and Rehabilitation* 24 (2002): 3.

15. Marcia J. Scherer, "From People-Centered to Person-Centered Services, and Back Again," *Disability and Rehabilitation: Assistive Technology* 9 (2014): 1–2.

16. Joyojeet Pal et al., *Technology for Employability in Latin America: Research with At-Risk Youth and People with Disabilities* (Seattle: Technology and Social Change Group, University of Washington, 2009); Joyojeet Pal et al., "Marginality, Aspiration and Accessibility in ICTD," in *Proceedings of the Sixth International Conference on Information and Communication Technologies and Development: Full Papers*, vol. 1 (New York: ACM, 2013): 71; Joyojeet Pal et al., "A Capabilities View of Accessibility in Policy and Practice in Jordan and Peru," *Review of Disability Studies: An International Journal* 10 (2015): n. p.; Joyojeet Pal and Meera Lakshmanan, "Mobile Devices and Weak Ties: A Study of Vision Impairments and Workplace Access in Bangalore," *Disability and Rehabilitation: Assistive Technology* 10 (2014): 323–31; Jasmine Jones and Joyojeet Pal, "Counteracting Dampeners: Understanding Technology-Amplified Capabilities of People with Disabilities in Sierra Leone," in *Proceedings of the Seventh International Conference on Information and Communication Technologies and Development* (New York: ACM, 2015), 1–10.

17. Alister C. Munthali, "A Situation Analysis of Persons with Disabilities in Malawi," August 2011, http://www.afri-can.org/D&R/Situation analysis of PWDs in Malawi Final Report.pdf.

18. World Health Organization, "World Report on Disability," 2011, http://www.who.int/disabilities/world_report/2011/report.pdf.

19. Nicolas A. Rattray, "Contesting Urban Space and Disability in Highland Ecuador," *City and Society* 25 (2013): 25–46.

20. Myriam dos Santos-Zingale and Mary Ann McColl, "Disability and Participation in Post-conflict Situations: The Case of Sierra Leone," *Disability and Society* 21 (2006): 243–57.

21. Jean-François Trani et al., "Access to Health Care, Reproductive Health and Disability: A Large Scale Survey in Sierra Leone," *Social Science and Medicine* 73 (2011): 1477–89.

22. Evariste Karangwa et al., "Community-Level Responses to Disability and Education in Rwanda," *International Journal of Disability, Development and Education* 57 (2010): 267–78.

23. Robin T. Petroze et al., "Injury, Disability and Access to Care in Rwanda: Results of a Nationwide Cross-Sectional Population Study," *World Journal of Surgery* 39 (2015): 62–69.

24. Joyojeet Pal et al., "Representation, Access and Contestation: Facebook and Vision Impairment in Jordan, India, and Peru," *Disability and the Global South* 2, no. 3 (2014): 811.

25. Ibid.

26. Ibid., 812.

27. Joyojeet Pal et al., "Smartphone Adoption Among Visually Impaired People in Urban Spaces: Cases from Seoul and Bangalore," India HCI Conference, 2017 (forthcoming).

28. Pal et al., *Technology for Employability in Latin America*, 41.

29. Joyojeet Pal and Meera Lakshmanan, "Assistive Technology and the Employment of People with Vision Impairments in India," in *Proceedings of the 5th International Conference on Information and Communication Technologies and Development* (New York: ACM, 2012), 310.

30. Pal et al., "Marginality, Aspiration and Accessibility in ICTD," 73.

31. Pal et al., *Technology for Employability in Latin America*, 70.

32. Pal et al., "Capabilities View of Accessibility," 76.

33. Joyojeet Pal, J., Priyank Chandra, Terence O'Neill, Maura Youngman, Jasmine Jones, Ji Hye Song, William Strayer, and Ludmila Ferrari, "An Accessibility Infrastructure for the Global South," in *Proceedings of the Eighth International Conference on Information and Communication Technologies and Development* (New York: ACM, 2016), 29.

So the actual page number is page 29 for the exact quote

34. Pal et al., "Marginality, Aspiration and Accessibility in ICTD," 71.

35. Ibid., 72.

36. Meen Raj Panthi, "The Disability Situation in Nepal," *Disability World* 24 (2004), http://www.blindcanadians.ca/publications/cbm/22/disability-situation-nepal.

37. Angi Stone-MacDonald, "Cultural Beliefs and Attitudes About Disability in East Africa," *Review of Disability Studies: An International Journal* 8 (2014).

38. Arthur Kleinman et al., "The Social Course of Epilepsy: Chronic Illness as Social Experience in Interior China," *Social Science and Medicine* 40 (1995): 1319–30.

39. Raymond Lang, "Understanding Disability from a South Indian Perspective" (paper presented at the 14th annual meeting of the Disabilities Studies Association, Winnipeg, Canada, 2001).

40. Blyden Potts, "Disability and Employment: Considering the Importance of Social Capital," *Journal of Rehabilitation* 71 (2005): 20

41. Pal et al., *Technology for Employability in Latin America*, 54.

16. ICT Access, Disability Human Rights, and Social Inclusion in India

I acknowledge the helpful comments and immense editorial assistance of Professor Michael Stein.

1. See General Comment No 2 of 2014 on Article 9 of UNCRPD: Accessibility, CRPD/C/GC/2, May 22, 2014, http://www.ohchr.org/EN/HRBodies/CRPD/Pages/GC.aspx.

2. See generally Lisa Schur, Douglas Kruse, and Peter Blanck, *People with Disabilities: Sidelined or Mainstreamed*, Cambridge Disability Law and Policy Series (Cambridge: Cambridge University Press, 2013).

3. To focus sharply on the social model of disability, I prefer the term "disabled persons" to its governmental counterpart "persons with disability," which leans toward a medical model.

4. See the concept note of the national conference "ICTs for Persons with Disabilities: Taking Stock and Identifying Opportunities," organized by UNESCO and the Department of Electronics and IT (Ministry of Communications and IT, Government of India), September 2014, accessed November 27, 2015, http://www.unesco.org/new/fileadmin/MULTIMEDIA/FIELD/New_Delhi/images/conceptnote_03.pdf.

5. Fiona Kumari Campbell, *Contours of Ableism: The Production of Disability and Abledness* (Houndmills: Palgrave Macmillan, 2009), 30.

6. Ibid., 45.

7. M. Warschauer, "Demystifying the Digital Divide," *Scientific American* 289, no. 2 (2003): 5, cited in Vandana Chaudhry et al., "Rethinking the Digital Divide in Relation to Visual Disability in India and the United States: Towards a Paradigm of 'Information Inequity,'" *Disability Studies Quarterly* 25, no. 2 (Spring 2005), http://www. http://dsq-sds.org/issue/view/29.

8. Chaudhry et al., "Rethinking the Digital Divide."

9. Ibid., 2.

10. World Programme of Action Concerning Disabled Persons, adopted by the General Assembly December 3, 1982, resolution 37/52, A/RES/351/Add. 1.

11. Standard Rules on the Equalization of Opportunities for Persons with Disabilities, A/RES/48/96, March 4, 1994.

12. See general comment on Article 9, CRPD/c/11/3, November 25, 2013, http://tbinternet.ohchr.org/_layouts/treatybodyexternal/Download.aspx?symbolno=CRPD/C/GC/2&Lang=en.

13. The CRPD was adopted on March 13, 2006, and entered into force on May 3, 2008, after its twentieth ratification.

14. CRPD, Article 2, para. 4.

15. Incheon Strategy to "Make the Right Real" for Persons with Disabilities in Asia and the Pacific, adopted by governments of the ESCAP region from October 29 to November 2, 2012, in Incheon, Republic of Korea. One of the goals set therein is "to enhance access to the physical environment, public transportation, knowledge, information and communication." Accessed December 25, 2015, http://www.unescap.org/resources/incheon-strategy.

16. Constitution of the Republic of South Africa 1996, Article 9.

17. Constitution Act 1982 Canada, Article 15.

18. Constitution of India, Article 14.

19. Ibid., Articles 19(1)a and 19(a)e.

20. Ibid., Preamble and Article 21.

21. *Amit v. Union of India*, MANU/SC/0481/2005; *Union of India v. National Federation of the Blind*, (2013) 10 SCC 772.

22. As a matter of fact, a number of Supreme Court and High Court cases have placed reliance on CRPD provisions. To this day, litigation pertaining to availing of enforcement of the right to accessible ICT has not arisen. This is in sharp contrast with

the position in the United States, the United Kingdom, Canada, Europe, and other countries where the matter has been seized on by the courts and has resulted in the evolution of some empowering jurisprudence.

23. See National Policy for Persons with Disabilities 2006, para. 16, http://socialjustice.nic.in.

24. The policy was made available on the department's website on March 31, 2010, for comments and inputs from stakeholders till May 15, 2010. See http://deity.gov.in.

25. NPOUEA 2013, sec. 2, p. 1, accessed January 2, 2016, http://www.ncert.nic.in/announcements/notices/pdf_files/Nationalpolicyonuniversal.pdf.

26. Ibid., sec. 4, p. 3.

27. Ibid., Preamble, p. 1, accessed December 12, 2015, http://www.ncert.nic.in/announcements/notices/pdf_files/Nationalpolicyonuniversal.pdf.

28. NPOUEA 2013, sec. 2, p. 1.

29. Ibid., sec. 4, p. 3.

30. Ibid., sec. 5, p. 4.

31. Ibid., sec. 6.2.1, p. 4.

32. Ibid., sec. 6.3, p. 5.

33. Ibid., sec. 6.5, p. 7.

34. See http://epgp.inflibnet.ac.in/ (sponsored by the Government of India). The Ministry of Human Resource and Development of the Government of India, under its National Mission on Education Through ICT (NME-ICT), has assigned work to the University Grant Commission for development of e-content in seventy-one subjects at the postgraduate level.

35. See the Consortium for Educational Communication (sponsored by the Government of India), http://cec.nic.in/edusat/Pages/default.aspx. EDUSAT is the satellite exclusively devoted to meeting the demands of the educational sector.

36. See http://www.epathshala.co.in/. ePathshala is a technology-enabled educational product that changes the way students learn anywhere and anytime. Sponsored by the National Council of Educational Research and Training, New Delhi (Government of India), it provides lectures and other educational resources in multimedia format to teachers and students of pregraduation levels.

37. "The New Delhi Declaration on Inclusive ICTs for Persons with Disabilities: Making Empowerment a Reality," 196EX/11, https://www.unesco.de/fileadmin/med1ien/Dokumente/Kommunikation/New_Delhi_Declaration_Inclusive_ICTs_Making_Empowerment_a_Reality_26_11_2014.pdf.

38. Ibid., para. 5.

39. Ibid., para. 9.

40. Ibid., para. 7.

41. Ibid., para. 2.

42. Ibid., para. 3.

43. Ibid., para. 2.
44. Ibid., para. 1.
45. Accessible India Campaign, accessed December 22, 2015, www.disabilityaffairs.gov.in. For critical analysis, see "Accessibility India Campaign: Unfolding the Package Prepared by 'Equals, Centre for Promotion of Social Justice' Chennai," http://www.equalscpsj.org/.
46. Accessible India Campaign.
47. Department of Empowerment of Persons with Disabilities, Ministry of Social Justice and Empowerment, Government of India, "Strategy Paper on Accessible India Campaign: Objective 5," accessed January 8, 2016, http://disabilityaffairs.gov.in/upload/uploadfiles/files/Strategy%20Papar%20(AIC).docx, 10.
48. Ibid, "Target 5.1," 10. Since then, the timeline for the target has been revised twice, to March 2017 (see "About Accessible India Campaign," accessed November 2, 2016, http://www. http://accessibleindia.gov.in/content/innerpage/about-accessible-india-campaign.php) and July 2019 (see "Accessible India, Empowered India," accessed November 2, 2016, http://ayjnihh.nic.in/AccessibleIndiaCampaign.pdf, 19).
49. Department of Empowerment of Persons with Disabilities, Ministry of Social Justice and Empowerment, Government of India, "Strategy Paper on Accessible India Campaign: Target 5.2," accessed November 2, 2016, http://disabilityaffairs.gov.in/upload/uploadfiles/files/Strategy%20Papar%20(AIC).docx, 10. See also "Accessible India, Empowered India," accessed November 2, 2016, http://ayjnihh.nic.in/AccessibleIndiaCampaign.pdf, 19.
50. See generally "Guidelines for Indian Governments Websites," accessed December 25, 2015, http://darpg.gov.in/darpgwebsite_cms/Document/file/Guidelines_for_Government_websites.pdf.
51. PRS Legislative Research (Government of India), accessed November 10, 2015, www.prsindia.org.
52. Draft bill no. 1 of 2014, "The Rights of Persons with Disabilities Bill, 2014," sec. 39.
53. Ibid., sec. 41.
54. Ibid., sec. 42.
55. Ibid., sec. 45.
56. Ibid., secs. 46(2) and 73)f.
57. Department of Empowerment of Persons with Disabilities, Ministry of Social Justice and Empowerment, Government of India, "Strategy Paper on Accessible India Campaign: Objective 7," accessed November 2, 2016, http://disabilityaffairs.gov.in/upload/uploadfiles/files/Strategy%20Papar%20(AIC).docx, 10.
58. Ibid, "Objective 7.1," 10. As of the date of this writing, this target has not been achieved because the National Media authority has not been established, nor is any progress reported on the development and adoption of National Standards of Captioning and Sign Language Interpretation.
59. Ibid, "Objective 7.2," 11.

60. Indian Copyrights Act 1957, secs. 31B and 52 (i)(VII)(zb) (amended in 2012), http://mhrd.gov.in/sites/upload_files/mhrd/files/upload_document/CRACT_AMNDMNT_2012.pdf.

61. Ibid., sec. 52(1)(VII)(zb), subclause (ii).

62. Ibid., sec. 52(1)(VII)(zb), subclause (i).

63. "Minutes for High Level Advisory Committee on Accessibility (December 30, 2014)." These minutes are made available by one of the members of the committee on a social media platform, accessed November 2, 2016, http://accessindia.org.in/pipermail/accessindia_accessindia.org.in/2015q1/100973.html.

64. Government of India, "Guidelines for Indian Government Websites," accessed January 15, 2016, http://guidelines.gov.in/#&panel1-1. These guidelines were developed by the National Informatics Centre (NIC). They were adopted by the Department of Administrative Reforms and Public Grievances (DARPG) in February 2009 and have been included in the Central Secretariat Manual of Office Procedures (CSMOP), Government of India.

65. "Minutes of High Level Advisory Committee on Accessibility."

66. "Smart-Card for Disabled Persons for Train Ticket Concession," http://www.railnews.co.in/i-card-for-disabled-persons-for-train-ticket-concession/.

67. For details, see "Delhi Metro Trains Staff in Sign Language to Handle Hearing Impaired Commuters," NetIndian News Network, New Delhi, April 21, 2013, http://indiarailinfo.com/news/post/delhi-metro-trains-staff-in-sign-language-to-help-impaired-commuters-indian-railways-news/130501. Chennai Metro rail corporation has trained thirty customer relationship assistants in sign language; see also "Chennai Metro Rail on Right Track for Differently Abled," *Deccan Chronicle*, December 2, 2014, http://www.deccanchronicle.com/141202/nation-current-affairs/article/chennai-metro-rail-right-track-differently-abled.

68. "Guidelines for Persons with Disabilities Scheme in Universities and Colleges XII Plan (2012–2017)," http://www.ugc.ac.in/pdfnews/5471032_person-with-disabilities.pdf. There are two schemes, A) Higher Education for Persons with Special Needs (HEPSN) and B) Financial Assistance to Visually-Challenged Teachers. See also "Scheme for Implementation of Persons with Disabilities Act, 1995 (SIPDA)," http://disabilityaffairs.gov.in/content/page/sipda-scheme.php, implemented from 2014. The grants-in-aid are provided under this scheme, inter alia, to autonomous bodies and universities to support activities pursuant to implementation of the provisions of the Persons with Disabilities (Equal Opportunities, Protection of Rights and Full Participation) Act, 1995, particularly relating to rehabilitation and provision of barrier-free access, making government websites at the state and district levels accessible to PWDs as per the guidelines for Indian government websites, and new product development and research.

69. See the schemes provided by the National Handicapped Finance and Development Corporation, New Delhi, http://www.nhfdc.nic.in/scholarship.html.

70. RBI /2012-13/191 DBOD. No. Leg. BC. 38/09.07.005/2012-13, September 5, 2012, https://www.rbi.org.in/scripts/NotificationUser.asp. See also Circular DBOD. No. Leg. BC. 91 /09.07.005/2007-08, June 4, 2008; Circular DBOD. No. Leg. BC. 123 /09.07.005/2008-09, April 13, 2009; and RBI Circular "Need for Bank Branches ATMs to Be Made Accessible to Persons with Disabilities," DBOD. No. Leg. BC.113/09.07.005/2013-14, May 21, 2014.

71. Indian Banks' Association, "Standards for Accessible ATMs," Circular No. CIR/RB/ATMVCP/6846, February 27, 2013, http://talkingatmindia.org/Download.aspx. IBA guidelines on providing banking facilities to visually impaired persons, November 18, 2008, http://www.eyeway.org/?q=iba-circular-providing-banking-facilities-visually-impaired-persons (sponsored by EYEWAY disability rights organization). See also the code of the bank's commitment to customers, January 2014, http://www.bcsbi.org.in/Codes_CommitmentCustomers.html (sponsored by Banking codes and Standards Board of India) stating, inter alia, at 2.1.7, "We will not discriminate you on the basis of age, race, gender, marital status, religion, disability or financial status."

72. Indian Banks' Association, "Standards for Accessible ATMs."

73. "Guidelines for the Purpose of Opening/Operating Bank Accounts of Persons with Autism, Cerebral Palsy, Mental Retardation, Mental Illness, and Mental Disabilities," DBOD-Master Circular on Customer Service, 2014, para. 9.2 and 11, 42–45, http://talkingatmindia.org/Resources.aspx. See also Vrinda Maheshwari, "Accessibility in Banking Services in India: A Report by the Centre for Internet and Society," accessed December 15, 2015, http://cis-india.org/accessibility/blog/banking-accessibility.pdf.

74. See DaisyIndia Forum, http://www.daisyindia.org/.

75. See Benetech USA, "Bookshare India," http://www.bookshare.org/cms/bookshare-india.

76. See http://ssa.nic.in/. Sarva Shiksha Abhiyan (SSA) is the government of India's flagship program for achievement of Universalization of Elementary Education (UEE) in a timely manner, compulsory education for children aged six to fourteen, and disabled students aged six to eighteen.

77. "Research," TATA Consultancy Services, http://www.tcs.com/research/Pages/TCS-Accessibility-Consulting-Services.aspx.

78. Centre for Internet and Society, http://cis-india.org/.

79. See generally "Report on the Training in the Use of eSpeak Hindi with NVDA" and "Report on Use of eSpeak Bengali with NVDA," http://cis-india.org/accessibility/blog.

80. Information gathered by the author from visually challenged ICT expert Deepender Manucha, Delhi.

81. "Soon, App to Help Visually Impaired Use Smartphones," *Times of India*, June 26, 2015, http://timesofindia.indiatimes.com/city/pune/Soon-app-to-help-visually-impaired-use-smartphones/articleshow/47821850.cms.

82. IIT, Delhi, in collaboration with Indiana University in the United States, organized the 2nd Indo-US Workshop on Emerging Accessibility Technologies for the Blind and Visually Impaired (BVI), February 11–13, 2016.

83. "A Compliant Mechanism Design for Refreshable Braille Display Using Shape Memory" (paper presented at the ASME 2015 International Design Engineering Technical Conferences & Computers and Information in Engineering Conference [IDETC/CIE 2015], Boston, August 2–5, 2015).

84. "World Report on Disability," 2011, http://www.who.int/disabilities/world_report/2011/report.pdf.

85. Rehabilitation Act 2000, sec. 508.

86. General Comment No. 2 of 2014 on Article 9 of CRPD: Accessibility, paras. 10, 23, 28, 31, 32.

CONTRIBUTORS

Jonathan Lazar is professor of computer and information sciences at Towson University and has served as director of the Undergraduate Program in Information Systems since 2003. He also founded the Universal Usability Laboratory at Towson University and served as director from 2003 to 2014. In the area of human-computer interaction, Lazar is involved in teaching and research on web accessibility for people with disabilities, user-centered design methods, assistive technology, and public policy. He has authored or edited ten books, including *Ensuring Digital Accessibility Through Process and Policy* (coauthored with Dan Goldstein and Anne Taylor), *Research Methods in Human-Computer Interaction* (coauthored with Heidi Feng and Harry Hochheiser), *Universal Usability: Designing Computer Interfaces for Diverse User Populations*, and *Web Usability: A User-Centered Design Approach*. He has published over 140 refereed articles in journals, conference proceedings, and edited books and has been granted two U.S. patents for his work on accessible web-based security features for blind users. He frequently serves as an adviser to government agencies and regularly provides testimony at federal and state levels, and multiple U.S. federal regulations cite his research publications. He currently serves on the executive boards of the Friends of the Maryland Library for the Blind and Physically Handicapped and the State of Maryland Work Group on Increasing the Teaching of IT Accessibility Concepts in State Universities. He has served in multiple roles in the Association for Computing Machinery Special Interest Group on Computer-Human Interaction (ACM SIGCHI), most recently, adjunct chair of public policy (2010–15) and Digital Accessibility Chair (CHI 2014). Lazar has been honored with the 2016 SIGCHI Social Impact Award, the 2015 AccessComputing Capacity Building Award (sponsored by the University of Washington and the National Science Foundation) for advocacy on behalf of people with disabilities in computing fields, the 2011 University System of Maryland Regents Award for Public Service, and the 2010 Dr. Jacob Bolotin

Award from the National Federation of the Blind. During the 2012–13 academic year, he was selected as the Shutzer Fellow at the Radcliffe Institute for Advanced Study at Harvard University to investigate the relationship between human-computer interaction for people with disabilities and U.S. disability rights law.

Michael Ashley Stein holds a J.D. from Harvard Law School and a Ph.D. from Cambridge University. Cofounder and executive director of the Harvard Law School Project on Disability and a visiting professor at Harvard Law School for over a decade, Stein also holds an extraordinary professorship at the University of Pretoria's Centre for Human Rights. He previously was professor at William & Mary Law School and also taught at New York University and Stanford Law Schools. His pathbreaking, prolific, and wide-ranging scholarship has been published globally by leading journals and presses, and he is the recipient of fellowships and awards from the American Council of Learned Societies, the National Endowment for the Humanities, and the National Institute on Disability Rehabilitation and Research, among others. An internationally recognized expert on disability law and policy, Stein participated in the drafting of the UN Convention on the Rights of Persons with Disabilities, works with disabled people's organizations around the world, actively consults with governments on their disability laws and policies, advises a number of UN bodies and national human rights institutions, and has brought landmark litigation. Stein has received numerous awards for his work, including the inaugural Morton E. Ruderman Prize for Inclusion, the inaugural Henry Viscardi Achievement Award, and the ABA Paul G. Hearne Award, and was appointed by President Obama to the United States Holocaust Memorial Council.

John Carlo Bertot is past president of the Digital Government Society (DGS) and served as chair of the International Standards Organization (ISO) Library Performance Indicator (ISO 11620) working group from 2002 to 2014. He is currently the associate provost for faculty affairs at the University of Maryland, where he is a professor in the College of Information Studies. He has served as chair of the American Library Association (ALA) Library Research Round Table and currently serves on the ALA E-Government Services Subcommittee. In addition, he served as editor of *Government Information Quarterly* from 2000 to 2015 and as coeditor of *Library Quarterly* from 2002 to 2014. Bertot's research has been funded by the National Science Foundation, the Bill and Melinda Gates Foundation, the Government Accountability Office, the ALA, and the U.S. Institute of Museum and Library Services.

Peter Blanck is University Professor at Syracuse University, the highest faculty rank, granted to eight prior individuals in the history of the university. He is chairman of the Burton Blatt Institute (BBI) and honorary professor, Centre for Disability Law and Policy, at the National University of Ireland, Galway. Blanck received a J.D. from Stanford University, where he was president of the *Stanford Law Review*, and a Ph.D. in social psychology from Harvard University. He has written widely on the Americans with Disabilities Act (ADA) and related laws. He has received more than $70 million in grants to study disability law and policy. Blanck also is chairman of the Global Universal Design Commission (GUDC) and president of Raising the Floor (RtF) USA. Before teaching, he practiced law at the Washington, D.C., firm Covington and Burling and served as law clerk to the late Honorable Carl McGowan of the U.S. Court of Appeals for the D.C. Circuit. Among Blanck's recent books is *eQuality: The Struggle for Web Accessibility by People with Cognitive Disabilities*.

Judy Brewer directs the Web Accessibility Initiative (WAI) at the World Wide Web Consortium (W3C). The W3C's work on web accessibility includes ensuring that W3C technologies support accessibility; developing accessibility guidelines for web content, browsers, media players, mobile devices, and authoring tools; developing resources to improve web-accessibility evaluation tools; providing education and outreach on web accessibility; coordinating with research and development that may affect future accessibility of the web; and promoting implementation of web-accessibility standards. WAI guidelines include the Web Content Accessibility Guidelines 2.0, which has been adopted by many governments around the world; the Authoring Tool Accessibility Guidelines and User Agent Accessibility Guidelines; and Accessible Rich Internet Applications (WAI-ARIA). Brewer is a principal research scientist at MIT's Computer Science and Artificial Intelligence Laboratory (CSAIL). She is the recipient of a RESNA Certificate of Appreciation for efforts related to assistive-technology policy development during national health-care reform, an Equality of Access and Opportunity Award from the American Foundation for the Blind for advocacy to increase the accessibility of the Windows 95 operating system, and an Access Advancement Award from the Association of Access Engineering Specialists for efforts related to web accessibility. Among her other awards are the Harry J. Murphy Catalyst Award, the Roland Wagner European Award for Computers Assisting People with Special Needs, the Susan G. Hadden Pioneer Award from the Alliance for Public Technology, SXSW's Dewey Winburne Community Service Award, and the Newell Perry Award from the National Federation of the Blind.

Joyram Chakraborty is a human factors engineer and assistant professor in the Department of Computer and Information Sciences at Towson University. His current work concerns internationalization of interface design, cross-cultural game design, and standardization of health-care records. This work relies heavily on the use of cognitive theories of decision making. Chakraborty has conducted several usability studies of cross-cultural gaming strategy to design more culturally inclusive video games. His collaborative works have been published in several peer-reviewed journals and have resulted in a U.S. patent in collaboration with IBM Research. He has also studied automated speech recognition (ASR) systems. This work investigated the use of cross-cultural behavior patterns to establish a cognitive framework to develop learning algorithms to support data centers. He has also investigated the cognitive processes involved in designing, comprehending, and maintaining user interfaces for telehealth devices in the support of emergency medical technicians (EMTs). He is currently collaborating with the Johns Hopkins University School of Public Health and the Bloomberg Foundation to improve user experiences in mobile-heath interventions and working on an Army Research Laboratory grant to develop algorithms based on user preferences.

Timothy Elder is a civil rights litigator specializing in high-impact disability discrimination and digital access cases. He has worked as counsel in a nationwide class action settlement involving Uber Technologies, helped secure injunctions against testing entities for their failure to accommodate students with disabilities, negotiated groundbreaking digital access settlements with publicly traded technology companies, tried and won employment discrimination claims before juries, and argued before numerous federal trial and appellate courts. He graduated magna cum laude from the University of California, Hastings College of the Law, and manages his practice from the San Francisco Bay Area.

Jim Fruchterman is a Caltech-trained engineer and the founder and CEO of Benetech, a Silicon Valley nonprofit technology company that develops software applications to address unmet needs of users in the social sector. He is the recipient of numerous awards recognizing his work as a pioneering social entrepreneur, including the MacArthur Fellowship, Caltech's Distinguished Alumni Award, the Skoll Award for Social Entrepreneurship, and the Migel Medal—the highest honor in the blindness field—from the American Foundation for the Blind. His first social enterprise idea was a machine that recognizes letters and words and uses software to read those words aloud to people who are blind. In 1989, after a stint as a rocket scientist and after creating two successful for-profit Silicon Valley companies, he founded a nonprofit to actually build reading machines. Since then, Benetech's work has grown to touch thousands of organizations and the lives of hundreds of thousands of people. Benetech's suite of tools and services has transformed the ways people with disabilities access printed information, at-risk human rights defenders safely document abuse, and environmental practitioners protect species and ecosystems. Today, through Benetech Labs, its innovation arm, Benetech explores new software-for-good ideas that have the potential to make life better for millions.

H. E. Ambassador Luis Gallegos obtained a law degree and also a J.D. degree at the Central University of Ecuador, and as a Humphrey Fellow Scholar, earned a master of arts degree from the Fletcher School of Law and Diplomacy. A prominent and career diplomat, Ambassador Gallegos has held many positions, including permanent representative of Ecuador to the United Nations in Geneva (twice); permanent representative of Ecuador to the United Nations in New York (twice); ambassador of Ecuador to Australia, ambassador of Ecuador to the United States; vice-president of the Commission of Human Rights; vice-president of the Assembly of the Member States of WIPO; vice-president of the 57th Session of the UN General Assembly; and three-time president of the Political Committee of the Non Aligned Movements. He was the chairman of the Ad-Hoc Committee on a Comprehensive and Integral International Convention to Promote and Protect the Rights and Dignity of Persons with Disabilities from 2002 to 2005, fostering a disability human rights treaty at the United Nations, and has supported its implementation globally, including his work as chairman of the board of trustees of the Global UN Partnership for Inclusive Information and Communication Technologies (G3ICT) and honorary chairman of the Global Universal Design Commission. Ambassador Gallegos has been the recipient of numerous awards for his work on human rights and humanitarian aid, and is considered an invaluable ally by the world's disability rights community.

G. Anthony Giannoumis is assistant professor of universal design in the Department of Computer Science at Oslo and Akershus University College and an international research fellow at the Burton Blatt Institute at Syracuse University. His research focuses on technology law and policy. He is currently researching the implementation of policies aimed at ensuring equal access to technology. His interests include universal design, international governance, social regulation, and standardization, and he has conducted research on assistive technology and intellectual property. He has acted as a researcher with DISCIT, a European Union (EU) project dedicated to making persons with disabilities full citizens, and a legal and ethical adviser for Cloud4All, another EU project that promotes the use of cloud platforms to ensure universal access for people with disabilities and for all. He was awarded a Marie Curie Fellowship in 2011 as part of DREAM Disability Rights Expanding Accessible Markets and has been a visiting researcher and guest lecturer throughout Europe, North America, Asia, and Africa.

Paul T. Jaeger is a professor in the College of Information Studies at the University of Maryland. His research focuses on the ways in which law and public policy shape information behavior, particularly for underserved populations. He is the author of more than 150 journal articles and book chapters, as well as twelve books. His recent books include *Disability and the Internet: Confronting a Digital Divide* (2012); *Public Libraries, Public Policies, and Political Processes: Serving and Transforming Communities in Times of Economic and Political Constraint* (2014) with Ursula Gorham, John Carlo Bertot, and Lindsay C. Sarin; *Digital Literacy and Digital Inclusion: Information Policy and the Public Library* (Rowman and Littlefield, 2014) with Kim M. Thompson, Natalie Greene Taylor, Mega Subramaniam, and John Carlo Bertot; and *Libraries, Human Rights, and Social Justice* (Rowman and Littlefield, 2015) with Natalie Greene Taylor and Ursula Gorham. His research has been funded by the Institute of Museum and Library Services, the National Science Foundation, the American Library Association, the Smithsonian Institution, and the Bill and Melinda Gates Foundation, among others. He is editor of *Library Quarterly*.

Sanjay S. Jain is associate professor at the ILS Law College, Pune, India. He coordinates two important centers, one of which is the Centre for Public and Equal Opportunity. In recognition of his research abilities, the college has also appointed him as the director of its Research Centre affiliated with Savitribai Phule Pune University, Pune. His doctoral thesis was "Feminism and Constitutional Law." He has twenty years of teaching experience and has published five books, including *Basic Structure Constitutionalism—Revisiting Kesavananda Bharati* (2011, coedited with Sathya Narayan). He has also published a number of articles in books and various journals. He is a disability rights activist. He has designed two novel research initiatives, the Constitutional Law Olympiad and the CONST ICON competition to promote analytic and rigorous study of constitutional law by students, and he drafted the Maharashtra State policy for the empowerment of persons with disabilities on behalf of the core group constituted by the government of Maharashtra. He has received a number of awards, including the Most Efficient Disabled Employee National Award at the auspicious hands of the president of India, the Honorable Dr. A. P. J. Abdul Kalam, in 2004.

Deborah Kaplan has been involved in technology accessibility in a variety of roles for many years. At the World Institute on Disability, where she also served as executive director for eight years, she pioneered projects on technology policy focused on universal design in technology as a goal. She headed the Accessibility Technology Initiative for the California State University system and currently is Section 508 Policy Lead in the Office of the Chief Information Technology Officer at the U.S. Department of Health and Human Services. She is also a member of the Executive Committee of the CIO Council Accessibility Community of Practice, the Steering Committee of the Web Accessibility Initiative of the World Wide Web Consortium (W3C), and the Planning Committee for the M-Enabling Summit. She has a law degree from Boalt Hall at the University of California at Berkeley and received a B.A. with honors from UC Santa Cruz. She lives in a cohousing community in Silver Spring, Maryland.

Raja Kushalnagar is associate professor and director of the Information Technology program in the Department of Science, Technology, and Mathematics at Gallaudet University in Washington, D.C. He has a J.D. from Thurgood Marshall School of Law, an LL.M. in intellectual property and information law from the University of Houston, and a Ph.D. in computer science from the University of Houston. His research focuses on the intersection of disability law, accessible technology, and human-computer interaction. His research on accessible technology focuses on enhancing educational access for deaf and hard-of-hearing students in mainstreamed classrooms; his research on disability law focuses on the impact of copyright and patent law on accessibility for people with sensory disabilities; and his research on human-computer interaction focuses on improving universal design and accessibility of personal devices. He has written several peer-reviewed publications in all three areas. He has received several grants to enhance accessibility for deaf, hard-of-hearing, and low-vision students enrolled in mainstreamed classrooms and to improve personal-device accessibility.

Fredric I. Lederer is Chancellor Professor of Law and director of the Center for Legal and Court Technology (CLCT), formerly the Courtroom 21 Project, at William and Mary Law School. He is a former trial lawyer and military judge and a law-reform expert. His areas of specialization include legal technology, evidence, technology-augmented trial practice, electronic discovery and data seizures, criminal procedure, military law, and legal skills. He is author or coauthor of eleven books, numerous articles, and two law-related education television series. As founder and director of CLCT, Lederer, along with his colleagues, is responsible for the McGlothlin Courtroom, the world's most technologically advanced trial and appellate courtroom, located at William and Mary Law School in Williamsburg, Virginia.

Janet E. Lord is a senior research associate at the Harvard Law School Project on Disability, where she collaborates on disability rights research and advocacy activities. A well-known and respected international human rights lawyer, she has taught at several universities and has worked with a variety of international organizations and donors, including the UN Office of the High Commissioner for Human Rights, the UN Disability Program, the U.S. Agency for International Development, the U.S. National Council on Disability, the European Union, and the World Bank. Her areas of specialization include human rights treaty negotiation and implementation, disability law and policy, health rights for marginalized populations, humanitarian assistance, political participation, and human rights education and advocacy. She has written extensively on disability law and policy issues, drawing on her experience of participating in the negotiation of the UN Convention on the Rights of Persons with Disabilities and subsequent implementation of that treaty globally.

Ravi Malhotra has been a disability rights advocate for more than twenty-five years and a member of the University of Ottawa Faculty of Law since 2006. He was called to the Ontario bar in 2001 and graduated from Harvard Law School in 2002, where he studied disability rights law under Professor Samuel R. Bagenstos, later principal deputy assistant attorney general of the United States. He is a member of the Human Rights Committee of the Council of Canadians with Disabilities (CCD). He is coauthor with Morgan Rowe of *Exploring Disability Identity and Disability Rights Through Narratives: Finding a Voice of Their Own* (2013), which examines the narratives and life experiences of twelve mostly young adults with physical disabilities. He is also editor of the interdisciplinary text *Disability Politics in a Global Economy: Essays in Honour of Marta Russell* (2016). This anthology explores the impact of globalization on disability politics in light of the writings of disability rights advocate Marta Russell and features the work of many prominent scholars from a number of disciplines. He has published widely in law reviews and has given invited lectures at McGill Law School, the University of Illinois–Chicago, and Yale Law School.

Jorge Manhique is program officer for Africa (Malawi and Rwanda) for the Disability Rights Fund and the Disability Rights Advocacy Fund. He is responsible for grant making, grants oversight, and technical support to disabled people's organizations in Malawi and Rwanda. He has over five years of experience working with persons with disabilities in Mozambique. He served as project manager at the Federation of People with Disabilities in Mozambique, where he was responsible for managing projects addressing implementation of the CRPD. He established the first monitoring unit within FAMOD with the mandate to advocate for law reform in critical areas, such as education, health, accessibility, and mental health. He represented FAMOD in the technical committee responsible for drafting the Disability Act and drafted the position document submitted to the ad hoc commission responsible for the constitutional review process in Mozambique. He led a project on inclusive education funded by the United Kindom's Department for International Development (DFID). He has an LL.M. degree in international and comparative disability law and policy from the National University of Ireland.

Mirriam Nthenge is a policy research officer with Kenya Dialogues Project-Society for International Development. She is holds an LL.M in international and comparative disability law and policy from National University of Ireland (2015). She is an Open Society Foundation Disability Rights Fellow (2014/2015) and a former Research Fellow with UN Special Rapporteur on the Rights of Persons with Disabilities-Catalina Devandas Aguilar. Mirriam is very passionate about human rights monitoring mechanisms, with her focus being national human rights institutions, treaty bodies, and special procedures. She has also conducted extensive research in the area of legal capacity and education.

Joyojeet Pal is an assistant professor in the School of Information at the University of Michigan, Ann Arbor, where he teaches user experience and accessibility. He uses qualitative methods to study a range of issues on accessibility and the information economy in the Global South. His work examines the use of accessible technology in the context of the existing economic and cultural impediments to employability and social inclusion for people with visual impairments. He received his bachelor's degree in commerce and economics at Sydenham College, University of Mumbai, and his Ph.D. in city and regional planning at the University of California at Berkeley.

Megan A. Rusciano received J.D. degrees from the University of Ottawa Faculty of Law and American University Washington College of Law (AUWCL) and has been admitted to the Maryland bar. She wrote "Situating Staley: Investigating the Constitutionality of Forcibly Medicating a Texas Death Row Inmate to Render Him Competent for Execution," published in American University's *Journal of Gender, Social Policy, and the Law*. She received the T. Morton McDonald Scholarship Award for legal research and writing on graduation from AUWCL. She interned at the Arc of the United States, the U.S. Department of Justice, and West End Legal Services of Ottawa. Currently she is an advocate for clients with special needs trusts at the Arc of Northern Virginia. Through ongoing volunteer work with the Nidus Personal Planning and Resource Centre in British Columbia, she promotes the use of supported decision making as an alternative to guardianship in both the United States and Canada. She continues to seek ways to become a more self-aware and responsive ally for people with disabilities.

David Sloan is user experience research lead for the Paciello Group (TPG), a digital-accessibility consultancy. He has spent over fifteen years as a researcher, educator, and consultant, helping people create great digital products and services that can be used by as many people as possible, regardless of disability. He joined TPG in 2013, having previously worked at the University of Dundee's School of Computing, one of the world's largest academic research groups investigating accessibility for older and disabled people. He received a Ph.D. in computing science and an M.Sc. in applied computing from the University of Dundee, and a B.Sc. in topographic science from the University of Glasgow.

Brian Wentz is an associate professor of management information systems at Shippensburg University of Pennsylvania, where he is frequently involved with applied research and projects that focus on the implications that web accessibility and usability can have on business, education, employment, public policy, and societal inclusion. For more than thirteen years he has been involved in a variety of projects related to web accessibility and usability for people with disabilities. Dr. Wentz received the 2013 Honorary Service award from the Pennsylvania Council of the Blind, and he has published over twenty-five refereed articles in journals, books, and conference proceedings.

Marco Winckler is assistant professor in computer sciences at the Université Paul Sabatier (Toulouse, France), where he is involved in education at undergraduate and graduate levels. He obtained a Ph.D. degree in informatics from Université de Toulouse 1 Capitole and a master's degree in computer science from the Universidade Federal do Rio Grande do Sul (Porto Alegre, Brazil). In 2006–7 he was visiting scholar at the Université Catholique de Louvain (Belgium). He is a member of the Interactive Critical System (ICS) research team, where he investigates models, methods, techniques, and tools to support development of reliable, usable, and effective interactive systems. His research combines topics of engineering interactive systems, human-computer interaction, and web engineering. Among his academic duties, he is responsible for the internship program of the master's program on human-computer interaction held by the Université Paul Sabatier and the École Nationale d'Aviation Civil (ENAC). He also serves as chair of the IFIP working group 13.2 on Methodologies for User-Centered Systems Design and secretary of the IFIP TC 13 on Human-Computer Interaction.

Mary J. Ziegler is program manager for online accessibility at the Massachusetts Institute of Technology Office of Digital Learning. Previously, she led the MIT Information Systems and Technology (IS&T) Accessibility and Usability Group (2009–15) and the MIT Assistive Technology Information Center (2005–9). Throughout her career, she has been instrumental in creating numerous initiatives, collaborations, and technology implementations, each designed to increase access for students and staff (and most recently global learners) with disabilities. She received an M.A. in German from Middlebury College, Vermont, and a B.A. in sociology and German from Dickinson College, Carlisle, Pennsylvania.

INDEX

Access Board. *See* United States Access Board
Accessibility for Ontarians with Disabilities Act (AODA) [Canada], 74, 94, 98, 103, 109
Accessibility for Ontarians with Disabilities Act Alliance (AODA Alliance), 109, 129–30
accessibility policy, 77, 78, 86, 91, 165, 241
accessibility testing, 85, 87, 275
accessibility training, 83
Accessible India Campaign, 270, 271, 277
Accessible Procurement Toolkit [Canada], 37
Accessible Rich Internet Applications (ARIA), 15, 63, 135, 166, 168
Access to Information Act [Canada], 129
access to justice, 111–24; case specific information, 115–17; court information, 114–15; hearings, trials, and courtrooms, 117–18; for persons with communication disabilities, 122; for persons with hearing disabilities, 122; for persons with intellectual disabilities, 122–23; for persons with mobility-related disabilities, 118–20; for persons with visual disabilities, 120–22
Access to Justice Task Force report [Australia], 111
Administrative Procedure Act (APA) [US], 127
Adobe, 148
Adobe Flash, 131
Alliance for Equality of Blind Canadians, 103
alternative dispute resolution (ADR), 113
American Library Association (ALA), 59, 62, 63

American Sign Language (ASL), 48, 195
Americans with Disabilities Act (ADA), 2, 3, 42, 43, 44, 50, 55, 56, 57, 67, 74, 82, 96, 97, 98, 102, 114, 115, 163, 164, 165, 189, 190, 221
Association for Research Libraries (ARL), 68
Association of the Physically Disabled of Kenya, 239
audiobook, 67, 144, 146, 147, 148, 151, 154
Australia, 30, 33, 35, 43, 91, 111, 117, 118, 129, 164, 166
authentication, 201, 204, 205
Authoring Tool Accessibility Guidelines (ATAG), 20, 21, 166, 168, 269
automated teller machine (ATM), 104, 203

Baker, David, 105
barriers to political participation, 26–27
Benetech, 274
Berne Convention for the Protection of Literary and Artistic Works, 191–92
Berners-Lee, Tim, 46, 54
biometrics, 201, 204, 205
bipolar, 49
blind or visually impaired, 2, 15, 26, 27, 29, 35, 36, 48, 50, 56, 57, 58, 68, 94, 96, 103, 104, 105, 106, 109, 115, 120, 121, 129, 130, 135, 143, 144, 147, 150, 156, 157, 161, 166, 173, 184, 192, 196, 203, 204, 205, 207, 208, 211, 216, 217, 219, 241, 258, 273, 274, 276
Bollywood Hindi films, 276
Bombay, 255
Bookshare, 147, 148, 153, 274
braille, 27, 35, 57, 59, 82, 121, 134, 144, 146, 147, 148, 150, 151, 152, 162, 203, 217, 238, 261, 267, 273, 276

Brazil, 91, 132, 136, 150, 164, 166, 188, 189, 217
Brazilian Sign Language, 217

California, 27, 57, 79
California State University (CSU), 79
Campbell, Fiona Kumari, 264
Campeche, 259
Canada, 37, 38, 69, 91, 94–110, 129, 266
Canadian Charter of Rights and Freedoms, 94, 103, 105, 106, 107, 110
Canadian Human Rights Commission, 95
Canadian Radio-Television and Telecommunications Commission (CRTC), 104
candidate recommendation, 17, 21
Captioned Films for the Deaf, 185
captioning. *See* closed captioning
Caracas, 256
censorship, 222
Center for Legal and Court Technology at William and Mary Law School, 119, 120, 121
Centre for Internet and Society, 267, 275
cerebral palsy, 161, 176, 218, 219, 221
Chafee Amendment, 147, 149, 151, 191, 192, 193, 195
Chaudhary, Vandana, 264, 265
Chennai, 258, 273, 274
China, 43, 117, 164
Civil Rights Act of 1964, 221
civil society, 25, 136, 232, 234, 235, 236, 239, 242, 268, 274
civil society organizations (CSOs), 136, 235, 239, 241, 242, 243, 268
closed captioning, 26, 33, 182–98, 275
closed-circuit television (CCTV), 35
Cognitive and Learning Disabilities Task Force, 23, 48
cognitive disabilities, ix, 3, 4, 20, 42, 43, 44, 45, 47, 49–51, 52–55, 56, 57, 135, 174, 204, 205, 206, 207, 221, 222, 273
cognitive load, 50–51
Colombia, 134
Committee on the Rights of Persons with Disabilities, 235, 239, 270, 277
Communications and Video Accessibility Act (CVAA), 6, 164, 187, 190, 191, 221
community service organizations (CSOs), 253, 256, 257, 259
complaints, 31, 32, 77, 87, 95, 138, 165, 189

Completely Automated Public Turing Test to Tell Computers and Humans Apart (CAPTCHA), 205, 273
Congo, 33
Constitution of India, 266, 267, 268
Constitution of Kenya, 238
Convention on the Rights of Persons with Disabilities (CRPD), x, xi, 3, 7, 13, 14, 25, 28, 36, 39, 40, 42, 44, 53, 55, 57, 61, 73, 90, 91, 92, 93, 99, 100, 101, 103, 104, 112, 135, 139, 143, 150, 154, 158, 162, 188, 202, 215, 216, 228, 234, 240, 241, 243, 244, 245, 247, 248, 249, 250, 251, 252, 259, 260, 261, 262, 265, 266, 267, 268, 270, 271, 272, 277
cookies, 46, 207, 210
copyright, 62, 96, 103, 104, 147, 149, 150, 151, 154, 155, 166, 167, 183, 184, 185, 189, 190, 191, 192, 193, 194, 195, 196, 197, 198, 222, 272
Correa, Rafael, 250
Costa Rica, 189, 247, 249, 250, 258
Council of Canadians with Disabilities (CCD), 104
Creative Commons, 145
CRPD committee. *See* Committee on the Rights of Persons with Disabilities
Cupertino, 79

DAISY Consortium, 148, 153, 155, 166, 274
DAISY Forum of India, 267, 274
Dart, Justin, 97
deaf, DEAF, and hard of hearing, 6, 14, 26, 29, 32, 33, 39, 48, 50, 56, 97, 115, 122, 135, 161, 173, 182, 184, 185, 188, 189, 193, 194, 197, 198, 204, 205, 211, 217, 239
deaf-blind, 174
democratic deficit, 233
Denmark, 91
Deuteronomy 16:20, 124
Digital Millennium Copyright Act [US], 191, 197, 222
direct data capture (DDC), 33
direct recording electronic voting devices (DREs), 36
Disability and Rehabilitation, 247
disabled peoples organizations (DPO). *See* disabled persons' organizations (DPO)
disabled persons' organizations (DPO), 26, 30, 31, 36, 38, 39, 228, 231, 235, 236, 237,

239, 240, 241, 242, 243, 253, 256, 268, 276, 277
document accessibility, 82, 83
Down syndrome, 47, 204, 205
Down Syndrome Ireland, 39

easy checks, 22
Ebola, 251
e-book, 46, 59, 66, 143, 144–46, 147, 148, 151–54, 155, 156, 157, 159
Ecuador, ix, 247, 248, 249, 257
edX, 56, 165
e-government, 24, 29, 66, 67, 199, 240
Eldridge, 107, 108
election commission, 26, 27, 28, 29, 31, 32, 33, 35, 36, 38, 39
elections, 2, 26, 30, 31, 32, 33, 36, 39
electronic discovery (e-discovery), 116
elementary education, 216
emergency, ix, 2, 7, 13, 14, 26, 53, 74, 101, 188, 208, 216
employment, 13, 60, 61, 62, 63, 66, 67, 70, 76, 78, 82, 97, 98, 100, 101, 102, 150, 157, 160, 206, 212, 214, 215, 216, 218, 220, 223, 239, 240, 251, 256, 258, 259
EPUB, 153, 156, 166
eQuality, 41, 42, 47, 51, 52, 55, 56, 57
Estey, Steve, 39
European Disability Forum (EDF), 235, 236, 242
European Norm 301 549 (EN 301 549; European Standard 301 549), 14, 92, 169
European Standards Organizations (ESO), 236
European Union (EU), 34, 39, 85, 91, 92, 93, 135, 138, 210, 228, 229, 230, 231, 232, 233, 234, 235, 236, 237, 239, 242
e-voting, 24, 26, 27, 28, 29, 31, 34, 35, 36
exercise, 219
exercise of rights, 14, 24, 26

Fairfax County, 114
fair use, 147, 149, 190, 193, 195, 196, 197
Federal Rule of Civil Procedure 34(b)(2)(E) [US], 116
Federation of People with Disabilities in Mozambique, 239
Finland, 91
France, 91, 209, 210
Freedom of Information Act [Australia], 129

Freedom of Information Act (FOIA) [US], 127–29, 130, 131
Freedom of the Press Act of 1766 [Sweden], 127

gaming, 55, 212, 213, 215, 216, 217, 218, 219, 220, 221, 222, 223
general comment on accessibility by the Committee on the Rights of Persons with Disabilities, 235, 266, 270, 272
geolocation, 12, 199, 206, 208, 209
Germany, 91
Global Initiative for Inclusive ICTs (G3ict), 92, 93
global positioning system (GPS), 7, 40, 46, 55, 208, 255
Global Public Inclusive Infrastructure (GPII), 54
Global South, 93, 229, 237, 240, 241, 242, 243, 244, 247, 254, 258, 259, 260
Government in the Sunshine Act [US], 129
Government of India Guidance for Websites (GIGW), 272
Guatemala, 39, 247, 249, 251

hard of hearing. *See* deaf, DEAF, and hard of hearing
Harvard University, 4, 7, 8, 56
HathiTrust, 68, 149, 196
healthcare, 5, 13, 15, 47, 53, 60, 95, 97, 107, 202, 210, 212, 214, 215, 216, 218, 220, 223, 250
Help America Vote Act of 2002 (HAVA) [US], 31
higher education, 4, 79, 148, 159, 163, 164, 165, 166, 167, 168, 172
HTML5, 17
human-computer interaction (HCI), 3, 4, 5, 43, 172, 201, 215, 246
human interaction proofs, 201, 204
Human Rights Code, Ontario [Canada], 95
Human Rights Tribunal of Ontario [Canada], 95, 96

Incheon Strategy, 266, 270
inclusion, 18, 39, 40, 43, 57, 62, 63, 64, 65, 67, 68, 70, 81, 92, 95, 96, 101, 102, 105, 107, 108, 109, 111, 113, 126, 136, 138, 150, 157, 158, 160, 161, 162, 195, 220, 223, 231, 251, 263, 272, 277

Inclusive Planet Centre for Disability Law and Policy, 267
India, 152, 166, 247, 249, 250, 253, 254, 255, 256, 258, 259, 260, 263–77
Indian Bank Association (IBA), 273
Indian Copyrights Act 1957, 272
Indian Institute of Technology, 275
Indonesia, 136
institutional change, 227, 228, 229, 230, 231, 232, 233, 237, 242, 243
Integrated Accessibility Standards Regulation (IASR) [Canada], 98, 99–102
International Federation of Library Associations and Institutions (IFLA), 62
International Standards Organization (ISO), 17, 85, 86, 169
Internet of Things (IoT), 55
Internet service providers (ISPs), 46, 66
Ireland, 37, 38, 39, 91, 92, 132
Israel, 45
Italy, 91

Japan, 19, 91
JAWS, 134, 254, 256, 257
Jodhan v. Canada, 94, 105, 105–7, 108, 109, 110
Jordan, 247, 249, 252, 253, 254, 258, 260

Kenya, 32, 45, 229, 237, 238, 239, 240, 241, 242
Kenya National Association of the Deaf, 33, 239
Koh, Harold, 96, 97

large print, 59, 67, 82, 144, 146, 151, 152, 162, 276
large print book, 67, 146, 152
Latin America, 189, 247, 250, 256
Law for the Integration of Persons with Disabilities [Venezuela], 250
Law on the Rights of Persons with Disabilities [Jordan], 252
Lepofsky, David, 97, 129
Ley Vigente Sobre Discapacidades [Ecuador], 248
Library for the Blind and Physically Handicapped, 68
Lima, 257
Louisiana, 38

Madison, James, 127
Malawi, 247, 248, 249, 254
Malkowski, Gary, 97
Marrakesh Treaty to Facilitate Access to Published Works for Persons Who Are Blind, Visually Impaired, or Otherwise Print Disabled (Marrakesh Treaty), 3, 28, 62, 103, 150, 151, 154, 167, 193
Maryland, 36, 68
Massachusetts, 35
Massachusetts Institute of Technology (MIT), 56
Massive Open Online Course (MOOC), 56, 159, 160
Media User Accessibility Requirements (MUAR), 22
Mexico, 39, 136, 247, 251, 252, 253, 259, 260
Milton, John, 126
Ministry of Electronics and Information Technology, New Delhi (MEITY), 268, 272, 275
mobile phone. *See* telephone
Moreno, Lenin, 250
movies, 46, 155, 184, 185, 276
Mozambique, 229, 237, 238, 239, 240, 241, 242
multi-stakeholder involvement, 18
My Opinion, My Vote, 38

National Association for the Blind [India], 267, 276
National Association for the Blind Delhi, 274, 276
National Association of the Deaf [US], 56
National Commission for Persons with Disability (NCPD) [India], 271
National Council for People with Disabilities [Rwanda], 252
National Council for the Care of Persons with Disabilities (CONADI), 251
National Federation of the Blind [India], 267
National Federation of the Blind (NFB) [US], 2, 57, 130, 149
National Handicapped Development and Finance Corporation, 272
National Instructional Materials Access Center, 148
National Library Service, 58

National Policy on Universal Electronic Accessibility (NPOUEA) [India], 268, 269, 270, 272, 274, 277
National System for Integral Family Development [Mexico], 252
New Delhi, 268, 269, 270, 276
New Delhi Declaration on Inclusive ICTs for Persons with Disabilities, 270, 272
New Zealand, 91
Norway, 91, 136

online assessment, 159, 176
online learning, 159, 160, 161, 162, 165, 166, 167, 168, 169, 170, 171, 172, 173, 174, 175, 177, 178, 179, 180, 181
Ontarians with Disabilities Act (ODA) [Canada], 96, 97, 98
Open Government Partnership (OGP), 136
Open Stand, 16
operable (Web Content Accessibility Guidelines), 19, 34

participatory processes, 232, 234, 236
password, 48, 201, 204, 206, 273
PDF, 82, 83, 115, 131, 132, 133, 159, 168, 169, 176
people with mental disabilities, 27, 44, 49, 157, 187, 206, 269
people with mental health challenges. *See* people with mental disabilities
perceivable (Web Content Accessibility Guidelines), 19, 29
perceived disabilities, 112, 113, 123, 124
Persons with Disabilities Act [India], 250, 267
Peru, 247, 249, 252, 253, 260
Philippines, 136
pivot, 229, 232, 237, 241, 242, 243
Placencia-Porrero, Inmaculada, 236
policy entrepreneur, 227, 228, 230, 231, 232, 242, 243
policy network, 227, 229, 230, 231, 232, 242
political participation, 24–40
pornography, 222
Portugal, 91
print disability (print disabled), 38, 103, 144, 149, 150, 156, 157, 193
privacy, 6, 15, 17, 55, 60, 189, 199, 200, 201, 202, 203, 204, 206, 208, 209, 210, 211
privacy policy, 209

procurement, 14, 31, 36, 37, 75, 76, 77, 78, 80, 83, 85, 86, 90, 91, 92, 134, 135, 148, 165, 169, 178, 181, 228, 229, 236, 242, 267, 269, 270, 272
public accommodations, 43

Quito, ix, 257

Radcliffe Institute for Advanced Study, 4, 7, 328
Raising the Floor (RtF) Consortium, 54, 55
reasonable accommodation, 28, 29, 34, 42, 50, 261, 265, 266, 268
reasonable modification. *See* reasonable accommodation
recreation, 47, 101, 213, 214, 215, 219
rehabilitation, 126, 202, 215, 218, 220, 221, 223, 250, 252, 269, 271
Rehabilitation Act of 1973: Section 504 of, 2, 76, 77, 163; Section 508 of, 2, 14, 73, 74, 75, 76, 77, 85, 88, 89, 90, 92, 93, 114, 115, 130, 136, 137, 164, 168
Reserve Bank of India (RBI), 273
Rights of Persons with Disabilities Bill [India], 271
robust (Web Content Accessibility Guidelines), 19
Rwanda, 33, 247, 249, 252
Rwanda National Association of Deaf Women, 33

Saksham Trust Noida (Saksham), 274, 275, 276
Santa Clara County, 27
Scherer, Maria, 247
Section 504. *See* Rehabilitation Act of 1973
Section 508. *See* Rehabilitation Act of 1973
security, 12, 15, 17, 22, 26, 32, 36, 89, 121, 200, 201, 202, 203, 204, 205, 206, 211, 258
Semantic Web, 46, 47, 54, 55
Serbia, 39
Sierra Leone, 247, 249, 251, 254
sign language, 14, 32, 33, 39, 48, 54, 100, 107, 115, 122, 123, 161, 174, 182, 195, 217, 238, 271, 273
SMS (short message service), 29, 32, 33
social exclusion, 24, 111, 215, 218, 221, 259
social justice, 58, 59, 60, 62, 63, 64, 65, 66, 70

344   Index

South Africa, 136, 266
South Korea, 91
Spain, 91, 237
Standard Rules on the Equalization of Opportunities for Persons with Disabilities, 187, 188, 265
Stark, Chris and Marie Laporte, 103
State Bank of India, 273
State of Maharashtra, 272
Stein, Michael, 119
Steinstra, Deborah, 104
Support for Canadians with Print Disabilities Act, 103–4
Sweden, 91, 127

talking book, 59
technical standard, 18, 20, 21, 44, 76, 88, 136, 167, 174
telephone, ix, x, xi, 7, 12, 13, 18, 19, 26, 29, 57, 106, 146, 152, 159, 202, 240, 241, 273, 274
television (TV), ix, x, xi, 12, 14, 26, 187, 191, 272
Television (TV) Decoder Circuitry Act of 1990 [US], 186, 191
terms of service, 209
text messaging. *See* SMS
touch screens, 27
Towson University, 7, 68
Twenty-First Century Communications and Video Accessibility Act (CVAA) [US], 6, 164, 187, 190, 191, 221

ubiquity of technology, 45, 159, 172
understandable (Web Content Accessibility Guidelines), 19
United Disabled Persons of Kenya, 239
United Kingdom, 43, 91, 119, 136, 164, 166, 188
United Nations Convention on the Rights of Persons with Disabilities. *See* Convention on the Rights of Persons with Disabilities (CRPD)
United Nations Decade of Disabled Persons, 187
United Nations Educational, Scientific, and Cultural Organization (UNESCO), 62, 269, 275
United Nations High Level Meeting on Disability and Development, 39

United Nations International Day of Persons with Disabilities, 270
United Nations International Year of Disabled Persons, 187, 265
United Nations Sustainable Development Goals (SDGs), 269
United States Access Board, 74, 76, 77, 89, 136, 164, 167, 168
United States Agency for International Development, 37
United States Department of Education, 165, 186
United States Department of Health and Human Services, 2
United States Department of Justice (DOJ), 2, 56, 69, 76, 115, 116, 131, 137, 163, 165
United States Federal Communications Commission, 6, 186, 196
United States Federal Trade Commission, 6
United States Library of Congress, 58, 59, 133
Universal Declaration of Human Rights, 25, 60, 61, 62, 66, 143, 149, 150, 185, 202
universal design, 28, 37, 51, 67, 104, 153, 154, 155, 157, 171, 263, 265, 266, 268, 269, 270, 271, 274, 276
universal design for learning (UDL), 67, 171, 179, 180
University of Colorado, Boulder, 165
User Agent Accessibility Guidelines (UAAG), 20, 21, 168, 269

Venezuela, 247, 249, 250, 251, 256
Via Rail, 107, 108
Victorian Electoral Commission's Election Access Advisory Group [Australia], 30. 33
Vienna Declaration and Programme of Action, 187
Voice over Internet Protocol services, 29
voice recognition (speech recognition), x, 15, 26, 35, 38, 161, 190, 197. 204, 205, 211, 216

Warschauer, Mark, 264
WCAG2ICT, 20
Web Accessibility Evaluation Tools List, 22
Web Accessibility Initiative (WAI), 11, 12, 18, 19, 20, 22, 23, 48, 135, 166, 168, 178

WebAIM, 49
Web Content Accessibility Guidelines (WCAG), 17, 19, 20, 21, 22, 45, 48, 53, 56, 74, 78, 81, 88, 91, 101, 102, 103, 105, 106, 135, 166, 168, 178, 181, 222, 269, 271, 275
Web Ontology Language (OWL V.2), 54
WGBH's Caption Center and the National Captioning Institute (NCI), 186
wheelchairs, 33, 34, 106, 107, 119, 206, 219, 253, 261, 273; users, 27, 28, 107, 119, 250, 253, 255, 256
women with disabilities, 27, 60, 269
World Bank, 240, 249, 263
World Intellectual Property Organization (WIPO), 103, 150, 167, 189, 193
World Programme of Action Concerning Disabled Persons, 187, 265
World System Teletext, 186
World Wide Web Consortium (W3C), 11, 12, 16, 17, 18, 19, 20, 21, 23, 43, 45, 54, 105, 135, 166, 168, 181

Xavier's Resource Centre for the Visually Challenged, 267, 274

years lost to disability (YLD), 249, 250, 251